EVOLUTION of the Spirit

OUR JOURNEY THROUGH THE UNIVERSE

by

Walter D. Pullen

OZARK MOUNTAIN PUBLISHING

PO Box 754, Huntsville, AR 72740

800-935-0045 or 479-738-2348 or fax 479-738-2448

www.ozarkmt.com

Library of Congress Cataloging-in-Publication Data
Pullen, Walter D., 1971-
Evolution of the Spirit, by Walter Pullen
Our spiritual journey through the universe. The evolution of our souls.
1. Spiritual Evolution 2. Planes of the Universe 3. Karma 4. Reincarnation
5. Kingdoms of Nature 6. Cycles of Evolution 7. 2010 8. Metaphysics
I. Pullen, Walter D., 1971- II. Spiritual Evolution III. Metaphysics
IV. Title
Library of Congress Catalog Card Number: 2010939625
ISBN: 978-1-886940-741

Cover Art and Layout: www.enki3d.com
Book set in: Times New Roman
Book Design: Julia Degan

Published by:
OZARK MOUNTAIN PUBLISHING
PO Box 754
Huntsville, AR 72740
www.ozarkmt.com
Printed in the United States of America

Table of Contents

Preface

"Truth is like beauty. It's relative, and often fades over time."
- I. Chris English

Spirituality is such a vast topic that it's challenging to express in words. The very essence of spirit is that which is beyond standard levels of thinking, and therefore can't be fully expressed by concepts such as language. That raises the questions: Where does spiritual information come from? How can such things be known in the first place? Can they be proven to be right or wrong? Finally, as the author of this book about spirituality, how do I know the things written in it are true?

Although spirituality is inherently abstract, at the same time spiritual knowledge isn't very different from material knowledge, even if it's harder to prove given our society's current culture and state of technology. Arthur C. Clarke said "any sufficiently advanced technology is indistinguishable from magic," meaning there's ultimately no difference between spirit and science. We often place things we label as "spiritual" on a high pedestal or make unnecessary fuss over them, when in reality everything is science, or more accurately everything is spirit.

Spiritual knowledge in general, and the content of this book in particular, comes from four main sources: references, experiences, deductions, and intuitions. A source of information can be on a personal or impersonal level, and it can be generated internally or received externally. These four combinations can be summarized in the following simple grid:

Sources of Knowledge		
	Impersonal	**Personal**
External	Reference	Experience
Internal	Deduction	Intuition

1) Reference: A reference is impersonal data received externally. Knowledge can be obtained from external sources, such as teachers or other guides, books, and so on. References reuse or repackage existing information, as opposed to other sources which gather new information. Unfortunately, it's not always clear how much a particular external source can be trusted because some are incomplete or even completely inaccurate. Fortunately, at the same time, often very different schools of thought present the same information, just in different forms. A skeptic might say various sources are merely copying each other there's certainly sharing going on. But when different reputable sources agree on a point it does give that information additional credence.

2) Experience: An experience is personal consciousness encountering something external. No amount of study can substitute for a direct personal experience. For example, if you have an out-of-body experience, the existence of the astral plane will become an experienced reality, and not just a learned theory. If you see a UFO land, the existence of extraterrestrials will also be real, and not just something to believe in. Skeptics may doubt, and suggest explanations such as mental hallucination or weather balloons for such phenomena. In some cases they're right, but in others they're just trying to fit everything into their more limited experience and vision. Personal experiences are limited to the individual in question, and tend to be doubted by others unless the person is considered a credible source; however, personal experiences do help validate other sources.

3) Deduction: Unlike references and experiences, which come from things external to one's self, information can also be determined internally. Deduction covers sources that would be considered original observation and research. This source includes gathering and analyzing new data, or taking existing data and making new connections and expanding upon it. Deduction can even include expressing existing data in a new way, although that comes closer to a standard reference.

4) Intuition: Finally, knowing can come from intuition. Intuition is similar to deduction since they both come from within; however, intuition has less of an impersonal intellectual focus. Sometimes something just feels right, or you know that something is true where it comes to you in a way that's much more than just imagining or making something up. Intuition is usually considered the least reliable source, since unlike deduction, it's very difficult to prove. However, intuition and feelings do play a role in all presentations of information, if for no other reason than they affect how one chooses to present their data and what they choose to focus upon in the first place.

Although this book is a non-fiction reference, its ultimate purpose is to share a feeling of awe. This book contains many specifics about aspects of the Universe; however, it's important to remember that the details themselves aren't the primary message, as much as the overall communication of a sense of vastness. Simply saying something like "spirit is amazing" doesn't have much impact. However, listing levels of consciousness so that one sees how high they go and how enchanting they are, and comes to their own conclusion that spirit is amazing, is much more effective. Technical descriptions of spirit won't reduce the impact of directly experiencing it, or even its mystery. The opposite is more often the case because the more we learn about spirit, the more we realize that there's so much we don't know!

In my own spiritual Path, I've encountered many good sources of wisdom. Some focus on philosophy, others on methods of personal development, and some on knowledge of the Universe around us. The other main purpose of this book is to link the various areas together, and attempt to present a coherent picture of spirituality as a whole. By describing all the colors in turn, hopefully we can see the rainbow.

Spiritual truth, and for that matter knowledge on any subject in general, is like the Chinese parable of three blind men feeling an elephant. The first felt a thick leg and considered an elephant to be like a tree, the second felt the trunk and considered an elephant to be like a snake, and the third felt the wrinkled ears and considered an elephant to be like a large bat. Each of them is right, and yet they only have a small piece of the whole. For something as expansive as spirituality, each of us is blind, and can only see a small part of it, no matter how much we try. However, we can at least work to continually increase our vision, understanding, and abilities.

Much of this book is an attempt to present esoteric content in a simple or more modern fashion. Because spirituality is such an extensive topic, I must emphasize that this book is merely a summary of spiritual evolution. Only the basic or most fundamental aspects of each area are described; many details aren't included. Each chapter of this book could easily be expanded into its own volume; indeed there are already quality works available in each area. The goal here is not to present a full picture, but lay a foundation for further exploration.

Hence, this book could be considered entry-level, describing the various aspects of spiritual growth to the neophyte. However, because it presents a comprehensive view, hopefully even experienced seekers will find parts to be of interest or areas that are able to "fill in the gaps." On a personal level, I've contemplated what book I might have most benefited from when I first started my own spiritual Path in this life. In other words, if I had the opportunity to send one book back in time to myself at a younger age, this book would probably be it. If it can benefit anybody else, even partially, it will have served its purpose.

This book is divided into two halves. The first part is about the mechanics of spirituality, which includes a description of the Universe we exist within and core laws around which it operates. The second part is more abstract, and covers spiritual practices and philosophies. The mechanics come first because many of the practices and philosophies make reference to them. In other words, the first part is about knowing spirituality on an impersonal level, while the second part is about becoming spiritual on a personal level. If the first part is the raw data about spirituality, the second part is the conclusions that have been drawn from it.

I sincerely believe everything in this book to be true, but I also recognize parts may be inaccurate if not completely wrong. I could preface every sentence with "in my opinion," but that would be unnecessarily verbose; the reader should realize the views presented are ultimately only those of the author. The goal is not to say "this is the answer" and get people to blindly accept that and stop questioning and learning, but rather the opposite: To inspire and encourage people to discover more about spirituality and ultimately, find their own answers and purpose.

Much of the writing here is really just describing the same fundamental truths that can be found elsewhere, but in slightly different forms (like is often seen between different religions). At the same time, some statements presented may go against established doctrine of certain belief systems. Depending on those beliefs, parts may even cause offense, which is of course not intended, but is sometimes unavoidable. I make no claim of being an Enlightened Master or anything close to it yet, but I am at least a part of the same Universe which contains us all. I only hope this text helps serve the plan of which all of us are a part, and can be one more drop of water added to the pool of Earth's wisdom.

As an example of how knowledge expands and becomes more accurate over time, consider science. Johannes Kepler made many great contributions to astronomy, although for much of his life, he incorrectly believed that the orbits of the planets could be described by the five platonic solids. Classical physicists such as Isaac Newton believed that momentum equals mass times velocity, which seemed correct at the time and applies in most instances. Later ,however, Albert Einstein discovered that formula was missing a factor to account for the speed of light. Einstein's formula is more complete, but it doesn't cover all instances either we now know different equations apply at the level of quantum mechanics.

Books are a continual improvement upon each other; every work "stands on the shoulders of giants" that have gone before. The world changes over time. Things that were true before aren't necessarily true today, and similarly things in this book that are true now won't necessarily be true tomorrow. Just as we evolve over time, so does spiritual growth itself evolve. If this book becomes obsolete, it will have served its purpose because that means others will have done better.

In our interconnected Universe of which we are all a part, no work is done in isolation. This book isn't just my own personal creation, but has been enabled by the encouragement and wisdom of many others. I'd like to acknowledge a few such people or groups that I've had the honor of interacting with in this life, without which this book would be vastly different or wouldn't have been written at all. These acknowledgments should not be taken to mean that they have reviewed or endorse the content. Special thanks to:

- Kent and Fay, my parents who provided me with a positive environment of morals, education, and appreciation of nature to grow up in.
- Jessica, my spouse and soulmate sweetie who encouraged me to actually take action to manifest this book on the physical plane, and has supported me in countless other ways.
- Sanktma, a fellow seeker whose own process of writing books inspired me to do the same.
- Arasia, for embodying service and who was present when I was first getting into spirituality.

- Selena, for providing fellowship and community to me and many others.
- Susan, part of my spiritual family who showed me the lighter side of spirit and that it doesn't have to be taken so seriously.
- Solara, for her tireless dedication in exploring the New, releasing the old, and most of all sharing how to Live Large.
- Dick Sutphen and the Sutphen Corporation, for presenting metaphysical growth and wisdom in a grounded and practical manner.
- The center of Astara, which has been a part of my Path for over half this lifetime.
- The Theosophical Society and its founders, whose writings have provided the basis for much of modern spirituality.
- The staff of Ozark Mountain Publishing, Inc. for believing in this work, and conducting the editing and everything else that goes into actually printing a book.
- Finally thanks to all those unmentioned, forgotten or unknown to begin with, on this or other planes of existence, who have inspired, supported, or otherwise assisted.

1:
Planes of the Universe

"The real voyage of discovery consists not in seeking new landscapes but in having new eyes."
- Marcel Proust

In exploring spirituality, one of our first tasks is to understand the different levels which compose our Universe. Ultimately, everything is a manifestation of the Divine, and there is no difference between spirit and matter where things just express in denser or lighter forms. In our normal physically awake lives, we experience the physical plane of existence. However, that is only one plane among many. There are seven different planes of the Universe, and our physical plane is the lowest or densest. These are the "many mansions in the Father's house" referred to in traditional writings. A plane both defines a density of matter, as well as a dimension or environment in which one may be conscious. Each plane in turn has seven subplanes or densities of matter within it.

The following is a list of the planes of the Universe. This table is best read from the bottom up, since the lowest or densest planes are at the bottom. We are most familiar with the physical plane; as we rise to higher spiritual planes, they become more abstract and harder to understand. The standard or most common name of the plane is listed, along with alternate names for the plane or names for particular sections of it. Finally, the focus of each plane is listed, which is also what that plane's material consists of.

Planes of the Universe			
Number	**Name**	**Alternate Names**	**Focus**
1	Logos	Adi / Godhead	Divinity
2	Monadic	Anupadaka / Christ	Essence
3	Atmic	Nirvanic / Spiritual	Spirit / Will
4	Buddhic	Intuitional / Akashic	Intuition / Love
5	Mental	Causal / Soul	Thought
6	Astral	Emotional	Feelings
7	Physical	Etheric	Matter / Form

Any object or being on a higher plane is invisible to objects and beings on lower planes. On the physical plane we can pass through higher plane objects as if they weren't present. We're generally not even aware of their existence. Touching planes above the physical is like trying to interact with radio waves where waving your hands in front of a television set won't affect the objects in the scene that's being transmitted. The broadcast images are in effect on a completely different plane.

Any object on a plane has a counterpart on all higher planes. For example, any physical object, or at least a counterpart or reflection of it, can be seen by an entity on the astral plane. Purely astral objects, however, can't be seen by physical plane entities. These behaviors reinforce the fact that the different planes aren't different locations, but rather different levels of vibration or consciousness.

Each living person has not only a physical body, but also a separate astral body and a body on each of the higher planes, although we're usually not conscious of them or in them. A planet on a particular plane also exists on all the higher planes, but generally on each higher level the planet seems bigger, like layers of an onion with the physical world at the center, because of additional matter that doesn't exist lower down. The smallest subatomic particle on any plane is formed of several particles of the next higher plane held together, which together form the larger and denser lower plane particle. One could conceivably subdivide particles into those of the next higher plane, and keep doing that all the way to the highest Divine plane.

Physical Plane

The physical plane is the lowest of the seven planes, and is where we spend our waking conscious lives. The physical plane is the plane of form and bodies where everything interacted with is an object. We are generally only aware of the three lowest subplanes of physical matter, which are the solid, liquid, and gas states of matter. That means we primarily interact with the lowest subplanes on the lowest plane of the Universe, which shows how uniquely special are our lives upon Earth!

The four higher subplanes form what's called the etheric plane, even though it's really just a subsection of the physical plane. These subplanes are composed of various subatomic particles. Modern science is continually increasing its knowledge of these particles and its ability to detect them. An etheric object is generally not visible to ordinary senses or equipment. Fairies and nature spirits exist etherically, as does the occasional earthbound ghost after physical death that hasn't yet made its proper transition to higher planes.

Astral Plane

The astral plane is the first higher non-physical plane that one frequently hears about it in paranormal writings. The word "astral" means related to stars; frequently, things on or from this plane appear with obvious auras or otherwise glow like stars. This plane is also called the emotional plane because the matter on it is what composes a feeling, desire, or emotion. The astral plane can also be called the plane of kama; "kama" is Sanskrit for desire and sexual love, and is also the name of a Hindu god of love.

A strong emotion may seem so intense that one can "almost touch it," and in a sense that's true, as emotions are just one plane away from the physical. On the astral plane itself emotions are many times more intense, and virtually impossible to hide from others, since there's no dense physical body in the way, and the higher astral vibrations don't have to be "stepped down" to the physical consciousness in order to be experienced. Because the astral plane is literally composed of emotion, you can see anyone's feelings in the aura around their body, just as easily as you can see material aspects like hair or clothing color in someone's physical appearance. This emotional realness and open communication can either be ecstatic bliss or horrifyingly annoying depending on the person.

Astral (and higher plane) objects and bodies can not only go through physical matter in the same space without adversely affecting either side, but they can also pass through each other without too much resistance, avoiding much of the collision aspect that happens with physical matter. One can still interact much like on the physical plane, such as walk on the ground or pick up objects; however, one can also fly, and even zoom to the other side of the world in a matter of seconds, at least with practice.

Negative or other "heavy" emotions such as hatred and fear exist on and form the lowest subplanes, also known as the lower astral, while positive "light" emotions such as affection and joy form the upper subplanes. Being conscious on the lower astral feels extremely unpleasant; this realm is the "hell" or purgatory of traditional religions. The highest astral subplanes form a "Summerland" or realm where everything seems pleasant and beautiful, and so can be called a heaven. In an out-of-body experience or near-death experience one is conscious on this plane. Similarly right after one dies and before they are born they are also on the astral. The first Angels are seen on this plane.

Note it is impossible for what we think of as "evil" to exist anywhere except on the lower half of the astral plane (and by extension the physical plane) by definition. It may be comforting to know that of the seven planes in the Universe, negativity can only ever influence 1½ of them. Even on the lowest planes, "negativity" serves an important educational purpose in our evolution. Stories about "devils" being able to invade and overthrow heaven and such are merely that: fictional stories. Heaven is a level of vibration, meaning you can't be conscious in it unless you're already filled with goodness. On the astral plane and above, changing your consciousness can automatically change the realm you see and feel around yourself. The concept that we see the world through the filter of our own energy and expectations is real enough on the physical, but on the astral where the whole plane is feelings, it's one of the most fundamental facts of existence. That is why the astral is also sometimes called the plane of illusion or glamour because so much of what we see and experience there is filtered through our own subjective biases.

Mental Plane

The next plane above the astral is called the mental plane because the "matter" on this plane composes thought. The lower subplanes express specific concrete thought, while the higher subplanes express abstract thought. For example, the general concept of "sphere" is upper mental, while a specific sphere such as "my newest yellow tennis ball" is lower mental. The higher subplanes form what's called the Causal plane because the true causes of things are often formed here before they descend into concrete effects on the lower planes. The mental plane can also be called the plane of manas; "manas" is Sanskrit for mind.

Just as rising to the astral plane leaves bodies behind, rising to the mental plane leaves emotion behind. In spite of that, this plane shouldn't be thought of as cold or purely intellectual. A different type of feeling permeates this plane where love and other, higher plane influences are much more apparent. Because the mental plane is higher than the astral, one shouldn't think that means thoughts are better than emotions. What it does mean is that thoughts are less dense than emotions. If physical bodies are like earth, emotions are like water, while thoughts are like air. That's an accurate analogy because based on the concept of "as above, so below," there is a correlation between the seven planes (starting with bodies, emotions, and thought) and the seven subplanes of the physical plane (starting with solids, liquids, and gasses). Altruistic thoughts free of any sense of selfishness that aren't entangled with desire that would confine their energy to the astral plane, rise to this level.

On the mental plane, everything moves as fast as thought. Thinking of the other side of the world instantaneously and effortlessly teleports you there. You can communicate with any being telepathically, and see the essence of each other's thoughts. Unlike on the astral and lower planes, thoughts no longer need to be translated into any language. You can change any aspect of yourself instantly; personality based concepts such as age and gender still exist, but aren't fixed in any way. After physical death, a soul can transition to this level from the astral plane after living on the astral for a short or long while. The mental plane can be considered the true Heaven. Its seven subplanes form the "Seven Heavens" described in religious literature. In the upper Causal part of this plane exists what we think of as our soul, which houses one's individual personality. Most Angels and other spiritual beings are found here.

Just as one can astral project and be conscious on the astral plane via an out-of-body experience, so is it possible to "mental project" to the mental plane. Doing that, however, is extremely rare. Being conscious on this plane while still physically alive is much more challenging because it requires a high state of spiritual evolution combined with a saintly level of devotion and love. This difficulty shows that having the energies of a plane in your consciousness is very different from being conscious on that plane itself. Everybody has emotions and thoughts, but few are able to be conscious on the astral or mental planes.

Buddhic Plane

From here on up we enter spiritual levels so high that our trying to conceive of them is like a fish trying to understand calculus! The Buddhic plane is the plane of all-encompassing Love and unity. The name "Buddhic" comes from the Sanskrit word "Buddha," meaning one who is enlightened or awake. This plane is also the plane of true spiritual insight and intuition, so is often called the Intuitional plane. Buddhic energies are still relatively rare to most of humanity; however, it's easy to mistake astral energies for Buddhic since they're both related to feeling. Standard psychic experiences and influences are astral, as is emotional love tinged with desire. True Buddhic Love and Oneness is a much higher energy. Angels and other radiant beings of a much higher sort than before can be experienced here, but now they're much harder to describe. If they descended to a level where we could visualize them in the first place, they would take forms such as "winged globes and fiery wheels" or gigantic entities with a hundred arms and a thousand eyes.

An experience of Buddhic consciousness is indescribably blissful as you feel One with everything. It can be considered the first level of Cosmic Consciousness or Samadhi. Because this plane leaves behind the concept of an individualized personality, one can't travel to it like they can lower planes. In a sense one can only experience the Buddhic plane via the "grace of God," where a desire to be on this plane prevents it from being so, since desire pulls one down to the astral. Again this plane is literally impossible to describe in words or visualize, because it's a plane higher than the mental, meaning thought has been left behind. Skeptics of metaphysical phenomena may focus on how spiritual things can't be intellectually proven. They're right because true Spirit can only be experienced, merged with, or become a part of.

While on the mental plane one sees their environment, on the Buddhic plane one becomes their environment. While on the mental plane one thinks, on the Buddhic plane one knows. Thoughts may be right or wrong, but true intuition is always right. In addition to a plane of Love, it is a plane of pure reason, containing the answer to everything. On the Buddhic plane one could conceivably ask any question, even things that should be impossible to determine, and get the correct answer. You don't ask specific questions like "how many people in the world are holding crystal spheres right now" and get a specific number in return, as much as you swim in the sum total of all possible questions and answers. A subjective question like "what is the meaning of life" would yield a burst of energy that would be felt. Of course, translating the answer down to the lower planes is the challenge. Just as any emotion drops one down to the astral plane, so does any thinking automatically drop one down to the mental plane.

The Buddhic plane is home of the Akashic Records, hence one may call that aspect of this plane the Akashic plane. The word "akasha" is Sanskrit for space or ether, and is like a fifth element beyond earth, water, air, and fire. The Akashic Records contain the history of everything everywhere. Everything that ever happens gets recorded in perfect detail. Viewing the Akashic Records can be like watching a 3D movie. Although the Akashic Records are ultimately on this plane, accurate reflections of them can be seen on the mental, and at least semi-distorted versions of them on the astral. In the heaven worlds, there are literally cinemas that tap into the Akashic Records, so you can watch any part of your past life or the lives of others.

Atmic Plane

The Atmic plane is the plane of Spirit, will, and consciousness itself. Atma is Sanskrit for "self," where this plane is one's true, innermost nature and expression. This plane of sacred and holy Spirit is the highest one you can experience before reaching Divine or semi-Divine levels. This is the plane of will because action on this level is free from any distorting or limiting influence. On the Atmic plane are found the great spiritual Masters, as well as any Enlightened spirit who has achieved Nirvana. Therefore, it is also called the Nirvanic plane. The word Nirvana is Sanskrit for "blow out," as in blowing out a candle. It means extinction or annihilation, and it literally is, at least to the concept of the separate self we're aware of on lower planes.

While on the Buddhic plane one experiences Oneness, on the Atmic plane one becomes Oneness on a much deeper level. While on the Buddhic plane one knows everything, on the Atmic plane one knows nothing. From that serene, quiet emptiness can be heard the sound or Word of the Divine. Stepped down many levels to the physical plane, a mere reflection of a reflection, we call that sound "Aum" or "Om." On this plane one truly enters the Unknown. Like the Buddhic plane, being conscious on this plane can only be described as Cosmic Consciousness where there are different levels or degrees of it. All words that could ever possibly describe this plane and level of consciousness have already been used in describing the Buddhic plane where all one can do is say it's exalted in countless additional ways to an immeasurably higher degree. No matter how blissful or expanded a state of consciousness can be, there are always deeper levels of Love!

Monadic Plane

The Monadic plane is the plane where Monads, the ultimate Divine spiritual spark in all things, express themselves and evolve and create on the lower planes. Every being, from the lowest to the highest, possesses a Monad. Your Spirit is a projection from your Monad, just as your soul and bodies are a projection of your Spirit. Spirits are at different levels of evolution; however, on the Monadic plane all are eternally equal. The word Monad is Latin for "unit" or "single," where the energies here go beyond even consciousness (whether separate or Unified) to something that can only be described as essence. This essence is beyond any type of matter or even dimension; not even the term "non-physical" is appropriate.

Space, time, and self were left behind long ago. If the Atmic plane is the Beyond, the Monadic plane is Beyond the Beyond.

As the Monadic plane is the penultimate or second highest plane, right before the Divine, this plane can, to use a religious term, be considered the "Son of God" and those on it as "Sons of God." The essence here can therefore be considered Christ energy. The word "Christ" means "anointed" or "messiah," and is a title that sometimes gets assigned to the greatest Masters, such as Jesus Christ. This plane is occasionally called the Anupadaka plane, which means "parentless." Note — Saying these energies have no origin (i.e. are parentless) and saying these energies have the Divine as their origin (i.e. are the Son of God) are basically different ways of saying the same thing.

Logos Plane

The Logos plane is the highest of the seven planes, and is the plane of Divinity. This plane is ultimate potential, and can be thought of as the eternally deep waters from which the Universe as we know it was Created. The Big Bang or birth of the Universe can be considered the Divine saying "let there be light," which resulted in the creation of the Monadic plane or level of vibration, followed by the lower planes one by one. This plane is sometimes called the Godhead plane, and sometimes called the Adi plane; "adi" is Sanskrit for "first" or "supreme." If the Atmic plane is the Unknown, the Logos plane is the Unknowable. To use terms from Christianity, if the light of the Monadic plane is the "Son," the infinite potential of the Logos is the "Father."

The word Logos (plural: Logoi) is Greek for "word" or "reason," and represents the Divine sound, vibration, and energy of the Godhead. A Logos is a deity that has the ability to be a Creator, i.e. to create Monads and breathe forth spiritual life from itself. The great beings whose physical bodies are planets, stars, galaxies, and beyond express on this level, assuming this state can be called a "level" in the first place. The being behind a planet is called a Planetary Logos, the being behind a solar system is a Solar Logos, and so on. That means there are different levels of Logoi (although it's really like comparing infinity to infinity) as a Solar Logos is formed from several Planetary Logoi, and a Galactic Logos has many Solar Logoi acting as cells in its body. Each human Monad is a cell in the body of the Planetary Logos of Earth. We are eternally One with and a part of it just as a molecular cell is always part of the body it belongs to.

Cosmic Planes

If the above wasn't expansive enough, the Universe or rather Multiverse actually extends beyond the seven planes presented. All seven planes, from the physical to the Logos, together form a single great plane called the Cosmic Physical plane. What we consider our seven planes, are actually what amount to subplanes of the Cosmic Physical. The Cosmic Physical plane is sometimes called the Cosmic Prakritic; "prakrit" is Sanskrit for "natural" or "vulgar," or in other words physical. The Cosmic Physical plane is the lowest of seven total Cosmic planes; each Cosmic plane is named after the corresponding standard plane. That is perhaps the biggest example possible of the concept of "as above, so below." Cosmic planes form the Divine. The Cosmic Astral can be considered the feelings of the Divine, the Cosmic Mental plane the thoughts of the Divine, and so on. Cosmic planes (other than the Cosmic Physical) are generally considered not to be subdivided into standard planes. The Creation of our Universe was the subdividing of the eternal Cosmic Physical plane into the seven standard planes.

Do all seven Cosmic planes together in turn form another single great plane, which is part of yet another set of seven? Do planes within planes continue like that forever like a fractal graphic? It's possible; however, at such high levels nobody can say for sure. The simplest answer is that the Cosmic planes are the highest possible. There's a lower limit where the subplanes of standard planes are as far as things can be subdivided. Therefore, there should be an upper limit, too. Cosmic planes are already Divine and eternal, so this concept doesn't put any sort of a limit on the infinity of Divinity.

The following is a more complete table of the planes of the Multiverse, showing the seven planes of our manifest Universe, how each of those planes is subdivided into seven subplanes and how all the planes together form the lowest Cosmic plane.

<table>
<tr><th colspan="5">Planes of the Multiverse</th></tr>
<tr><td colspan="5">Cosmic Logos Plane</td></tr>
<tr><td colspan="5">Cosmic Monadic Plane</td></tr>
<tr><td colspan="5">Cosmic Atmic Plane</td></tr>
<tr><td colspan="5">Cosmic Buddhic Plane</td></tr>
<tr><td colspan="5">Cosmic Mental Plane</td></tr>
<tr><td colspan="5">Cosmic Astral Plane</td></tr>
<tr><td rowspan="49">Cosmic Physical Plane</td><td rowspan="7">Plane 1</td><td rowspan="7">Logos</td><td rowspan="7"></td><td>Subplane 1</td></tr>
<tr><td>Subplane 2</td></tr>
<tr><td>Subplane 3</td></tr>
<tr><td>Subplane 4</td></tr>
<tr><td>Subplane 5</td></tr>
<tr><td>Subplane 6</td></tr>
<tr><td>Subplane 7</td></tr>
<tr><td rowspan="7">Plane 2</td><td rowspan="7">Monadic</td><td rowspan="7"></td><td>Subplane 1</td></tr>
<tr><td>Subplane 2</td></tr>
<tr><td>Subplane 3</td></tr>
<tr><td>Subplane 4</td></tr>
<tr><td>Subplane 5</td></tr>
<tr><td>Subplane 6</td></tr>
<tr><td>Subplane 7</td></tr>
<tr><td rowspan="7">Plane 3</td><td rowspan="7">Atmic</td><td rowspan="7"></td><td>Subplane 1</td></tr>
<tr><td>Subplane 2</td></tr>
<tr><td>Subplane 3</td></tr>
<tr><td>Subplane 4</td></tr>
<tr><td>Subplane 5</td></tr>
<tr><td>Subplane 6</td></tr>
<tr><td>Subplane 7</td></tr>
<tr><td rowspan="7">Plane 4</td><td rowspan="7">Buddhic</td><td rowspan="7">Akashic Records</td><td>Subplane 1</td></tr>
<tr><td>Subplane 2</td></tr>
<tr><td>Subplane 3</td></tr>
<tr><td>Subplane 4</td></tr>
<tr><td>Subplane 5</td></tr>
<tr><td>Subplane 6</td></tr>
<tr><td>Subplane 7</td></tr>
<tr><td rowspan="7">Plane 5</td><td rowspan="7">Mental</td><td rowspan="3">Causal subplanes</td><td>Subplane 1</td></tr>
<tr><td>Subplane 2</td></tr>
<tr><td>Subplane 3</td></tr>
<tr><td rowspan="4">Lower mental</td><td>Subplane 4</td></tr>
<tr><td>Subplane 5</td></tr>
<tr><td>Subplane 6</td></tr>
<tr><td>Subplane 7</td></tr>
<tr><td rowspan="7">Plane 6</td><td rowspan="7">Astral</td><td rowspan="3">Upper astral / Summerland</td><td>Subplane 1</td></tr>
<tr><td>Subplane 2</td></tr>
<tr><td>Subplane 3</td></tr>
<tr><td rowspan="2">Mid-astral</td><td>Subplane 4</td></tr>
<tr><td>Subplane 5</td></tr>
<tr><td rowspan="2">Lower astral / Purgatory</td><td>Subplane 6</td></tr>
<tr><td>Subplane 7</td></tr>
<tr><td rowspan="7">Plane 7</td><td rowspan="7">Physical</td><td rowspan="4">Etheric subplanes</td><td>Subplane 1</td></tr>
<tr><td>Subplane 2</td></tr>
<tr><td>Subplane 3</td></tr>
<tr><td>Subplane 4</td></tr>
<tr><td>Gasses</td><td>Subplane 5</td></tr>
<tr><td>Liquids</td><td>Subplane 6</td></tr>
<tr><td>Solids</td><td>Subplane 7</td></tr>
</table>

Spatial Dimensions

The physical plane is three dimensional, meaning it contains three dimensions of space. The astral plane, at least when fully experienced, has four actual spatial dimensions. Above the astral, the mental plane has five dimensions, the Buddhic six, the Atmic seven, while the Monadic and above can be considered to have infinite dimensions, or more accurately are beyond the concept of dimension altogether. Sources that refer to people or the Earth transitioning from the 3rd to the 4th dimension (or to higher dimensions) ultimately refer to evolving into being able to sense and interact with these higher plane vibrations. One potential way of understanding or getting in touch with the spiritual energies of higher planes is meditating upon or visualizing multidimensional objects.

The basic element of existence is the point, which has no size, so can be considered the 0th dimension. If a point moves in any direction, it draws out a line. That line is the 1st dimension. If a line moves in a new direction, it marks out a flat plane where a plane is the 2nd dimension. A line segment (as opposed to a line that stretches infinitely in both directions) moving marks out a quadrilateral, such as a square or parallelogram. If a plane moves in another new direction, it marks out a solid or section of space where a solid is the 3rd dimension.

A 4th dimension of space can be hard to visualize. Each new dimension goes in a direction perpendicular to all existing directions. As the first three dimensions already cover forward/backward, left/right, and up/down, a 4th dimension perpendicular to the first three has to tunnel into spiritual realms. The prefix "hyper" is used to describe a higher dimensional version of something. If a 3D cube moves in a direction perpendicular to its three spatial dimensions, it marks out a 4D object called a hypercube. A hypercube effectively has infinite volume, since there are infinite solids that can fit into it along its 4th axis. That is like how a standard 3D cube effectively has infinite area, since flat 2D squares can be stacked on top of each other forever without filling it up. Any three dimensions taken from a 4D or higher dimensional object form a solid or hyperplane. A hyperhyperplane or hypercube is a 4D region of space, while a hyperhypercube is a 5D cube.

Time is a different class of dimension. Time can be considered a 4th dimension when combined with our three physical space dimensions. One way to visualize an object of any dimension is by visualizing an object of one dimension lower moving over time. For example, a 3D cube is a flat 2D square moving through the 3rd dimension over time. The end result of the motion is like two copies of the original object at the start and end locations, plus lines connecting each pair of vertices, faces connecting each pair of edges, and so on.

An object of any dimension can be measured by parameters of the lower dimensions. For example, a 1D line segment has two 0D endpoints, a 2D square has a 1D perimeter, and a 3D cube has a 2D surface area (as well as a 1D length). Similarly a 4D hypercube has what can be considered a 3D "surface volume," and 2D (as well as 1D) "lengths." Just as a 3D scene can be depicted by projecting it or flattening it upon a 2D surface, the same can be done with higher dimensions. That means when dealing with locations on the astral and higher planes, one can, at most, point to a physical location where the higher dimensional place would be if projected into our three dimensions.

The following table summarizes spatial dimensions and characteristics of an object in that dimension. For example, a cube in the 3rd dimension (corresponding to the physical plane) has 8 points, 12 edges, and 6 faces. Notice how the number of points doubles in each higher dimension. In general the number of any element in any dimension is equal to twice that element from the previous dimension plus the number of the next lower element from the previous dimension. For example, the number of 1D edges or lines on a 3D cube (12) is equal to twice the number of edges on a 2D square (4 x 2 = 8) plus the number of points on a 2D square (4). In other words, when moving a square through the 3rd dimension, you get the number of edges on the start and end position squares, and also get an edge for each point on a square that becomes a line when moved.

Spatial Dimensions					
Plane	**Dim.**	**0D Points**	**1D Edges**	**2D Faces**	**3D Solids**
-	0	1	-	-	-
-	1	2	1	-	-
-	2	4	4	1	-
Physical	3	8	12	6	1
Astral	4	16	32	24	8
Mental	5	32	80	80	40
Buddhic	6	64	192	240	160
Atmic	7	128	448	672	560

The following table shows objects in the various dimensions projected onto a flat 2D surface. The objects seem more complicated the higher in dimension they go because additional dimensions or axes are depicted. In a sense, however, the reverse is true since objects become less dense the more spiritual they become. The lower planes are built on top of or formed from elements of higher planes. Another way of looking at it is that as an object becomes less dense, it's able to move through and express in additional dimensions. For example, a very heavy physical object is stuck on the ground or limited to falling down to the ground in one dimension, a lighter object can be rolled around on the surface of the ground in two dimensions, something truly weightless can fly around through three dimensions, and finally spirit can not only fly, but travel through space and time in four or more dimensions.

A 2D square

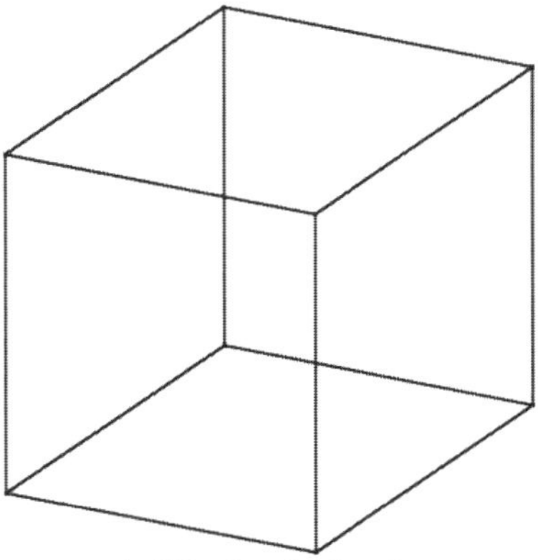

A 3D physical cube

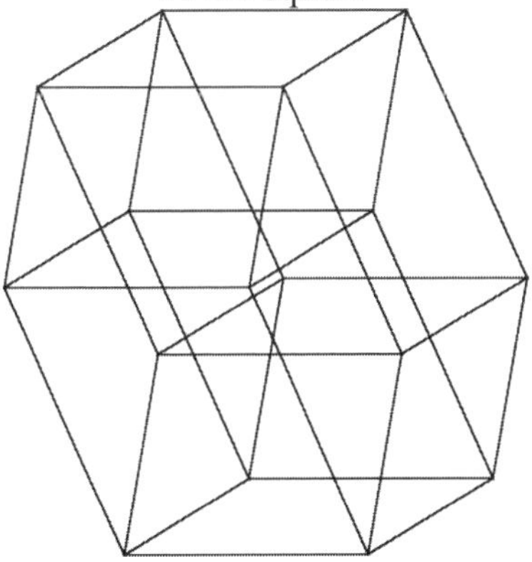

A 4D astral hypercube

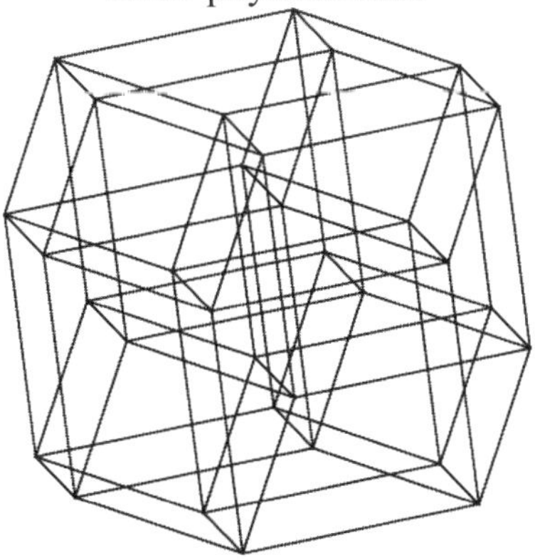

A 5D mental hyperhypercube

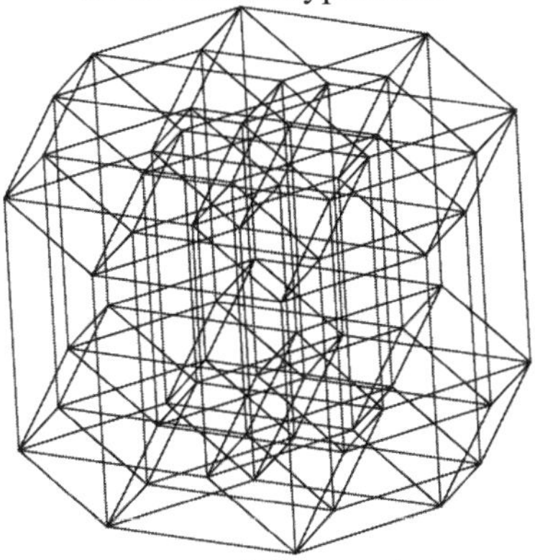

A 6D Buddhic particle

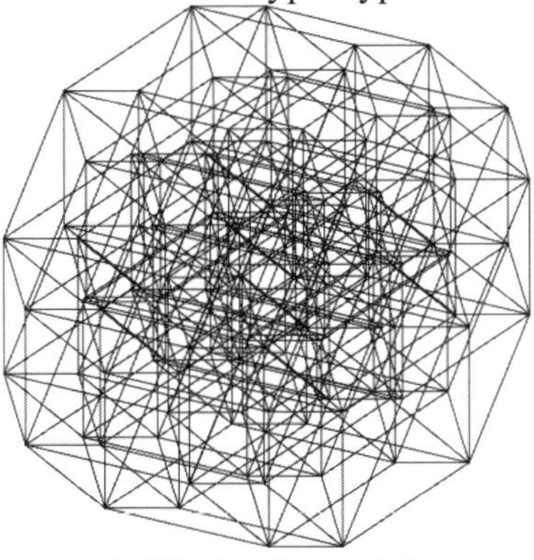

A 7D Atmic particle

2:
Rays of Divinity

"We all live under the same sky, but we don't have the same horizon."
- Konrad Adenauer

Having familiarized ourselves with the landscape of the Universe as defined by the seven planes, the next area of interest is the energies that play through it. The most fundamental powers in the Universe are called Rays. A Ray is nothing less than an emanation from Divinity itself. Picture the Divine as a great central sun or the center of a flower where the Rays are like rays streaming forth from the sun, or the unfolding petals of a flower. There are seven Rays total, each defining or expressing an aspect of existence.

The seven Rays can be considered the "Seven Beings before the Throne of God," since they're just one step removed from Divinity. As the Rays stream forth from the Divine, galaxies, stars, planets, and evolved beings act as receiving and transmitting stations, until eventually the Rays shine upon each of us. In this respect the Rays are like drinking water or electricity in a city. The water starts from a master reservoir or power generation station and gets distributed and stepped down to substations until it reaches individual homes.

Each of the Rays exists on all planes, from the Logos to the physical, and in a sense they are a more fundamental way to divide or classify the Universe than the planes themselves since the action of the Rays actually manifested the planes and created the Universe in the first place. If the planes of the Universe are a "noun" because they're similar to places, the Rays are more like a "verb" because they're energy. If the planes are the amplitude of a vibration, the Rays are the frequency of the vibration. If the planes are a way of dividing everything in the Universe "vertically" into higher and lower, the Rays are a way of dividing the Universe "horizontally" into flavors.

The seven Rays are listed in the following table. In addition to a number, each Ray has a name that indicates what aspect of Divinity it covers. Included is the most fundamental word that describes the Ray's essence, its traditional name as most commonly seen in other sources, along with additional keywords associated with that Ray.

The Seven Rays			
#	**Name**	**Traditional Name**	**Keywords**
1	Will	Will / Power	Purpose, Conviction
2	Wisdom	Love / Wisdom	Compassion, Life
3	Activity	Active Intelligence	Creativity, Invention
4	Synthesis	Harmony Through Conflict	Balance, Art
5	Awareness	Concrete Science	Knowledge, Discipline
6	Appreciation	Devotion	Idealism, Commitment
7	Expression	Ceremonial Magic	Order, Ritual

Notice the odd numbered Rays are more yang or traditionally masculine, and focus on forms of manifestation, while the even numbered Rays are more yin or traditionally feminine, and focus on forms of love. In addition, the first three Rays compose a class called "Rays of Aspect," since will, wisdom, and activity form a primal trinity of the fundamental aspects of the Universe. The last four Rays are called "Rays of Attribute," since they build upon or combine the first three Rays to create new attributes or energies. Finally, each Ray is most similar to the plane of the same number, although it's again important to emphasize that each Ray exists on all planes, and that no Ray should be considered more spiritual or evolved than another. Earlier Rays may seem better since they deal with more fundamental energies, while later Rays may seem better since they encompass the earlier ones.

Correspondences to the Seven Rays				
Number	**Name**	**Type**	**Class**	**Plane**
1	Will	Yang	Aspect	Logos
2	Wisdom	Yin	Aspect	Monadic
3	Activity	Yang	Aspect	Atmic
4	Synthesis	Yin	Attribute	Buddhic
5	Awareness	Yang	Attribute	Mental
6	Appreciation	Yin	Attribute	Astral
7	Expression	Yang	Attribute	Physical

Each Ray defines a characteristic of Divinity, and continues the "divine story" told by all the previous Rays. That means one could continue the story and consider additional energies beyond the seven described here. Some sources consider there to be twelve Rays total, with the last five Rays added to the list referring to various aspects of spiritual growth. Those additional Rays are ways of combining the first seven, just as the last four Rays are ways of combining the first three. Just as there are additional more subtle chakras beyond the seven within our physical bodies, so are there additional more subtle Rays beyond the main ones described here. In a sense, there are an infinite number of Rays. Earlier Rays are like the branches of a tree, and later Rays are like the leaves of a tree.

Most everything can be classified as being on one of the seven Rays, including people. Each person has their soul on one of the Rays, and their personality on another Ray. One is the Ray of your true spiritual nature and purpose, and the other, the Ray that indicates how you're expressing in this particular lifetime. The personality Ray is usually different from the soul Ray, as a way of defining the internal versus external Ray influences in a person's life. More subtle aspects of ourselves, such as our bodies, emotions, minds, and even Spirits, can also be associated with one of the Rays. One can determine their personality Ray by just reading the definitions and picking the one that fits them the most. The soul Ray is a deeper influence and therefore harder to verify, since knowing it ultimately requires soul consciousness or awareness of past lives, but with appropriate contemplation it too can be intuited.

The seven Rays are similar to the twelve signs of the zodiac in astrology, in that they're both ways of dividing the spectrum of inner characteristics into discrete buckets. The Rays can be treated as a system similar to astrology. One can determine compatibility between Rays, beneficial times for people of each Ray, and so on. Just as some people have their zodiac sign fit them very well, while others are affected by multiple signs, the same is true with Rays. Some people seem almost a pure incarnation of a particular Ray, while others seem to express a number of them equally. As with zodiac signs, each of the Rays can be expressed in a negative as well as a positive manner, while one is learning the lessons of a Ray or how to handle it properly. Just as the rays of the sun affect different areas of the world at different times, so does each of the Rays have cycles of increased and decreased activity. These Ray activity periods can affect areas small and large, ranging from an individual person's life to the world as a whole.

The following table is an example of specific things associated with the Rays. Certain gemstones are pure expressions of a particular Ray. Each Ray has a primary mineral that most strongly embodies it, along with other minerals that are also associated with it. One way of getting attuned with a Ray is through meditation upon these minerals.

Minerals of the Seven Rays		
#	**Main Mineral**	**Other Minerals**
1	Diamond	Clear Quartz, Zircon, Magnetite
2	Sapphire	Lapis Lazuli, Turquoise, Sodalite
3	Emerald	Aquamarine, Jade, Malachite, Peridot
4	Jasper	Agate, Tiger Eye, Chalcedony, Serpentine
5	Topaz	Citrine, Chrysoberyl, Amber
6	Ruby	Tourmaline, Garnet, Carnelian, Red Coral
7	Amethyst	Kunzite, Porphyry, Violane

As the Rays express the Universe, there are numerous other things that can be associated with them. There are several ways one can map Rays to colors, such as simply using the seven colors of the rainbow. Traditionally, each Ray has an outer or exoteric color for external expression and a different inner or esoteric color for spiritual expression. I've found the best overall color for a Ray to be that which is based on the minerals that correspond to it. This arrangement nicely has white and purple covering the end Rays, and the middle Rays covered by the rest of the rainbow in sequence.

Colors of the Seven Rays			
Number	**Mineral Color**	**Outer Color**	**Inner Color**
1	White	Orange	Red
2	Blue	Purplish Indigo	Light Blue
3	Green	Black	Green
4	Yellow	Cream	Yellow
5	Orange	Yellow	Indigo
6	Red	Red	Silvery Rose
7	Purple	White	Violet

Ray #1: Will

The 1st Ray is the beginning of everything, and is the most fundamental energy possible. All things started from an act of will, including the Universe itself. The 1st Ray is the infinite power of will. People on the 1st Ray are leaders, with a strong sense of purpose. The strength of this Ray gives one the conviction and courage to keep going no matter what obstacles may present themselves, even if others disapprove.

The 1st Ray is like the axle in the middle of a wheel, which helps hold all the spokes together. That's a secret of the 1st Ray and leadership in general: Confident in its own state of being, the 1st Ray doesn't need or seek additional power, but rather uses its power to provide the space for the other Rays to do their magic.

Unevolved, the 1st Ray is controlling, egocentric, arrogant, stubborn, narrow minded, isolated, and destructive. The 1st Ray is associated with the number one, since it sees the Oneness in all people in the positive sense, or focuses on the gratification of the separate individual in the negative sense.

Ray #2: Wisdom

The 2nd Ray provides a Divine counterpoint to the 1st. The 2nd Ray nurtures wisdom and intuition. Through wisdom comes compassion for others, making this the Ray of unconditional love. A focus on others makes one aware of life energies, making this nothing less than the Ray of life itself.

While the 1st Ray is powerful, the 2nd is serene. If the 1st Ray is the Divine Father, the 2nd is the Divine Mother. The 1st Ray may have willed the world into being, but the 2nd Ray makes the world go around, just as "love makes the world go around." While 1st Ray people are leaders, 2nd Ray people are teachers. The 2nd Ray can produce good leaders as well, but they lead more quietly by example as opposed to giving orders. The 2nd Ray is the ultimate philosopher, who seeks to embody qualities internally as opposed to manifest them externally.

Unevolved, the 2nd Ray presents itself as lazy, apathetic, weak-willed, overly shy and self-effacing, snobbish, or spiritually proud with a condescending attitude toward those who seem less spiritual.

Ray #3: Activity

The 3rd Ray expands the polarity of the first two Rays into a triangle, resulting in numerous ways of interacting and expressing. All this potential bursts forth as the Ray of dynamic creativity. If the first two Rays are parents, the 3rd Ray is their enthusiastic child. This Ray is traditionally called the Ray of "Active Creative Intelligence," which covers the points that there's lots of energy, that energy is directed into manifesting things, and that there's conscious intelligence behind it. The 3rd Ray is intellectual, but in an abstract philosophical way, and so makes a good professor or inventor. The 3rd Ray is traditionally associated with astrology.

The 3rd Ray is ambitious, focused, and communicative, and therefore often successful in business, especially as an entrepreneur where they have the freedom to do what they want. It loves novelty, change, and efficiency, such as that produced by machinery and new technology. Both the 3rd and 2nd Rays make inspiring teachers; however, the 2nd Ray person teaches more by example, waiting for you to come to them when you're ready, while the 3rd Ray teaches in a more outgoing manner, to all who they can get to listen.

Unevolved, the 3rd Ray acts absent minded, unreliable, inaccurate, deluded, secretive, manipulative, or overly ambitious. Individuals on the 3rd Ray may be unable to control or quiet their minds, can be active or creative for selfish as opposed to altruistic reasons, or just let themselves get overly busy and eternally distracted.

Ray #4: Synthesis

The 4th Ray is the combination of the powerful 1st Ray and the peaceful 2nd Ray. This Ray is traditionally called the Ray of "Harmony through Conflict," since it learns about and achieves inner harmony through outer struggle. The 4th Ray covers all couples, dualities, and opposites. This is symbolized by being the middle Ray, and the number four being two plus two. More importantly this Ray deals with the interaction, balance, union, and marriage of opposites, making it the Ray of synthesis, or the whole that's greater than the sum of the parts that compose it.

The tension and swirling energies held by the 4th Ray makes it the Ray of artistic expression, drama, and adventure stories. It's a Ray for all those who work with or seek fairness, such as judges, journalists, and social activists. This is one of the most passionate Rays, with the most life in it! Both the 4th and 1st Rays are associated with politics; however, the 1st Ray tries to impose its views, while the 4th seeks balance, or at least eventually achieves balance after supporting one side and fighting with the other side for a long while, before realizing that the only way to truly get rid of an enemy is to make them a friend. The 1st Ray may embody the concept of Oneness; however, the 4th Ray is our epic journey into Oneness.

Unevolved, the 4th Ray feels unbalanced, erratic, overly dramatic, rebellious, full of negativity, and is unable to control its extreme emotions.

Ray #5: Awareness

Having balanced energies in the 4th Ray, the Divine now becomes conscious of itself, seeking and transmitting the light of understanding. The 5th Ray is the combination of the strong 1st Ray and insightful 3rd Ray. The 5th Ray is about awareness, which often expresses itself as knowledge. This Ray is traditionally called the Ray of "Concrete Science," which certainly applies, however, there is much more to it than just intellectual materialism. The 5th Ray is about the mind, and by extension, meditation and discipline. It provides form, stability, grounding, and self-reflection, which are often overlooked virtues. The 5th Ray is also about acceptance and truth. More than any other Ray, the 5th sees and accepts things accurately the way they really are here and now, with no illusions about how things could be or how one might wish they were.

Both the 5th and 2nd Rays are psychological; however, the 5th deals with the intellectual or theoretical parts of inner development, while the 2nd the more intuitional or feeling parts. Both the 5th and 3rd Rays are intellectual; however, the 3rd is more abstract and chaotic, while the 5th is more concrete and regulated. The most inspired genius is a combination of the 5th and 3rd Rays where the 5th provides the ability to organize what's known, and the 3rd allows expanding it in new directions.

Unevolved, the 5th Ray seems detached, unemotional, critical of others, closed minded about anything that can't be seen physically or proven scientifically, and with intellectual pride considering itself better than those who seem less intelligent.

Ray #6: Appreciation

Having become aware of itself in the 5th Ray, the Divine now turns inward and appreciates itself. The 6th Ray is the combination of the loving 2nd Ray and the abstract 3rd Ray. The 6th Ray is the Ray of loving devotion. This devotion can be directed toward anything because regardless of what seems to be doing the appreciating and what seems to be appreciated, ultimately everything is a part of the Divine! Most traditional religions or belief systems, especially ones that focus on faith in a Deity or Master teacher, are an expression of the 6th Ray. This Ray also covers selfless service, which is another way of showing appreciation for others or the Divine. The focus on faith makes this the Ray of unrestricted idealism, with imaginative dreams of how things could be or should be.

Both the 6th and 1st Rays are committed; however, the 1st is committed because it makes a decision to, and willfully stays committed despite all obstacles, while the 6th is committed out of an inner feeling because it desires to be. Both the 6th and 2nd Rays are about love; however, the 2nd loves in a more abstract or Universal sense, while the 6th feels love toward something specific in a more real and passionate sense. Both the 6th and 3rd Rays are visionary; however, the 3rd is idealistic as a means to create things or discover secrets, while the 6th is idealistic for its own sake because it enjoys the feeling. Both the 6th and 4th Rays are emotional; however, the 4th works with feelings in general, while the 6th directs those feelings toward a particular purpose.

Unevolved, a person on the 6th Ray feels fanatical, intolerant of those with different beliefs, blind to their own shortcomings or those of people around them, trapped in their own fantasies and illusions, withdrawn from the world, overly sensitive and self-sacrificing, or vain with too much narcissism and pride.

Ray #7: Expression

The 7th and final Ray is the combination of the first three Rays; all energies are present. The Divine having appreciated itself, now does the final step: truly expressing itself. The 7th Ray is about all forms of expression, both individual and group, and both spiritual and physical. The 7th Ray is associated with spiritual orders and Mystery Schools, especially pagan or Tantric belief systems that focus on magic, ritual, ceremony, nature, and celebration. Being the last standard Ray, the 7th also opens the door and acts as a bridge to higher levels of understanding. On a more material level, the 7th Ray expresses as structured organizations such as clubs, companies, the military, and nations.

Both the 7th and 3rd Rays are active; however, the 3rd Ray creates and invents new things in an abstract manner, while the 7th Ray expresses or makes use of existing things in a concrete manner. Both the 7th and 4th Rays are artistic; however, 4th Ray art is more traditional and static, such as painting and sculpture, while 7th Ray art is more worldly and dynamic, such as dancing and parades. Both the 7th and 5th Rays are disciplined and ordered; however, the 5th Ray is more internally disciplined, while the 7th Ray applies order to external activities. The most inspired art is a combination of the 7th and 4th Rays. The 4th provides a deep inner meaning and the 7th a beautiful outer form.

Unevolved, the 7th Ray expresses as bureaucratic, rigid, and cliquish, with too much pride in one's own Path and dislike of those on different Paths. The 7th Ray can also be overly materialistic and focused on external things, or too involved with hedonistic pleasures such as sexuality.

The Three Outpourings

Even though the Rays are being treated as energies, they're more accurately Universal archetypes, and therefore are not something that can be readily measured like standard energies. This subtlety or abstraction is beyond the level of even spiritual energies, which are already something not normally perceivable by physical senses. However, the first three Rays, the Rays of Aspect, do correspond to fundamental concrete energies in the Universe. These three energies are called Outpourings because they are sent forth by the Divine to create, populate, and evolve our Universe.

The First Outpouring is fohat, which means cosmic electricity or force. Fohat is the essence of all energy not directly related to a living being. On the physical plane it manifests as the Universal force behind influences such as electromagnetism, gravity, and the force within atoms. This Outpouring happened first because it created the Universe, and is therefore associated with involution, since it created the lower planes and prepared the way for them to be inhabited by entities. The First Outpouring is related to the 3rd Ray, since they both deal with creative activity.

The Second Outpouring is prana (pronounced prah-nuh), which is Sanskrit for "breath of life." Prana is the essence of life itself, and is something all beings, from the highest to the lowest, make use of. Many physical and mental health problems are caused by a lack of prana or improper bodily processing of it. Pranayama is a type of yoga that focuses on controlling the breath, and by extension, improving the flow of prana. The Second Outpouring followed the first, and became the life force to ensoul the environment created by the First Outpouring. The Second Outpouring is related to the 2nd Ray since the loving awareness of the latter is the essence of life.

The Third Outpouring is kundalini (pronounced koon-duh-lee-nee), which is Sanskrit for "spiral" or "coiled." Kundalini is the energy of evolution, or the gradual spiraling path we all take upward toward Spirit. This Outpouring is nothing less than the pressure of the Divine will itself! It happens last because kundalini is something that all life eventually awakens to, or an entity first activates after starting their spiritual Path. Kundalini could be considered a destructive energy, since it dissolves old or lower forms as it rises back to Divinity. Kundalini exists within all people. Its presence within and influence on the human body is described more in the chapter "Spiritual Bodies." The Third Outpouring is related to the 1st Ray, since they both deal with will.

As described above, the three Outpourings correspond to the first three Rays, but in reverse order. Why is that? From the standpoint of the Divine as represented by the Rays themselves, the Universe is first Created through an act of will (represented by the 1st Ray) and then later the Universe is populated with life and activity (represented by the 2nd and 3rd Rays). However, from the standpoint of beings perceiving and evolving within the Universe, the first energy is activity or external existence (represented by the First Outpouring). Life and will (represented by the Second and Third Outpourings) are qualities we evolve into expressing and knowing. Notice that the three Outpourings deal with manifesting, existing within, and transcending the Universe, making them similar to the trinity represented by the Hindu deities Brahma the Creator, Vishnu the Preserver, and Shiva the Destroyer.

3:
Spiritual Bodies

"I am in my body the way most people drive in their cars."
- Laurie Anderson

In studying spirituality, one of the most relevant things to do is see how it applies to our own lives. Having defined the planes of the Universe, it follows to see what's contained within them, or what parts of ourselves exist on the various planes. Any object on one plane exists on all higher planes, or has higher plane counterparts. Since we live in physical bodies, with the physical plane being the lowest, that means that we also have bodies on all the higher planes. Each body is usually named after the plane it exists on. Our astral body is our body on the astral plane, our mental body is our body on the mental plane, and so on.

Any body is a superset of the bodies on lower planes. Anything on a lower plane has higher plane counterparts; however, many things on higher planes aren't visible lower down. That makes higher bodies effectively larger than lower ones, or have what amounts to auras that extend out farther the higher one goes. One way to depict the bodies is with the physical as a dense circle in the middle, and other bodies as increasingly large and less dense circles surrounding it. The outermost circle, for the Logoic or Divine plane, should really be considered to have no boundary, since the Divine is eternal and infinite. Note: bodies aren't limited to human bodies; the same concept applies to most everything in the Universe. For example, Earth has an astral body; our planet appears "larger" on the astral plane. Expanding bodies can even apply to the Universe itself. The entire physical plane is really a small subsection created within a much larger Universe and can be considered the physical body of God itself.

Interpenetrating Bodies

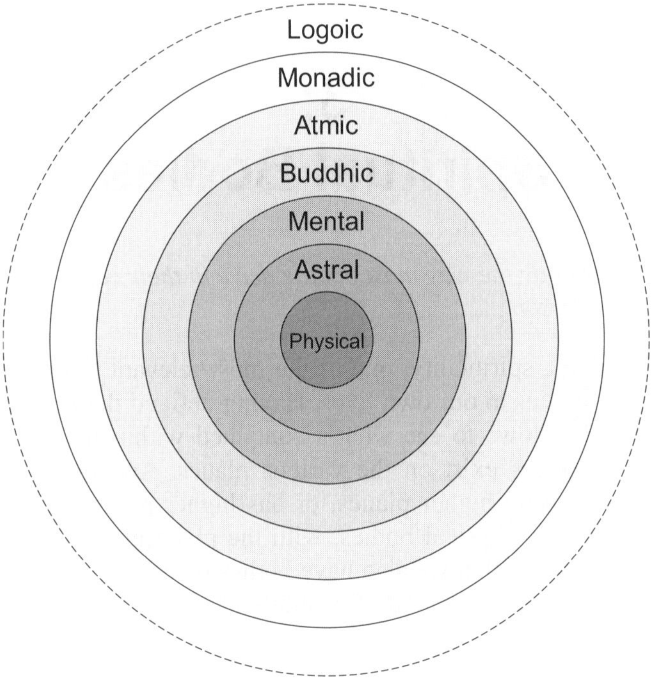

Personality

The physical, astral, and lower mental bodies together form one's personality. The personality is everything that defines us within a particular lifetime, which includes our dense body, emotional inclinations, and intellectual nature. For example, all our desires are stored in or expressed by our astral bodies, while our knowledge, beliefs, and memories are stored in our mental bodies. This trinity formed by the three lowest bodies is called the lower triad. All three bodies are mortal; they are created before birth and discarded after death. Since all things are composed of spirit in different densities, that means even the physical body can be considered one of our "spiritual bodies."

The physical plane is divided into dense physical and etheric subplanes. These halves are different enough from each other to almost be considered separate planes. The part of our physical body on the etheric subplanes is called the etheric double. The etheric double is the same size as the physical body and looks very similar, except it has an aura extending out from it. This aura can be seen with psychic vision or sensed intuitively. People's health and moods can be seen in the strength and coloring of their aura.

Our consciousness is always focused in one of our bodies, usually the lowest. Upon physical death, consciousness is forced to move to the astral body because the astral is now the new lowest body. Out-of-body or near-death experiences are one way one can experience consciousness in a higher body while a lower body still exists. Note — Just because one doesn't consciously inhabit a body doesn't mean one isn't using it. For example, any emotion is reflected in the astral body, and any thinking uses the mental body.

Everything in the Universe is alive, which means each of our bodies is alive separate from our consciousness inhabiting it. Feelings such as hunger, an addiction to a physical substance, or the need to procreate are more influences coming from our physical and astral bodies, than desires we create ourselves. The astral body, when considered separately from ourselves, is called the desire elemental, and the mental body when considered separately is called the thought elemental. Many emotional responses are due to the desire elemental reacting out of past habit or due to its current composition, which then affects one's consciousness, instead of an intentional choice by the person. Having a "song running through your head" is the thought elemental doing the same thing over and over again on its own, which your consciousness senses.

It's important to be aware of what things are consciously chosen by you, versus are just influences coming from one of the bodies of your personality. Many people let their bodies control them, which is like a horse leading its rider. Substances such as alcohol and drugs can deaden higher influences, allowing the lower bodies to do things one regrets later. A significant part of spiritual growth is exercising, training, and refining our bodies, so they can be our willing and effective servants instead of our masters. That doesn't mean one shouldn't ever be gentle and understanding with their bodies.

Sometimes bodies need to have fun or relax, just as pet dogs sometimes need to be able to run around without a leash.

Soul

"You don't have a soul. You are a soul. You have a body."
- C.S. Lewis

Above the personality exists the soul. The soul is frequently called our higher self. The soul is sometimes called the ego, even though the term "ego" is more often used to refer to one's lower or selfish nature. Unlike the lower personality bodies that continually get recreated and destroyed before and after each lifetime, the soul is effectively immortal, since it exists across all our lifetimes. Ultimately, even the soul has a beginning and an end. It was created at the beginning of our human evolution and will eventually be transcended after we become Masters and graduate from the human kingdom.

The mental plane is divided into a dense lower mental half and an upper Causal half. These are different enough from each other to almost be considered separate planes. The mental plane is similar to the physical plane in this respect, since both are divided into two halves. The part of our mental body on the higher mental subplanes is called the Causal body. The soul can be considered the consciousness with the Causal body.

The Causal body stores our virtues, wisdom, and talents across lifetimes. This home of the soul is sometimes called the "house not made with hands." If the Causal body is a bathtub, each lifetime is like a pitcher of water. The lessons and experiences we acquire in a life are like adding food coloring to that pitcher. After death, the water in the pitcher gets poured into the bathtub, allowing the bathtub or soul as a whole to grow and improve over time.

The soul is on a high enough plane that it only contains that which is good and positive. Note that often what we think of as negative in our lives actually helps develop higher qualities. For example, we learn discipline and endurance through difficult experiences, we often don't know how much we love someone until they're no longer with us, and so on. The soul never contains anything negative, and can never be adversely affected no matter how evil one may be on lower planes. What we think of as evil simply can't exist on the mental plane. The closest that can happen is analogous to bringing a video of a horror movie into a sacred temple. The video is just an inert concept; even if it's played, it's still only an image as opposed to reality.

Not only is each soul growing, but the number of souls in existence increases over time. Just as the Universe is expanding, so are new souls being created. If the Universe is a garden, we are the plants growing in it, and the gardener maintaining the garden can be considered "God." Eventually, the older plants grow enough to help out the gardener, or in other words go to seed and cause additional plants to sprout themselves. In the unfathomably distant future, we'll grow enough to be able to give birth to new souls altogether, instead of just giving birth to new physical bodies to house existing souls for one lifetime as we do now.

Spirit

Above the soul exists the Spirit. Like the soul, the Spirit is everything that defines us across lifetimes. The Spirit is sometimes called the oversoul, although the term oversoul can also just be another way of referring to the soul itself. The Spirit includes our bodies on the upper Causal, Buddhic, and Atmic planes. In other words, the Spirit means our abstract knowing, love, and will aspects. The trinity formed by these spiritual bodies is called the Higher Triad. It's sometimes called the trinity of Atma, Buddhi, and Manas; "manas" is Sanskrit for mind.

Bodies on such spiritual planes are hardly bodies in the traditional sense of the word, but are rather principles or expressions of energy. Since these spiritual planes are so high and filled with Oneness, there's no longer any concern about bodies acting independently or in negative ways. The challenge with the higher bodies is awakening and becoming aware of them in the first place.

The Higher Triad of Spirit and the lower triad of the personality are similar; their three aspects are related to each other in reverse order, forming lower and higher octaves of the same energies. The mental body (highest part of the personality) and the upper Causal body (lowest part of the Spirit) cover concrete and abstract forms of thought, the lower and higher forms of knowing. The astral body (middle part of the personality) and the Buddhic body (middle part of the Spirit) cover emotion and love, the lower and higher forms of feeling. The physical body (lowest part of the personality) and the Atmic body (highest part of the Spirit) cover existence and will, the lower and higher forms of action.

The highest aspect of Spirit is the Monad, which exists on the second highest or Monadic plane. Monads are the ultimate Divine sparks within everyone. Every creature in the manifest Universe, from the lowest to the highest, has a Monad. All Monads are effectively equal. The only difference between the Monad of a rock and the Monad of an Archangel is the Archangel's Monad has more experience on the lower planes. The Spirit and its trinity of aspects is actually a reflection or division of the essence of the Monad. If the Monad is white light, the Atmic, Buddhic, and Causal bodies are that light classified into a rainbow of colors. The Monad has each of the three aspects of Spirit within it, but at the same time, the whole is greater than the sum of the parts. Our spiritual bodies and especially our Monads are effectively immortal, since they exist just once, and don't get recreated for each physical incarnation.

The Monadic principle is the highest "body," where there's nothing higher other than the eternal Logos plane. If the Monad is a ray of white light, the source of that light is a Divine Sun on the Logos plane. Each of us is ultimately a ray of light from the same Sun, making us all part of the same Divine Being. The Monads of everyone in the human race put together are like cells in the body of the One Being that encompasses the human lifewave as a whole.

Sutratma

Our bodies aren't separate from each other. In a sense we have just one body where the parts on different planes are just different densities of the whole. What amounts to a thread or pipe runs through all our bodies, connecting them to each other and allowing spiritual life to flow down from above. This stream of life is called the sutratma, which is Sanskrit for "soul thread."

On the astral plane, the sutratma appears as a "silver cord" connecting the astral body to the physical, which can sometimes be seen or felt during out-of-body experiences. When the sutratma reaches the physical plane, it turns into something called sushumna. Sushumna (Sanskrit for "grace") runs down the spinal cord, and can be considered the etheric counterpart of the physical body's central nervous system. On either side of sushumna are two related lines called ida and pingala. Ida (Sanskrit for "pale") is to the left of sushumna, and focuses on yin, traditionally feminine, lunar, or calming influences. Pingala (Sanskrit for "reddish") is to the right of sushumna, and focuses on yang, traditionally masculine, solar, or energizing influences. Sushumna, ida, and pingala are the three main nadis in the body. A nadi (Sanskrit for "conduit" or "stream") is an etheric channel through which prana or life force flows.

Antahkarana

Related to the sutratma is the antahkarana. The antahkarana is also a thread that runs through our bodies and overlays the sutratma. The antahkarana acts as a communications wire or access road, allowing spiritual influences and consciousness to move in both directions. The word antahkarana is Sanskrit for "work between," where it's often called the "rainbow bridge" because it connects our diverse bodies together. It's also called the "bridge between heaven and earth," since it connects the personality to the soul and spirit, and is the channel by which one travels into spiritual Enlightenment.

Unlike the sutratma that always exists, the antahkarana must be built from the physical body up. Each soul has the task to develop or construct their antahkarana. Initially one isn't aware of their higher bodies or principles. As one develops spiritual qualities, the antahkarana grows and expands, allowing one to receive impressions from the next higher plane, and to start using the next higher body. Early in one's evolution the antahkarana exists only as a potential, and is like a thin thread, weak and basically unusable. Gradually the antahkarana strengthens and expands until it's large enough to act like a wide multilane freeway.

As with many aspects of spirituality, what exists for the individual exists on a greater level for humanity as a whole. There is a group antahkarana which is formed of the threads of everyone's individual antahkaranas. As we grow individually, the human antahkarana grows. Once the majority of humanity is spiritually

Enlightened, the One Being that we together form will also be Enlightened.

Permanent Atoms

Each body has a central or primary point called a permanent atom. This point can be considered the location in the body where the sutratma runs through it. A permanent atom, as the name indicates, is a permanent part of a body. Normal bodies are constantly replacing cells, or otherwise taking in new matter and expelling old matter, but the permanent atom always remains a part of it. A permanent atom even survives the death of a body. After death the permanent atom for the discarded body gets drawn up into higher planes and becomes dormant. Before physical birth, the permanent atom acts as a seed around which the rest of the new body is formed.

Permanent atoms exist on all planes for which one has bodies, and are named after the plane in question. The physical permanent atom exists on the physical plane, the astral permanent atom exists on the astral plane, and so on. The lower mental and Causal halves of the mental plane are different enough in energy to have separate permanent atoms. The permanent atom for the lower mental plane is called the "mental unit." The permanent atom on the Monadic plane is the Monad itself.

The function of a permanent atom is to store a history of everything that has ever happened to the surrounding body. A permanent atom is similar to the Akashic Records in this respect. It's also similar to the virtue storing Causal body; however, unlike the Causal body, the permanent atoms can also store negative vibrations (assuming they're in the personality bodies where negative vibrations can exist in the first place). The permanent atom also broadcasts these recorded vibrations, allowing it to attract energy of a similar nature. Before birth, the permanent atom draws around itself matter of similar quality, allowing one to more or less continue their growth where they left off in a previous lifetime. During life, the permanent atom helps implement karma, by drawing experiences that fit the vibrations being given off.

In spirituality the term "atom" refers to the smallest element of matter possible on a plane, which on the physical plane would be a subatomic particle quite a bit smaller than what's called an atom in mainstream science. The highest subplane of each plane is usually called the atomic subplane because atoms are again one of the smallest things possible, and the highest subplane is the least dense and containing the finest matter. Permanent atoms always exist on the atomic subplane of each plane, with the exception of the mental unit, which is on the highest subplane of the lower mental plane.

Permanent atoms can't ever be constrained or interfered with through mechanical or even energetic means. The physical permanent atom wouldn't even be harmed or affected by a nuclear bomb because it's already the smallest element possible that's still on the plane to begin with. Once more of society becomes aware of permanent atoms, authors will likely start writing science fiction stories based on the premise of villains capturing permanent atoms of people and adversely modifying them in some fashion, even though such a thing isn't possible. For practical purposes, consider the physical permanent atom on a higher plane altogether, even though technically it's still on the physical plane.

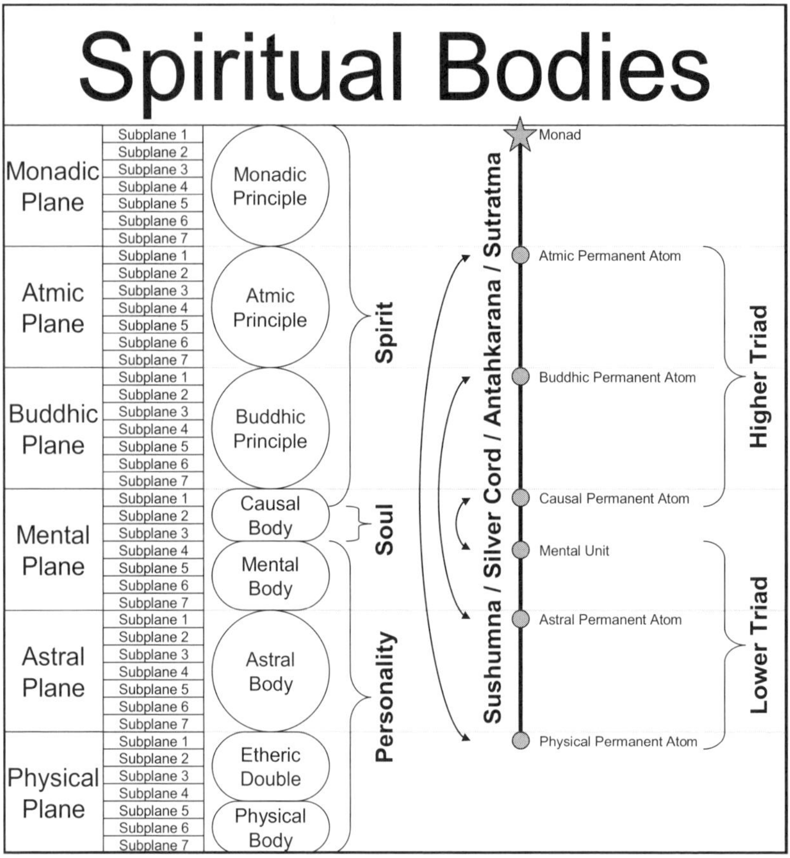

Chakras

Within the etheric double are centers of energy called chakras. The word chakra (most commonly pronounced chock-ruh or shock-ruh, although it's technically pronounced chuck-ruh) is Sanskrit for "spinning wheel." Each chakra receives and transmits certain types of energy, meaning the chakras serve a similar function to the organs in the dense physical body. Chakras are spinning vortexes of energy, and look like whirlpools or cones, with the point of the cone placed along the spine and the base of the cone extending out to the surface of the body. The higher up in the body a chakra is located, the more spiritual its energy. Lower chakras work with more physical or bodily energies.

There are seven main chakras in the human body, which are listed in the following table. Each chakra corresponds to a gland from the endocrine system in the physical body, and has at least a somewhat similar function to that gland. Chakras also look like flowers. Each chakra seems to have a number of petals with higher chakras having smaller but more numerous petals. Each chakra corresponds to a color of the rainbow. Psychically seen, the chakras often, but not always, appear to be that color. For example, the heart chakra may appear rosy pink, or the crown chakra may appear golden white. Each chakra also corresponds to a musical note in an octave. Notice the odd numbered chakras are more yang or traditionally masculine in energy, while the even numbered chakras are more yin or traditionally feminine.

The Seven Chakras							
#	**Name**	**Sanskrit**	**Gland**	**Petal**	**Color**	**#**	**Type**
7	Crown	Sahasrara	Pineal	1000	Violet	B	Yang
6	Third Eye	Ajna	Pituitary	96	Indigo	A	Yin
5	Throat	Vishuddha	Thyroid	16	Blue	G	Yang
4	Heart	Anahata	Heart	12	Green	F	Yin
3	Solar Plexus	Manipura	Adrenals	10	Yellow	E	Yang
2	Navel	Svadhisthana	Ovaries	6	Orange	D	Yin
1	Root	Muladhara	Testes	4	Red	C	Yang

Root: The first or root chakra is located at the base of the spine. In Sanskrit this lowest chakra is called the Muladhara, which means "base." This chakra deals with physical life itself, basic health, and security. A yang polarity chakra, it's also associated with the physical act of sex, hence its link with the testes in men, and the outer genital area in both genders.

Navel: The second or navel chakra is located a couple inches below the navel or belly button. This is often called the sacral chakra because of its proximity to the sacrum or pelvis area. In Sanskrit this is called the Svadhisthana (sometimes spelled Swadhisthana with a "w") which means "sweetness." It deals with nurturing, sensation, pleasure, and sensuality. A yin polarity chakra, it's associated with reproduction, hence its link with the ovaries in women, and the internal reproductive organs in general. The navel chakra also deals with the distribution of physical food and etheric prana, and so is related to the lower digestive system.

Solar Plexus: The third or solar plexus chakra is located in the gut area. In Sanskrit this is called the Manipura which means "bright jewel." This is the chakra of energy and personal power, especially since it's associated with the main adrenal glands and adrenaline. It deals with energy, drive, purpose, action, self-image, and effectiveness.

Heart: The fourth or heart chakra is located in the center of the chest between the breasts. In Sanskrit this middle chakra is called the Anahata which means "unstruck sound" or the inner sound of silence. It deals with love, compassion, peace, centeredness, and beauty. The heart chakra is like a cup or chalice that can receive spiritual Love raining down from above. The Christian legend of the Holy Grail, or the mystical chalice of Jesus Christ, ultimately refers to this chakra. The concept of a quest to find the Holy Grail is such a challenge because the Holy Grail actually exists within each person, and is only found when one matures enough to open their heart chakra, allowing them to feel the Love taught by Jesus. Note — The physical permanent atom is located within the heart chakra.

Throat: The fifth or throat chakra exists at the base of the neck. In Sanskrit this is called the Vishuddha (sometimes spelled Visuddha without the first "h") which means "purification." It deals with self-expression, creativity, knowledge, clarity, and ethics. The throat chakra's color is sky blue or electric blue, and is associated with the breath and respiratory system. This chakra is the dividing point or link between the head and body, so it also deals with communication. Hence, it's associated with the thyroid gland, which regulates other glands in the body, effectively communicating with them.

Third Eye: The sixth or third eye chakra exists between the eyebrows. In Sanskrit this is called the Ajna which means "perceive." Its color is indigo or deep blue. The 96 petals of this chakra seem to be divided into two groups, which look like wings on either side. The third eye facilitates both outer and inner vision, and deals with intuition, imagination, introspection, reflection, and psychic ability. The highest yin polarity chakra, it's effectively the queen of them. Being in the head, it's associated with the pituitary gland which controls all the other glands in the body (even the thyroid gland which regulates under guidance from the pituitary).

Some associate the third eye with the pineal gland, although most consider the pineal to be associated with the crown chakra. The tilak or bindi worn on the forehead by many Hindus is placed over the third eye area.

Crown: The seventh or crown chakra exists on top of or slightly above the head. Psychically seen, the vortex of this chakra can look like a ring hovering over the person's head. This is most certainly the origin of halos that seem to be above the heads of spiritual people. Depending on the source or what one considers a petal when psychically viewing this chakra, it has 960, 976, or exactly 1000 petals. Yes, psychics actually do count them! Either way the crown chakra is often called the "thousand petal lotus." In Sanskrit it's called the Sahasrara, which means "thousandfold." The crown chakra is associated with consciousness, pure awareness, wisdom, understanding, bliss, and our connection to Spirit and the Divine. The highest gland in the body, the small and seemingly inactive pineal, is associated with the crown chakra. The pineal gland helps regulate sleeping and waking cycles in the physical body (i.e. normal consciousness and unconsciousness), but spiritually it's the doorway to higher forms of consciousness altogether. The crown chakra can be stimulated by jewels in actual crowns. More enlightened kingdoms are sure to have used crowns not as a way to flaunt wealth or status but rather as a way to assist their rulers in maintaining appropriate consciousness to properly administrate and serve their kingdom.

Chakras are considered open or closed, based on whether they're actively spinning or lacking energy. This reflects the person's personality or current tendencies in the associated areas. For example, if the solar plexus chakra is closed, one tends to be meek or lacking willpower, while if that chakra is over-stimulated, one tends to become controlling or egocentric. Unevolved people tend to have their lower chakras open and their higher chakras blocked, since they rarely focus on anything loving or spiritual. Once one starts evolving spiritually, the higher chakras start opening. In the early stages of a spiritual path, one sometimes does the reverse and has their higher chakras open and their lower ones blocked because they judge their "lower nature" to be bad. The ultimate goal is to have all chakras open, so we can be both spiritual and effective in physical life. The lower chakras should be a receptacle for higher influences, just as physical life in general is a way to accomplish spiritual goals.

When a chakra opens or is otherwise stimulated, it can often be felt by sensitive people. For example, a tingle above the head likely means the crown chakra is opening, and indicates you've developed increased wisdom. A glow in the heart area likely means the heart chakra is open, indicating increased compassion. Being around someone who's intentionally or unintentionally draining your energy can feel like tightness in the area of the solar plexus chakra because your personal power is being threatened. There are often purely physical reasons for feeling something, such as just an itch, but a chakra truly opening to any great extent tends to be an unmistakable experience. Of course, not feeling anything doesn't necessarily mean a lack of chakra activity. Just as some people are more in tune with their physical bodies, the same is true with their etheric bodies.

There exist additional chakras lower and higher than the seven main ones. For example, below the root chakra is a simple chakra with only two petals that deals with animal instinct, which has mostly been transcended by today's humanity. Above the crown chakra, i.e. above the physical body altogether, are a few chakras that deal with spirituality or unified consciousness, which again in most people are unopened and exist only as potentials. There also exist numerous minor chakras within the human body. Some are between the main chakras and associated with other glands, while others are on the extremities, such as in the palms of the hands and the soles of the feet.

The chakras we have change over time as the human species evolves. For example, animals only have six chakras out of the main seven because they lack the crown chakra. However, in animals the lower instinct chakra is presumably much more active. In the distant future, humanity will evolve into active use of higher chakras, while at the same time we'll eventually outgrow and stop using our current lower chakras. The way we use existing chakras also changes over time.

Here is a future vision of our chakras which will be at a time in the distant future when the bodies we inhabit will be vastly different and more spiritual. What we now consider the 8th and 9th chakras will have come into being. At the same time the lowest two chakras, the root and navel, will have "scrolled off the bottom of the screen" so to speak. In the etheric bodies we'll inhabit, there's no longer need for the physical root chakra, and with reproduction coming from the spirit instead of the body, there's no need for the navel chakra. The throat chakra will sustain us through processing breath, instead of the navel chakra through distributing food. Communication will move from the throat chakra to the heart. Our lowest chakra will be the solar plexus, our individual manifestation or source of power in the world.

The concept of chakras isn't limited to our own bodies. Other things in the Universe have what amount to chakras, too. The seven continents can be considered chakras in the body of the Earth (with islands being minor chakras), the largest planets can be considered chakras in the body of the solar system (with minor planets and asteroids being minor chakras), and so on.

Even physical atoms have what correspond to chakras. Inside of each atom exists seven main vortexes of energy called spirillae. Mainstream science doesn't know about this aspect of atoms yet, but will eventually discover them. Just as our chakras open as we evolve, so does each atom get its spirillae activated one by one. As an example of another effect we have on our environment, our activities can help open these spirillae. Most atoms on our planet have four spirillae opened. Some atoms, especially those in the bodies of spiritually focused people, have five or even six spirillae opened. In the distant future, atoms will have all seven opened.

Kundalini

At one end of the sutratma is our eternal Monad, while at the other end is the root chakra. The root chakra, being the lowest, is in a unique and special position. Spiritual evolution is part of the Divine will; that influence can push up on the sutratma from below, meaning it pushes up through the root chakra. Picture an elevator lifting up under your feet with the feet as the focal point through which the elevator acts upon you. Hence, there's a lot of potential power accessible through the root chakra where this energy is called kundalini.

Kundalini (pronounced koon-duh-lee-nee) is Sanskrit for "spiral" or "coiled." It's often associated with the serpents or snakes, and is sometimes called the "serpent fire." Images of deities, pharaohs, and other important figures sometimes show them carrying serpents or with serpents coming out of their foreheads, which is a symbol of their having awakened and mastered kundalini within themselves.

As with the other chakras, feeling a tingling in the root area can indicate this chakra opening. If the tingling is especially pronounced, or the chakra feels like it's on fire or getting shocked by electricity, it can indicate the stirring of kundalini. When kundalini actually awakens, the experience is completely unmistakable! A feeling of liquid light will rise through the body, as if the body were an open tube. As it rises, it energizes each chakra it passes. Kundalini usually stops and exits through one of the chakras, after which the body more or less returns to normal. The higher it rises the better; that is one way of measuring a person's attainment. The goal in a kundalini experience is for it to spiral or flow all the way to the crown chakra, at which point it brings illumination. Eventually, generally at the time when one becomes a spiritual Master, one has not only done this, but is also able to keep kundalini permanently awakened.

Since kundalini is in effect part of the Divine will, having it awaken corresponds to one beginning to fulfill their ultimate destiny. Therefore, kundalini rising sometimes results in metaphysical abilities manifesting, such as psychic foretelling, intuitive healing, astral projection, or many others. These occult talents aren't meant to be "powers" to enhance one's ego, but are rather gifts to pass on in service. Anybody can learn to channel, but one whose Spirit wants to serve the Universe as a communicator is certain to be the best at it. This makes each person's experience of kundalini unique, so there's only so much that can be written about it.

Kundalini will awaken and rise in its own time as one evolves spiritually. The amount it has progressed can be treated as a measure of one's growth, similar to the number of opened chakras. One doesn't need to do anything to make it happen and shouldn't try to force it. Still, there exist forms of kundalini yoga or specialized rituals to help awaken it and guide it upward. If one engages in such activity, it should only be done under the guidance of someone experienced, who knows what they're doing and how to assist with whatever situations may occur.

Kundalini is one of the few things in spirituality that has the potential to be dangerous. Since kundalini is nothing less than the will of the Divine, it's in effect an unstoppable force. Awakened prematurely, it will force its way through any blockages in the chakras, which can cause physical or spiritual pain. Some sources describe people awakening kundalini and feeling like they're going to die from the unpleasant process. It's even possible for kundalini to get roused, and then fall downward from the root chakra and stimulate the animalistic instinct chakras, generating karma of a most unpleasant nature. That would only happen if one were very unevolved to begin with, or for some reason made the colossal mistake of intentionally trying to increase the power of their lower nature.

Proper kundalini awakening is like running down a beautiful garden path, with soft grass under your bare feet. Improperly, it's like running on hot coals through the nastiest of thorn bushes. In other words, one should work to clear out the weeds and cultivate a clear path before trying to travel down it. Kundalini shouldn't be feared as it's a natural process we all eventually go through, but it's important to be aware of it and how to properly approach it.

4:
The Law of Karma

"Have you ever noticed how, when you point your finger at someone else, there are three fingers pointing back at you?"
Karen Millar

The Universe runs according to various laws. Understanding these laws helps us become more aware of the Universe and more able to work in harmony with it. One of the primary laws of the Universe, and one of the most fundamental aspects of spiritual living, is karma. Karma means cause and effect, or the consequences of your actions. The word karma is Sanskrit for "deed" or "action." There are many popular sayings that refer to karma: As you sow, so do you reap. What you put out is what you get back. What goes around, comes around.

Karma is related to the Law of Reciprocity or the Golden Rule which says "do unto others as you would have them do unto you." Karma features prominently in philosophies such as Buddhism and Hinduism; however, most every religion has a way of expressing a similar concept. For example, the Christian Bible has the verses: "Whoever sheds the blood of man, by man shall his blood be shed" (Genesis 9:6), and "So in everything, do to others what you would have them do to you, for this sums up the Law and the Prophets" (Matthew 7:12). Karma can even be seen in science. Newton's Third Law of Motion states that "for every action there is an equal and opposite reaction." If you push on a wall, the wall pushes back on you just as hard.

The Threefold Law from Wicca and other pagan belief systems expresses karma and states that your deeds return to you three times over. Why three times, and not ten times or just once? One way of looking at it is that when you do a bad deed, it adversely affects you in three ways: First, you have to make up for what you did, by making amends to whoever you wronged, or letting them "pay you back" so to speak. Second, it fills your consciousness and aura with negative vibrations, which attract energies and people of a similar level. Third, it's a lost opportunity in which you could have done a positive act or otherwise have evolved forward. Fortunately, doing good deeds has a similar threefold effect.

Karma is also related to the Law of Attraction, which means that the things that happen to us are based on our own actions. Everything you think, feel, say, or do (or don't do for that matter) creates karma. People often think of karma just in terms of the major deeds they do, but since karma is simply the energetic union between action and reaction, even the most minor actions create karma. Turn on a faucet, and out comes water.

Karma can be labeled good, bad, or neutral based on whether the things that come to us are liked or disliked; however, all types of karma are the same fundamental concept. The difference between good and bad karma is based on one’s viewpoint; different people can interpret the same event differently. Sometimes an event that seems bad at first turns out to have been for the best when looked back upon later, or vice versa.

Traditional sins such as stealing or murder are obvious examples of actions that create bad karma. Enabling or restricting life is perhaps the strongest way to generate karma. Being a parent generates good karma on many levels since it creates life and gives a soul an opportunity to grow on the physical plane. Adopting a child, assuming the child is loved and given both guidance and freedom, is one of the best generators of karma, since it gives someone a life they wouldn’t have had otherwise. Conversely, abusing a child creates extremely bad karma, since it can damage a person for life, and sometimes even result in a cycle of them being abusive in turn when they grow up, which is additional bad karma for the originator.

The intent behind an action can be just as important as the action itself. Unintended harm that results from good intentions may generate some bad karma due to carelessness or lack of wisdom, but it will still generate good karma from wanting to help in the first place. Consider two soldiers fighting in the same army where it doesn’t matter whether that army is fighting for a good or a bad cause. One soldier passionately hates the enemy and desires to kill, while the other is working to serve and save lives. Both may do exactly the same things on the battlefield, and both will get a certain amount of similar karma for those actions; however, the former soldier is generating additional negative karma and the latter positive karma. Just as needless killing is one of the worst acts, so is being willing to give up your life for another person or worthy cause perhaps the ultimate act of service.

Ultimately, action and reaction are one, even if they seem separated by years or distance. One can think of karma as "do something bad, and later something else bad will mysteriously happen to you." It often seems like that; however, that's a limited way of looking at karma, which forgets that spirit transcends time and space. Just as pushing a wall and the wall pushing back is one action, so is karma a single event when seen from a high level. If I plant a seed today, in many years I'll have a tree.

Karma, like many spiritual concepts, exists in both individual and group forms. Karma is usually considered in terms of each individual and the results of their separate actions. However, groups of people also have karma, such as families, nations, ethnicities, and the human race as a whole. Because the Universe is an interconnected whole, individuals can experience karma from things done by those around them, even if it's to a lesser degree than if they do it themselves. For example, if a government implements harmful environmental policies, that cause creates an effect that's eventually felt by all the people in that nation, if not the world.

Living with Karma

It's important to be careful and sensitive when talking about karma with others, especially those not on spiritual Paths that are likely to misunderstand the concept. (The same is true for many other metaphysical topics for that matter.) If you tell someone who had a bad experience that it's just due to their karma and that they shouldn't be upset about it, that just adds insult to injury. You can expect a hostile reaction from them in such a circumstance, which would be your own karma for being insensitive. Treat others the way you would like to be treated when your own karma comes up.

People might think karma means they shouldn't help others or stand up for themselves, under the assumption that anything bad that happens to someone is his/her karma. Fortunately, that's not true! It may be someone else's karma to fall down, but it's our karma to see them fall and to be in a situation with them where we have to decide whether to help, and how we behave determines our own karma. If in doubt between two choices, pick the compassionate one.

Karma and its causes can be subtle. To hate something gives it power and can draw it to you since that's what you're focused upon. Learning to love or otherwise deal with it is the best way for you to grow. To avoid something can manifest it as well because refusal to admit reality can make you trip over it in your path since you're not aware of what's right in front of you. Some people start spiritual paths or create spiritual organizations not because they love spirituality, but because they dislike the realities of the world. Such activities with negative roots rarely succeed or last long because what was avoided inevitably comes up again in their new environment. Spirituality is more about loving everyday life than ascending from it.

The best way to respond to a challenging situation is with acceptance and love; doing so won't maintain any energetic attachment to it. And even if such a situation ever does come to you again, it won't bother you! Spiritual people avoid fighting whenever possible, but they don't deny that self-defense is sometimes necessary. In other words fight if needed, but do so with love, or at least don't hatefully fight the situation. Both weakly submitting and hatefully resisting can draw similar situations to you as future karmic lessons. If you're meek, you may attract aggressive people into your life if your karma is to learn to stand up for yourself. If someone acts like a victim, their karma may be drawing to them someone who acts as a perpetrator. That doesn't make the perpetrator right since the perpetrator creates their own karma for what they do. However, the victim in such a circumstance should recognize how they contributed to the situation, so they don't fall into the same trap again.

Karma explains why evil intentions are doomed to fail. You can't harm someone unless it's their karma to be harmed. Things don't happen pointlessly. Everything happens for a reason. We are all interconnected; actions between seemingly separate individuals are ultimately interactions within the greater One Being we all form. In other words, you really can't ever harm another person. Only they can choose to allow themselves to interact on a certain level for their own growth. If you choose to engage in evil acts, you don't significantly change other people's realities, but you do affect your own. You've created or entered a reality where people can be adversely affected by evil, meaning you can expect events to backfire or for you to encounter like-minded people to fight with in such a manner.

One shouldn't be afraid to create karma. Karma and its implications may make one hesitant to do things for fear of potentially creating bad karma. Of course, being too timid in life creates its own karma, by losing opportunities for growth. Some actions create both good and bad karma. Sometimes the best karma happens when one is willing to do what's right, even if it generates some unpleasant repercussions in the process. (Of course, sometimes the worst karma is generated when one makes up excuses to justify bad acts.) Be willing to take the bad with the good since life consists of both. More importantly, we can learn from both.

Reasons for Karma

"Now as Jesus passed by, He saw a man who was blind from birth. And His disciples asked Him, saying, 'Rabbi, who sinned, this man or his parents, that he was born blind?' Jesus answered, 'Neither this man nor his parents sinned, but that the works of God should be revealed in him.'"
- John 9:1-3

Karma tends to be one of the more difficult metaphysical concepts for one to accept or believe in, due to its deep philosophical implications. Karma means being responsible for our actions. It also means being responsible for what happens in our lives, and letting go of blaming other people or external sources for what happens to us. If there were no karma, we would be in a random and unfair Universe. The Universe is mysterious, and life often seems unfair on Earth; however, that's just due to our limited Earthly perspective. Karma is a beautiful and freeing concept because it means we truly create our own reality and are in control of our own destiny. When you smile at everyone, everyone seems to smile at you, or at least you see the world through a positive filter. A loving person lives in a loving world, while an angry person lives in an angry world.

Although karma is ultimately an impersonal law of the Universe, in our own lives karma helps us grow, and karmic events are lessons which help our evolution. There are no accidents or things happening at the wrong time, even if it seems that way to physical plane eyes. Everything happens in accordance with the soul's wishes. The soul is often braver than the personality in what it's willing to undergo, and arranges experiences we might not choose ourselves. And of course, most people aren't yet aware of soul consciousness while physically alive, meaning they're not aware of the karma planned for their lifetime. We can't control what happens to us, but we can control how we react to it and whether we choose to learn from it.

One of the most challenging questions for spiritual philosophies to answer is "why bad things happen to good people." Karma explains that, in a sense, bad things never happen to good people. Either the person isn't completely good when the full picture of their karma is considered, or the seemingly bad thing isn't so negative when more closely examined. Some people have bad things happen to them because they did something similarly bad before. Fortunately that's not always the case; there's a lot more to what happens in life than the depressing concept of "an eye for an eye" or feeling that if something bad happens, it must be due to one being unevolved in some way. An excellent example of this is Jesus, who was crucified not due to any bad karma on His part, but rather because He intentionally chose that destiny to benefit all of humanity. There are several reasons a seemingly bad event can happen to someone. The following is a list of seven types of seemingly negative karma, all of which serve a positive purpose.

1) Punishment karma: The most traditional type of bad karma is punishment for an earlier bad deed. This helps the perpetrator to learn that having bad things happen to you hurts, and to not do them to others in the future. Such a direct experience of pain teaches one more effectively than any attempt at external teaching can. Ultimately this helps one learn compassion for others. Even this scenario can be considered positive since the negative karma is now balanced.

2) Backfiring karma: Bad karma often happens due to the original action backfiring. Karma is often looked at as a reaction seemingly separate from its action. For example, if you steal from someone, someone will steal from you in your next life, in a seemingly unconnected event. However, sometimes the effect is directly traceable to the cause, even in physical life. For example, if you're mean to people, you may find yourself without friends.

Backfiring karma may be subtle and happen due to unintended consequences. For example, a city building roads to try to reduce traffic congestion may actually increase traffic because the new roads make driving more appealing to people who would otherwise travel using other means.

3) Experience karma: Negative karma can be a way to learn about suffering. If one has experienced suffering firsthand, they're better able to help others avoid or overcome it. Some people who are burdened with challenges never did anything bad, but rather intentionally chose them ahead of time as opportunities to learn how to help others. Some people whose souls are training to become Master healers or Guardian Angels pick a different challenge each incarnation. For example they were blind in a past life, are paralyzed this life, will be schizophrenic their next life, and so on. It's a lot easier to help someone when you've experienced the problem yourself.

4) Virtue karma: Negative karma is sometimes given to one, or intentionally chosen, as a way to build strength, fortitude, non-attachment, or other virtues. For example, a bad experience can make an unnaturally isolated person reconnect with others out of necessity, or a non-emotional person get in touch with unhealthily repressed feelings. Karma can even make one contemplate the reasons for things, and learn about spiritual concepts like karma itself. Life is sometimes painful, but through adversity we become stronger in ways we never would be able to in lives containing only pleasantries. Sometimes we lose things in order to learn that we can get along without them. Just as diamonds, the hardest gemstone, are made that way through extreme pressure, so are we made strong through facing hard challenges.

5) Appreciation karma: Negative karma can be a way to make others or ourselves appreciate things more. Sometimes we don't appreciate loved ones until they're gone, or until we hear about someone else's loss and realize that it could happen to us, too. Some souls volunteer for bad experiences as a way to serve, to make the rest of us appreciate more the good things we have. Consider a survival story where a person survives a sinking ship until they're rescued a month later. Hearing about it makes us thankful for the everyday things we have and focus on what's important in life. One person's challenging experience, if shared, can benefit many people.

6) Example karma: Sometimes negative karma, or more importantly the actions that lead to it, are done intentionally as an example to others of how to act or not act. The things we do on Earth are like roles in a great play where there are many roles one can choose or roles that need to be filled. Some people really are here just to be an example to others! Before birth, some souls choose to be tricksters who teach through bad examples, intentionally doing things improperly and experiencing the resulting bad karma to show the rest of us those ways don't work. For example, before a group of souls is born, an Angel or some other being may come to them and ask if anyone wants to be a drug addict this lifetime. One person's major mistake can be a great asset, if it's shared and is used to prevent many from making the same mistake in the future.

7) Testing karma: Negative karma is a positive opportunity to see how much we've learned. Like a test in school, sometimes life tests us not because we've done anything wrong, but to see how well we're able to respond to a situation. Regardless of whether we seem to "pass" or "fail" a test, we still gain experience from the lesson that helps us along our path. For that matter good karma, and every other situation in our lives, is also an opportunity to grow and serve. With this view, ultimately there is no "good" and "bad" karma; those are just labels we give to specific experiences. When the positive potential is seen in everything, negative karma no longer exists.

Implementing Karma

Karma happens due to the law of attraction. We draw to ourselves experiences in accordance to the vibration or energy we give off. Good deeds attract good energy, while bad deeds attract bad energy. An important part of karma is that the result may not happen immediately, and may not seem related to the original event, at least not to physical plane eyes. This can explain the concept of a random good or bad event making up for something similar one did earlier. Often there isn't enough time for good or bad karma to manifest in one's lifetime. One may receive their karma in the afterlife or in a future life. Karma is therefore closely related to the process of reincarnation, which will be described more fully in a later chapter.

Karma happens automatically due to vibration, and doesn't require Lords of Karma or other spiritual beings to make it happen.

If I jump in the ocean, I'm going to get wet. Still, there are many evolved spirits that help coordinate events on Earth. Before being born, Guardian Angels and such help many souls plan their upcoming lives, by determining what they want to learn in it, what karma they want to have come up, and so on. Older souls are able to choose their own karma to experience in life, just as older students choose what classes they want to take in school.

Sometimes the fulfillment of karma requires intervention from spiritual realms. Some spiritual beings (who are of course part of the Universe) work in harmony with the Universe to help implement its laws. For example, a person may get a strong message (that seems to be outside their own thoughts and intuition) not to cross a bridge, which collapses a few minutes later. It wasn't their karma to die there that day, and so they needed an extra nudge to avoid it. A stronger example involves someone whose karma is to be helped by a passing stranger when his/her car breaks down in the desert; however, there's nobody else on the road, so an Angel in disguise needs to do it. This can happen with negative karma, too. Maybe the driver who cuts you off on the road while making a rude gesture with his middle finger is actually an Angel! He needed to do the deed himself since all the other drivers were being nice that day, and there was nobody else for you to be energetically linked with to experience your "car-ma" in that manner.

The above implies that some people we meet (usually good, but they may seem bad to us) are actually spiritual beings. Such beings can not only implement karma, but also absorb our actions. If we're rude to a stranger, they again may be an Angel, because no humans were available at that time whose karma it was to receive rudeness. Of course, we shouldn't make too big a distinction between Angels and ourselves, as we all experience karma together. Humans are also spiritual beings that help implement the laws of the Universe, while Angels themselves are growing and learning too.

Transcending Karma

Karma can be modified. Once a deed is done, the karma for it isn't fixed in stone. If you throw a rock up into the air, you can expect your karma to be to have a rock hit you on the head in a few seconds. Simply step out of the way if you want to avoid that "bad karma." Both seeking forgiveness and acquiring wisdom can erase karma, since those are actions no different from any other. Of course, that only helps to a certain extent. Feeling regret for hurting someone is good, apologizing to them is better, and making up for it is the best; however, none of those new actions change the fact that the original deed was still done and had an effect on the other person and yourself.

For most people, learning to avoid things that result in bad karma and doing things that create good karma is enough. A spiritual person who understands karma will take the next step and seek to resolve any bad karmic debts from their past. This is one reason spiritually-oriented people often have such challenging lives. As you grow and become wiser, you're able to handle more, so your higher self or Guardian Angel is likely to bring forth more past karma to deal with in this life. That may seem unfortunate, but the work needs to be done eventually. Once individuals have fully balanced the scales and finally dealt with all their karma, they're close to being Masters themselves.

Once one gets far enough on the spiritual Path, they should realize that even good karma can be a hindrance. Doing good deeds just because you want a reward or don't want to generate bad karma still results in merit but to a lesser extent. A life of good deeds may result in individuals going to heaven after their death where they're surrounded by gold streets, jeweled buildings, and the like. That's certainly a worthy goal; however, such a realm isn't the highest possible heaven or state of consciousness. In other words, in a subtle sense, good deeds can inhibit one's growth as much as bad deeds, since they both create attachments. However, true altruistic action without thought for reward rises beyond the planes of cause and effect to the soul. Such deeds do not result in a corresponding reward in heaven or a future life; however, they do improve the soul itself and improve one's connection with it. That greatly benefits the spiritual seeker, which is in effect their proper karma.

Karma may seem a depressing concept where all of our actions are exactly balanced, and nothing good comes to us without effort. Although that's technically true, it is important to remember that we aren't alone in the Universe. The Divine will is that we evolve, meaning there is a lot of loving support and guidance behind every one of us, even if it often doesn't seem like it. In other words, we are floating down a Divine river where even when doing nothing, we're still slowly moving forward. A spiritual Path is merely swimming forward with the current, to move faster than the current would carry you on its own.

A related concept that helps us grow is that good actions create more good karma than bad actions create bad karma. That's not wishful thinking, but is simply because good is a less dense vibration, which affects higher and more powerful planes. When thrown with equal strength, a light object travels farther than a heavy object. Unevolved people tend to fill their lives with many evil acts and few good acts; one might think they're creating an overwhelming amount of bad karma for themselves. Fortunately, the strength of good karma allows even wayward souls to still grow and gain benefit from each lifetime.

Even Angels, Enlightened Masters, and celestial bodies are subject to karma since all results happen according to actions. Only when one reaches Divine planes so high that everything is One could they say karma no longer exists. On such planes, there's no longer the concept of action or time as we think of it, and no real separateness between consciousness and the Universe. Karma can't ever be avoided; however, one can transcend it. This is done by moving beyond the levels of cause and effect altogether. Masters don't liberate themselves from karma. It's more accurate to say they become one with karma and achieve liberation from themselves. In other words, when you're One with the Universe, there's no longer a separate individual doing separate actions, but rather everything is experienced as one unified, indescribably beautiful whole.

5:
The Cycle of Reincarnation

"Live as if you were to die tomorrow. Learn as if you were to live forever."
- Mahatma Gandhi

One of the deepest questions considered by philosophers is what happens to us after we die. A related question is what happened before we were born. To many, this question has a definite answer: We reincarnate. Each person had past lives before their current life, and will reincarnate again in a new body after their current physical body dies. A soul evolves through projecting physical incarnations. Each life brings back experiences and wisdom, which get assimilated before the soul reincarnates again.

Reincarnation is a basic tenet in philosophies such as Buddhism and Hinduism. Belief is less common in American and European cultures, although exposure to the concept is increasing. Like karma, reincarnation can be a hard concept to accept at first. Reincarnation makes one consider related spiritual concepts, such as a soul that can inhabit bodies, and spiritual planes that one can return to between lifetimes.

The main alternative to reincarnation is the single life view. That means each person only has one lifetime, and afterward they stay in spirit forever, usually in some form of eternal heaven or hell world, depending on how well they lived their life or whether they followed the "correct" religion. The concept that a single mistake can affect your situation for eternity is imbalanced and not in alignment with karma. What happens to souls who die in infancy, and never get an opportunity to experience much of life? What happens to souls who live out their lives in a secluded indigenous culture and never get a chance to learn about the "correct" religion? Note the concept of "only passing this way once" does have at least some truth to it. Although our souls reincarnate, the personalities we have in each life can vary greatly. Our souls are effectively immortal, although each individual life is unique and temporary.

The other alternative to reincarnation is that there is no life after death at all, which means that upon physical death our consciousness just ends and we cease to exist. That is sometimes the view of the intellectual who isn't aware of or interested in anything spiritual and refuses to consider that there might be something beyond just the physical world.

Tenzin Gyatso, the 14th Dalai Lama, has described reincarnation as removing old clothes when they get worn out and putting on new clothes. Our bodies die because after enough decades of physical existence, we need time to rest. Besides, being in the same body forever would be limiting and boring. Reincarnation gives us the opportunity to explore and learn from different aspects of life that we ordinarily can't change, such as having different genders, ethnicities, family members, and so on.

Physical Life

"Here is the test to find whether your mission on Earth is finished: if you're alive, it isn't."
- Richard Bach

Our world is full of repeating cycles. They may be short, such as heartbeats or breaths, or long, such as days or years. All of these cycles contain periods of activity or manifestation followed by periods of inactivity or rest. For example, the wakefulness of day is followed by the sleep of night, the activity of summer is followed by the quiet of winter, and so on. In Sanskrit the active part of a cycle is called a manvantara (Sanskrit for "within era") while the inactive part of a cycle is called a pralaya (Sanskrit for "dissolution").

Reincarnation is one big cycle where the activity of physical life is followed by rest and review in the afterlife before we're born again. Because our consciousness is currently within physical bodies, our focus is often too much on physical plane life, not realizing that's only a small part of a much larger whole. After physical death we don't immediately reincarnate, but rather physical life is one phase among several that the soul goes though during the cycle.

The term samsara (Sanskrit for "course of life") means the long cycle of birth, suffering, death, and rebirth. Life is often challenging or involves suffering because that's a very effective way to grow. The wheel of death and rebirth isn't eternal. Like a real wheel, each turning of it moves one farther along the path. Souls eventually evolve beyond the need to physically incarnate when they become Enlightened Masters. Note that physical life and reincarnation shouldn't be considered something negative that we need to liberate ourselves from, as it's a natural process and is how we learn the most and learn the fastest. However, it's also important to realize that we all eventually graduate from physical reincarnation and move on to other types of existence.

It's not easy to remember past lives, for the simple reason that the physical body and hence the physical brain we use to think is new each life. You can remember some of your spiritual history through psychic means such as past life regression, channeling on your own or through someone else, or just meditating on these issues and listening to your own intuition. However, those means often produce distorted results. For example, an impression of a past life isn't necessarily your own memory. It could be someone else's, like watching a vivid movie of another person's experience. To completely and properly remember past lives requires soul consciousness, which means having the connection to your soul fully open while physically alive, or waiting until after death when you return to your soul on the Causal plane.

Philosophically, it's often important not to be able to remember past lives, so karma can have its appropriate impact. Knowing that we did something bad in a past life would create dread of upcoming karma that would interfere with our experiences before it eventually happens, or would allow preparation to reduce its effect. When born, we usually don't remember our spiritual history or Earthly "mission" we want to accomplish. Even Gautama Buddha started out his last incarnation on Earth much like an average person, and only later started seeking spirituality and expressing his true nature.

We're in Earth school to learn certain things. When you're in a math class, you want to focus on the math lessons at hand not daydream about your other classes or what you're going to do after you graduate. Those things can be done between classes. Of course, for humans on a spiritual path, being able to sense their souls may be what they're here to learn in the first place. It's indeed a challenge to remember or connect with soul characteristics on Earth. Those are high energies we're gradually learning to sense and work with. Getting in touch with the soul is like a fantasy role-playing game such as "Dungeons and Dragons"®, if your Elf Wizard or whatever character at the time becomes aware of the real life person who's playing it.

In each incarnation, one usually repeats the experience of spiritual initiations they've attained before. Eventually one catches up to the highest level they ever had in past lives, meaning future growth in that life breaks new ground. Just as an unborn fetus resembles different more primitive life forms during its development, so do the early years of life repeat earlier experiences. For example, the first seven years of life tend to be focused on getting used to being incarnated in the first place. After that, ages 7 to 14 years are focused on physical development (which is why children often seem full of physical energy), ages 14 to 21 years are focused on emotional development (which is why teenagers often seem emotionally wild), and ages 21 to 28 years are focused on intellectual development (when one does higher education and establishes a career). After age twenty-eight individuals have generally caught up to their spiritual state in past lives where future activities are new growth. Age 49 (or 7 times 7) is another significant point, when one is heading toward retirement and really has the opportunity to progress on a spiritual Path. Of course, all these times are very rough estimates because individual lives can vary greatly.

Some personality characteristics are a reflection of the soul, while others are specific to just the current incarnation. Consider an artistic soul (who usually incarnates as an artist) choosing to incarnate as a scientist this time, in order to work on their intellect. To use an analogy from college, consider a literature major taking a math class, or a math major taking a literature class. It's interesting to contemplate what characteristics about ourselves or others are things we're temporarily focusing on (just as a college student needs to study a breadth of subjects to be able to graduate) versus traits that span multiple incarnations and define who we are as souls (just as a college student needs to study a subject in depth or have a major to be able to graduate). Something one is very passionate about isn't necessarily a soul trait. Such an interest may just be something their soul set up via astrology or some other mechanism to ensure they actually learn a little bit about that subject this time around.

Physical Death

"Once the game is over, the king and the pawn go back in the same box."
- Italian proverb

It's good to learn about and be prepared for death. We're often afraid or at least concerned about unknown or major events. Death is probably the most significant event in our lives. We study to prepare for tests in school, and we research a new neighborhood before moving there, so why not do the same before death? One of the most accurate publicly available sources of what exactly happens upon death, how one can prepare for it, and even help others who have already made the transition is the "Bardo Thodol." That title is Tibetan for "Liberation through Hearing in the Intermediate State," although the text is commonly known as the "Tibetan Book of the Dead."

What happens when one physically dies? What does their consciousness experience? The first thing that occurs upon death is one finds himself/herself outside his/her body. They may, for example, look down on their body from above, as sometimes happens in near-death experiences. Usually, individuals are aware of the moment of transition where their consciousness leaves their physical body. If people die in their sleep, as frequently happens, they'll still experience leaving their body. They'll become conscious any dream they're having will stop, although they probably won't physically wake up.

In a very sudden death, such as a being struck by lightning or being hit by an unseen car, one initially may not even be aware that they've died. If they see their body, or consider a circumstance such as "the airplane I was just in was a few seconds away from crashing," they might figure out that they're now dead. However, people are sometimes so attached to life, they're initially unprepared or unwilling to admit that they've died.

If one has experienced astral projection, they'll find the experience familiar, since the process of consciousness leaving the body is the same. Of course, astral projecting can only prepare one to a certain extent because death is always a special and unique experience, even for a living Master. When astral projecting, individuals are still connected to their physical body by their silver cord where like a person half awake, they probably never experienced astral consciousness to the fullest extent.

Occasionally a dying person will start seeing the next world, and still have a connection to this world, allowing them to physically speak about what they're experiencing. These words will usually be rapt remarks about how indescribably beautiful everything is.

The period between physical death and when one starts their new life on the astral plane is called the bardo. The word bardo is Tibetan for "intermediate state." Technically there are many different bardos in the cycle of reincarnation. Even physical life itself can be considered a long bardo between periods in the afterlife. Remember, we are spiritual beings having a physical experience. Spirit is our natural state, even if upon death, returning to spiritual planes initially seems new and unusual.

Once one has fully left their body, usually they soon enter what gets experienced as a long tunnel. This is more a tunnel through consciousness than a tunnel that moves them any distance. The tunnel can be manually entered, or one can seem to get sucked into it, depending on how accepting they are of the situation. It's best to be accepting of this and all aspects of death, and not be afraid or attached to physical life. In other words, if you find yourself dead, look around for a tunnel (or some other way to make your next step) and dive in!

On the far side of the tunnel, one usually encounters an indescribably brilliant Light. This clear white Light is brighter than the Sun but doesn't hurt your eyes. Individuals are never afraid of this Light because they always feel filled with immeasurable peace and love. This Light can be your soul, your Spirit, or the Divine itself. If you see the Light, seek to merge and become one with it since ultimately you are a part of it. Unless you've achieved ultimate Enlightenment, the Light eventually fades. The Light sometimes returns again to a lesser degree, e.g. the light of your Spirit is replaced with the light of your soul. Either way, seek to merge with it again. Some people, such as young souls or older souls who are distracted, don't see the Light at all. The experience of the Light is always based on vibration, so one sees as much as they're capable.

Picture the planes of the Universe as floors in a building. When one dies, they leave the physical floor and go up to the astral floor. The transition process is more than just taking stairs or an elevator from one floor to another. A better analogy is to say that one is briefly in a stairwell or elevator shaft, and has the unique opportunity at that time to look up the stairwell or elevator shaft all the way to the top of the building, or at least as high as they're capable of seeing and understanding. Therefore, the moment of death provides an opportunity for higher consciousness far beyond what one may expect. Enlightenment or ultimate liberation sometimes happens at the moment of death, assuming one is evolved enough to be close to achieving that state.

After the Light, one experiences a review of their life just completed. This process is like watching a movie of your life on fast forward where you can see the significant events and their positive or negative effects. The review may be part of where the concept of "your life flashing before your eyes" comes from, although here it's happening after death instead of when one barely avoids death. The life review process takes about three days. Apparently everyone, regardless of their evolutionary level, experiences it. This time period seems to be why it took Jesus Christ three days before He rose again after His crucifixion.

The review process is very subjective because many of individuals' experiences are based on their religious views. For example, the "Bardo Thodol" describes one seeing both good and wrathful deities. These images are illusions, and are how the positive and negative energies in play manifest to that particular person. A Christian might see images of Jesus and the devil praising or criticizing him. The review process is an excellent and unique opportunity to honestly look at your life, and ask forgiveness or give forgiveness where necessary. It doesn't erase the karma experienced later on the astral plane or in your next incarnation, but depending on how one reacts it can significantly reduce the amount of it.

Upon death, the physical permanent atom is withdrawn from the body where it moves to a higher plane and becomes dormant until one's next life. The physical permanent atom stores a history of all one's physical acts, and gives off a vibration attracting suitable karma. Pulling it out of the body at the same time consciousness is leaving the body is like pulling a hot dinner out of the oven, or like taking a movie projector out of a bag. One is likely to feel the warmth or see the images; this is presumably the technical cause behind why the life review happens.

Due to the significance of death, it's best to die in peaceful surroundings and in a loving state, to assist the bardo experience. That's not always possible of course, and fortunately isn't necessary for a positive bardo experience. Being an organ donor whose organs are removed soon after death may be a bit disturbing to someone who has just crossed over, at least if they're still attached to their body; however, the good karma of such an act should override any bumpiness in their bardo.

Dying through suicide is negative on many levels. Some philosophies even say that those who commit suicide get sent to "hell," or even get kicked out of the human kingdom and sent all the way back to the mineral kingdom. Fortunately, those are mostly just exaggerations to scare suicidal people into not going through with the act. It is true that suicide can create bad karma for future lifetimes. Committing suicide or refusing to participate in life and its evolutionary process can be seen as acting against the Divine will or trying to throw oneself off the ladder of evolution. Such a person often wants to cease to exist. Their self-created afterlife experience is likely to have them trapped on the lower astral plane in a lonely realm where they seem to barely exist anymore. One can't escape their karma. Rejecting the physical world causes one to have to solve their issues in the astral world or their next life, a process that's much harder and slower. Most of us commit suicide several times during our human evolution; experiencing the karma of it and learning the value of physical life the hard way is simply another lesson in our journey. Note: suicide to escape from personal problems (bad karma) is very different from giving up one's life in service to a worthy cause (good karma). Voluntary euthanasia where a terminally ill or permanently comatose patient chooses to "have their plug pulled" isn't a bad thing although it's still a serious decision that shouldn't be taken lightly.

Astral Plane Life

"We see things not as they are - but as we are."
- Ken Keyes Jr. in "Handbook to Higher Consciousness"

Once the death bardo is completed, one enters the astral plane and begins a new life in his/her astral body; they wake up on the appropriate higher or lower subplane based on their vibration. Unless one is stuck on a low subplane, they're usually immediately greeted by loved ones who have passed on before, along with their Guardian Angel and other teachers and guides, in a very joyful, spiritual reunion!

Life on the astral plane initially seems pretty similar to physical life. Language is still a barrier, and people congregate and form communities along cultural or religious lines. One still has all the biases they had in life, although many of the reasons for them are no longer relevant. There's no struggle for existence in the astral world because there's plenty of room and resources for everyone. You can't starve or be physically injured since pain can only exist emotionally.

On the astral plane, you can walk around using your feet; however, you can also hover and fly, and reach distant destinations at speeds that seem close to teleporting. You can touch and move astral matter; however, you can also make yourself pass through it, which of course feels very strange at first. Astral objects like houses exist; however, you can enter through the walls in addition to opening a door. You can even go through other people, and do things like reach inside your own body. Opportunities for intimacy on the astral plane are much higher, when you can hug another person and enter the same space together. It takes newcomers to the astral plane awhile to get familiar with astral abilities, such as flying and passing through objects. Often an astral wall will feel like a solid physical wall just because one believes they can't pass through it.

Your astral body initially looks identical to the body you ended your physical life with. Any health problems with that physical body don't exist on the astral. For example, amputated limbs are restored, scars are gone, blind people can see, and so on. As time goes on, people can adjust their body within certain limits. For example, older people can make themselves young again, and children can make themselves older. You can also change things like your weight and the length and color of your hair. Your personality still exists, so you can't change fundamental aspects of yourself like race, gender, or species, although the astral plane with all of its fluidity allows one to create very advanced illusions. A transsexual for example would be able to look and feel closer to their ideal gender than they ever could on Earth.

Food and sleep are unnecessary on the astral plane. One can still gain enjoyment from eating or otherwise feeling the vibration of food if they want to. Yes, you can eat as much as you want and never get fat! Although sleep is no longer required, one can still rest or daydream in a manner similar to sleep. On the astral, one can work ceaselessly for years without getting tired. For example, it's easy to read a novel or a whole series of novels in one sitting. One is still limited by his/her discipline, and feeling bored is often more likely on the exciting astral plane. Astral life is a great opportunity for one to grow spiritually and serve, since they no longer have mundane jobs or other obligations and struggles. Of course, only some people choose to invest their time this way. The astral plane is full of potential distractions, which can sometimes delay one's journey to higher realms. Feel free to enjoy the many astral pleasures but recognize them for what they are.

Just as the physical body lives until the physical parts stop working for one reason or another, the astral body lives until there are no longer any strong desires or emotions to keep one there. On the astral plane, desires gradually work themselves out and disappear. Any unfulfilled desire or emotional inclination one has doesn't go away upon death. Rather, the person faces it on the astral plane and stays with it until that passion disappears. Transcending this desire can happen through either satisfying it or deciding that it's no longer needed. For example, a person with a desire to write a book will stay on the astral plane until they write it or until they let go of their need to do so.

The seven subplanes of the astral plane each contain different densities of astral matter. Lower subplanes contain coarser matter which is used to form more “negative” emotions. Although the astral plane is only one plane, the matter in your astral body affects how you see your surroundings. This seemingly divides the astral plane into seven realms. The concept of “hell” doesn’t happen due to intentional punishment by higher beings, but happens naturally due to one’s own vibration. Thus, a person with dense matter in their body experiences heavy surroundings. As one transcends passions and desires, the corresponding matter drops away from one’s astral body. Once all matter from a subplane is gone, one “rises to the next subplane” and sees their environment differently. Once a new subplane is reached, one can’t involuntarily fall back down to a lower subplane because the ability to form such a negative emotion is no longer present. As astral life proceeds, everything (which includes other people, the world around you, and you yourself) appears increasingly better. Bad qualities are continually disappearing, and good qualities are continually becoming more apparent.

You can shift between subplanes without moving, and see better or worse versions of your environment. You can choose to descend lower than your subplane, for example, to visit people who are still on those levels; however, just as you can’t fit a large peg into a small hole, the dense matter in your body prevents you from being able to visit higher subplanes before you’re ready. Occasionally, spiritual teachers will take students down to the lower astral in order to learn about it.

Post-incarnation life on the astral plane		
Subplane	**Environment**	**Vibration overcome**
1	Clouds, light, bliss	Desire for love, Intellect, Pride
2	Jeweled temples, living flowers	Desire for spiritual growth, Service
3	4th dimension, altered forms	Desire for self improvement, Vanity
4	Exalted life	General Earthly desires, Attachment
5	Ordinary life	Arrogance, Separation, Greed
6	Purgatory, slums, dark mists	Fear, Anger, Lust, Sorrow
7	Hell, evil blackness	Evil, Hate, Physical addictions

The table above lists the seven subplanes of the astral plane, the general environment, and the passions or emotional vibrations overcome there before one rises to the next subplane. Because the astral plane is so dynamic and fluid, the environments and vibrations overcome should only be considered typical examples. More or less extreme versions of desires manifest on lower or higher subplanes. Here are more details about each subplane.

Subplane 7: The lowest subplane forms the “lower astral,” or the traditional “hell” of religions. It’s not everlasting, but it often seems like that to its inhabitants, who sometimes get stuck here for years. Given the heaviness of lower matter, this subplane tends to exist below the surface of the Earth, making one seem buried and unable to see any distance around them. The energy is so dense here that traditional astral abilities, like being able to pass through objects, are mostly absent; one is trapped as strongly as they’d be in a physical cell. Only people with the worst passions are conscious here, such as hardened criminals or those who would be considered “evil.” Because this subplane is closest to the physical plane, those with an attachment to physical things or who try to hold onto physical life can also be found here. A strong addiction to a physical substance such as drugs or tobacco can also temporarily draw one here until they “detox.” This shows the importance of overcoming any physical addictions before dying, as the withdrawal process is much more unpleasant on the astral where emotions are much more intense.

Subplane 6: The next three subplanes form the mid-astral plane. Their matter tends to coincide with the surface of the Earth. Hence astral people on these subplanes can see and guide physical people, although not the other way around unless the physical person has awakened their psychic senses. This subplane seems like a slightly degraded version of Earth life, like slums in a city where it seems eternally nighttime and somewhat misty. Unlike the lower astral, it's not painful existing here, although it is a bit depressing. The "hell" of before is now just a "purgatory." Even this plane offers freedoms beyond the physical. For example, you can fly, although with difficulty. Here people let go of harmful passions such as anger, prejudice, fear, strong lust, or extreme sadness.

Subplane 5: This subplane is closest to normal physical life, and looks and feels neither better nor worse. Here, people let go of unhealthy desires that don't directly harm others, such as greed and arrogance.

Subplane 4: This subplane is like physical life again, although the connection with the physical world is rapidly becoming less distinct. It may seem like Earth, although everything is slightly improved. Things are brighter and cleaner, flowers and sculpted trees may exist where they didn't before, and there's a subtle happy or exciting feeling in just being alive. It is here that people let go of general desires and attachments. For example, a longing to visit Egypt would manifest here. One would either visit the location on the astral to satisfy their desire or otherwise stay on this plane until they no longer feel the need to visit Egypt.

Subplane 3: The highest three subplanes of the astral plane form the upper astral, which is sometimes called Summerland, due to its beautiful and comfortable environment. Given the lightness of higher matter, these subplanes tend to be far above the surface of the Earth, and no longer have any obvious connection with the physical. Astral concepts or abilities such as the fourth dimension and changing your appearance are much more apparent. Good examples of the atmosphere on this subplane can be seen in various fantasy art images of fairies, temples, and nature at its most beautiful, in which everything seems to have a glowing aura. The people in such art usually have body types and flowing clothes that are challenging to have physically without extensive plastic surgery or unhealthily starving themselves. On the astral plane, however, one can adjust their body proportions however they like. For example, if you've ever wanted to look like a fairy, you can (minus the wings, although it's easy to create yourself an illusion of wings). More subtle desires manifest here, such as vanity and self-improvement.

Subplane 2: On this subplane, things can be as grand (or as simple) as you want. The traditional heavenly view of gold streets and buildings made of jewels are found here, along with rivers of light, plants that seem alive, sparkling crystal landscapes, and countless other wondrous enchantments. People can manifest whatever dream home they desire, as large and fantastic as a private city if they want. Life can seem like one big Renaissance Faire; everyone's happy and playing the roles they want. This may seem like heaven to the inhabitants, especially with the increasing presence of Angels one can meet and learn from, although true Heaven is actually higher still. On this subplane are primarily found people with more beneficial desires, such as wanting spiritual growth or to give teachings to others. The playful energy of the previous subplane is increasingly changing to a more sacred feeling.

Subplane 1: On the highest astral subplane, almost all emotion has been released, resulting in a much more serene and quietly blissful environment. Only the highest feelings still exist, such as a desire for love, or a subtle sense of self or pride. A fair amount of thought exists here, due to this subplane being just one step below the mental plane. By this point, people tend to no longer dress in wildly unique ways, due to vanity having been overcome. Clothing has become unified; most wear the same type of white robe. People no longer desire to create vast temples and such things. The environment tends to be much simpler, not unlike the traditional view of heaven being a realm of clouds and light.

Mental Plane Life

Once one has released all their desires, there's nothing left on the astral plane to keep them there. At this point consciousness rises out of the astral plane altogether, and moves to the mental plane. The astral permanent atom is withdrawn and becomes dormant, just as the physical permanent atom was withdrawn upon physical death. Rising from the astral to the mental plane is called the Second Death, since like the First Death or physical death, it involves one "dying" on a plane, and moving to the next higher plane.

Some sources use the term "Second Death" to mean the destruction of the soul; they assume that truly evil people can have their soul destroyed. The soul can never be harmed or degraded; such a view is just another version of the archaic concept that one can be sent to an everlasting hell. Like eternal damnation, some misguided people use the threat of having one's immortal existence terminated as an attempt to manipulate others. The worst that ever happens to someone is they create a large amount of negative karma. It's actually more sobering to know that no matter how bad individuals act, they reap all the karma for it and have to dig themselves out of their own very deep hole.

Just as physical death results in a physical corpse, astral death also results in the remnant of the astral body, composed of the astral matter the person was using. This astral remnant is called a shade or shell. Like a recently dead body, the shade still looks like the person, although it eventually fades away over time. Because astral matter and elemental essence is much more active than physical matter, a shade can still seem alive in many respects, and may move around on its own based on the desires the person had. This phenomenon is similar to the way in which a decapitated chicken can still run around for a few seconds, but much more lifelike. An inexperienced person, whether living on the astral plane or viewing it psychically, may mistake the shade for the person themselves. The shade is the remnant of what the soul didn't take with them to the mental plane, meaning a shade contains the more negative traits of the person. Just as cremation removes the rotting physical corpse, a similar action on the astral plane can ensure there's no animated astral corpse floating around and potentially causing problems.

When one starts life on the mental plane, they enter what's called devachan. The word devachan is based on the Sanskrit word "sukhavati," which means "shining place" or "blissful realm." Although it's called the "mental plane" because it's the realm of thought, it's also the realm of the deep feeling and love because all lower emotions and desires have been left behind on the astral plane, and the higher love of the Buddhic plane is much closer. The mental plane is the true Heaven world, which can be divided into seven levels, with each subplane being the next higher Heaven. In spite of this talk about heaven, one should realize that heaven is ultimately a state of mind; even physical life within the wheel of reincarnation can be heaven.

On the mental plane, one experiences the reality of all their good actions, feelings, and intents. In other words, anything expressed in their life that rose above the astral plane exists and is encountered here. While astral plane vibrations get overcome, mental plane vibrations get appreciated and enjoyed. For example, if you truly loved someone, you'll get to experience the joy of being with them in your heaven. If you wanted to serve the planet by say ending war, you'll get to experience a world without war and the love and gratitude of such a world.

All people exist in their own heaven world. That heaven world is the highest they can conceive, and is exactly what they want it to be. To an external observer, each person exists within their own unique shell. Inside that shell they have thought forms of their friends and teachers, and play out the results of their highest actions and aspirations, not unlike experiencing a very good movie. Those thought forms of other people may seem like illusions, but they're really much more than that because they're actually used and in a way embodied by the other souls in question. One soul may exist in the heaven worlds of many people (meaning you don't have to pick and choose who to spend time with) and may have many thought forms to express through. A soul is able to use them all simultaneously, even if doing something like that seems difficult to us. Playing out your own aspirations may also seem like an illusion, but again the energy of it is deeper and stronger than anything on lower planes. Interaction on the mental plane is far truer and more real than anything in the astral or physical worlds, even if it seems a bit weird or abstract to us.

Like every other plane, the mental plane or heaven world offers unique opportunities for growth. The thought forms in your heaven world aren't just static, but are real links that can be interacted with and learned from. For example, if you've ever wanted to sit at the feet of the Buddha or be a disciple of Jesus and receive wisdom from them, you can, assuming you appreciate them and such interactions enough for that to be a part of your heaven! Such thought forms actually have a connection with the Master in question. You can receive as much benefit as you're capable of receiving.

In spite of the mental plane being the true Heaven, the spiritual seeker should still realize that they are in a world of their own making. Evolved souls are able to see through their own heaven shell, and get an even more accurate view of the mental plane around them. For example, one can see Masters, Angels, and other beings tending younger souls in their heaven worlds like gardeners, and one can get opportunities to grow and serve on higher levels.

On the mental plane, there's no rising between subplanes. One immediately jumps to the highest level they're capable of experiencing or that they expressed in their previous life. Each subplane can express everything all the lower subplanes can and then some.

Very young souls who haven't yet learned many virtues experience little or no time on the mental plane. The person still returns to and touches his/her soul, as everyone does; however, they're more or less unconscious during the process, and seem to go directly from astral life to a period of sleep to their next life. Similarly, after physical death extremely spiritual people can sleep through most of if not the entire astral plane, and initially wake up on the mental plane.

After experiencing a long or short time on one of the subplanes of the lower mental plane, consciousness moves to one of the subplanes of the Causal plane. The lower mental body dies just as the lower bodies did, and the mental unit is withdrawn and becomes dormant. On the Causal plane, one sees, experiences, and blends consciousness with their soul. There's no longer a distinction between personality consciousness and soul consciousness; they're now one and the same. This is the high point of the reincarnation cycle where the previous incarnation has been fully completed.

Post-incarnation life on the mental plane			
Subplane	**Heaven**	**Environment**	**Vibration expressed**
1	7th	Souls complete	Soul unified with Spirit
2	6th	Souls growing	Soul consciousness evolving
3	5th	Souls resting	Soul consciousness
4	4th	Seemingly infinite bliss	Love for spiritual growth, art
5	3rd	Even more indescribable bliss	Love for service to others
6	2nd	More indescribable bliss	Love for groups
7	1st	Indescribable bliss	Love for individuals

The table above lists the seven subplanes or Heavens of the mental plane, the general environment felt, and the vibration expressed on that subplane. Here are more details about each subplane:

Subplane 7 (1st Heaven): On the lowest subplane people express love for particular individuals, such as spouses, family, close friends, and even pets. This subplane is nothing less than utterly indescribable bliss.

Subplane 6 (2nd Heaven): On the next subplane people feel love and devotion for higher entities, such as deities, teachers, or groups of people such as the planet as a whole. This plane is also utter bliss, and can only be described as "more blissful" than before. All superlatives that could possibly be used to describe something have already been used to describe the previous subplane.

Subplane 5 (3rd Heaven): On this subplane people love higher entities again, but this love is expressed as service to others, instead of just adoration to the entity in question. For example, heartfelt prayers to a Master express on the previous level, but service inspired by them or in their name would express on this level.

Subplane 4 (4th Heaven): This subplane is the highest in the lower mental plane, and the highest subplane before one reaches their soul. This subplane catches anything not covered by the earlier heavens. For example, this is the subplane of true spiritual growth. Here one expresses spiritual growth out of love with no desire to do so for self-enhancement. This is also the subplane of ultimate service where one loves service and does it for its own sake, not because they want to please someone. Even the highest forms of literature, art, and science can express on this plane, but only that expressed out of love and not because one wants recognition.

Subplane 3 (5th Heaven): Here is the first Causal level subplane. On this level exists the soul itself; this is the first subplane of pure soul consciousness. On this level one can finally remember all past lives because the Causal body constantly exists and unlike lower bodies, isn't continually destroyed and recreated. The soul can look over its previous life as a whole, and plan what it wants to do in its next life. Young souls will be guided in this process by other beings, while older souls take increasing larger roles in deciding their own evolution.

Subplane 2 (6th Heaven): Most souls are on the previous subplane one level down. To rise to this subplane requires the soul itself to evolve. All souls on this level are on a spiritual Path, are conscious on the Causal plane itself, and are no longer absorbed in their own private heaven worlds.

Subplane 1 (7th Heaven): The highest subplane or highest Heaven is one step short of the Buddhic plane of Oneness. Only the most evolved souls exist here, namely those that have a conscious connection with their Spirit above, such as Masters or those close to it.

Physical Rebirth

Eventually, the afterlife period comes to an end. The soul has fully reviewed the previous incarnation and grown all it can from it. Just as a person who wakes up wants to get up and begin a new day, so does the fully rested soul want to begin a new incarnation. We are multidimensional beings who exist in both Spirit and matter where enough time experiencing Spirit makes one want to experience form again. The desire for rebirth is called trishna, which is Sanskrit for "thirst" or "longing."

The process of rebirth is similar to the process of death in reverse. First the soul activates its dormant mental unit, which draws around itself lower mental matter, creating a new, lower mental body. This body attracts matter of a quality according to its vibration, giving one a similar mental body to where they left off in their previous incarnation. Consciousness moves from the soul or Causal body into the lower mental body. This lower expression makes one lose touch with true soul consciousness, although they're still conscious in the Heaven world.

Next, the soul activates its dormant astral permanent atom, which draws around itself astral matter of appropriate vibration, creating a new astral body similar to the one they had in their previous incarnation. This new astral body has matter from multiple subplanes, but it's generally purer than the one they had when they died. Rising through the subplanes after their previous life causes all the denser subplane matter to fall away; however, general tendencies or habits for that lower expression are still present in their astral permanent atom. Babies and children have relatively pure astral bodies. Unfortunately, they usually get rapidly filled with astral matter from lower subplanes due to their previous emotional tendencies from past lives which reassert themselves. In addition, discordant energies on the physical plane or karmic events make them react negatively. The above demonstrates how important it is to treat children with love and kindness. Their new and sensitive astral bodies can remain light and open or be quickly corrupted based on the energy they receive from their parents and environment.

Finally, the soul activates its dormant physical permanent atom. Here, however, the soul doesn't form the new physical body on its own, but rather it seeks and finds a suitable physical body formed by the conception of a couple on Earth. A soul choosing its next body is similar to a person buying a new house. Just as house buyers often have real estate agents help them, souls often have their new Guardian Angel or other guides help them decide which new body is right for them. This choice isn't made carelessly, but rather a body is found over a period of time, with suitable parents chosen that should assist the soul in fulfilling its karma.

Once the right embryo or fetus is found, the soul attaches itself to it. Usually this happens at the moment of conception where a soul is hovering around a couple making love waiting for the sperm to meet the egg. (On higher planes, it's much easier to know whether conception will happen.) It follows that a potential form of birth control is to psychically see whether any souls are hovering nearby or form a psychic shield to keep out any souls seeking rebirth. Once inside a fetus, the soul sometimes leaves it, just as someone moving into a new house is sometimes away from it. Only at birth is a soul locked into a particular physical body. Occasionally the soul may even be replaced by a different soul, if a better set of parents is found or the parents make choices during pregnancy that make the environment unsuitable for the first soul.

A miscarriage or abortion doesn't force the soul to go through the entire death cycle again. Rather the soul stays on the astral plane and finds a new body, which will often be with the same parents if they conceive again. The debate about "when life begins" doesn't have a clear answer. Conception is a special time, as it's when a soul reserves a body. Birth is a special time, as it's when a soul is fully reincarnated. Between the two events, the soul is continually involving itself more and more with the fetus, like moving into a new house. The event of quickening around the middle of pregnancy, when the baby can be felt moving, can be considered when the soul is truly inside its new body, and is often when the mother starts feeling like the baby is a separate being. If one dies as a baby or child, then they do go through the whole death cycle, although they're certain to reincarnate quickly due to the shortness of their life. Dying very young may seem sad, although presumably the soul chose to have that specific experience, for example to experience the afterlife through a child's eyes without any preconceived notions.

The total period between physical incarnations can vary greatly. This time between lifetimes is influenced by several of factors. Dying at a young age tends to shorten the time while dying old lengthens it, because the longer one is physically alive the longer it takes to process the time on earth before being ready to return. Younger souls tend to reincarnate more quickly because they have more attachment to physical things and have done less on higher planes. Similarly more evolved people usually incarnate less frequently because their studies and good karma keep them more active on higher planes. In addition, souls may choose to reincarnate faster or slower than normal in order to be able to meet up in physical life with other souls with whom they are connected or to be present for historical events. The unprecedented changes on Earth at this time are one reason why the population is much higher than in previous centuries. In other words, many souls want to be present now.

For a specific example, there exists a group of rather evolved souls characterized by emotion or will that on average spend 700 years between lifetimes. That means a number of people alive today were last incarnated in the 1200's. It takes them roughly ten years in the afterlife to process each year on earth. There's a parallel group of souls with a more intellectual focus that incarnates less often, closer to every 1200 years on average, because their mental nature causes them to have less attachment to the physical and to analyze each life in more detail. The intellectual group, however, doesn't evolve any faster than the emotional group. Although they may get more from each life, they have fewer incarnations over time.

Physical life is only a small part of our existence. We are spiritual beings having a physical experience, more than we are physical beings having a spiritual experience. Physical incarnations are like exercising or playing a game. You may occasionally have an extended session, but you're usually not doing it. Some suggest you can be reborn right after death if you're too attached to the physical, or allow yourself to get distracted by sexual desires in the bardo. Fortunately, that isn't true and shouldn't be a serious concern. Being distracted can certainly reduce the benefit of one's bardo experience or influence the astral subplane one initially ends up on, but a cause that minor won't have an effect as big as skipping the heaven worlds and potentially starting one's next incarnation centuries prematurely.

Highly evolved souls near the Master level sometimes choose to do immediate reincarnations. Such an action is called "renouncing your devachan," because the advanced soul is choosing to forgo the extended time in the heaven world they've earned during their incarnation. True Masters can do much to serve the world, so once a soul gets close to that point, they often want to finish as soon as possible. This situation is analogous to staying late at work to finish an important project.

The total number of souls in the human kingdom is about 60 billion. With a current world population of six billion, that should mean one in ten souls are incarnated at this time. Presumably world population won't ever approach 60 billion, even in the distant future when we're able to live in large space stations without concern for the limits of area and resources on Earth. If people kept reproducing, presumably it would be arranged for souls from a completely different lifewave to inhabit the physical bodies being created.

The following table depicts the reincarnation process. It starts with physical life, when one is conscious in their physical body. It then moves through the death phases where the physical, astral, and finally lower mental bodies die and are discarded with their respective permanent atoms made dormant. At this point one has a short or long period of union with their soul in their Causal body before the rebirth process begins. New lower mental, astral, and then physical bodies are created or found, with their respective permanent atoms reactivated.

The Cycle of Reincarnation

	Physical Life	Astral Life	Mental Life	Soul Union	Mental Rebirth	Astral Rebirth	Physical Rebirth
Causal Plane	Causal body	Causal body	Causal body	Conscious in causal body	Causal body	Causal body	Causal body
Lower Mental Plane	Mental body	Mental body	Conscious in mental body	Mental body dead and mental unit dormant	Conscious in mental body	Mental body	Mental body
Astral Plane	Astral body	Conscious in astral body	Astral body dead and astral permanent atom dormant	Astral permanent atom dormant	Astral permanent atom to be awakened	Conscious in new astral body	Astral body
Physical Plane	Conscious in physical body	Physical body dead and physical permanent atom dormant	Physical permanent atom dormant	Physical permanent atom dormant	Physical permanent atom dormant	Physical parents sought and physical permanent atom to be awakened	Conscious in new physical body

Reincarnation in Media

Several movies, although fictional stories, accurately depict aspects of life after death:

"Defending Your Life" (1991) is a warm movie that takes place almost entirely in the afterlife world. It's about people reviewing the good and bad parts of their past life, under the guidance of more experienced beings. It shows the concepts of reincarnating upon Earth again versus moving on to higher realms where one can learn more, and how one's afterlife surroundings are improved based on their merit. The only differences are that it actually takes thousands of lifetimes instead of just a few to graduate from physical incarnations on Earth, and that the goal of life on Earth is to express love as opposed to just letting go of fear.

"What Dreams May Come" (1998) is an artistic movie that also mostly takes place in the afterlife world and addresses the issue of loved ones finding themselves on different levels in the afterlife, specifically where one person is in purgatory and the other isn't. It also depicts many aspects of the afterlife, such as we each create our own afterlife world according to our own views and wishes, we can voluntarily visit lower realms, and that guides and loved ones can help people rise out of lower realms. The only differences are the implication that someone can stay in "hell" forever, while those regions are overdramatized.

"The Five People You Meet in Heaven" (2004) is another touching movie that, excluding flashbacks, takes place entirely in the afterlife world. It basically depicts a man's bardo experience where he encounters people who have things to teach him that he didn't learn in life. It shows the importance of giving and asking for forgiveness. It also reveals how each person's heaven is different and thus it shows how people can see the same situation differently. It does a good job showing how our lives are interconnected and affect each other, and how seemingly ordinary jobs are sometimes the most significant or helpful to others. The only difference is that we're not limited to meeting five people in our bardo experience, but depending on our lives, we may encounter fewer or many more.

"Flatliners" (1990) is more of a dark thriller movie, but it still contains several accurate points. This film is about people trying to experience the afterlife by intentionally stopping or "flat lining" their hearts. It worked but resulted in realistic hallucinations concerning negative things they had done in their lives. Thus it was that they experienced the bardo or purgatory prematurely while still alive.

"The Divine Comedy," an epic poem written by Dante Alighieri in the early 1300's, describes a journey through the afterlife worlds. Dante's poem is divided into three canticas or volumes. In "Inferno" (Hell), people are trapped and suffer according to the sins they committed in life. In "Purgatorio" (Purgatory), people are working to overcome the various sins. In "Paradiso" (Paradise), people experience heaven. In spite of being written during the Middle Ages in an environment of fundamentalist religion, it's surprisingly accurate in many respects. Dante's Hell is similar to the lower astral plane where in both, souls are trapped and suffer based on the wrongdoings they committed. Dante's Purgatory is also like the astral plane, except in that location souls are consciously working on themselves. Dante's Purgatory describes seven terraces where the souls climb each, cleansing themselves of one of the Seven Deadly Sins in the process, which is very similar to rising through the seven subplanes of the astral plane. The only real difference between *hell* and purgatory is whether one is repentant and working toward higher realms. Dante's Paradise is like the mental plane; here souls experience the highest heaven of which they're capable. The main difference in the Divine Comedy is that again there's no permanent *hell*. A soul can transition from *hell* to purgatory anytime; it's only their ignorance or holding onto passions that keeps them trapped.

College as Life

The concept of "as above, so below" applies to many aspects of spirituality where many of the deep truths of the Universe can be seen in everyday things. Reincarnation and the grand scheme of humanity's spiritual evolution are very similar to the process of going to college.

In college, we begin each semester or quarter with several classes we intend to take. If we fail one or more of our college classes, we have to take them again next semester. In each college class we have professors and faculty guiding and teaching us, and judging our performance and recording the grades we will get after the semester is over. In college we get tested; however, ultimately it doesn't matter whether we pass or fail our tests. What matters is what we learned in the process. We often learn more from looking at the problems we got wrong than the problems we got right. One can experience many fun activities in college, although the main goal is still education. Ultimately, even though the outer purpose of college is learning lessons, the vast experience in and of itself plays a big part in one's life.

Similarly, we begin each physical incarnation with several things we intend to learn. If we fail our karmic lessons, we have to try again in some future life. In life we have Guardian Angels and other spirit guides assisting us. Some record our performance and help us review the results afterward. In life we get tested, however ultimately it doesn't matter whether we pass or fail our tests, what matters is what we learned in the process. We often learn more from reviewing the things we did wrong than the things we did right. One can experience many fun activities in life, although the main goal is still learning. Ultimately, even though the outer purpose of physical incarnation is learning lessons, the vast experience in and of itself plays a big part in one's overall evolution.

After each semester is a break where we review the semester just completed, relax, and plan what classes we intend to take next semester. Some students we work with in classes are our friends, and we enjoy their presence during the break. Certain students have the same major as us and we see them in many consecutive semesters and classes. Some friends are close enough that we were with them before or will still be with them after the college experience.

Similarly, after each physical incarnation is a break on the higher planes where we review the lifetime just completed, relax, and plan what karma we want to experience in our next life. Some people with whom we interact in life are our friends, and we remain friends with them in the afterlife. Some souls are close enough that we were with them before we started human incarnations in the first place, or we will still be with them after graduating from the human kingdom.

College is not an unending wheel of semesters and vacations. As there was an original enrollment, eventually there comes a final graduation. In order to graduate, one needs to have made the grade on a standard distribution of courses and also obtained a required number of credits. Every year there is a graduation day where students who are advanced enough graduate. Those who aren't remain and take classes for another year until next year's commencement. The university isn't filled with everyone at the same level. Instead there are freshmen who have only been around for a semester or so, seniors who have taken many classes, and various grades in between. Classes get more advanced and abstract as one approaches graduation.

Similarly, life is not an unending wheel of incarnations and afterlives. As there was an original entry into the human kingdom, eventually there comes a graduation from it. In order to graduate, one needs to have learned a standard set of virtues and also obtained a required number of experiences. At the end of every era, there is a graduation period when those who are advanced enough move on. Those who are not remain on Earth and have incarnations until the next era's special period. The planet isn't filled with everyone at the same level. There are young souls who have only been around for a lifetime or two, old souls who have been through many lifetimes, and various levels in between. Life lessons get more advanced and spiritual as one approaches Mastery.

The vast majority of students entered college from various high schools, and take four years to graduate. However, students who are making rapid progress may enter the realm of college in their early teens, skipping most or all of high school. Some students come in, take many classes each semester and graduate quickly. Others students take it slow and easy, with only a few classes each semester, or are slow learners, and remain in college for many years, perhaps taking a break or even changing their major. Since college is such a vast and effective place to learn, some people come back as adults to take more classes or get another degree. There are higher levels beyond normal college degrees where students can continue to learn, such as graduate school.

Similarly, the vast majority of souls entered the cycle of human incarnations from various animal forms and takes a number of eras to graduate. However, souls who are making rapid progress may enter the next phase of evolution early, skipping most or all of certain eras. Some souls come in, take on many lessons each lifetime and graduate quickly. Other souls take it slow and easy, with only a few lessons each lifetime, or are slow learners, and remain on Earth for many eras, perhaps taking a break or even changing their soul purpose. Since physical life is such a vast and effective place to grow, some souls come back as Masters to have more lifetimes or acquire more experiences. There are higher planes beyond normal physical incarnation still connected with Earth where Enlightened spirits can continue to learn.

In addition to needing a certain amount of breadth in their courses, students also have a major in a particular area, which explains why there is such a diverse variety of people on campuses. After graduation each student will leave college and start a career in this area of expertise. There are numerous things in the world that the college graduate can do, although there are several main categories. Most people leave college altogether and do work in various areas. Some, however, stay in college in a position of teaching to help others learn. The college experience isn't absolutely required for a person to do many things in life, but it certainly helps, so most seek it because it allows fast and thorough growth even though it may be challenging at the time. In the middle years of college, frequently students don't pay much attention to what they will be doing after graduation, but as they get closer to graduation, they start looking at job opportunities.

Similarly, each soul, in addition to needing a certain amount of breadth in their experiences, also has a focus in a particular area, which explains why there is such a diverse variety of people on Earth. After Enlightenment, souls will leave the Earth plane and start fulfilling their true spiritual purpose. There are numerous things in the Universe that the Master can do although there are several main categories. Most spirits leave the Earth plane altogether to do work in various areas. Some, however, stay on Earth as spiritual teachers to help others learn. The human experience isn't absolutely required for a soul to do many things, but it certainly helps, so most seek it because it allows fast and thorough growth even though it may be challenging at the time. Frequently, in the middle of evolution one doesn't pay much attention to what they will be doing after Enlightenment, but as one gets closer to Ascension, this becomes more apparent and they start considering their spiritual purpose.

Most students spend all their time at one university. However, there are other colleges out there, which also have students. Some colleges are larger, more advanced, or preferred by some over others, while some are focused on particular trades. In the course of studies, students may leave one college and enter another. It is possible for a student who's particularly inappropriate in one college to leave or get expelled and go to another. Such things can happen with large groups of students as the colleges themselves change, are built, or closed down. That means that some of the people in one's own school were at one time in semesters in another college. Visitors from other universities sometimes come for various purposes or events. The various universities communicate and work together, although usually on the level of the faculty and graduate school students that is beyond the knowledge or concern of a normal student's studies.

Similarly, most souls spend all their time on one planet. However, there are other dimensions or planets out there, which also have souls. Some planets are larger, more advanced, or preferred by some over others while some are focused on particular purposes. In the course of evolution, they may leave one planet and go to another. It is possible for a soul who's particularly inappropriate on one planet to leave and get sent to another. Such things can happen with lifewaves of souls as the planets themselves change, are created, or destroyed. That means that some of the people on one's own planet were at one time experiencing lifetimes on another planet. Extraterrestrials from other planets sometimes come for various purposes or events. The various planets communicate and work together, although usually on the level of Angels and Masters and beyond the knowledge or concern of the normal soul’s growth process.

6:
Kingdoms of Nature

"In every color there's the light. In every stone sleeps a crystal. Remember the Shaman, when he used to say: 'Man is the dream of the dolphin.'"
- David Fairstein

Evolution happens throughout all planes of the Universe, and affects all levels of being. The process of a human becoming interested in spirituality and then following a spiritual Path is a very important part of evolution, and tends to be the phase we're most aware of since we're actually experiencing it now, but it's still only one phase among many. Not only do we exist in multiple human bodies through the cycle of reincarnation, but we existed and were evolving long before we became human in the first place, and will continue to grow after we become Enlightened and leave the human kingdom altogether.

Looking at the big picture, each entity's journey began when it was first Created, when a Divine Logos first breathed forth the entity's immortal Monad as part of some lifewave. A new Monad is as spiritual as any existing Monad; however, it's not yet aware of or familiar with the Universe around it. All Monads are inherently equal; however, younger Monads aren't as capable of sensing or manipulating the environment around themselves. Each Monad projects a Spirit or has a Spirit act as a reflection of it. One's Spirit exists on the high Atmic, Buddhic, and Causal planes. This Spirit is in turn young and inexperienced, so Spirit projects itself into the lower mental, astral, and physical planes in order to evolve.

This process of becoming aware of the planes of the Universe, and eventually mastering them, is the journey of involution and evolution. Involution is the first phase. Here one's Spirit gradually projects itself and anchors an aspect of its consciousness into denser and denser planes. Once the physical plane, the lowest and densest level, has been reached, the return journey of evolution begins. Evolution proceeds from lower planes to higher planes where an entity is continually raising the level of vibration they're able to feel and work with. One experiences, expresses, and finally masters continually more spiritual planes, until all planes up to the level of Spirit itself have been mastered. Once consciousness has fully returned to Spirit, the young entity has completely grown up, and has become an Enlightened Spirit of the Universe.

There exist several kingdoms of nature through which entities evolve in sequence. From the moment Spirit first projects itself into the lower mental, astral, and physical planes, to the time when the return journey is complete where Spirit is aware of itself and a Master of the lower planes, there are seven main phases. Each phase is covered by a kingdom of nature, during which the Spirit expresses through the form covered by that kingdom.

The following table shows the seven kingdoms of nature. Listed are the planes covered by the bodily forms of each kingdom. Humans, for example, span the physical through mental planes since we all have bodies, emotions, and minds. Also listed is the purpose of each kingdom or the goal toward which entities in it are working. As each successive kingdom either involves to the next lower plane or evolves to the next higher plane, one could deduce the kingdoms and their meanings independently, based on knowledge of the planes.

The Seven Kingdoms of Nature			
Number	**Name**	**Planes covered**	**Goal**
1	Causal Elemental	Causal	Involve to Mental
2	Mental Elemental	Mental	Involve to Astral
3	Astral Elemental	Astral	Involve to Physical
4	Mineral	Physical	Evolve to Etheric
5	Vegetable	Physical through Etheric	Evolve to Astral
6	Animal	Physical through Astral	Evolve to Mental
7	Human	Physical through Mental	Evolve to Spiritual

Elemental Kingdoms

Elemental Kingdoms are the first three kingdoms of nature, which cover the involution half of the journey, when a Spirit is reaching farther and farther down into matter. Each of these kingdoms has Spirit expressing itself as a single atom on one of the planes. The entity acts as and experiences being "matter" on that plane. The goal of each elemental kingdom is to involve down to the next denser or lower plane. Younger specimens of an elemental kingdom tend to be on the higher subplanes of the plane they are on, while older specimens tend to be on the lower subplanes, because they're getting closer to the next lower plane, which means getting closer to graduating to the next kingdom.

The first elemental kingdom begins when a Spirit projects itself into the higher mental plane, also known as the Causal plane, and attracts an atom to use as a "body." This becomes the Causal permanent atom, which stays with that Spirit throughout its evolution. Once that atom is able to express on the lower mental subplanes and be used as specific instead of just abstract thoughts, the Spirit graduates to the second kingdom. The second elemental kingdom has the projection from Spirit extended to the lower subplanes of the mental plane. A second permanent atom is acquired on the lower mental plane. This atom expresses as parts of concrete thoughts until it's able to be dense enough to become an emotion, at which point Spirit graduates to the third kingdom. The third elemental kingdom has the projection from Spirit extended again to the astral plane. A third permanent atom is acquired on the astral plane. The atom expresses as emotions until it's able to be dense enough to become physical matter, at which point Spirit graduates from the elemental kingdoms to the mineral kingdom.

It's important to realize the elemental kingdoms are involving, meaning they're trying to reach lower planes. Humans are evolving, meaning we're seeking to reach higher planes. The term elemental essence refers to a collection of elemental kingdom entities. These entities are found throughout the astral and mental planes, and even within our own astral and mental bodies. Elemental essence may seem to work at cross purposes to us, since it's heading in the opposite direction. For example, astral elemental essence wants to become physical, so naturally it gravitates toward or seeks out denser emotions. A burst of anger is in a sense appreciated by astral elemental essence since anger expresses on the lower astral subplanes.

In spite of this, elemental essence shouldn't be disliked or thought of as a negative influence. The downward and upward heading kingdoms actually form a symbiotic relationship. Elemental essence helps us evolve higher: We struggle against our lower natures and the "gravity" of elemental essence, which tends downward. Elemental essence acts like a test where there would be less of an incentive to push upward; if there wasn't, the alternate option would be drifting downward. Similarly, we help elemental essence involve lower: As we refine our natures, the elemental essence within instinctively dislikes being raised higher, so feels forced to leave our bodies. That independent action to become denser on its own, as opposed to getting a free ride when we express negativity, causes the elemental essence to truly become denser. The physical body grows stronger when pushing against weight, and similarly our souls grow stronger when pushing against (or dancing with to use a more positive term) the elements.

Mineral Kingdom

The fourth kingdom, the mineral kingdom, is the middle point of the seven kingdoms of nature. Here involution ends and evolution begins. Note that some sources skip the three elemental kingdoms, or combine them with this one into one large kingdom of matter, and so consider minerals the first kingdom of evolution, with just four kingdoms total before reaching Enlightened levels.

In the mineral kingdom, the Spirit has reached the densest or physical plane. Finally the involutionary journey from Spirit is complete. Upon entering this kingdom, one last permanent atom is acquired on the physical plane. The complete set of permanent atoms is like beads on a string, and they will stay with the Spirit through the rest of its evolution. The seed has been pushed into the ground, and now it's time for that seed to grow upward.

An entity in the mineral kingdom now has a "body" beyond just a permanent atom, which consists of a chunk of earth; however, it only has a body that can't really feel or think anything. The goal of the mineral kingdom is to master the concept of having some physical form and then start evolving upward. This upward journey means becoming aware of ever higher plane vibrations. For minerals the goal is just to be able to feel the etheric subplanes of the physical plane.

As rocks, veins of ore, and so on tend to exist for millions of years, only the occasional chemical reaction changes them. Entities attached to rocks don't treat them as bodies that are born and die. Rather, there are guiding Angels or other evolved beings that place an entity's physical permanent atom inside a suitable rock, then retrieve it after enough time has passed (which may be many thousands of years). An individual rock may have more than one entity inhabiting it. In a sense, all mineral kingdom entities on this planet can be considered to share one big body: the Earth itself.

The type of mineral one gets attached to is based on the spiritual Ray they exist on. In general each mineral type exists on one of the seven Rays, and any entity inhabiting such a mineral is also of that Ray. See the chapter "Rays of Divinity" for information about the gems associated with each Ray. During the early phases of the mineral kingdom, the physical permanent atom gets attached to simple, soft rocks, or even sand or dirt. That's because the young entity isn't capable of existing in dense rock yet. It's still used to the softer astral vibrations. Evolved minerals are attached to crystals or gems because they offer the most organized structure and the densest surroundings, which younger minerals aren't able to handle or take advantage of. The primary gem at the head of each Ray is usually inhabited by an entity when it graduates to the vegetable kingdom.

With a high level of psychic vision, one can actually see the permanent atoms within rocks. Given the number of rocks composing our planet, not every rock has a permanent atom attached to it. With gemstones being rare, things like crystals and especially cut jewels more frequently have a permanent atom attached to them. The stone in an engagement or wedding ring is almost certain to have one. Jewelry is good for evolved minerals because the cutting of the stone and being worn by people results in subtle vibrations the entity can feel and benefit from. A "pet rock" may be more alive than you realize!

Vegetable Kingdom

The fifth kingdom, the vegetable kingdom, is the first kingdom fully on the evolution side of our journey. The Spirit has fully anchored its existence on the lowest or physical plane and now is working on being aware of these planes. This is accomplished through having a simple body, namely a plant, in which the entity can grow in. This is the first kingdom to have what is similar to physical incarnation. The guiding Angels place permanent atoms in plants when they sprout, and they retrieve them when the plant dies.

The goal of the vegetable kingdom is to be able to feel emotion. Being able to refine your emotions, such as learning to feel love or control hate, is a much later task. Here the objective is just to be able to feel emotions in the first place, or in other words be conscious of and able to manipulate the matter of the astral plane. Plants are obviously alive. They can feel in a rudimentary sense, such as react positively as they enjoy sun or water or react negatively if they lack either or get cut down. Once a plant stops just subconsciously reacting to physical things and is able to feel its environment and, more importantly, likes doing plant activities, such as grow taller, it's not far from graduating to the animal kingdom.

Young entities evolving in the vegetable kingdom are attached to simple plants like mosses. More evolved entities inhabit flowers and bushes, and the most evolved inhabit trees. As with the mineral kingdom, not every plant has a permanent atom attached to it. Every plant is alive in its own right, but not every plant is acting as the body of an incarnated Spirit. There are many Spirits in a lifewave, but not enough for every last blade of grass or bit of seaweed to house one.

Garden plants often have permanent atoms, since the cultivation allows the indwelling entity to feel its environment and have the opportunity to grow in supportive surroundings. The largest and grandest trees like Redwoods or Sequoias usually have several permanent atoms attached to them. Sharing a body with other entities may seem strange, but it's no different from conjoined twins in the human kingdom. Plant bodies often have indistinct boundaries. Plant trunks sometimes split near the ground, effectively forming two plants that share the same root system. Below ground roots gradually blend into and become one with the earth. Some plants even have runner roots which sprout up some distance from the original plant as a seemingly separate plant.

Animal Kingdom

The sixth kingdom, the animal kingdom, continues the evolutionary journey. The Spirit is now rising through the planes, increasing its awareness of them. The animal kingdom features fully independent bodies that the indwelling entity can control and move with developed sensory organs. Plants can feel things and are somewhat aware of their environment, but not nearly to the extent that animals are.

Animal consciousness primarily makes use of the astral plane; animals can express the full range of emotions. Animals also have at least the beginnings of mental development and can think to some extent. Animals also act instinctively and usually just follow their genetic programming. Sometimes even when an animal seems to express caring, that's only due to instinct or blind emotion as opposed to a conscious choice to act in a loving manner.

The goal of the animal kingdom is to be able to manipulate the matter of the higher mental or Causal plane, such as being able to express unselfish love, think abstractly, or develop free will and stop just acting and reacting instinctively. Once an animal entity is able to express a higher quality, it graduates to the human kingdom.

Simple animals such as bugs are the bodies for entities that have recently entered the animal kingdom, while more developed animals such as domestic cats and dogs represent the most evolved entities in the kingdom. Many beloved pets seem “practically human.” In fact, they are. The five most common animals from which one enters the human kingdom are cats, dogs, horses, elephants, and monkeys and related primates. Most regions of the world have at least one of these animals, so graduation to humanity can happen most anywhere. It’s possible but rare to graduate from other animals. The most evolved animals tend to be associated with humans because we act as role models, expressing the qualities that animals are working toward developing themselves.

Human Kingdom

The seventh kingdom, the human kingdom, is of course where we all are now. This is the last kingdom before one reaches the Master level, and achieves union with their Spirit. The goal of the human kingdom is to consciously finish this return journey to Spirit, or in other words become aware of and be able to work with the matter of planes higher than the mental. Note the word "human" here means the human level of evolution, not just humans on this planet. Most people on this planet have been members of the human kingdom, using some form of body or another, long before Earth evolved the Homo sapiens bodies we’re currently occupying.

The human kingdom rises up another level of awareness, to include the Causal plane. Humans, therefore, have physical bodies, emotions of all sorts, and thoughts which include the higher mental qualities covered by the Causal plane. We’re able to think abstractly or philosophically, love altruistically and, most importantly, make the choice to do so. Humans are unique in this respect, since we have a developed free will, which allows us to choose to act positively or negatively, and reflect on what it means to be human in the first place. Plants and animals may sometimes seem better than people, since they don’t start wars, ruin the environment, and so on, but they also don’t have any choice in the matter. Humans have choice, so can express both the highest good and lowest evil. A big part of the human kingdom is evolving to make the right choices.

Time within the human kingdom can be divided into several phases. Early in the human kingdom, the soul focuses on developing and refining its body, emotions, and mind. Young souls may seem unevolved and controlled by lower passions, but they're really where they most need to be. Such dense experiences help them become more aware of and able to work with astral energies. A loud and dirty construction site must be present before a beautiful temple gets finished. Those that have been human longer generally have their emotions developed and under control, but their challenge is now their undisciplined or inflexible minds where they may spend their time in frivolous distractions or dislike anything that can't be proven. One of the main dividing points in thc human kingdom is when one becomes interested in spirituality, and begins a spiritual Path. That event is called the First Initiation. The chapter "The Great Initiations" describes this and the phases of the Path in more detail.

Once one graduates to a new kingdom, they never go back to the previous kingdom. Entering a new kingdom is like being born, since one is literally emerging into a new world or level of awareness. That means once one becomes human, they never again incarnate as an animal, no matter how negatively they may behave. Naughty children get disciplined, not sent back to their mother's womb. It is possible for a human to act like an animal by expressing lower animalistic passions. Very young human souls may still feel a connection with the animal kingdom and whatever animal form they graduated from. It's even possible for ghosts (misguided souls who after physical death resist moving to the afterlife) to temporarily attach themselves to some animal's body, seeking a way to stay near physical existence; however, that doesn't make them an animal any more than dressing up in an animal costume does.

The human kingdom ends after one becomes a Master and ascends into conscious union with their Spirit. The post-Enlightenment or superhuman state of being could be considered an 8th kingdom since evolution still happens, although it's fundamentally different from the kingdoms one inhabited before, since now one is a fully grown up Spirit instead of just a spirit in training.

After the human kingdom, one may or may not keep their permanent atoms, depending on the Path they choose to follow afterward. If they incarnate again as a teacher or otherwise stay close to the world in order to serve, then they will maintain them. Otherwise, the permanent atoms are lovingly discarded, having served their purpose. Just because they no longer have their permanent atoms doesn't mean they're no longer able to descend to lower planes. Such Spirits can manifest a temporary form to express and feel things although it would be different than experienced in a standard body. Of course, after Enlightenment most Spirits don't ever have a need to return to lower planes, any more than adults have a need to return to an elementary school classroom.

Group Souls

Our soul is the part of us that exists on the Causal plane, from which our many incarnations get projected, and which stores our virtues, such as wisdom and love collected in each life. Entities inhabiting animals and all the earlier kingdoms technically don't have souls, which means they aren't conscious of or able to manipulate Causal plane matter. Spirits are always close to the Divine planes of being while their current bodies are down on the physical plane. Before they become aware of the Causal plane, they're effectively cut off from or unconscious of their Spirit and have no place to store or way to transmit the things that are learned. How can a young Spirit link with its body when it has no connecting soul?

All kingdoms before the human kingdom make use of a "group soul," which is a construct on the Causal plane. A group soul can be considered similar to a government-assisted group housing project for those unable to live on their own, or even just an apartment that young people rent before they're able to buy their own homes. A group soul serves the same purpose as a soul, except that multiple entities make use of one. In spite of containing the word "soul," a group soul is more a managed collection of energy and not an independent being in its own right. A group soul doesn't have its own Spirit although each entity using it is, of course, connected to its Spirit through that group soul.

Group souls are created and coordinated by Angels and other evolved beings who guide placements or incarnations of minerals, plants, and animals from and back into each group soul until the time an animal evolves enough to express soul characteristics and acquire its own individual soul. A group soul is like a school classroom. People enter, grow up, learn, and eventually leave to begin their own careers. Most children aren't grown up enough to learn on their own, so they need the structure of being led to school and taught by teachers.

When a Spirit is using a group soul, its experiences after each life return to that group soul as a whole. That's like pouring a glass of juice (representing virtues collected during an incarnation) into a collective bathtub (the group soul) instead of your own personal pitcher (your individual soul). That means that if one is using a group soul, the good things they do benefit the group soul as a whole, instead of just themselves. It's similar to having roommates in an apartment where cleaning (or not cleaning) the apartment positively (or not so positively) affects everyone there. Having your "personal harvest" spread among the group soul isn't a personal loss because you, in turn, benefit from the work of all the other entities using the group soul.

In spite of plants and animals being in kingdoms associated with evolution, they're still focusing on differentiation, which is technically an aspect of involution. Differentiation means they're separating from others and developing their own uniqueness, as opposed to re-combining with others in Oneness. Over time, growing Spirits have increasingly different experiences. This gets reflected in group souls. Group souls gradually divide over time, or entities using them upgrade into different and smaller sized group souls. Eventually, a group soul has just a single Spirit inhabiting it, at which point that Spirit is very close to the point of getting its own soul. When that happens, the Spirit recycles what's left of the group soul as starting material for its own new individual soul. It's similar to a "rent to own" arrangement where if one rents or leases something long enough, he/she gets to keep it.

For example, in the Causal elemental kingdom, presumably the entire kingdom uses a single group soul. In the mental and astral elemental kingdoms, there are several giant group souls that cover each Ray or each subplane of the lower mental and astral planes. In the mineral kingdom, there's a group soul for each class of rock, such as a group soul for quartz, a group soul for diamonds, and so on. In the vegetable kingdom, there are several group souls for each plant species and subspecies, such as a group soul for wild red roses, and another for red roses in greenhouses. In the animal kingdom, there are quite a few group souls for each species and breed while later species have more group souls than earlier species. For example, there are only a few group souls covering mosquitoes, but a very large number covering cats.

Focusing on the animal kingdom, consider a group soul for "dog," which eventually through the differentiation of experiences had the group soul for "Labrador Retriever" split off, which had "Labradors in England" split off, which had “well trained English Labs” split off, which had "English Labs serving as seeing eye dogs for the elderly" split off, and so on until their experiences become unique enough that group souls have just a few Spirits or a single Spirit using them. Once a Spirit is able to express that uniqueness on its own, it becomes truly independent and can run its own soul instead of needing to have an Angel hold the link between Spirit and body for them.

Animals can differentiate themselves when the group soul they’re in divides, and also by leaving a group soul for a different and higher group soul with fewer members. Consider a mountain lake. As water flows out of the lake, other water streams into it. Similarly, as some entities break away from a group soul, either due to getting their own souls or due to transfer to more evolved group souls (such as being promoted from coyote to domestic dog), other entities transfer into that group soul from some simpler animal. Note: group souls themselves slowly evolve over time, as the animal species or subspecies they represent evolve their physical forms. That’s similar to how an apartment building evolves as it gets decorated, gets storm windows added, and so on.

Individualization

The point in time when a Spirit acquires its own soul is called individualization. Individualization is one of the most significant events in a Spirit’s entire evolutionary journey. It’s the beautiful, powerful, spiritual moment when an animal breaks away from a group soul and creates its own soul. Individualization happens when an animal becomes loving enough, or smart enough, or develops free will enough to express qualities that belong to the Causal or soul plane of existence. That's also the moment when a spirit graduates from the animal kingdom to the human kingdom. The fundamental difference between animals and humans is that animals don't have individual souls, and humans do. By definition, using a group soul means it's an animal, and having an individual soul means it's human or at least on the human level of evolution.

Individualization usually occurs through emotion, intellect, or will. Individualizing through emotion happens when feeling love or affection to such a degree that your astral body temporarily reaches up to the Buddhic plane, and that connecting thread becomes the start of your new soul. Individualizing through intellect happens when thinking or contemplating concepts to such a degree that your lower mental body reaches up to the Causal plane, and that abstract link starts your new soul. Individualizing through will happens when taking independent action to such a degree that your physical body connects to the Atmic plane, the ultimate plane of free will, and that independence breaks you away from the group soul.

The way one individualizes has an effect on their evolution throughout the human kingdom. Sometimes you can intuit which method a person did by observing them, in the same way you can sometimes sense what Ray they're on, what their astrology is, and so forth. Physical, emotional, and mental people tend to have respectively individualized through will, emotion, and intellect. That isn't always true, because there's a difference between a fundamental soul characteristic and how one may be expressing in a particular incarnation. Before one graduates from the human kingdom, they need to develop all three qualities of will, love, and intelligence. An Olympic marathon runner likely individualized through will, but they could also be an intellectual soul that's focusing on developing their body and discipline in this particular incarnation.

The above are the most common ways of individualizing. The healthiest methods involve reaching up to a higher plane for the first time, and receiving the downpouring blessing. However one can also break away from a group soul due to negative actions, although these methods are rare. For example, it's possible to individualize through pride where people feel separate enough to disconnect themselves from any group soul. It's also possible to individualize through fear, by an overstimulation of feeling while trying to avoid suffering, or even through hatred where one seeks the suffering of others, which is also a very separating influence. Someone who individualized through disharmonious means is likely to have a long evolutionary path that features quite a bit of negativity before becoming positive. For example, they may have incarnations as sociopaths, evil sorcerers, political dictators, and so on. But Enlightenment is the destiny of everyone; presumably the Spirit chose to have such a challenging path to fulfill a higher purpose, even if such a purpose is hard for most to understand. For example, some souls act as tricksters or testing influences, others may want to experience evil firsthand to know how to teach others to avoid it, and so on.

It's important to treat animals with kindness and patience. Animals are influenced by humans to a greater degree than we expect. Cruelty to animals has far reaching implications, both to the animals themselves and by association our own karma. Mistreating an animal has the effect of either "peeing into their group soul bathtub," or in a very extreme case individualizing the animal negatively. Similarly, one shouldn't try to prematurely individualize an animal. Forcing an animal to individualize by say showering it with more affection than it can understand or handle may do more harm than good. Like a womb, the animal kingdom serves an important purpose. An animal that individualizes too quickly is like a baby born prematurely or a butterfly forced out of its cocoon before it's ready to emerge, which ultimately delays the entity's journey into their new world.

Individualization happens before Spirits unite together in Oneness, which is a later phase in our evolutionary journey. Individualizing and leaving the group soul is like a college class graduating; students separate and move on to their own new lives. The class as it was is no more, although it will be replaced by next year's students. The grown-up students may eventually work together in society, but that will be on a much higher level than the class, even if it's a somewhat similar concept. In order to truly come together in Oneness, one needs to be separate first.

In summary, the evolutionary process involves first being in a group soul, which is a type of Oneness, but you don't have any choice in the matter. You then individualize or separate from the group soul since you've built your own unique soul. That seems like separateness, but at least you chose it, and now have free will. Finally, you become aware of your own Spirit and the Universal Spirit, which is Oneness again. You're now conscious of it and have chosen it. We start from unconscious unity, involve into conscious independence, and finally evolve into conscious unity.

Fairy Kingdom

"And though you should live in a palace of gold, or sleep in a dried up ditch,
You could never be as poor as the fairies are, and never as rich."
- Rose Fyleman

There exist forms of expression or kingdoms of nature other than the seven kingdoms humans evolve through. There are still seven basic phases or levels of awareness; however, other tracks of evolution exist on our planet that go through additional kingdoms of nature. Beyond that, this chapter has been focusing on just the evolution of entities with spiritual Monads expressing through them, but that's certainly not the only thing in the Universe. There exist other life forms that we can't even conceive where, in a sense, everything in the Universe is alive, even abstract concepts. A house is an evolving entity as we fill it with objects and memories, the internet is an evolving entity, and so on.

The first alternate kingdom of nature is the fairy kingdom. Fairies actually exist, but their bodies are on the etheric subplanes of the physical plane, so they can only be seen or interacted with psychically. Consider the fairy kingdom as kingdom number 6½, half way between animals and humans, and overlapping half of each. In other words, the average fairy is as evolved as the smartest animal, and also as evolved as the dumbest human. The least evolved or dumbest fairies are as smart as the average animal, while the most evolved fairies are as smart as the average human.

A completely different lifestream, separate from all the human lifewaves of various levels, evolves through the fairy kingdom. Insects, fish, and birds are thought to be the animal forms of entities that will eventually graduate to the start of the fairy kingdom, while mammals are the animal forms for those who will become human. Dolphins and whales are a special case, since they're quite evolved. They're most likely part of the fairy lifestream. Entities inhabiting them will eventually become fairies; however, it's possible they're a different lifestream that's already individualized.

Fairy bodies tend to be small, ranging from a few inches to a few feet in height. They usually have humanoid form but with various parts in different proportions, such as longer limbs or pointed ears or heads, and they often have wings, as well. Since fairies don't have dense physical bodies, their experience of life is very different from animals and humans. They experience none of the struggles of survival or making a living, and they don't feel pain or fear. Fairies, as with all non-physical entities, see the life within each form, as opposed to the form surrounding each life. Fairies tend to be very emotional and act like human children in many respects. They can be consumed by some emotion quickly and have it disappear just as quickly.

Fairies primarily act as nature spirits, helping the vegetable kingdom grow or looking after the elements. Sometimes they're connected with a particular plant, looking after it similar to how a Guardian Angel looks after a person. For example, a dryad is a tree fairy. The dryad, a member of the fairy kingdom, is separate from the tree itself, which is a member of the vegetable kingdom. Not all plants have fairies connected with them, although any plant that is blessed with fairy attention is sure to grow much better.

Many fantasy forms from popular culture actually exist as fairies. Since all fairies have etheric bodies, one can't find physical evidence of them, but they can be seen with psychic vision, or intuitively felt. Creatures similar to pixies, trolls, unicorns, dragons, and many other creatures exist, just with non-physical bodies. Gnomes are fairies that exist within the earth, undines are fairies of the water, salamanders (very different from the amphibian creature of the same name) are fairies of fire, and sylphs are fairies of the air. Sylphs are generally considered the highest form of fairy, both in intellect and in compassion. They look like beautiful humans, and sometimes even look after people in a similar fashion as Guardian Angels, and are friendly enough they may be mistaken for Angels. Eventually, when mainstream science discovers the etheric levels of the physical plane and is able to see etheric creatures, they'll classify creatures in the fairy kingdom just as they do animals and plants. Just as humans are "Homo sapiens" in the scientific naming system, the fairy kingdom in turn will eventually be divided into phylum, class, order, family, genus, and species!

Fairies are carefree and fun loving, and tend to lack the discipline and structure humans value. Fairies aren't evil, but they may act in ways we dislike, since they're different in so many ways. They have a reputation as capricious tricksters and mischievous pranksters for a good reason. Most however are shy and, like wild animals, try to avoid humans. Since fairies have intelligence combined with more spiritual bodies, they're sometimes able to manifest minor occult powers, such as change their form, make themselves visible enough to be seen by sensitive people, or even lead people in the wilderness astray with "glamour" or illusions. Since fairies can readily see people's feelings, they can imitate what's on our minds. When people psychically see demonic monsters, they're often just seeing fairies playing "dress up." Such a person may get scared thinking there are evil forces out to get them, especially if the fairy pursues them. The fairy doesn't have any malicious intent, but rather doesn't know any better, thinking the person's reaction is just part of a game.

In general, once an entity enters a kingdom, it stays there until it masters that kingdom and is ready for the next one. There are however occasional crossovers between kingdoms. As humans are on the whole more evolved than fairies, it's possible for an entity to jump from the fairy kingdom to the human kingdom. People who love fairies or seem especially connected with them may have been one in a past life, although such cases are extremely rare.

For example, the "fairy tale" story of "The Little Mermaid" by Hans Christian Andersen features a mermaid (a type of water fairy) who fell in love with a human prince. More importantly, she wanted to have her own soul and so got herself magically transformed into a human. In the original version of the story, she refused to kill her prince after he chose to marry another person, even though not doing so would result in her death. Her compassion and loving sacrifice in this instance should be enough to individualize her, and move her to the next higher kingdom (or at least graduate her to the next higher class of fairy, as happened in the story). Due to her attachment to humans in general or her prince in particular, her next life should be as a human instead of continuing to follow the fairy lifestream. In other words, "The Little Mermaid" is probably based on a true story, or at least things like that can actually happen!

Angel Kingdom

"People think Angels can fly because they have wings. Angels fly because they can take themselves lightly."
- Lynn M. McDougal

The other main kingdom on Earth is the Angelic kingdom. Angels are sometimes called Devas. The word Deva (pronounced day-vuh) is Sanskrit for "intelligent agent" or "shining one." There are numerous types of Angels. The youngest Angels may be found as low as the astral plane and are as evolved as the average person. The oldest Angels are incredible, indescribably vast beings just shy of Divinity or the Logos plane. There's no limit to the different things Angels do; however, the simplest summary of their activity is that they look after or guide things. Many act as Guardian Angels for people while others look after districts of land, guide groups of people (such as large companies or nations), or embody a certain virtue.

Every human gets a Guardian Angel assigned to him/her at birth. That Angel acts as a spirit guide, although it isn't necessarily the only spirit guide one might have. They lovingly watch over the person throughout their lifetime, quietly encouraging them toward good things, and caring sympathetically when they do wrong or face challenges. Most people aren't aware of their Guardian Angel or get to meet them until after death. It's a thankless job, especially if you're a Guardian Angel for any younger souls who still tend to create negative karma for themselves. However, it's an important job where their positive influence, if subtle, can't be overemphasized. It's comforting to know we're never alone in life's journey, even if it sometimes seems like it. Note: Angels work with energies more than specifics, so one shouldn't feel self-conscious or think an Angel is watching their every move.

Angels look similar to humans, and usually express in what looks like human form. Angels, especially the more evolved kinds, can also be balls of light or forms that are downright indescribable. One way to distinguish a human from an Angel is that a human's aura looks like a misty cloud that gradually fades the farther it gets from their body, while an angel's aura is more pronounced with a distinct boundary, looking like overlapping flames. This difference in intensity is reflected in how the respective kingdoms express themselves. Humans, even evolved ones, tend to focus on or communicate one thing at a time, while Angels can express many feelings and concepts at the same time. Interacting with a human is like sucking on a piece of hard candy. Connecting with an Angel is like biting down on that candy, resulting in a forceful explosion of flavor in your mouth all at once.

Angels technically don't have wings, at least not of the sort that are bodily appendages sticking out of their backs. With their wide and distinct auras, the part of their aura behind their backs can look like wings of light; the individual "flames" forming their auras can look like feathers. Psychic visions that perceive this are likely the origin of Angels being considered to have wings and being shown with them. Of course, Angels are masters of traveling through the spiritual planes and are so full of love that they "take themselves lightly," which are other reasons they get associated with flying.

Fairies acquire souls and enter the Angel kingdom after individualization. Just as higher animals frequently individualize through a connection with humans, so do fairies usually individualize through a connection with Angels. Since fairies on average are more intelligent than animals, that means the fairy lifestream tends to individualize later in evolution than the human lifestream. This is probably due to the nature of the respective lifestreams. Humans keep physical bodies until they become Masters. We're a very diverse kingdom with lots of individuality, expressing on all the planes at once. Fairies are a more homogeneous life form since they express fewer aspects, avoiding the dense physical plane. Fairies can be emotional and even intelligent for long period of time before touching abstract thought or love that's enough to individualize them.

Humans can become Angels as well. Most Angels have never been human, but a certain percentage of them have had human incarnations in the past. Joining the Angel evolution is one of the Seven Paths available to a person once they become a Master and graduate out of the human kingdom. Since the Angel kingdom partially overlaps but on the whole is ahead of humanity, it can be considered kingdom number 7½. The option of becoming an Angel is a natural and "official" path of evolution, as opposed to a fairy becoming human which is very rare and "abnormal." Presumably, a human that's a crossover from the fairy kingdom will choose to become an Angel after Enlightenment, since they would have become an Angel had they stayed in the fairy kingdom. Given the philosophy that everything happens for a purpose, the Angel that got to inhabit both the human and fairy kingdoms will use their relatively unique experience to help fulfill their future destiny.

The following chart shows all nine kingdoms of nature on Earth, and the planes they cover and are working towards. The first columns are the seven kingdoms humans progress through. The last two columns cover the kingdoms in the fairy/Angel lifestream.

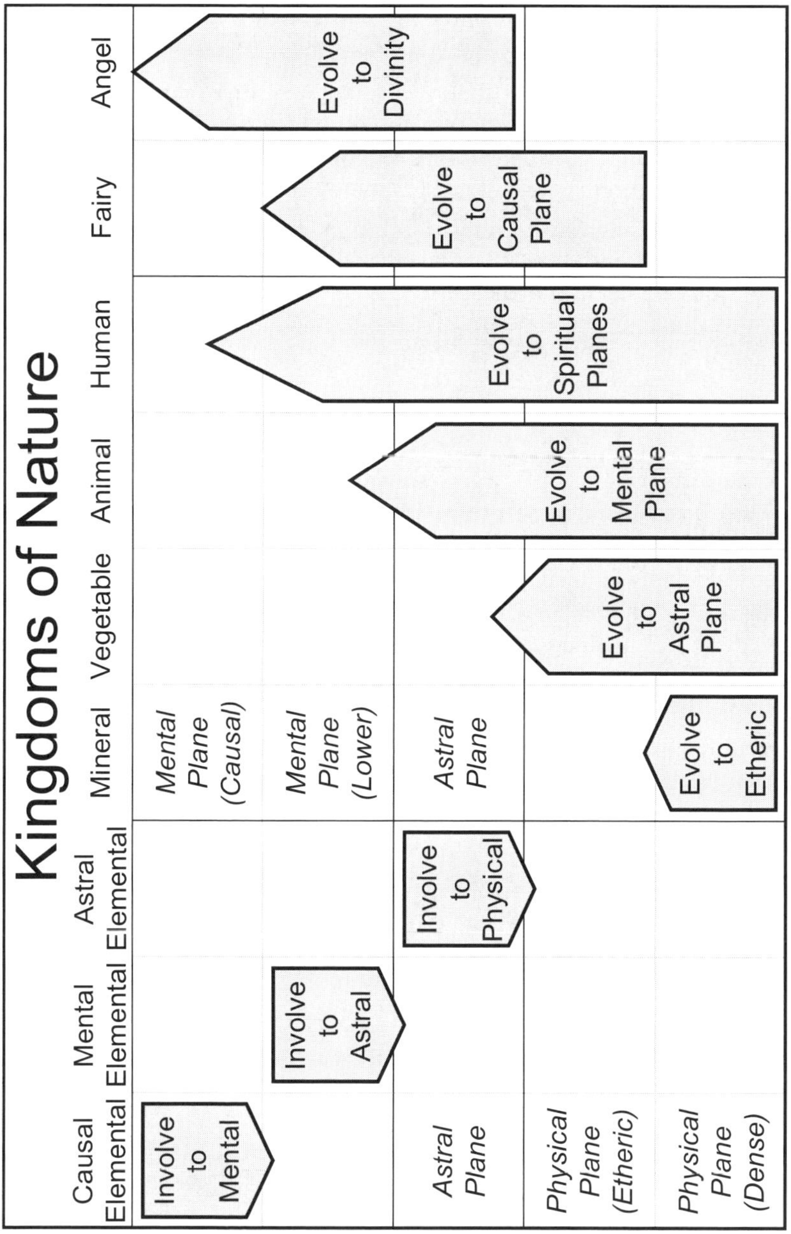
Kingdoms of Nature
Causal Elemental
Mental Elemental
Astral Elemental
Mineral
Vegetable
Animal
Human
Fairy
Angel
Involve to Mental
Involve to Astral
Involve to Physical
Astral Plane
Physical Plane (Etheric)
Physical Plane (Dense)
Mental Plane (Causal)
Mental Plane (Lower)
Astral Plane
Evolve to Etheric
Evolve to Astral Plane
Evolve to Mental Plane
Evolve to Spiritual Planes
Evolve to Causal Plane
Evolve to Divinity

The following chart shows the paths of progression the various lifestreams take through the kingdoms from the moment one was first created and breathed forth, all the way to when one becomes Divine himself/herself. The two horizontal lines divide the kingdoms into three important phases. The lower line is the moment of individualization where one graduates from a group soul and acquires his/her own soul. The upper line is the moment of Enlightenment when one reaches the Master level and has completed their journey back to their Spirit.

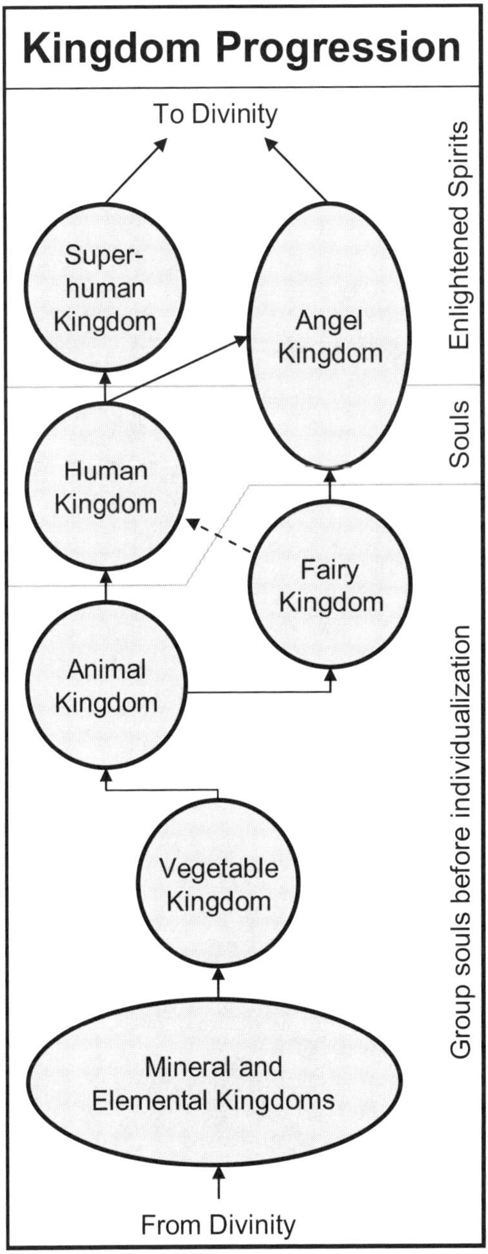
Kingdom Progression
To Divinity
Enlightened Spirits
Super-human Kingdom
Angel Kingdom
Souls
Human Kingdom
Fairy Kingdom
Animal Kingdom
Group souls before individualization
Vegetable Kingdom
Mineral and Elemental Kingdoms
From Divinity

7:
The Great Initiations

"Faith is taking the first step even when you don't see the whole staircase."
- Martin Luther King, Jr.

In the spiritual journey to Enlightenment and beyond, there are signposts along the way. They can be used to divide our long journey into more readily understandable phases. One method of mapping evolution within and beyond the human kingdom is via the nine Great Initiations. Each Initiation marks a very real change in one's soul or Spirit and is an emergence into a new level of consciousness. These Initiations are recognized and honored by various beings and groups. There actually exists a Great Initiator on spiritual planes who welcomes each entity to its next level. This Great Initiator does what corresponds to handing out a diploma but in a much vaster sense.

The main attribute that defines an Initiation is that the seeker has mastered one of the planes of the Universe, is free from its limitations, and, therefore, is ready for the next level. Mastering one plane means one has touched the next higher plane for the first time and has started to work with it. As one increases their awareness, they're welcomed onto the next higher floor of the Divine Mansion, so to speak. Hence, much of the information about these Initiations one could deduce independently from knowledge about the planes. The energy of Initiation can be considered the energy of the next plane pouring into your consciousness.

The popular image of "initiation" is that given by the leaders of some secret society where they make someone feel important on an outer personality level. Real Initiation is much more sacred and happens on a much deeper level. Initiation isn't something given to you, as much as it's just something that acknowledges your attainment after you already meet all the qualifications. Being Initiated is like being promoted at work and means increased responsibility where more is expected of you. It is important to realize it's not the outer personality that gets Initiated, but rather the soul or Spirit. Hence, it's possible to receive at least the earlier pre-Enlightenment Initiations and not be consciously aware of them, since your higher self got Initiated on higher planes while you were asleep. Initiations do, however, frequently correspond to a spiritual event in physical life.

Since Initiations cover such vast leaps in consciousness, the time period between each Initiation can be vast, covering potentially thousands of lifetimes or millions of years. It can also be quite short; two Initiations can be taken in consecutive lifetimes or even in the same lifetime. It's like considering how long one spends within each room of an art gallery – they can rush through it or spend a very long time experiencing each image. The same is true in spiritual growth; neither slower nor faster is necessarily better. Each incarnation, one tends to repeat the experiences of the earlier Initiations they've attained to a certain extent, even though they're not actually being Initiated again. Eventually, one catches up to the highest level of attainment they ever achieved in past lives, meaning future growth breaks new ground, and may lead to the next Initiation. For example, Gautama Buddha became a Master during his last lifetime on Earth, but he started out that incarnation much like the average person and needed certain experiences before he started seeking.

The following table summarizes the nine Initiations. The Initiation name column is what the Initiation is traditionally called beyond its number. The personal name is what one who has taken that Initiation is called or rather what they become. Each Initiation is determined by one having achieved mastery of or freedom from a particular influence and is marked by a certain activity. Finally, there is listed the approximate number of people currently incarnated on Earth that have taken each Initiation. These numbers can change over time. There are "primitive" time periods where there are few spiritual people of any grade on the planet, and other periods where high percentages of the people present have been Initiated. Earth is similar to a classroom and may be holding a class of kindergarteners at some time periods and a class of high school honor students at others. Currently, Earth is rapidly moving from a relatively primitive period to a spiritual period, meaning the numbers of people incarnated on all levels are similarly increasing.

The Great Initiations

#	Initiation Name	Personal Name	Mastery of / Freedom from	Marked by	Number on Earth
1	Birth	Aspirant / Seeker	Physical body	Seeking	100 million – 600 million
2	Baptism	Disciple	Astral body	Commited Path	10 million – 60 million
3	Transfiguration	Initiate	Mental body / personality	Service / Cosmic Consciousness	100,000 – 600,000
4	Renunciation	Arhat	Buddhic plane / pride / soul	Oneness / Crucifixion	1000 – 6000
5	Revelation	Master / Adept	Atmic plane	Ascension / Enlightenment	10 – 60
6	Decision	Chohan	Monadic plane	7 Choices / True Purpose	0
7	Resurrection	Manu / Bodhisattva	Divine plane / Spirit	Divinity	0
8	Transition	Lord / Buddha	Consciousness	Divinity	-
9	Refusal	Logos	Everything	Divinity	-

To put the enormous magnitude of growth covered by the nine Initiations into perspective, here's a simpler to understand analogy showing nine phases of how one's relation to a school can change over time as they grow. The school of course represents our planet, which is the Great School we all grow in. There's at least a minor relation between each stage here and the corresponding spiritual Initiation.

1: Your pregnant mother researches the schools you'll eventually attend.
2: You're a baby in pre-school.
3: You're a student in grade school.
4: You've graduated from grade school and have gone off to college.
5: You're an adult and get a job working at the school as a janitor.
6: You get a job working at the school as a teacher teaching students.
7: You're the principal of the school.
8: You're the superintendent of the entire school district.
9: You retire.

Here's another analogy that uses climbing a mountain; the mountain, of course, represents spirituality.

1: You see a mountain and gaze up at it in wonder.
2: You pick a route and start climbing to the top.
3: You reach the top of the mountain for the first time.
4: You move out of your home and live on top of the mountain permanently.
5: You jump up from the mountaintop and fly free above it.
6: You start building your own mountain.
7: You become a mountain.
8: You become One with the entire world.
9: You leave the world altogether.

A third analogy for the Great Initiations involves the evolution of a seed.

1: An underground seed is warmed by the earth.
2: The life within the seed pushes against the seed's outer shell.
3: The seed cracks and the sprout inside becomes visible.
4: The sprout leaves the seed behind and pushes up through the dirt.
5: The sprout breaks the surface of the earth and sees the world around it.
6: The new sprout knows what type of plant it will be.
7: The sprout becomes a full grown plant.
8: The plant goes to seed and creates new plants.
9: The plant dies and the life within it moves on.

Each Initiation contains within it all the qualities of previous Initiations. For example, a Disciple of the Second Initiation is still drawn to experience spirituality like an Aspirant of the First Initiation. Similarly, the discipline expressed by a Disciple doesn't go away after they take higher Initiations. This containment is similar to how one doesn't forget their high school lessons when they go to college, or how the foundation of a building doesn't go away when the higher stories are constructed.

Consecutive Initiations are related. Odd numbered Initiations signify revelations where one is exposed to a new level of consciousness. Even numbered Initiations signify effort where one works to master the quality presented in the previous Initiation. After the First Initiation, one becomes interested in spirituality while after the Second Initiation, one commits to spirituality and works on himself/herself. After the Third Initiation, one is exposed to Oneness and the consciousness of Spirit while after the Fourth Initiation, one has worked to surrender his/her consciousness to Spirit and express Oneness at all times. After the Fifth Initiation, the Master experiences higher worlds while after the Sixth Initiation, the Master has worked to become a part of these higher worlds. After the Seventh Initiation, the Master touches the Divine while after the Eighth Initiation, the Master has worked to transition themselves into being a part of the Divine.

Initiations 5 through 8 are similar to Initiations 1 through 4. Each group of four Initiations covers similar phases, except the first set happens to the soul, while the second set happens to the Spirit. The First and Fifth Initiations expose one to soul and Spirit and a completely new area of growth. The Second and Sixth Initiations are where one works to understand and express on a soul or Spirit level. The Third and Seventh Initiations feature Spirit pouring down on soul, or the Divine pouring down on Spirit. The Fourth and Eighth Initiations are one leaving behind soul or Spirit in preparation for graduating to the next area.

These relations between the Initiations are summarized in the following table. For each Initiation, listed is its type concerning whether it's a revelation of a new quality, or effort in developing that quality. Qualities include being on a spiritual Path to begin with, expressing Oneness and service, complete Mastery and finally merging with Divinity. Also listed is the area where growth is taking place, be it soul or Spirit, and the phase at which one is within that area. Phases include initial exposure to an area, commitment to developing that area, a downpour of higher energies as a result of previous work, and finally transcending the area.

Relations between the Great Initiations					
#	**Name**	**Type**	**Quality**	**Area**	**Phase**
1	Birth	Revelation	Path	Soul	Exposure
2	Baptism	Effort	Path	Soul	Commitment
3	Transfiguration	Revelation	Oneness	Soul	Downpour
4	Renunciation	Effort	Oneness	Soul	Transcend
5	Revelation	Revelation	Mastery	Spirit	Exposure
6	Decision	Effort	Mastery	Spirit	Commitment
7	Resurrection	Revelation	Divinity	Spirit	Downpour
8	Transition	Effort	Divinity	Spirit	Transcend
9	Refusal	Revelation	Cosmic	Divine	Exposure

Why are there nine Initiations and not seven like in so many other aspects of spirituality? Initiations actually do form groups of seven where in one sense, the first two aren't full Initiations like the others since they mostly happen on a personality level. In another sense, the last two Initiations aren't like the others since they happen at Divine levels. Instead of focusing on either the first seven or the last seven Initiations, it's best to include all of them, to give the most comprehensive view before, during, and after each phase.

Initiations, or rather the processes leading up to them, are often scary or even painful to a certain extent. That is because they embody the ultimate in change, involve death of the old way of life, and signify making the leap into the new. For example, before the First Initiation, seekers are faced with the concept of leaving the safe comfort zone of their old mundane existence and experiencing a new and unknown spiritual existence, a process which they might fear will utterly change their life (and they're right). Before the Second Initiation the seekers are faced with the concept of truly committing to spirituality and letting go of their old attachments. Before the Third Initiation they are faced with letting go of personal ego, and so on.

Before one reaches the Master level, it's not readily apparent what Initiations they have taken. The linear progression presented here gets distorted by the realities of physical life and the uniqueness of each individual. For example, spiritual seekers may seem to have the qualifications of the Third Initiation, but they also have a drug addiction, which would seem to imply they lack physical control and hence haven't taken the First Initiation yet. Sometimes a soul may have taken an Initiation in a past life, but in this life they're focusing on learning something, so they may not seem that spiritual outwardly or express it in their lives. Situations like this are another reason one shouldn't place too much emphasis on where they or other people seem to be.

The Great Initiations are not the only set of signposts along our spiritual Path. There are also ways of dividing one's growth between the major Initiations where one could define what amounts to sub-initiations. Also, the definitions for terms used here are not the only ones available. For example, spiritual organizations may describe their members as disciples or initiates, which is different from what it means when one becomes a true Disciple or Initiate after taking the Second or Third Initiations. One can be an "initiate" in a group while still an Aspirant as described here. Similarly, some consider an Arhat to be one who has already attained Enlightenment while here it's defined the phase immediately before.

Initiation #1: Birth

The First Initiation marks the point where one becomes interested in spirituality in the first place. One has "heard the call," and is responding with an inner longing. After this point one begins to explore, study, and seek spiritual experiences. This Initiation is called "Birth" because it indicates a birth into a major new era of their evolution. The term being "born again" as used by some traditional religions refers to this utter change in life and perspective. One may not be aware of it yet, but they've differentiated themselves from the masses of humanity, and have started upon a path that will ultimately lead to Divinity. The vast majority of people have no interest in spirituality, although their numbers are increasing daily (both in total and as a percentage of the population).

Those who have taken the First Initiation are called Aspirants or seekers because they now aspire to spiritual growth and, more importantly, seek it out on their own. This Initiation may be marked by a metaphysical experience, such as seeing a UFO or having an out-of-body or near-death experience. Such an awe-inspiring, mind-blowing event makes one aware that there's much more to life than mundane reality. At the current time, roughly 10% of the incarnated population qualifies as an Aspirant. Attending religious services doesn't necessarily make one an Aspirant since he/she may be doing so out of obligation or fear. Similarly, many Aspirants are "solitary" and don't follow any formal school of thought. If you meet an Aspirant, he/she'll seem open minded or friendly with a clarity or intelligence about them.

The other defining aspect about the First Initiation is one has mastered their physical body, and are free from controlling physical influences, such as addictive substances or other unhealthy physical habits. Without control over one's own body, one can't hope to use it as a proper foundation for future growth. Once one has mastered the physical aspects of being human, the door is open to the next step: Spirituality.

To use another term from traditional religion, after the First Initiation one is considered "saved," meaning they're on a spiritual path for good and will never again return to a non-spiritual way of life. That doesn't mean there won't be (potentially big) mistakes made or (potentially multiple lifetime) delays along the way, but it does mean the Aspirant is guaranteed of being able to find his/her way to Enlightenment on their own eventually. In spite of this, the period after the First Initiation is sometimes called the "probationary" part of the Spiritual Path, meaning the Aspirant hasn't fully demonstrated his/her commitment to it yet.

Initiation #2: Baptism

The Second Initiation marks the point where the "Path" part of the Spiritual Path truly begins. One makes a conscious commitment to spiritual growth, is aware of the concept of Enlightenment, and is working to achieve it for himself/herself. One who has taken the Second Initiation is called a Disciple because he/she is now following some Path. Disciples may physically move to an ashram or become a traditional disciple of a Master or follow a school of thought in some less obvious way. From now on, the Disciple is part of a network and has very definite links to others—peers that are on the same chosen Path, Masters, guides, or other Disciples further along that Path.

While the Aspirant looks upon the mountain, playing around its base or on its lower slopes while dreaming of the summit, the Disciple has chosen a route and begun the work to actually climb it. For example, while the Aspirant just learns about karma, the Disciple accepts the law of karma and lives his/her life appropriately, working to clear their negative karma and create positive karma. Note: the focus is on working on self. The words "disciple" and "discipline" have the same root.

Disciples recognize the validity of most Paths, but they've also chosen a Path right for them and no longer "beat around the bush" with respect to growing. True Disciples no longer make the mistake of seeing their Path as the only way; however, because they've experienced some success on their Path, they're happy to share it with others. If you meet a Disciple, he/she is likely to seem intense, if not passionate about his/her growth. At the current time about 1% of the population qualifies as a Disciple.

The name "Baptism" for this Initiation comes from the religious practice of anointing with water or being accepted into a Path. Note: having been baptized via a traditional religion doesn't necessarily mean one has taken the Baptism Initiation while at the same time, most Disciples have never gone through a baptism ceremony.

Traditional baptism is done with water. Similarly, the Baptism Initiation is related to the watery astral plane. The other defining aspect of the Second Initiation is the seekers have mastered their astral bodies. Their emotions are calm, they're able to embody positive emotions, and they don't let negative emotions control them.

If they have an overwhelming passion, it's for union with the Divine. This doesn't mean they are unemotional, but rather their feelings are appropriate for the moment and are a healthy influence on themselves and those around them. With a serene nature and healthy emotional life, they are able to meet the many challenges of the Path, clear their bad karma without creating new negative karma, and create an inner sacred space allowing them to grow into taking the next steps.

The period after the Second Initiation is the most critical and potentially hazardous of all the Initiations. Disciples are beginning to awaken their own power, develop psychic or other metaphysical talents, and undertake significant projects. This phase of spirituality is analogous to being a teenager who has power and the desire to use it but not necessarily the wisdom to use it properly. A teenager may crash the car, overdose on drugs, or accidentally get pregnant. Similarly Disciples should be vigilant they don't make reckless mistakes that may have long lasting repercussions.

Initiation #3: Transfiguration

The Third Initiation marks conscious connection with your Spirit. This Initiation is called the "Transfiguration" because the energy utterly and irrevocably changes your makeup. You used to only live in your personality, as projected from your soul. Your world consisted of body, emotions and mind (i.e. you were active on the physical, astral, and mental planes). Now you're aware of Spirit, and are starting to live in intuition, universal Love, and will (i.e. the Buddhic plane, the next plane higher than the mental).

The Third Initiation also marks the mastery of the threefold personality. Body, emotions, and now mind are calm and developed, acting as faithful servants instead of controlling influences. Many people have calm emotions, but very few have calm minds. Most minds are continually running from one random thought to another like a hyper puppy where the moment one stops using it, the internal babbling resumes. As with your body and emotions, even your thoughts can become something you observe and bring forth from a quiet place inside, instead of something that's the primary seat of your consciousness.

The first two Initiations were focused on you, the individual, and your own individual growth. This is the first Initiation that's not just about you, but also about the world. From now on, whether or not you're conscious of it yet, you're a channel through which spiritual energies flow to Earth. For that reason, the Third Initiation can be considered the first true Initiation; when one has taken it, he/she can truly be called an Initiate. This is the first initiation of Oneness; the seeker is aware of the Greater Being we all form and are forming. After this Initiation, one begins a life of true service. That doesn't mean one didn't serve before, but now service is something one does because it feels right and is an innate part of their being, as opposed to something they do just because they know it's the right thing or will help them grow. Ego or selfishness has been reduced to almost nothing. From now on, you care about the growth and evolution of those around you as much as you do your own because you and others are One.

While Aspirants learn about karma, and Disciples work on resolving their past karma, with the Initiate all of their "negative" karma has finally been balanced, and the path of higher growth before them lies fully open without anything from the past dragging them down or otherwise distracting them. That doesn't mean there won't be extremely challenging experiences in the future, just that they will all be more directly focused on growth.

The Third Initiation can be marked by one or more experiences of Cosmic Consciousness or Samadhi, or in more technical terms their consciousness has touched the Buddhic plane. You've reached the top of the mountain, and for the first time can see what lies beyond. If you meet an Initiate, they're likely to have a beautiful glow about them, and perhaps seem Angelic in a way, since the energy of their Spirit is starting to shine through them into their life and the world. At the current time, there are approximately a few hundred thousand Initiates in incarnation. The closeness of this number to 144,000 may be the cause of "the 144,000 souls" one hears about doing good works from various sources.

The Transfiguration Initiation is similar to the Biblical transfiguration of Jesus. When He took a few of His disciples to a mountaintop, He glowed radiantly and the voice of God was heard affirming Jesus as His Son. Similarly, upon Initiation one feels themselves to be a child of God or the Divine, as opposed to just knowing it intellectually. Being an acknowledged child of the Divine does not separate you from others, but rather makes you feel connected with and compassionate for everyone and everything. It does not make you feel individually superior, but rather you see the perfection and beauty of everything unfolding at its proper pace throughout eternity.

Initiation #4: Renunciation

The Fourth Initiation marks one moving on from their personality and soul. This process requires renouncing the lower planes that have served them for so long, hence the name of this Initiation. The personality has been mastered, and the soul is perfect and complete, so the next step is to Ascend on to the Spirit above. One who has taken the Fourth Initiation is called an Arhat (pronounced are-hut) which is Sanskrit for "deserving" or "meritorious."

While the Third Initiation marked the pinnacle of the human experience, and the initial experiences of Cosmic Consciousness, by the Fourth Initiation one is able to experience Cosmic Consciousness frequently, if not continuously. More technically, they've mastered the energies of the Buddhic plane of love and unity. For this reason people near Mastery seem to spend a large amount of time in meditation. Before, one was conscious on the lower planes, and reached up to and experienced Spirit. Now they are conscious on the higher planes, and are reaching down to experience and do things in the lower realms. While the Initiate reached the top of the mountain, then returned home, the Arhat lives on top of the mountain permanently, and is getting ready to jump up to fly higher. An Arhat is truly a Spirit having a human experience, and no longer a human having a spiritual experience.

Although Renunciation is a conscious decision, it's important to realize it doesn't happen due to any dislike for "lower" forms of existence. That would be a dualistic way of looking at it where the Arhat is beyond duality. Renunciation happens because one can be the old way no longer, like a baby being pushed out of the womb. Once the student has learned all they can, it is time for them to leave their Master. Similarly, once the soul is complete and has served its purpose, it's time to lovingly renounce it. The soul is renounced by moving consciousness above the Causal plane level of the soul, after which the soul fades away naturally. The Arhat can still use lower plane bodies and have what would be considered a soul; however, it's no longer necessary for their evolution and no longer the seat of their consciousness.

The Fourth Initiation deals with Oneness in a much more comprehensive sense than the Third. Pride is traditionally the last illusion or limitation to fall away before one becomes a Master. The Arhat has finally overcome all aspects of personal egotism, including the subtle case of being proud of having overcome pride! They no longer cast judgment, and don't even judge others or themselves if they make judgments. They're full of eternal love, and even love others and themselves if love seems to be absent. They fully live in the now, even when they choose to consider the past or future. This state of consciousness may be hard to understand; the Arhat has mastered all the seeming paradoxes and contradictions of life as often described in Zen koans. Their feelings are radiant like the sun, their mind is like lightning, and their soul and Causal body have been perfected.

The Arhat has not only resolved all their negative karma, but they've resolved all their positive karma as well. They truly have no attachment to physical existence. Arhats no longer need to physically incarnate, although they usually choose to do so for continued growth and service. At the current time, there are only a few thousand Arhats in incarnation. They often live in seclusion or under the close watch of a physical or discarnate Master, doing the last steps necessary so they can Ascend (see the next Initiation). Arhats may also have disciples of their own; they may be considered living Masters, even if that technically isn't true yet by our definition here. If you meet an Arhat, they're likely to have incredible energy; the radiance of their spiritual growth is likely to be a catalyst for your own.

The Fourth Initiation is sometimes called the Crucifixion initiation because the process of leaving your personality and even soul behind feels like being crucified. It's perhaps the ultimate frightening experience, since it's in effect the ultimate death. Just physical death and discarding your outer body after a single incarnation is disturbing enough, much less sacrificing your perfected soul that for so long has acted as your higher self. You have to abandon your old life before you can live in a new life, but that means having neither during the transition process. What one goes through during Renunciation is depicted in a literal sense by Jesus Christ on the cross. You may feel utterly alone in the Universe, seemingly abandoned by all things within and without that you traditionally receive comfort from where even God has forsaken you. You have to totally surrender everything possible about yourself. It may be uncomfortable, but it serves a much higher purpose. You're removing yourself from the "cross" of the reincarnating personality, and are moving to Spirit.

Initiation #5: Revelation

The Fifth Initiation marks ultimate mastery of the human kingdom; hence, one who has taken this Initiation is called a Master. The word "Master" implies control; however, what the Master has achieved control of is himself/herself. They are also called Adepts since they're adept at all aspects of being human. A Master is the highest level one can go and still be a member of the human kingdom. The Ascension process begun after the Fourth Initiation has been completed and one has transferred consciousness from their soul to their Spirit. The traditional concept of an "Ascended Master" refers to one who has gone through this process.

This Initiation is called "Revelation" because, for the first time, one can truly see the spiritual planes accurately and see them from the vantage point of Spirit itself without any barriers, illusion, or ignorance. One is completely Enlightened, meaning the light of Spirit is upon them. They've jumped off the top of the mountain and are soaring totally free. While the Fourth Initiation was characterized by a significant amount of what we'd consider suffering, from now on, one lives and grows in eternal bliss. Spiritual growth still happens after one achieves Mastery, but now one is permanently infused with Spirit or rather has become Spirit.

A Master may incarnate to serve or teach, and a few do, but most move on to other things. While the Arhat mastered the spiritual energies of love, the Master has gone a step further and mastered the energies of will or pure Spirit. All three aspects of one's Spirit are now developed: abstract thought, love / intuition, and will. The Master primarily works on the Atmic plane, and is able to see and touch their Monad for the first time on the next higher plane.

If you meet a real Master, it's likely to be so beautiful an experience it will make you want to cry. At the same time, a Master usually seems very humble, and very "human." It's not a frightening experience in any way unless your own filters or biases seriously distort things. Rather, it makes you feel truly yourself. At the present time, there are only a few dozen true Masters on Earth making use of physical bodies in order to serve. Some Masters are publicly recognized as such, some run ashrams with disciples, while others work more behind the scenes.

Initiation #6: Decision

The Sixth Initiation marks the Master graduating from the human kingdom and deciding what to do next. There are several choices before the Master of things they can do to serve and continue their own evolution. For more about these choices, see the next chapter "Post-Enlightenment Paths." The name "Decision" has deep meaning here since the Master's will is so powerful, and they're finally free from (or rather one with) karma or the forces of cause and effect. One who has taken this Initiation is consciously one with their Monad where they primarily work on the Monadic plane.

A new Master is effectively a baby, from the standpoint of the new superhuman world they've entered. Before Mastership, you're like a seed underground, slowly reaching up through the soil. Enlightenment is when you break the surface, and the real world is revealed to you for the first time. You then start a new phase of growing from a seedling. Around you can be seen trees, bushes, and flowers of numerous flavors. After the Sixth Initiation, the Master has decided what type of plant they want to be in the real world. In that respect the Sixth Initiation is related to the Second, since they both involve making a commitment to a new stage of growth and activity. One who has made this great Decision is called a Chohan, which is Tibetan for "lord of dharma." A Chohan is nothing less than a chief or leader of Masters.

Chohans generally don't physically incarnate since they're so evolved. They're more likely to just physically manifest themselves if needed. Chohans don't even incarnate on Earth to teach, except during highly evolved eras or significant times in history. A college professor could certainly teach a kindergarten class, but the kids would only be able to understand so much. It's better for the professor to work with college graduates. When a Chohan does manifest, in the wake of their passing is almost always a long-standing religion.

If you were to meet a Chohan, assuming one were to manifest on the physical plane in the first place, their presence would be so powerful you'd want to avert your gaze or steady yourself on the ground. This is part of the origin of bowing before those in a position of honor as a gesture of respect. It wasn't done to show submission as much as an actual physical necessity.

Initiation #7: Resurrection

The Seventh Initiation is the last initiation related to growth on our planet, so in one sense this is the final Initiation. It marks when one has mastered his/her Spirit; their Monad is perfect and complete. One has fulfilled their chosen form of service to the planet, and through doing that has mastered the energies of the Monadic plane. One now is raised or resurrected from the six planes of evolution to the seventh or Divine plane. Such a Being has truly become a "son of God." Since the Divine has been touched, future Initiations are related to one's Divine growth. Just as the Third Initiation marks one mastering his/her personality/soul and touching Spirit, the Seventh Initiation marks one mastering his/her Spirit/Monad and touching the Divine.

One who has taken the Seventh Initiation can become a Manu. The word Manu (pronounced mah-new) is Sanskrit for "man" and refers to the Being who created the first humans. On very rare occasions, a Manu will manifest on Earth for an important purpose, such as to create the next Root-Race of bodies to be used by a lifewave. In general, a Manu is one who oversees or embodies a major aspect of the world or divine Plan. Note that there are several classes of Manus, starting from being the Manu of a Root-Race of humanity and extending up to a Manu of an entire Chain of Globes; these higher Manus are on levels beyond the Seventh Initiation. Manus are described more in the chapter "Cycles of Evolution."

After the Seventh Initiation, one can also become a Bodhisattva or World Teacher. The word Bodhisattva is Sanskrit for "perfect knowledge and being." They are ones who are worthy of Nirvana but have chosen to stay in close touch with Earth to continue to serve. The Manu and Bodhisattva are only two examples of options and Paths available at this point. These "demigods" may fulfill a number of other different but just as important purposes of which we can't conceive.

A Manu is so far beyond our experience, that if one were to manifest before you, you'd probably keel over unconscious with no memory of the event, if not physically explode or burst into flame from an overdose of ultimate love!

Initiation #8: Transition

The Eighth Initiation marks one making the Great Transition to full and permanent Divinity, hence the name "Transition" for this Initiation. One leaves the seven planes of the Universe, the seven planes forming the Cosmic Physical plane, that have formed our evolutionary environment since our Monads were first breathed out in a lifewave from a divine Logos. There's no real name for such a Being, beyond "Lord" or "King" or "Buddha", since they're now qualified to act as a Lord of the World, be it the administrator of a planet or some other similarly significant aspect of the Universe.

While the Fourth Initiation marked one leaving the soul behind, the Eighth Initiation marks leaving one's Spirit behind. While in the Seventh Initiation, one's Spirit touched Divinity for the first time, in the Eighth Initiation, one fully enters Divinity. One leaves individual spiritual consciousness behind to be replaced with Divine Consciousness. Consciousness, at least the way we think of it, is ultimately an illusion. It consists of us experiencing that "I am this" or "I am not this," which is a limitation. The Eighth Initiation is the ultimate in Oneness since finally you are truly One with everything. No words can ever hope to describe the depth of compassion or the radiant potential that comes with this ultimate state of Being.

These "gods" (if such a term may be used) are so vast, there's no ordinary way to communicate with them or meet them. Not only are they not physical, even the term "non-physical" doesn't do them justice anymore! In a way they're all around you and within you, everywhere you look. You can't communicate with them in the standard sense any more than a cell can communicate with the body it's in. To use the reverse analogy, what would you say to a cell in your body? Your forms of feeling and thought are so beyond that of the cell. It's like a professor trying to teach calculus to a fish; not only does the fish have no hope of understanding it, the fish doesn't even understand the language you're using or even the concept of "language."

Initiation #9: Refusal

The Ninth and last Initiation marks one leaving our world altogether, in a sense refusing further involvement with it. The name "Refusal" for this final and highest Initiation may seem puzzling. After all the effort of becoming One, doesn't this imply a separation? Everyone who has reached this point has spent a lot of effort merging into Divinity and serving the world. But eventually even service comes to an end, and even service can be considered a form of limitation. After the Eighth Initiation, one became fully Divine but was still attached to our world and in service to it from higher planes. Through the nine Great Initiations, one has grown from ordinary human to their ultimate destiny: Divinity. The child has fully grown up and now is ready to leave home and make his/her own life in the Universe. There's again no real name for one who has taken this Initiation beyond Logos where they've reached the level of a Logos themselves.

An example from fiction may be able to shed some light on what happens in this Initiation. The science fiction television series "Babylon 5" featured the two most powerful and ancient races in the Galaxy, who had guided the rest of the races for eons. They were the Vorlons who represented law and good, and the Shadows who represented chaos and evil. The time came when their presence was no longer needed, and they decided to leave the roles they had fulfilled for so long and no longer be involved with the Galaxy. They went "beyond the rim," past the "ring pass not," and were free from everything. There were other "First Ones," beings harder to understand than even the already strange Vorlons and Shadows, which had made the same transition earlier. The Vorlons and Shadows left to join them.

What happens after the Great Refusal? Yes, there are further Initiations that happen. They're different from those experienced thus far since the Being who holds the office of the Great Initiator is now your equal, if not someone you're more evolved than. The Great Initiator used to be a godlike being you knew little about, and now he's a "drinking buddy" so to speak. Once you're at the level of a Logos, you can breathe forth your own lifewaves, creating new Monads, who will eventually make their way through the entire evolutionary process and become Divine, too. As a Logos you can literally become a planet, then evolve into being a star with planets working for you, or have planets as organs in your body. After that you can eventually evolve into being a Galaxy, with stars as cells in your body. Being a Planetary or Solar Logos is only one option among many you have at this point. They're just the Divine states most readily apparent to us since planets and stars have physical manifestations we can see. Most possibilities at this point are unconceivable to us. Those who are Logoi now presumably were that way at the time the Universe was Created, at which point they manifested and embodied the initial Galaxies and Stars. At this level, you're so Divine that you exist beyond the end of the Universe and presumably can play a role in designing a future one.

Just as the standard planes of the Universe are encompassed by a single Cosmic Plane on a higher level, so are the nine Initiations encompassed by a single Initiation on a higher level called a Cosmic Initiation. Little is known about them, only that the First Cosmic Initiation occurs after the Ninth Initiation. A Planetary Logos has taken the First Cosmic Initiation and is working toward the second. A Solar Logos has taken the Second Cosmic Initiation and is working toward the third. Presumably, a Galactic Logos has taken the Third Cosmic Initiation and is working toward the fourth, and so on. Just as the standard Initiations involve one mastering the various standard planes, the Cosmic Initiations apparently involve one mastering the various Cosmic Planes or aspects of Divinity.

8: Post-Enlightenment Paths

"When you reach the top, keep climbing."
- Zen proverb

In spiritual growth, most of our attention is focused on where we are here and now, and how we can take our next step. However, there's also benefit to considering where our Path leads in the future, even in the far distant future. The only potential downside is if one puts too much emphasis on a potential future, such that they disregard where they are on their journey now, or forget the magic of being human. We grow through the journey itself; destinations only mark what we've done up to that point.

After one reaches the state of an Enlightened Master, he/she has graduated from the human kingdom, and several choices or options for future activity become available. These are the Seven Paths where the Master decides to take one at their Sixth Great Initiation. Enlightenment is more the beginning of a Path, than the end of one. It can be interesting to meditate on what Path you, or those you know, may end up taking. It's like a child considering what they want to be when they grow up. Often what we end up doing has no relation to our earlier interests while at the same time, some know inside what they're meant to do at an early age.

Having seven paths should not be seen as limiting or confining spirits to "boxes" in any way. The post-Enlightenment state is eternally blissful; these Seven Paths just classify the infinity of options in more easily understood categories. If Earth is college, the Paths describe what you can do after you graduate. After one graduates, one could say the seven categories of things they can do are enter graduate school, be a homemaker, get a blue or white collar job, join the military, enter politics, or just take time off and relax.

Certainly there are countless different ways one can express each of these options.

In general, once one decides on his/her Path, he/she stays on it permanently. This isn't due to any forced requirement but rather is due to their awakened Spirit having found its true purpose and place in the Universe. Occasionally, Masters do move between Paths just as one may switch jobs on Earth.

The following table lists the Seven Post-Enlightenment Paths, presented in order from the most readily understandable to the most abstract. The Focus column shows what aspect of Spirit the Path primarily expresses. All Paths have elements of each although each Path tends to emphasize one over the others. Note: none of the Paths focus on intelligence, love/intuition, or will. The Master by definition has already mastered these three primary aspects of Spirit (as expressed on the mental, Buddhic, and Atmic planes) where these Paths define how the Master chooses to use those core energies. The Earth analogy column shows what Earthly career is most similar to the Path in question. Although the Paths are on a level we can barely conceive, the concept of "as above, so below" applies; knowing the choices available on Earth gives at least a slight hint to those available in Spirit. Finally, each Path has a similar focus to the energy of one of the seven Rays.

Post-Enlightenment Paths			
Path Name	**Focus**	**Earth Analogy**	**Ray**
Earth Service	Wisdom	Graduate school	2
Nirmanakaya	Compassion	Homemaker	4
Logos Training	Power	Politics	1
Builder	Creation	Manufacturing job	5
Angel Evolution	Light	Service job	3
Staff Corps of the Logos	Service	Military service	7
Nirvana	Bliss	Time off traveling	6

Earth Service

The Path of Earth Service is a deep calling to help others grow spiritually. This is the path most readily apparent to us on Earth since we occasionally see those on this Path incarnating as Masters to teach. That's not the only way to help Earth grow, of course. Others on this path may not incarnate or may be more focused upon the evolution of the animal or other kingdoms of nature. None of the other Paths involve the Master physically incarnating since none of the others are focused on direct interaction with younger souls. This Path mainly expresses spiritual wisdom since it's about teaching and guiding. One may teach or make a commitment or vow to serve others before Enlightenment, of course. There is great need for servers of all levels; however, the Master is able to serve on a much deeper level and in many unconceivable ways.

The earthly analogy of this Path is most similar to going on to graduate school after you graduate from college. It involves you still being connected with your school, except now you're taking on a larger role, and are a teacher yourself of younger souls. Just as a graduate student or professor still studies and grows while teaching, so does the Master still grow while doing Earth Service, even if it seems to us that they're just teaching. Just as faculty is involved with running the school, so is an Earth Service Master involved with the spiritual Hierarchy of our planet.

This Path is more commonly chosen in the earlier stages of a human lifewave, such as the present where a low percentage of people have reached the Master level. Later, when Masters become more numerous, there will be enough Spirits teaching already, so the other Paths will be emphasized more. The need for teachers early on is one example of where a Master may choose to switch Paths. The earliest souls to attain Enlightenment tend to choose Earth Service initially since the need is so great, and then they continue on their true Path later.

Nirmanakayas

A Nirmanakaya is an embodiment of spiritual compassion, an Enlightened being who forgoes the Nirvana they've earned. Instead, they choose to silently and lovingly watch over the world as a guardian. The word Nirmanakaya is Sanskrit for "created body." Such beings have no need for bodies, but they manifest them so they can still be in touch with the lower planes of Earth. A Nirmanakaya may manifest as low as the mental plane, but they rarely go below it, and they don't ever physically incarnate. This is similar to the Path of Earth Service since both sacrifice in order to benefit Earth from relatively lower planes, but Nirmanakayas play a subtler if just as important role. Think of the Nirmanakayas as forming a ring around the world, meditatively protecting and sending loving energy to it. There are no words that can ever hope to describe the beauty and exalted Love of a Nirmanakaya.

This Path is most similar to being a homemaker who stays at home to rear children as a loving and nurturing parent. Both roles require great patience and compassion, along with sacrifices of time and resources that one could spend elsewhere if they were so inclined. Fortunately for us on Earth, there are people who desire to be parents, and we're similarly blessed that some Enlightened Spirits are called to be Nirmanakayas.

Logos Training

The Path of Logos Training involves the Master training to be a Planetary Logos who will presumably eventually evolve into a Solar Logos or even a Galactic Logos in the distant future. For that reason, this may seem like the most ambitious of the Paths since one's sights are upon literally becoming a planet. They'll be a true Creator, able to breathe out new lifewaves. With such majesty and responsibility forthcoming, this Path can be seen as an expression of spiritual power. Power doesn't mean control in a negative sense. The Master evolved beyond misuse of power long ago, although it does mean authority and opportunity.

This Path is most similar to joining politics and running for or holding political office. Just as there are politicians on many levels, from a member of the city council to the president of a nation, so are there many levels of Logos. A Logos or one training for it is like the ideal politician, working to serve society as opposed to his/her own interests. A true king isn't the ultimate ruler but is rather the ultimate public servant. This Path is perhaps the most challenging since so much is necessary and so much is expected. The president may have influence, but he/she has also made a significant sacrifice since he/she no longer has the freedom to do many things the average person can. As a Logos can create new lifewaves, this Path also has an analogy to being a parent and giving birth, although the Nirmanakaya Path tends to better capture the nurturing aspect of parentage.

Evolutionary Builders

A Builder is one who helps create or coordinate the environment in which we evolve. For example, they may literally construct a planet or Globe in preparation for the human or other lifewaves that will evolve on it. At the end of each evolutionary Chain, Builders create the set of Globes to be used in the next Chain. Like most Masters, Builders never physically manifest. They commonly work with the Causal plane energies, setting causes into motion that eventually have physical effects. This Path is most similar to having a manufacturing or "blue collar" job. It may seem less spiritual at first, but really a Builder expresses spiritual creativity, and so is a minor Creator in their own right. This is the most creative and "hands on" of the Paths.

Just as construction often needs to remove the old before the new can be built, so do some Builders focus on the destruction side of creation. They help coordinate "Earth Changes" when they happen, ranging from earthquakes or other seeming disasters to the eventual dissolution of the entire planet in the far distant future when its purpose is fulfilled. Whether creating or destroying, it's all done in Love and service so the next phase of being may be brought forth.

Angelic Evolution

One Path open to the Master is to become an Angel or Deva and enter the Angelic kingdom. The human kingdom ends after Enlightenment, but the Angelic kingdom continues on to the doorstep of Divinity. Most Angels have never been human, but as this Path shows, some have been human in their evolutionary past. Other than this case, switching between kingdoms of nature is extremely rare. Angels that have evolved to this level serve on the mental plane and higher, although Angels in general can exist on or descend as low as the astral.

The types of things Angels do, the energies they work with, and the things they express just by virtue of being are too numerous to list. Since Angels tend to work with others or guide more abstract energies, the closest Earthly analogy to what they do is a "white collar" service job. One easily understood example is that of the Guardian Angel which all humans have watching over them.

Guardian Angels past the Master level tend to work on higher levels with groups of souls unless the individual in question is close to Enlightenment himself/herself.

The Staff Corps of the Logos

The Staff Corps of the Logos is a unique group of Spirits who serve our Planetary Logos, and eventually our Solar Logos, in whatever way is most needed. All the other Paths are relatively steady, focused on a particular aspect of Spirit. This Path has elements of all the others in it, and so is eternally dynamic and changing. For that reason, this can be considered one of the most challenging, and therefore the most respected Paths. The Staff expresses Service in its truest sense, since it's not about doing what you want to, but doing what's most beneficial to the whole. Some souls seem like eternal wanderers, never settling down. Their ultimate future may be as a member of the Staff. Preparing for this destiny can also be the reason for the challenging or unique evolutionary paths some spirits take on their way to Mastery, such as Individualizing through negative means, crossing over to humanity from the Fairy kingdom, or just an abnormally extended period of creating and resolving bad karma.

Among the many things a member of the Staff may do is be sent to incarnate as a Bodhisattva or World Teacher for a planet, which has a young lifewave on it, one too young for any of its members to have yet reached the Master level themselves. The spiritual offices or positions still need to be filled. Until a lifewave evolves enough to take care of itself, it gets guidance from others. Spirits on the Path of Earth Service focus on their own lifewave, but the Staff may assist completely different lifewaves. This Path is most similar to joining the military. The military, in its ideal non-violent sense, is a group of "few and proud" who serve all the other Paths and do odd jobs nobody else wants, deploying themselves where needed. Other Paths may act as the organs or bones in the body of a lifewave, but the Staff Corps of the Logos exists in the spaces in between, and deserves credit for being the cartilage and ligaments that hold it all together.

Nirvana

Last but certainly not least, an Enlightened Spirit may choose to enter Nirvana, the ultimate paradise. The word Nirvana is Sanskrit for "blow out," as in blowing out a candle. It means extinction or annihilation, and it literally is, at least to a Spirit's old way of life. Nirvana is the ultimate goal as described in both Buddhism and Hinduism. The Enlightened state of the Master is already eternally blissful, no matter what Path is taken afterward. Nirvana can only be described as "more blissful." The drop returns to the ocean where the Spirit stays on the Nirvanic plane, never descending below it.

Nirvana is rarely chosen by the earliest souls in a lifewave to reach Enlightenment because initially there's such a strong need for leaders and teachers, i.e. for Spirits to be on the Path of Earth Service. Much later, when there are many Enlightened Spirits serving in the various roles, and there are "enough cooks in the kitchen," so to speak, Nirvana becomes more common. As a lifewave is really one great being whose destiny is to do great things together as One, individual Spirits who reach the far shore early can wait for others to catch up. In the final phases of a lifewave, when almost all Spirits have become Enlightened, and most have continued evolving toward their ultimate destiny, Nirvana becomes rare again, as the laggard Spirits don't want to fall too far behind.

There's nothing wrong with choosing this Path, even if it seems lazy in comparison to the others. Spiritual growth isn't a rush or a race. Just as students have summer vacation between school years, so do seekers rest at many points on their eternal spiritual journey. They may not seem to grow while in Nirvana, but they do, just as some of the most educational experiences youths have are while taking time off doing things such as traveling. If you've reached Enlightenment, feel free to take a billion or at least a few million years off if that calls to you. You've earned it!

9:
Cycles of Evolution

"All rising to a great place is by a winding stair."
- Francis Bacon

In spiritual growth, we mostly focus on ourselves and in the here and now. However, there's also benefit to looking outside our individual selves at the wider environment in which we live and grow, and seeing the big picture of how that spiritual school changes over time.

Two important concepts will appear throughout this chapter. Involution is the process of separating and densifying while evolution is the return journey of unification and spiritualization. On many levels, something first becomes more dense and individual, then turns around and grows back toward Spirit. An analogy on a simple everyday level is the concept of going on a camping trip, getting dirty and enjoying "roughing it," and then returning home afterward, richer from the experience. Our entire lives are like this because we descend from our souls, incarnate in physical bodies, and then return to our souls after "death." Involution and evolution even applies to the Divine creating and experiencing the Universe itself.

The purpose of the process of involution and evolution is to allow Spirit to become more aware of itself. For example, sometimes we don't truly appreciate the convenience of our homes until we experience living in a tent and eating before a campfire. Camping is fun, yet also requires effort and a bit of courage and initiative to make the journey, just as physical life in general does. It's like going to the gym to exercise; the process can be uncomfortable and tiring, but it's worth it afterward.

Root-Races

Our planet Earth has a long, rich history and a vast, spiritual future. Many have heard about the ancient civilizations of Atlantis and Lemuria. Those civilizations were indeed real; we've experienced many different past civilizations and will build many in the future. Human evolution on our planet Earth is divided into seven great time periods called Root-Races. Each Root-Race has its own civilization and group of people.

A Root-Race is different from the popular definition of race. When most say "race," they really just mean ethnicity, which doesn't differ much beyond skin pigment. A Root-Race is an entire species; the difference between an earlier and later Root-Race is like the difference between Neanderthals and modern Homo sapiens. Both are of humanoid form, and have human souls inhabiting them, but one has certainly evolved more than the other. One however shouldn't go too far in saying later Root-Races are better than or superior to earlier ones, any more than they should say 12th grade students are better than 1st graders, just because they've been around longer. Although each Root-Race builds upon the experience of the previous ones, each also has its own focus. Neanderthals wouldn't be able to make a living in modern cities anymore than modern Homo sapiens would be able to survive long in the Stone Age.

The following table lists the Seven Root-Races we've had or will have on Earth. Each Root-Race has a primary focus that it's meant to express and develop. Root-Races three through seven roughly correspond to the first five Planes of the Universe: Activity is related to the physical plane, emotion to the astral plane, intellect the mental plane, love the Buddhic plane, and being the Atmic plane. Just as the first five Planes of the Universe are three dimensional through seven dimensional, so can the first two Root-Races be considered one and two-dimensional preparatory work. Root-Races overlap to a certain extent, and the rough timeframe covered by each is listed. Notice each Root-Race covers less time than the one before. Just as today's society seems to be speeding up, so do later Root-Races with their accelerated rate of vibration fit more into a given time period than earlier ones.

The Seven Root-Races of Earth				
#	Name	Focus	Plane	Timeframe Covered
1	Borean	Anchoring	-	200 million to 60 million years ago
2	Hyperborean	Building	-	100 million to 6 million years ago
3	Lemurian	Activity	Physical	10 million to 600,000 years ago
4	Atlantean	Emotion	Astral	1 million to 10,000 years ago
5	Kraunchan	Intellect	Mental	100,000 years ago to 10,000 years from now
6	Aquarian	Love	Buddhic	600 to 40,000 years from now
7	Pushkaran	Being	Atmic	30,000 to 60,000 years from now

#1. Borean: The first Root-Race on Earth was called the Borean. They existed on a continent called Borea, which was located near the North Pole. They weren't entirely physical, existing on the higher etheric subplanes of the physical plane, and so are also sometimes called the Etheric Root-Race. Therefore, they weren't even remotely like the humanity of today; there was never any visible manifestation of their presence. As the first Root-Race, its focus was on anchoring human life on the planet in the first place.

#2. Hyperborean: The second Root-Race was called the Hyperborean. They existed on a continent called Hyperborea, which was located in what is now northern Asia. The prefix "hyper" means beyond; the Hyperborean civilization basically built upon on the work started by the Borean. This Root-Race was the first that was fully physical, meaning we could see and interact with them if we traveled back to that time period. Their "bodies" however were amoeba-like blobs, very unlike human bodies today. All traces of this Root-Race and its landmasses have long since vanished from Earth.

#3. Lemurian: The third Root-Race was the called the Lemurian. Their continent of Lemuria (sometimes called Mu) existed in what today is the Pacific Ocean, until it was broken up by great earthquakes and volcanic activity. Some say today's Rapa Nui (Easter Island) is a remnant of it, since it's in the right location, and its unique large *moai* statues have Lemurian features. The Lemurian bodies developed modern bone structure, so were the first to have a humanoid appearance. Their bodies were much larger and stronger than human bodies today; they were on the order of 12 feet tall. The Lemurian Root-Race started as hermaphrodites. By the end of the Root-Race, male and female genders had separated from each other.

The Lemurian civilization was characterized by activity, and developing and enjoying the physical form. Humanity was fully present physically; however, the emotions, intellect, and, most importantly, free will that we're familiar with today had yet to be fully developed. During the early part of Lemuria, spiritual entities such as Angels and non-human Masters were physically present and guided humanity. From this came the many legends of humanity being founded by gods, extraterrestrials, and so on. Lemurians worked in harmony with these entities, however, only out of instinct as opposed to their own virtue. This state was the mythical "Garden of Eden" referred to in Christianity. Lemuria developed individual free will, meaning humanity "fell from" or left the Garden of Eden, and the evolved entities withdrew from obvious involvement with Earth. This wasn't a bad event but was planned and a natural part of our evolution. From this point forward, each human had the freedom of choice to fully express both good and evil and work on his/her growth independently. A child can only learn so much living with his/her parents. Eventually he/she has to move out and follow his/her own path, even if it means making mistakes.

#**4. Atlantean:** The fourth or middle Root-Race was called the Atlantean. It existed from roughly a million to 10,000 years ago. The continent of Atlantis was actually a few different large landmasses in or around what today is the Atlantic Ocean, which broke up over a period of time. The final island of Atlantis sank beneath the sea in a sudden disaster around 10,000 years ago, causing a large flood around the world. This historical Great Flood is referenced in the writings of many religions and cultures. Atlanteans generally looked human, different but not to an extreme from humanity of today, with the most obvious difference that some Atlantean ethnicities had blue skin color. Since the blue skin was present during the more developed periods of Atlantis, this may be part of the origin of some Hindu deities and Masters being depicted with blue skin today.

This civilization both developed and was characterized by emotion, meaning it expressed both positive and negative emotional extremes. Hence certain periods during Atlantis were very peaceful and spiritual, while others were filled with strife and warfare on both physical and occult levels. When warfare happened, it was on a level and intensity far beyond anything known in today's history. If humanity ever seems selfish or violent, take comfort in knowing the things people do today don't even come close to some of the wild things that went on during Atlantis! Much of our fantasy literature and role-playing games such as "Dungeons and Dragons"®, with their magic and fighting various monsters, are inspired by actual history on a subconscious level. Atlanteans had use of psychic energy that we have yet to rediscover on a mass scale. Their civilization had airships, but they were more like balloons that hovered and propelled themselves through psychic energy, as opposed to the motorized flying machines we have today. Atlanteans could think, and in many respects were like ourselves, but they didn't have the intellectual development we have today. For example, they never developed mathematics to any degree. Things as simple as multiplication were considered a form of magic and done by memorization or with tables as opposed to understanding the abstract formulas behind them.

#5. Kraunchan: Humanity of today is a part of the fifth Root-Race. It began roughly 100,000 years ago, and is still active and in development. Asia can be considered the main Kraunchan continent since that was the Root-Race's birthplace and is the largest landmass on Earth today. The Root-Race has, of course, since expanded to cover all continents. The term Kraunchan comes from "Krauncha," the Sanskrit name of the fifth Root-Race landmasses.

The fifth Root-Race is traditionally called the Aryan race. The name "Aryan" here has nothing to do with the Caucasian ethnicity although, unfortunately, due to misuse that word sometimes gets associated with ethnic biases. The term Aryan actually refers to the ancient Indo-Europeans who were the parents of all peoples from India to Europe, which is different from the "Aryan" Root-Race as described here which covers basically all of today's humanity and all ethnicities. The word Aryan itself comes from the Sanskrit word "Arya" meaning honorable or noble. It's likely the country name "Iran" has the same roots. Kraunchan is a more accurate term for the fifth Root-Race, and it's also more consistent since all the other Root-Races are named after their landmasses.

Our Kraunchan civilization is characterized mostly by intellect. To avoid repeating the problems of Atlantis, it values the concepts of ethics, law, trust, self-improvement, and giving and keeping one's word. Although not directly spiritual, these moral concepts do lay a good foundation for those who want to embark upon the spiritual Path. The fifth Root-Race has put less of an emphasis on psychic development and has focused on technological development, and experiencing both the positive and negative potentials of the mind and technology. On the whole, the world today is more orderly and, therefore, more peaceful than Atlantis; however, there are also new risks. The freedom of emotional potential developed in Atlantis is combined with modern technology. On the occasion when Kraunchans let negativity or hate control them, the potential for destruction is greater. Atlantis was destroyed by outside forces, but we have the potential to destroy ourselves. Fortunately, nothing that bad is in our destiny, but we still have to finish learning the lesson of our harmonious and disharmonious potentials and how to use that potential properly.

#6. Aquarian: Following our civilization will come the sixth Root-Race, which will develop and be primarily characterized by love and wisdom. It won't begin to appear for another 600 years or so. This Root-Race doesn't have a name yet, but a logical name for it is the Aquarian Root-Race since it will be born during the "Age of Aquarius," the soon to come extended period of world peace and harmony. Just as the intellectual Kraunchans still have many Atlantean emotions, so will humanity of the unified Aquarian Root-Race not only be loving and wise, but will also integrate most of the positive characteristics of previous Root-Races. They'll be intelligent, taking benefit of the technology the fifth Root-Race developed, but not letting technology disconnect them from grounded living. They'll be emotionally expressive, but without letting passions control them. They'll be physically strong and beautiful at least by natural standards since they know to take care of themselves on all levels.

The main Aquarian continent will be located in what's now the Pacific Ocean, roughly the same location as ancient Lemuria. By the time the continent of "Aquaria" raises itself from the ocean, North America as we know it will be gone. That means spiritual predictions that say California will fall into the sea are wrong, since actually the reverse is true: California will remain, but most of the rest of North America is eventually going to sink beneath the ocean! Before rushing to buy real estate in California, know that North America is completely safe for at least another thousand years, and probably for another five thousand. By that time the technologically-oriented Krauchans will mostly be living in space, or at least have a standard of living so high they can fully detect and prepare for Earth's movements, and migrate to new safer locations without putting strain on the population.

#7. Pushkaran: The seventh and final Root-Race on our planet will manifest deeper and more abstract levels of being. It's usually referred to as the Pushkaran Root-Race. "Pushkara" is Sanskrit for "blue lotus" and "seventh realm." One could also call it the Atmic Root-Race because the mastery of existence it will express is similar to the energies of the Atmic plane. By this time human bodies will start to become less physical, and like the first Root-Race will be more on the etheric than the dense subplanes of the physical plane. Etheric bodies will fundamentally change the way we live, such as reproduction will be done more through an act of will instead of just the body, and we'll likely no longer have separate genders. Lovemaking will still exist and will be exquisite beyond our current imagining; however it will no longer be tied to reproduction.

The seven Root-Races fit into the involution followed by evolution model. The first three Root-Races were the involution side. Borea marked the beginning of our journey on Earth where we began as etheric beings. During Hyperborea and Lemuria, we became more involved with Earth and physical life. The last three Root-Races are the evolution side. In the Kraunchan and Aquarian civilizations, we will evolve toward Spirit, finishing with the Pushkaran civilization where we'll be more etheric again—just like we started. The fourth Root-Race of Atlantis was the middle turning point with the strongest amount of physicality, individuality, and separateness. Atlantis was unique in this respect. It was here that involution and evolution, Spirit and matter, good and evil, and all other dualities struggled for dominance with no side being stronger.

Each Root-Race is divided into seven subraces. Each subrace is somewhat similar to the Root-Race of the same number with the fourth subrace of any Root-Race being more emotional and artistic, the fifth being more mental and technological, the sixth being more spiritual and sensitive, and so on. The different subraces exist simultaneously but first appear in order. The newest subrace of our fifth Root-Race is the sixth, which only started appearing a century or so ago. There are subtle physical characteristics that can indicate one's subrace; however, there are many mixtures. Subraces (and Root-Races for that matter) are more fundamentally defined by one's inner qualities as opposed to their outer appearance. People of the sixth subrace are sensitive and graceful souls with heightened intuition and spiritual inclinations, who often want to bring forth a "New Age." Children belonging to the sixth subrace are sometimes called "Indigo Children," where indigo is the sixth color of the rainbow. Each subrace can, in turn, be divided into seven branch races or "nations," but there isn't as strong of a distinction there.

The nature of intellect, as characterized by the fifth Root-Race and its fifth subrace, is to classify and compare. Seeking the best in things can result in disliking that which is perceived as inferior. That explains aspects of our Root-Race's history, such as caste systems, racial divisions, and so on. The start of the sixth subrace, with its focus on love and unity, is part of the increasing movement to appreciate diversity and respect all ethnicities and cultures. Things will continually improve in this area over the next 600 years through the development of the sixth subrace, until the sixth Root-Race itself begins, at which point we can finally say we have a paradise on Earth, with no war, poverty, and related problems. However, note that even in what will feel like a utopia, growth and learning will still be taking place and continually deeper levels of love and wisdom will be explored and expressed.

Each subrace usually has a spiritual Master physically incarnate among it, who guides it and helps establish its philosophy. That Master's teachings and influence tends to get adopted by the subrace and surrounding culture, and turned into a long-standing religion. There are of course other Masters that physically incarnate beyond those that guide subraces. Each Root-Race in turn has a greater Master called a Manu, who among other important purposes, incarnates to help set the physical form of that Root-Race. Most of these Masters and Manus are known in our history. Often a subrace Master is the Manu itself, just incarnating in a different body and expressing a different purpose. As a result, a number of different religious figures around the world were actually incarnations of the same overriding Spirit. That makes conflict between religions all the more illogical; sometimes groups who argue that "my Prophet is superior to your Prophet" are unknowingly referring to the same Master, just incarnated in a different time and culture!

Globes

What happened before the first Root-Race, and what will happen after the seventh? Outside the time period covered by the seven Root-Races on Earth, our lifewave of humanity was or will be on different planets! The term Globe means one of these planets that we evolve on. The period that we spend on any Globe is called a World-Period or Globe-Period. Each World-Period contains its own seven Root-Races. Earth is one Globe among several on which we evolve in sequence. We pass through seven different Globes in our solar system, which are called Globe A through Globe G in the order that we visit them.

Not all of these planets are physical like the Earth. The endpoint Globes A and G are on the lower mental plane while Globes B and F are on the astral plane. Globes C and E are physical, but the life on them is etheric while only the middle Globe D is fully physical. The presence of Globes B and F means that on the astral plane, two more planets will be apparent in our solar system while on the mental plane, two more will appear. Life on such planets is very different than life on Earth. The biggest difference is, of course, there's no physical incarnation since the planets aren't physical.

The following diagram shows the seven Globes, their names, and the planes on which they exist.

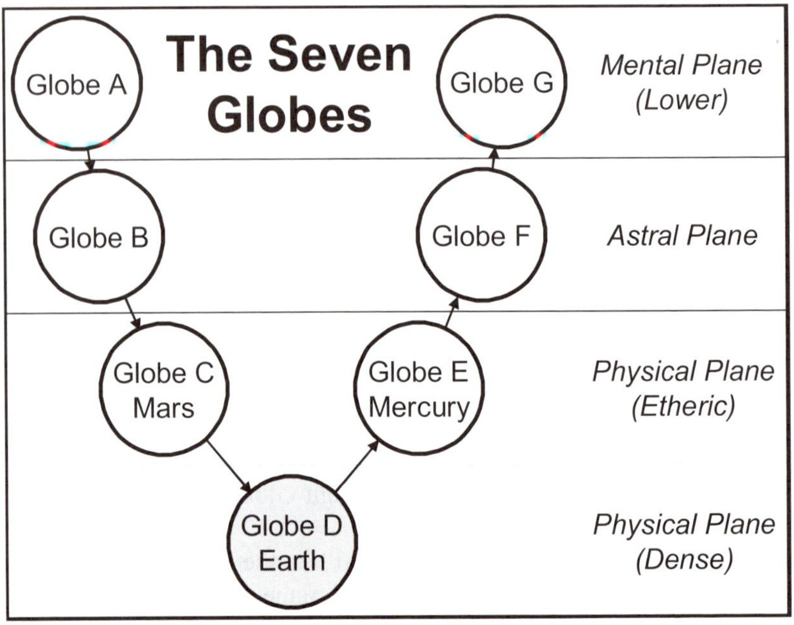

Our Earth is the fourth Globe, which is Globe D. Globe C is the planet in our solar system we call Mars while Globe E is Mercury. That means many of us had incarnations on Mars in the distant past and will be living on Mercury after our lifewave leaves the Earth after its seventh Root-Race! That also means technically there is life on Mars, but like fairies on Earth, it's not readily detectable.

The seven Globes form a group; these groups of seven can be seen in so many aspects of spirituality. Within these ubiquitous groups of seven, the third generally deals with activity, as seen in Lemuria, the third Root-Race; the fourth deals with emotion as in Atlantis the fourth Root-Race; and the fifth deals with intellect as with our present Root-Race. The same concept can be applied to our Globes, meaning Globe C, Mars, is focused upon activity, and Globe E, Mercury, is focused upon intellect. This is very similar to the astrological meanings Mars and Mercury have. Since our Globe D, Earth, is focused upon feelings, that means the general focus of our evolution at this time is learning love (sixth subrace) in an intellectual civilization (fifth Root-Race) on an emotional world (fourth Globe).

Just as each Root-Race has a Manu who coordinates its activities, so does each World-Period have a greater or more evolved Manu who administrates the entire sojourn on the planet, called the Lord of the World. A simplified analogy of the arrangement is each World-Period Manu is like a manager in a company; the Root-Race Manus are like employees who work for them. The current Lord of the World on Earth is named Sanat Kumara, which is Sanskrit for "eternal youth" or "eternal virgin."

The span of time covered by a World-Period, i.e. the amount of time spent on each Globe, can vary. Presumably earlier World-Periods take longer than later World-Periods, just as earlier Root-Races take longer than later Root-Races. Based on the length of the Root-Races that compose it, our current World-Period on Earth covers roughly 200 million years. Assuming that's average, the length of time to traverse all seven Globes is roughly 1.4 billion years.

Rounds

Continuing to expand our view of our evolutionary environment, the next questions to ask are what happened before the first Globe, and what will happen after the seventh? We don't just visit each planet once, but seven times total. Each traversal of the seven Globes is called a Round. There are seven Rounds total. We are presently in the fourth Round. That means some of us, in the far distant past, were on Earth three times before in the three previous Rounds. As with the Root-Races and Globes, each Round has a main theme with, for example, the fourth Round developing emotion in a grand sense, the fifth developing intellect, and so on. This reinforces the emotional aspect of our evolution at this time, since we're on the fourth Globe in the fourth Round.

The following diagram shows our journey through the seven Rounds on the seven Globes. Upon each Globe, the seven Root-Races forming each World-Period can be seen as numbered boxes. Our current Root-Race, which is the fifth Root-Race on the fourth Globe in the fourth Round, is shaded.

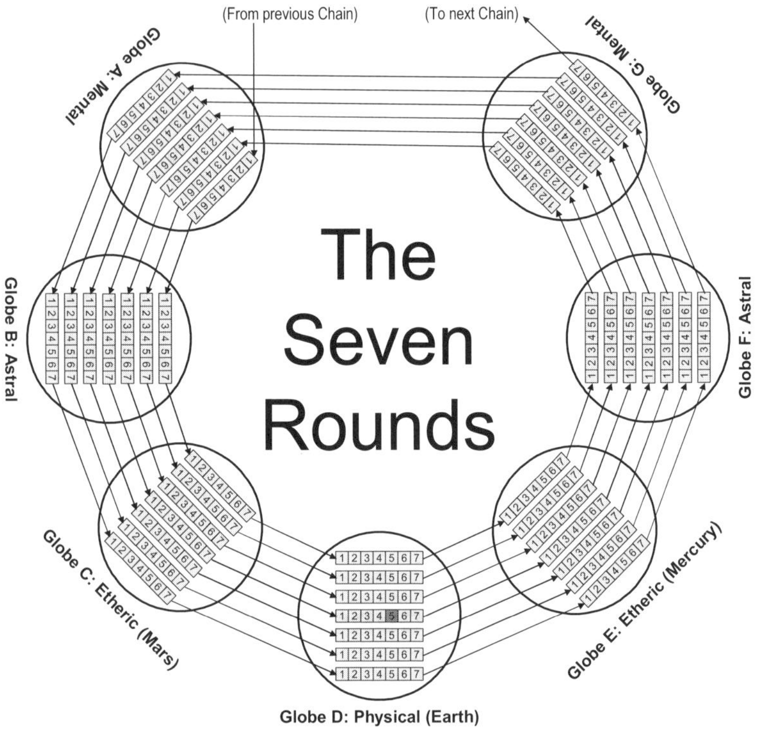

Each Round has a great Round Manu who administrates it. If the individual World-Period Manus are like managers, the Round Manu is the president of the company who directs each manager. The seven Globes can be considered the ingredients of a great recipe; a Round is the process of stirring them together. Our lifewave is like a spoon that moves around the bowl, touching each part of the mixture in turn. Even when the spoon is touching and transforming one part of the recipe, the other parts not being touched are still there, quietly waiting until the spoon comes around to them again.

Almost all of a lifewave exists on whichever Globe is active during a Round. However, the other six Globes aren't entirely empty during that period. A small percentage of souls from the human and other kingdoms of nature exist on the other Globes. This is similar to how the majority of activity on Earth is in those areas where it's daytime; however, that doesn't mean there isn't at least some activity going on all night. The souls on the non-active Globes act as caretakers, knowingly or unknowingly, keeping the Globe in order until the majority of the lifewave comes around again. Each World-Period evolves its own Root-Races; however, not necessarily from scratch. Remnants from previous Rounds can be used as a head start for what the latest Round wants to accomplish.

As the lifewave moves through each Globe, learning its lessons, inevitably there are souls who fall behind for one reason or another. This is similar to how a small percentage of students flunk a grade in school, so have to take that grade over again. Some of these lagging souls get left behind on whatever Globe while the bulk of the lifewave proceeds to the next Globe. The lagging soul then becomes part of the small group that stays on a non-active Globe. They remain there for six more World-Periods, which should definitely be enough time for them to learn whatever it was they were supposed to. They rejoin the main lifewave in the next Round when it comes around to that Globe again. The reverse occasionally happens too; sometimes a soul is progressing so rapidly, they're not learning much with the rest of their lifewave. They then do something similar to a "gifted" child skipping a grade in school; they jump to the next Globe prematurely before the bulk of the lifewave moves there. The fast learning soul rapidly learns the lessons of that Globe, then moves on to the non-active Globe after that, repeating the process until they catch up to the main lifewave again. When a soul either gets held back a Round or does an "extra credit" Round by evolving on the non-active Globes, this process is called taking the "Inner Round."

If one Round takes up roughly 1.4 billion years, then the length of time from the beginning of the Earth to where we are now in the middle of the fourth Round is roughly 1.4 x 4½ = 6.3 billion years. That's greater than mainstream science's current calculation of 4.5 billion years for the age of the world, but still close. Just as the first Root-Race on Earth was etheric where it took a Root-Race before life became fully physical, so was the entire first Round more etheric where it took a Round for the Earth to fully manifest itself physically. Subtracting that etheric Round from the age of the world makes the spiritual and scientifically calculated ages of Earth very close.

Chains

All seven Rounds together are called a Chain or a Chain-Period. A Chain technically refers to the set of seven Globes, upon which the seven Rounds take place. Note: even an entire Chain is still part of a larger picture. Chains evolve in a sequence of seven Chains, each with its own seven Globes and seven Rounds of evolution around them. The series of seven Chains follows the principle of involution followed by evolution. The Globes on the endpoint Chains are on higher planes, and the Globes in the middle Chains are on denser planes. Within each Chain, each of the Globes in turn is more etheric on the endpoints and denser in the middle. With Root-Races also involving then evolving themselves, this is a great example of the concept of cycles within cycles, or “wheels within wheels.”

More specifically, for the first and seventh endpoint Chains, Globes A and G are on the Atmic plane and composed of Atmic matter, Globes B and F are of Buddhic plane matter, Globes C and E are of higher mental or Causal matter, while Globe D is of lower mental matter. For the second and sixth Chains, everything drops a level, with Globes A and G on the Buddhic plane, Globes B and F on the Causal plane, Globes C and E on the lower mental plane, and Globe D on the astral plane. On the third and fifth Chains, the Globes have densified again, with A and G on the Causal, B and F on the lower mental, C and E on the astral, and Globe D on the etheric or higher physical plane. Finally, on the middle or fourth Chain, Globes A and G are lower mental, Globes B and F are astral, Globes C and E are etheric, and Globe D is dense physical.

We are presently in the fourth Chain. Note: of all 49 Globes in all seven Chains, only one features fully physical life, which is our planet Earth. That shows how rare and unique our current situation on Earth is. Even if physical life sometimes seems challenging or annoying, it shows how special it is to have the honor and opportunity to incarnate on the densest levels. For the less dense worlds, note the term "Globe" for planets on the high Buddhic and Atmic planes is somewhat a misnomer. On such spiritual levels, they are more concentrations of energy and consciousness. Since these “planets” are above even the Causal plane, life on them is fundamentally different from life on Earth. During such World-Periods, people not only don’t incarnate or project anything from their souls, which exist on the Causal plane, but they exist entirely on spiritual planes higher than the soul itself.

The following diagram shows our journey through the seven Chains; our Earth can be seen as the fourth Globe in the fourth Chain. This diagram shows all Chains at once where only the seven Globes from the active Chain exist at any one time, excluding a few retired remnants from a previous Chain like our Moon.

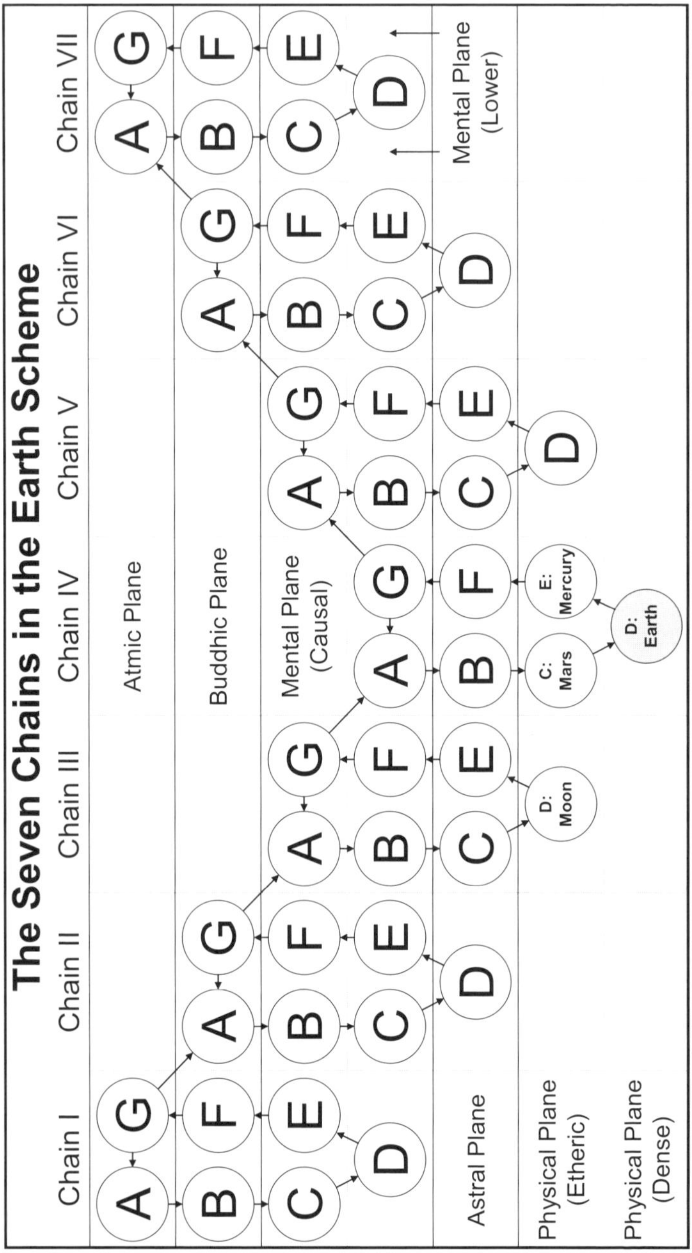
The Seven Chains in the Earth Scheme
Chain I
Chain II
Chain III
Chain IV
Chain V
Chain VI
Chain VII
Atmic Plane
Buddhic Plane
Mental Plane (Causal)
Mental Plane (Lower)
Astral Plane
Physical Plane (Etheric)
Physical Plane (Dense)
A
B
C
D
E
F
G
D: Moon
C: Mars
D: Earth
E: Mercury

After each Chain, the Globes or planets in it "die" by breaking up and gradually disintegrating, and a new set of seven Globes is created for the next Chain. Our solar system isn't static with regard to its planets, but rather the planets and the number visible on any plane change over billions of years as Chains leave and come into existence. Sometimes remnants of the Globes from a previous Chain can still be seen in the next Chain. Earth's Moon was the densest or Globe D of the third or previous Chain. In the long distant past, our Moon was much larger, predating the Earth and our other Globes, such as Mars and Mercury. Many of us evolved on the Moon during the Rounds of the "Moon Chain." But no more evolution happens on our Moon any more, and no more lifewaves visit it. Eventually it will fully disintegrate and disappear in a later Round of our Earth Chain.

The Moon is sometimes called the "Eighth Sphere," since it has a physical presence, yet is no longer an active Globe of any Chain. In one sense the Moon is a garbage dump for that which is physically and spiritually unfit for inclusion in our current evolution. Another perspective is that the Moon is our retired Mother, quietly resting with a rich history and many lessons and secrets. In a sense both points of view are true; together they lend to the feeling and mystery of our Moon. Astrologically, the Moon represents emotion and nurturing, which fits well given the Moon's history as the "mother" of Earth. The Moon was the fourth Globe in its Chain; the fourth Root-Race, Round, and so on are designed to develop emotion.

Just as each Round is coordinated by a Round Manu, so is each Chain coordinated by three different Chain Manus. The first Chain Manu begins the process by creating the Globes and receiving the lifewaves from the previous Chain, the second Chain Manu administrates the seven Rounds, while the third Chain Manu passes the lifewaves to the next Chain and dissolves the old Globes. These three aspects of creating, preserving, and destroying our worlds are similar to the trinity represented by the Hindu deities Brahma the Creator, Vishnu the Preserver, and Shiva the Destroyer. If a Round Manu is the president of a company, the Chain Manus are the mayors or elected officials who administrate the district the company is located within.

Schemes

An entire series of seven Chains is called a Scheme of evolution. The one we are in now is called the Earth or Terrene Scheme. There are other Schemes in our solar system, which the physical planets other than Earth, Mars, and Mercury, along with many non-physical planets, belong to. Our solar system is composed of ten Schemes total. Each of these Schemes goes through seven Chains, and is presently in a particular one of them with its seven Globes. Of the ten Schemes, only seven have any physical planets at this time. These seven physically present Schemes can be considered to form the seven chakras or the seven Rays of our solar system. The following is a brief description of the ten Schemes, listed in order from most evolved to least evolved. Schemes are usually named after the densest planet in their current Chain.

#1. Venus Scheme: This Scheme is in its fifth Chain; that is, it has one physical Globe with etheric life (Venus itself), two astral Globes, two lower mental Globes, and two Causal Globes. As the Venus Scheme is the only one in its fifth Chain, entities in it are the most highly evolved in the solar system. Venus is like a big sister to the Earth. Entities from Venus have helped our planet in the past, such as by providing spirits to incarnate here as Master teachers before we on Earth evolved enough to start producing our own Masters. The Venus Scheme is believed to be in its seventh or last Round, which means that Venus itself will soon ("soon" meaning in a billion years or so) disappear as the Venus Scheme moves into its sixth Chain with all non-physical planets.

#2. Earth Scheme: This is our Scheme, which is presently in its fourth Chain. It has three physical Globes (Mars, Earth, and Mercury), two astral Globes, and two lower mental Globes.

#3. Neptune Scheme: Like the Earth Scheme, this Scheme is in its fourth Chain like ours and has three physical Globes, two astral Globes, and two lower mental Globes. One of the physical Globes is definitely Neptune. Pluto is likely one of them, too, even though it has an eccentric and tilted orbit unlike all other physical Globes. Another is likely Eris, also known as 2003 UB313 or "Xena," a recently discovered body that's actually slightly larger and more massive than Pluto even though its orbit is even more eccentric. The second most highly evolved Schemes in the solar system are our own

Earth Scheme and the Neptune Scheme. Because Globe D in the Neptune Scheme is fully physical, it should have physical life instead of just etheric. This means that there should be visible extraterrestrial life on this planet with whom we can physically interact! Neptune itself is probably Globe D, since it's the largest, just as Earth is larger than Mars and Mercury. Neptune's gaseous atmosphere is most likely to be able to support some form of life, although such life wouldn't be remotely like our own. If it turns out there's no dense physical life on Neptune at this time, it's possible Neptune is in one of the earliest or latest Rounds or Root-Races, during which the life is more etheric, even on Globe D. Note: Pluto's moon Charon is not unlike Earth's Moon; both are relatively large in comparison to the planet they orbit. That means Pluto could also potentially be Globe D in the Neptune Scheme, and Charon could be the remnant of Globe D from its third Chain.

#4. Vulcan Scheme: This Scheme is in its third Chain. It has one physical Globe with etheric life, two astral Globes, two lower mental Globes, and two Causal Globes. If this Scheme is fully in its third Chain, it needs to have a physical planet somewhere; however, where is it? People used to believe in the presence of a planet inside Mercury's orbit, which they called Vulcan. Since there doesn't seem to be any readily visible object with physical gravity, another explanation is needed. It's possible that the Vulcan Scheme's Globe D is fully on the etheric subplanes of the physical plane, which could be due to it being in the first Round of the third Chain. Since Vulcan's astrological meaning is very similar to the Sun's, another theory is the physical Sun itself could be being used as Vulcan's Globe D. There's certainly a lot of room both on and within the Sun for evolution to take place—at least for etheric civilizations that wouldn't get incinerated by the Sun's heat!

#5-7. Jupiter, Saturn, and Uranus Schemes: All three of these Schemes are in their third Chain, Here they each have one physical Globe with etheric life (Jupiter, Saturn, or Uranus), two astral Globes, two lower mental Globes, and two Causal Globes. As these Schemes are one Chain behind Earth, perhaps we will eventually assist these Schemes in their evolution, just as Venus has assisted us?

#8-10. Asteroids, Kuiper, and Venus II Schemes: The final three Schemes are all in their earlier Chains, either the first or second, and, therefore, have no physical Globes. Scheme eight is usually called the Asteroids Scheme because when it enters its third Chain, its first physical planet will be where the asteroid belt between Mars and Jupiter is now. Some physical matter is already available there to be consolidated for it. Scheme nine can be called the Kuiper Scheme, since its first planet may appear in the Kuiper belt, an area beyond Neptune's orbit containing various small bodies not unlike the asteroid belt. As the Venus Scheme is in its last Chain with any physical Globes, after it transitions to a non-physical Chain, there will be room in its orbit for planets from younger Schemes to be created at in the future. Hence, for lack of any other name, Scheme ten can be called the "Venus II" Scheme.

Of the final three Schemes, it is likely that two are in their second Chain while the last is in its first Chain. That arrangement makes all ten of our solar system's Schemes symmetrically organized with one in its first Chain, two in their second Chains, four in their third Chains, two in their fourth Chains, and one in its fifth Chain. It seems fitting that the creation of Schemes is a process that, like human life, begins gradually, increases in intensity in the middle, and finishes just as gradually. Note, however, that because the different Schemes are in different Rounds in their current Chains, switching between Chains happens at different times for different Schemes, instead of everybody moving forward at once.

The following diagram shows the ten Schemes in our solar system, specifically the presently existing Chain of Globes within each Scheme.

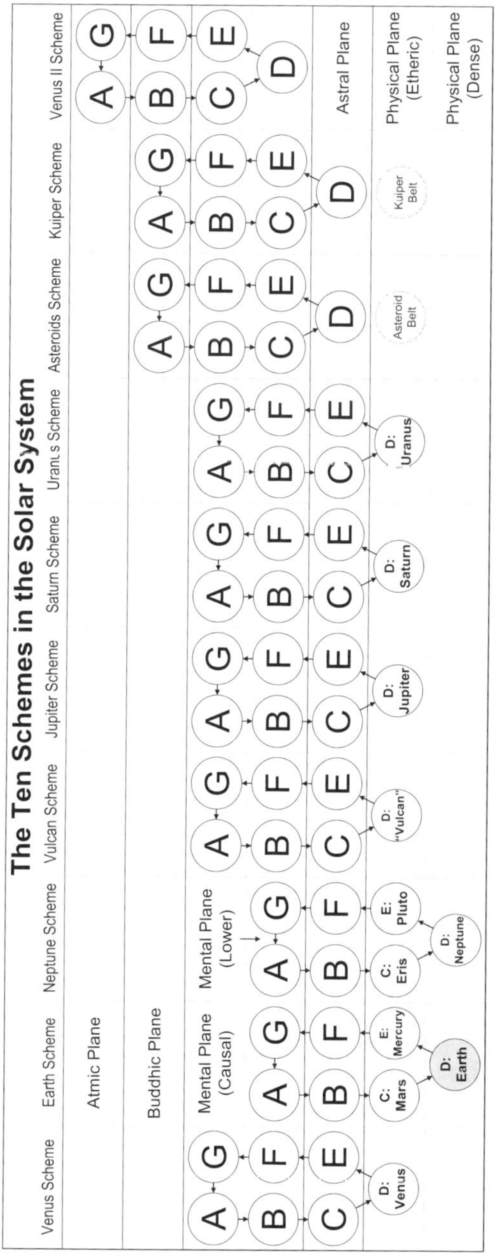
The Ten Schemes in the Solar System
Venus Scheme
Earth Scheme
Neptune Scheme
Vulcan Scheme
Jupiter Scheme
Saturn Scheme
Uranus Scheme
Asteroids Scheme
Kuiper Scheme
Venus II Scheme
Atmic Plane
Buddhic Plane
Mental Plane (Causal)
Mental Plane (Lower)
Astral Plane
Physical Plane (Etheric)
Physical Plane (Dense)
A
B
C
D
E
F
G
D: Venus
C: Mars
D: Earth
E: Mercury
C: Eris
D: Neptune
E: Pluto
D: "Vulcan"
D: Jupiter
D: Saturn
D: Uranus
Asteroid Belt
Kuiper Belt

Looking at all ten Schemes together and assuming that of Schemes eight, nine, and ten, two are indeed in their second Chains while the other is in its first Chain, we have the following totals for the number of planets in our solar system: On the physical plane are 11 planets, two with dense physical life and the other nine only supporting etheric life. Discounting the Earth, and counting the Sun and Moon, that gives us 12 physical bodies visible from Earth corresponding to the 12 signs of the zodiac. On the astral plane are 16 planets, or 27 when also counting the 11 physical planets with their astral counterparts. If one astral projects, that should more than double the number of planets visible in the sky! On the mental plane are 35 planets (19 on lower mental subplanes and 16 on Causal subplanes) or 62 total counting the lower plane counterparts, which again more than doubles the number of planets on all the lower planes. On the Buddhic plane are 6 planets (or 68 total counting lower plane counterparts), and on the Atmic plane are 2 planets. There is a grand total of 70 planets in our solar system, seven from each of the ten Chains currently manifest.

One can get a rough idea of the main focus of evolution happening in any Scheme, based on the astrological influence associated with its physical planets. For example, Neptune and the other physical planets in its Chain such as Pluto, have a general theme of aspects of consciousness in their evolution, and in our astrological influences assigned to them. Our own Earth Scheme, involving Earth, Mars, and Mercury, forms a general theme that can be summarized as doing, experience, or will. The Earth, Globe D of our Chain, is perceived from other planets as an influence of emotion or willful feeling, which is similar to the astrological meaning we have assigned our Moon, Globe D of our previous Chain.

Solar Systems

An entire Scheme of evolution is the activity of one great being called a Planetary Logos. All ten Schemes put together are part of a greater being called the Solar Logos, which is the Divine spirit of our solar system. Take note of the word "part," where the Solar Logos is so vast, that the ten planetary Schemes are just one of a number of different forms of evolution taking place in our solar system. A

Planetary Logos can be considered a child of the Solar Logos, a disciple of the Solar Logos, or an organ in its body.

Even solar systems form groups through which evolution proceeds in sequence. Our entire solar system was preceded by a previous solar system that finished its evolution and "died," where our solar system inherited much of its matter. That matter was brought to a certain level of evolution. Part of the current solar system's purpose is to evolve that matter to the next level. In billions of years, after our solar system has run its course, it will in turn be replaced with a third solar system. This is a macroscopic version of how Globes in one Chain get disintegrated and eventually form the Globes of the next Chain.

In summary, seven subraces make a Root-Race, seven Root-Races make a World-Period, seven World-Periods make a Round, seven Rounds make a Chain, seven Chains make a Scheme, and ten Schemes make a Solar System. The total count of each subelement forming each element is listed in the following table. Looking at all the levels, right now most of us are in the sixth subrace of the fifth Root-Race of the fourth Globe of the fourth Round of the fourth Chain of the second Scheme of the second solar system.

How Many in the Solar System?						
	Scheme	**Chain**	**Round**	**World**	**Race**	**Subrace**
Solar System	10	70	490	3430	24,010	168,070
Scheme		7	49	343	2401	16,807
Chain			7	49	343	2401
Round				7	49	343
World-Period					7	49
Root-Race						7

In turn, solar systems form ever larger groups, which have ever vaster Great Beings looking after them. Enough stars eventually form an arm of a spiral galaxy, which could be considered the spirit of a sign of the zodiac. All the arms or parts of a galaxy form a Galactic Logos, which is the spirit of an entire galaxy and can be considered to have stars as cells in its body. Groups of galaxies form galactic clusters, and groups of galactic clusters in turn form galactic superclusters. Eventually, we have a Divine Great Spirit acting as and coordinating the entire Universe, which one might choose to call "God."

Lifewave Progression

The length of time an evolving entity spends in any of the kingdoms of nature is about one Chain-Period. Since there are seven kingdoms of nature and seven Chains per Scheme, that means the entire length of one's evolution though all the kingdoms, from the Logos initially breathing forth their Monad to post-human Enlightenment, is about the period of one Scheme. Many of us who are human now were animals on the Moon, in our Scheme's third Chain where we individualized and graduated to the human kingdom in one of its later Rounds.

In other words, being human in the current fourth Chain means we were animals in the third Chain, plants in the second Chain, rocks or physical minerals in the first Chain, astral plane elements in the seventh Chain of some previous Scheme in the previous solar system, lower mental plane elements in the sixth Chain of that previous Scheme, and first entered evolution altogether as Causal plane elements at the start of the fifth Chain.

Although we were supposed to be physical minerals during the Earth Scheme's first Chain, and astral elements during some previous Scheme's seventh Chain, that wasn't entirely possible. The lowest Globe in any first or seventh Chain is on the mental plane, meaning there is no physical or astral matter available for such entities to directly involve in. One can only say the great Manus coordinating such evolution meditate upon the kingdom's advancement so it progresses in a similar manner. Therefore, many of us got what amounts to a free ride through the astral and physical elemental kingdoms. So, don't complain the next time you have a lot of work to do, since you effectively got to vacation for a few billion years during an earlier part of your evolution!

Entities progress at different rates, and there are earlier and later lifewaves, so graduation to the next kingdom can happen at various times. With multiple Rounds per Chain, one can roughly classify souls into categories based on which Round they individualized into the human kingdom. The advanced people we regard as Masters became human in an early Round. Most of us on a spiritual Path today entered the human kingdom one Round behind them. Non-spiritual but generally moral, intelligent, or cultured people began in the next Round after that, and so on. People we generally consider without virtue aren't "evil" but are rather just younger souls, who more recently entered the human kingdom and, therefore, haven't had time yet to evolve higher human qualities.

It takes an entire Chain to proceed through one kingdom of nature; however, one isn't active during the entire time period. An entity doesn't incarnate in every single Root-Race, World-Period, or Round. There are periods of rest where one enters an extended state of spiritual sleep, while waiting for conditions that will benefit their growth to present themselves again. As Root-Races and other cycles progress, the vibration of the environment rises, becoming appropriate for a higher class of soul. The active Globe is like a school classroom; the conditions on the planet during any time period are designed for a particular grade of student, and periodically the classroom switches to the next higher grade.

An advanced soul doesn't need to spend time in the earlier Rounds of a Chain, the earlier Root-Races of a World-Period, and so on because the earlier periods aren't evolved enough for useful growth. It would be like a high school student attending an elementary school class. The student wouldn't learn anything in such a simplistic environment, so they should wait until the classroom features a high school class, at which point they'll start showing up. Some souls who were human in the later Rounds of the Moon Chain have only just recently entered the Earth Chain, on this very Globe, even within the last century in our own Root-Race. Earth's past has featured struggling for survival, good vs. evil conflict, and so on that would have been too jarring for their sensitive natures. Besides, as old souls they've already "been there and done that." As time progresses and Earth's vibration continues to rise, ever more enlightened "boatloads" of souls will arrive and incarnate on Earth. Of course, there are also groups that incarnate earlier than their level in order to help out or serve in some fashion.

The reverse happens too where younger souls don't spend time in later periods. As the average evolutionary state in a Root-Race, World-Period, and so on becomes more advanced, there are points in time when less evolved souls drop out and stop incarnating. They eventually continue growing again in the earlier part of a future Root-Race, Round, etc. The classroom analogy is an elementary school student in a high school classroom. The higher level of learning and maturity is too much for the kid who needs to play, so they effectively get taken out of the classroom, to wait until an earlier grade is present again. A young soul in the presence of too high vibrations is likely to just have their lower passions inflamed, just as a young student in a too advanced class is likely to just get confused and turned off by learning in general. From the standpoint of the advanced souls, they need an "adults only" environment where there aren't criminals, wars, and so on causing chaos or distracting them.

Such points in time when all entities get spiritually evaluated for whether they can continue are given the dramatic sounding name "Judgment Days." A Judgment Day happens near the middle of each Root-Race, World-Period, Round, and Chain. Roughly one third of souls get temporarily held back after any Judgment Day, while two thirds continue evolving at the normal rate. The Inner Round where a soul stays on a Globe until the lifewave comes around again in the next Round, is one way this can be implemented. Judgment Days sometimes but not always are reflected on the physical plane as some sudden or not-so-sudden disaster, and so are the basis behind the "Earth Changes" one hears about that have happened in the past or might happen in the future. For example, the main sinking of Atlantis was the Judgment Day for Earth's fourth Root-Race, which of course caused many entities to leave physical incarnation at once. Some say the two World Wars or environmental changes, such as global warming, were or will be the Judgment Day for our current fifth Root-Race.

The greater order Judgment Day for our entire World-Period hasn't happened yet but likely will soon. That upcoming event is the main inspiration behind the predictions that Earth is about to change in some very special way that's never happened before or hasn't happened in a very long time, which we can be a part of if we take advantage of the opportunity. This situation is one of the reasons behind the high population on the planet at this time; numerous souls want to incarnate now, either to help out during this transition period or to try to quickly learn enough so they can stay on Earth. The school analogy is many souls are cramming for the final examination the night before. At the same time, the roller coaster ride of increasing vibrations on Earth is causing a number of souls to say what amounts to "Stop the world—I want to get off!" In other words, some souls are intentionally deciding to leave the planet.

Note: Judgment Days in general and "failing" them in particular shouldn't be considered a bad thing. If you get held back after one such event because you were slightly below the bar, that just means you'll be near the top of the class in the next group. Spiritual growth isn't a race. There's nothing wrong with getting off the train when the vibrations become too high and waiting on the station platform for the next train to come by, so to speak. The best place to be is not necessarily on the highest level but rather where we can learn the most. For those whose destiny is to be a leader, they may intentionally want to stay behind even if not required to do so, so they can guide or help out the next group.

Judgment Days again don't necessarily have an obvious physical manifestation like a disaster. In later periods, when the entities present are more evolved, they often happen quietly. The younger souls simply stop incarnating, and successive generations start seeming all the more spiritual. In the most spiritual periods, all souls are conscious co-creators of their evolution, and both older and younger souls choose the most appropriate times to start and stop incarnating. This is similar to how children are sent to school and have classes chosen for them while young adults choose their own classes and know enough to pick courses that are neither too basic nor too advanced.

10:
Our Extraterrestrial Cousins

"We're space aliens because Earth is in space!"
- Gary Murphy's three year old son

Just as we are not separate individuals but rather form One Being with the rest of our planet, the same is true with respect to our planet and solar system. Life on Earth isn't alone in the Universe, but rather there are numerous other civilizations on solar systems throughout the galaxy. Most exist only on spiritual levels, but a good many have a presence on the physical plane. We can see and interact with them while physically alive. In other words, extraterrestrials exist and sometimes visit Earth.

How do we know any extraterrestrial civilizations exist? Could we be alone in the Universe? Even without any direct evidence or experience of extraterrestrials, it's clear our situation isn't unique. Earth is just one planet around one average star on the edge of one galaxy. There are 100 billion to 500 billion stars in our own Milky Way galaxy, and at least 100 billion galaxies in the observable universe. Astronomers have already detected planets in other solar systems. The accuracy of those observations is increasing rapidly, so planets of Earth's size and orbit are sure to be detected soon.

Assuming that extraterrestrial civilizations exist, can they ever actually come to Earth? After all, contemporary physics says nothing can travel faster than the speed of light in a vacuum. Thus it should take many years for a spaceship to travel to the nearest star and much longer to arrive at our solar system. That, however, is a limited way of looking at the matter. We shouldn't assume it's impossible to go any faster, any more than a medieval knight should assume it's impossible to move faster than 50 miles per hour just because that's the fastest a horse can gallop. The same concept applies to how we should think of civilizations that are thousands or even millions of years ahead of us in technology. Extraterrestrial beamships truly travel through space, instead of just sliding across the surface of space. Think of this travel like going through a "wormhole" or the immediate speed of calling someone on the phone vs. the process of sending them a letter.

Another reason the existence of extraterrestrials is frequently doubted is the lack of widespread evidence. Since they haven't yet publicly revealed themselves to humanity, some claim that they don't exist. The word "publicly" is emphasized because many claim to have psychically communicated with, seen, or physically interacted with extraterrestrials. Direct personal experiences certainly prove their existence to those individuals but not to the rest of society. The naysayers frequently negate the stories of those who claim contact with extraterrestrials by stating that they're lying, hallucinating, and so on.

Some don't believe in extraterrestrials because the concept is simply too weird to consider, and, once accepted, it has many ramifications that may be just as disturbing. Existence of extraterrestrials challenges our current social order in many ways. For example, knowing that Earth is only one culture among millions upsets religions who believe that their view of God is the only one or the only path to truth. Acknowledgement requires some letting go of pride since we on Earth will go from being a big fish in a small pond to a tiny fish in an ocean. For example, we have world records for fastest runner, largest maze, and many other accomplishments that will become insignificant when compared to achievements done by the galactic community.

Extraterrestrials even challenge assumptions in this book. The previous chapter "Cycles of Evolution" presents an ordered system where planets are created as part of Chains, and physical forms are evolved under the direction of the beings working for the Planetary Logos. That's still true; however, it's not the only influence to consider. Presumably those extraterrestrials with whom we're able to interact physically are from Globe D of the fourth Chain in a Scheme in their own solar system since that's the only planet with physical life. If they're technologically and spiritually advanced enough to visit us, they're probably in the latter part of their fifth Root-Race (like Earth), or else they're in their sixth or even seventh Root-Races. That assumes other solar systems arrange their Schemes in the same manner that ours does, which is very likely but not necessarily true in all cases.

If Earth were the only planet with life, that would be just as mind boggling. Being alone in the Universe would imply certain traditional religious views are true, that humans were created by God, and that the rest of the Universe is just a big "waste of space." Unless one claims that extraterrestrials don't exist based on religious beliefs, one can't prove they don't exist. It's easier to prove the existence of extraterrestrials, since all you need is to just find one alien. Of course, not being able to produce an extraterrestrial doesn't mean they don't exist. It just means the evidence hasn't been presented yct.

Unfortunately, writing about extraterrestrials is difficult to do accurately. There's a huge amount of information available, and regrettably a large percentage of it is distorted. People often either make up events or misinterpret accurate data. Even if you're one of the lucky (or unlucky, depending on your preference) few who has had a direct experience with extraterrestrials, it's challenging to fit that experience into a larger picture. Nevertheless, there are some important general things that can be said. Extraterrestrials are an important part of understanding the Universe, so the subject shouldn't be avoided altogether. Over time our knowledge of them will continue to improve.

Extraterrestrial Philosophy

If alien civilizations are so advanced, why don't they come to Earth and stop wars, end poverty, and solve all our other problems? The reason is that doing so would ultimately cause more harm than good, since it would deprive our society and the souls within it of learning how to take care of problems on their own. Parents don't do their schoolchildren's homework for them because then they don't learn anything, and they would also develop an unhealthy dependence upon their parents. Modern anthropologists are careful when visiting indigenous peoples to have a minimal impact on their culture, and extraterrestrials have the same attitude toward us.

When we do prove ourselves worthy of interaction with extraterrestrials, it will have a major effect on our society. For example, on a mundane level, once we're able to exchange goods and technology, it will put many companies out of business when people buy from extraterrestrial sources that can produce better things for much cheaper. At the same time, it will be a great business opportunity when markets of a few billion people become potential markets of many trillions of creatures across the galaxy.

Accounts of humans meeting extraterrestrials often include us asking them how their beamships work, specifically how they're able to travel faster than light. They of course reply that they're not allowed to reveal such information. The most that's been determined is that the drive works though adjusting space-time. A beamship more or less just flies normally from one star system to another, but adjusts the passage of time so it appears to happen instantaneously from the reference frame of both those inside the spacecraft as well as outside observers in the respective star systems.

It takes more than just technology to travel through space. Each solar system has its own unique vibration. To travel to it, you have to be able to link up with that vibration. In turn, that requires the travelers to be able to control their own vibrations, which takes a certain level of organization and evolution. In other words, it takes spiritual consciousness to travel through physical space. You need to navigate through space, time, and vibration to reach another civilization.

Thus, one reason "evil" races can't invade or even interact with Earth is because we're on different levels of vibration. Just as nobody can harm you if it's not your karma, the same is true on a planetary level. If negatively-oriented races did somehow travel to Earth, they'd probably see an ancient past or distant future version of our planet, or find it uninhabited altogether. They may not even be able to detect our planet or solar system to begin with, and would see the whole area as empty space. The different civilizations on so many vibrational levels may be the cause of the invisible "dark matter" that seems to form so much of the mass of the Universe.

Although we've established that any extraterrestrial race that's successfully traveled to Earth is at least reasonably spiritually evolved, that doesn't mean one should worship aliens any more than one should put blind faith into any other teacher. One should still be their fullest selves, and not do anything they don't prefer or aren't ready for. If one meets an extraterrestrial (whether in an inner out-of-body state or in full physical consciousness) he, she, or it may ask you to do things such as help spread positive messages. There's probably benefit to either yourself or the planet in doing them, but you should still exercise your free will and only proceed if that path feels right.

Many extraterrestrial civilizations have humanoid bodies very similar to our own. Although each Planetary Logos is unique and forms its own lifewave, they do share with each other, just as human individuals share ideas or trade with each other. For example, the Planetary Logos or the Manus implementing a new race, when it comes time to evolve bodies for the human kingdom, will often borrow a template from another planet or get one at what amounts to a "galactic grocery store" instead of creating their own from scratch. Extraterrestrials may come from another planet and form colonies on Earth, and the bodies present start being inhabited by souls from our own lifewave instead of the alien lifewave. Extraterrestrials may at times intermarry with the bodies we currently have on Earth, to move the current DNA toward a more evolved ideal, or some existing set of DNA can just be used as something to evolve toward.

Earth is relatively unique among planets with humanoid lifeforms because we have wide ethnic diversity with people of many different skin pigments and cultures. Races on other planets tend to be more homogeneous in their looks and culture. One thing that happens when a planet develops a global society, which is starting to be seen on our own planet, is that culture inevitably starts blending, and through intermarrying ethnicities start to blend over time as well.

The most effective way for an extraterrestrial to visit and interact with Earth is not to fly here from their home planet in a beamship but rather to actually inhabit a human body. A walk-in occurs where a human soul willingly leaves a body and gets replaced by another soul. Walk-ins are usually other human souls from Earth's own lifewave or even just a more awakened aspect of one's own soul, but sometimes a walk-in is an extraterrestrial soul. Crawl-ins occur when an extraterrestrial soul is born in a human body. Walk-ins know that they're extraterrestrials in human bodies (even if they choose not to share it), but crawl-ins usually have to work to remember their true origins. A crawl-in is completely indistinguishable from a normal human since they have a human body, but the personality may be a bit "alien." Walk-ins are similarly indistinguishable although there's often a significant change in personality when the soul inhabiting a body changes. Those who don't know better may consider a walk-in to have some form of multiple personality disorder; however, only a small percentage of those with multiple personality disorder are actual walk-ins.

Both walk-ins and crawl-ins only happen through permission of both Earth's spiritual hierarchy and the extraterrestrial's own spiritual hierarchy. There's a long line of souls that want to incarnate on Earth at this time. For an alien to be able to "cut in line," they're probably here to help fulfill a mission in service to the planet or at least here to learn something important to help with their own growth. Extraterrestrials aren't allowed to openly visit or interfere with Earth, not even to fix our problems, but they are allowed to "help from the inside" so to speak.

A much more common scenario is for extraterrestrials to visit Earth on the astral or higher planes. If they want to interact with human individuals, they can contact our souls or visit us in the dream state. The main reason extraterrestrials visit Earth in the first place is to learn about us or to help teach, both of which can be done from higher planes much easier than on the physical. It's only when they actually need to do something on the physical plane, or if their civilization is physical enough that most of them aren't yet conscious on the higher planes, that they need to visit Earth in a physical beamship.

Space is the natural habitat of intelligent life. As a civilization develops technology, it tends to establish a presence in and eventually live in outer space. Civilizations may also emigrate to other planets and terraform them to conditions suitable for their civilization's lifeforms. Even if the initial evolution into physical life is very rare, all it takes is one civilization willing to expand to other planets before most star systems in the galaxy contain physical life. This is one reason extraterrestrial civilizations can exist in star systems that ordinarily seem too young to support Earthlike planets, such as the Pleiades.

Earth is our mother, but children don't live with their parents forever. A planet is like a nest for a lifewave; eventually, that lifewave grows up and is able to live without depending on it. The best way to save our environment is to not impact it in the first place. Some believe we'll gradually emigrate from the planet altogether, slowly returning land to indigenous cultures or those souls who feel a strong connection with the Earth. We can still return to visit, just as grown up children still visit and have a relationship with their parents. That won't happen for thousands of years, of course, but we can still set positive causes in motion today.

The galaxy is full of planets with physical life, much of which is humanoid in form. Some are more technologically and spiritually advanced while others are younger. Earth isn't unique in this respect, because we're extraterrestrials to the various other solar systems. Once we learn the external and internal techniques of space travel, we will visit other planets ourselves and be seen as the extraterrestrials we are. With the older civilizations, we'll interact as equals. For younger civilizations that aren't yet ready for open contact, we'll visit more secretly or on spiritual levels just as we're being visited today.

Extraterrestrials in Media

Extraterrestrials play a role in countless fictional stories. Most are grossly inaccurate with respect to reality. To create drama, the stories focus on conflict and often present the extraterrestrials as a negative invading influence. Nevertheless, a few fictional movies stand out among the rest for how accurately they depict aspects of extraterrestrials.

"2001: A Space Odyssey" (1968) and its sequel "2010: The Year We Make Contact" (1984) did a good job of showing how mind-bogglingly spectacular and *alien* other races can be. The mysterious black monoliths of various sizes captured the viewers' attention. These movies also demonstrated how some extraterrestrials spread life through the galaxy and assist younger societies in their evolution.

"Close Encounters of the Third Kind" (1977) is a classic that helped popularize many aspects of extraterrestrials. For example, the concept of close encounters of the first, second, and third kind represent respectively sightings, physical evidence, and actual contact. The movie is a good example of how extraterrestrials can communicate messages to people psychically or intuitively and even visit in controlled circumstances. It also shows how governments often want to hide such evidence, not out of maliciousness, but more from a standpoint of their own uncertainty and concern for society.

"Communion" (1989) is based on the true story of the Whitley Strieber contact case where he encountered a race of extraterrestrials called the Greys. Seeking answers for what happened and how to integrate it into his life, he underwent hypnosis and attended a support group with others who had similar experiences. This is probably the single most accurate movie about the "alien abduction" phenomenon. It also clearly presented how such experiences may seem frightening at first and/or be extremely weird.

"Contact" (1997) is the reverse of most movies whose plots feature extraterrestrials visiting Earth whether we want them to come or not. Instead this film has us leaving Earth to visit the extraterrestrials! The aliens sent our planet radio messages telling us how to build the great Machine that let us travel to them, but it was still up to our society to choose to visit them or ignore the message. This movie also helps demonstrate why extraterrestrials don't openly visit Earth yet. In the movie just certain knowledge that they existed on other planets caused great social upheaval on Earth.

"Star Trek," the science fiction television series, is notable because it presents a philosophy called the "Prime Directive" that states that the United Federation of Planets should not interfere with the natural development of less evolved societies. For example, one can't expose younger civilizations to advanced technology, the existence of extraterrestrials, or try to fix their problems. Younger civilizations can still be researched, as long as the Federation doesn't reveal its presence or otherwise interfere. When a society develops its own faster than light *warp* drive that allows them to explore other star systems, then the Federation lands and introduces itself. Star Trek's Federation with its many member civilizations and Prime Directive philosophy is surprisingly accurate with respect to the way things actually are in our galaxy.

Extraterrestrial Races

"Canst thou bind the sweet influences of Pleiades, or loose the bands of Orion?"
- Job 38:31

There are countless extraterrestrial races throughout the Universe. They exist on other planets, solar systems, galaxies, and dimensions. The following are the main civilizations that have a relationship with Earth.

Venus: Venusians come from the planet Venus in our own solar system but still count as extraterrestrials. Life on Venus currently exists on etheric levels, so they no longer visit Earth physically. Venusians usually interact with humanity on higher planes and sometimes act as walk-ins or crawl-ins.

As our big sisters in the solar system, the Venusians have played an important role in Earth's evolution. Currently, humanity is on the fourth Globe in the fourth Round, in the exact middle of the Chain (and the exact middle of the Earth Scheme since we're in the fourth Chain as well). At the middle point, there was a big switch from involution to evolution, as well as a big push in that direction from some of the most evolved entities in the solar system. This switch happened during Lemuria, one of the middle Root-Races. During Lemuria, there was a great event where a large number of Venusians came to Earth and even physically manifested themselves for a period of time. Their coming had the effect of accelerating the growth of many kingdoms of nature. For example, many animals entered the human kingdom, and many humans became more aware and intelligent. Earth's current fourth Round is meant to develop emotion, but we've already developed intellect a great deal as well. Growing intellect is meant to be the focus of the fifth Round, so in that sense we're an entire Round ahead of where we would be otherwise. Venusians are sometimes called "Lords of the Flame" or "Children of the Fire Mist" because their coming to earth appeared physically as large masses of fire, and their effect upon us was to quicken the fire within.

Sirius: Sirians come from the star system Sirius, the brightest star in the sky. They're a very advanced civilization similar to the Venusians. They're non-physical; however, they have a connection with the cetaceans or aquatic mammals, such as dolphins and whales. Just as Venus is a big sister to Earth, Sirius is like a big brother to our own Sun. One of the options before the Enlightened Master is to spiritually travel to Sirius and continue to learn and serve at a Lodge or Mystery School there. This situation is similar to your graduating from high school and then moving away from home and attending college so you can continue your studies.

Pleiades: Pleiadians come from the Pleiades star cluster. They look almost identical to Scandinavian or Nordic humans with their blond hair and blue eyes. They're considered to be 300 to 3000 years ahead of Earth in technological and spiritual development. The Pleiadians are probably the race that has the most involvement with Earth and physically visits us the most often. Their goal is to assist in our spiritual awakening. The Pleiadians say they are here to aid us until we learn to help ourselves. If the human race is like a teenager, the Pleiadian civilization is like a young adult in their 20's. Their more advanced technology and healthy practices allow them to live much longer. They would be considered physically attractive by today's Earth standards. Culturally, they tend to be playful and uninhibited with deep feelings while simultaneously approaching everything in a sacred manner.

Most Pleiadian beamships are saucer-shaped. The Billy Meier contact case where he learned from the Pleiadians over a period of time, mentions they have built a large, completely self-sufficient mothership whose main living section is a giant sphere 10½ miles in diameter. To give an idea of that size, a 10½ mile sphere is equivalent to a building with over 5500 stories. The middle stories would each cover 86 square miles. If the entire sphere were spread out, it would cover a square about 500 miles on each side or an area larger than the state of California. That's enough volume to give a billion people each their own 3000 square foot home with over half the sphere left over for parks and other community use. This shows that living in space doesn't have to be cramped or dangerous like Earth's extremely primitive spaceships of today. Instead it can be a very pleasant experience that a large percentage of the population participates in.

Vega: Vegans come from the star system Vega, one of the brightest stars in the northern hemisphere. They're about the same level of technology as the Pleiadians or even a bit more advanced. Since they've had fewer physical wars in their history, they have had less need to rebuild their civilization. Many of the challenges that Earth is facing now, other races have dealt with while growing up, too. Vegans also look very human and could pass as humans on Earth.

The Vegans encountered so far have very dark skin. However, note that as we learn about extraterrestrial civilizations, it's important not to make assumptions or stereotype, any more than we would about cultures or people in them closer to home. For example, we shouldn't assume all Vegans are dark-skinned just because all the ones seen and described so far look that way. It's very possible that's true; however, until we acquire more information it's possible there are orange or green-skinned Vegans running around as well.

Lyra: Lyrians come from a planet in the constellation Lyra. This planet was the first to evolve humanoid lifeforms and is the mother of the template from which many other planets have borrowed. The Pleiadians, Vegans, and other civilizations originally emigrated from Lyra. The Lyrians are a very old civilization with a rich history. At times their physical manifestation has been highly advanced. Other times, they've been quite primitive after wars or other disasters have set them back. Presently, they're about the same level of technology and spirituality as the Pleiadians and work with them closely. They look very human and have average skin tone, much darker than the Pleiadians but lighter than the Vegans.

The Lyrians, Vegans, Pleiadians, and almost every other race in our galaxy that exists physically and has both spiritual and technological understanding is part of a group called the Intergalactic Confederation. The Intergalactic Confederation is to the various solar systems as Earth's United Nations is to the various nations on our planet. Once a race evolves enough to be aware of other civilizations, they're allowed to join the organization. The Intergalactic Confederation tends to focus on physical races. Once a race evolves beyond the physical plane altogether, it becomes aware of higher groups and more spiritual ways of interacting with the rest of the galaxy.

Reptilians: The concept of "Reptilians" or "Reptoids" refers to any race whose physical form looks like an intelligent reptile. Just as humanoid bodies inhabit many star systems, there are various other bodily templates in use. Some are similar to reptiles, amphibians, insects, and other forms totally indescribable. Reptilians often get a "bad rap" in literature; they're considered an evil influence that wants to invade Earth or some other conspiracy theory. In actuality the Reptilians aren't better or worse than any other race and shouldn't be discriminated against or called derogatory names like "lizzies" any more than one should dislike a person of a different ethnicity. Reptilians make convenient targets for the xenophobic because they're different and ugly by our standards of beauty (as opposed to the playful Pleiadians with their supermodel bodies) and also because many people have an instinctive fearful reaction against reptiles such as snakes.

One thing that is true about Reptilians and other non-humanoid races is that they're very different from us. For example, it's easier to interact with Pleiadians or other human like races because their culture and even physical brain structure is similar to our own. Reptilians are like people from a vastly different culture where they approach and think about things in a very different manner than we're used to.

Orion: The Orion Empire from the constellation of Orion is an example of a race that at one time actually did express negativity on an interplanetary scale, which means they seemed to conquer or establish control over physical races on other solar systems. Usually a Planetary Logos evolves lifewaves relatively independently. It's only when they become spiritually advanced that they form connections with other solar systems. This is an example where such connections were formed earlier, when the planets were still growing and working out their karmas. The Orions never interacted with Earth, although they did battle with the Intergalactic Confederation a long time ago. Today the Orion civilization is about as spiritually advanced as Earth, rapidly evolving and releasing the last remnants of ineffective ways of being.

In addition to the Orion Empire, there were other civilizations in the constellation of Orion that are and always have been positively oriented. The "good versus evil" conflicts that took place there formed a powerful duality, one of the strongest ever seen. The vast drama that took place was an incredible growth experience for everyone involved, and allowed the souls directly involved, as well as external observers, to grow in many ways, especially in learning the nature of duality and our inherent connection with others. In other words, today Orion is increasingly serving the galaxy as a gateway from separateness to Oneness, for those civilizations that have yet to make the transition.

Andromeda: Adromedans are any beings (physical or non-physical) that come from the Andromeda galaxy. Andromeda is the largest galaxy in a group of a few dozen galaxies that form the Local Group, which includes our own Milky Way. Spiritually, these are beings from a different Galactic Logos, as opposed to merely a different Solar or Planetary Logos. The Andromeda galaxy, also called M31, has a spiral shape like our own galaxy, but is larger and acts like a big sister to us. Beings from the Andromeda galaxy are on average more evolved than beings from our own. Just as the Intergalactic Confederation is formed by a group of solar systems coming together, so is there a High Council in Andromeda that oversees connections between different galaxies in our Local Group.

DAL Universe: The DAL Universe refers to an alternate dimension or reality. It suggests there may be more places in the Multiverse for beings to exist other than positioning in time and space among the physical and non-physical planes of the Universe. The DAL Universe is like an antimatter Universe that's a reflection of our own. If it's formed of actual antimatter, then there are appropriate barriers to prevent the matter and antimatter dimensions from meeting and exploding! Presumably there's a way to flip your vibration to travel between the dimensions. At least one humanlike race exists in the DAL Universe, who is more evolved than all of the races described so far that aren't entirely on spiritual planes. The DAL's assist the Pleiadians with their spiritual growth similar to the way the Pleiadians assist us.

Interestingly, DAL Universe beamships land flat on the ground. This is in comparison to Pleiadian, Vegan, and Lyrian ships that always hover in the air or levitate over a beam of plasma or light. Related to this behavior, DAL Universe ships are entered by simply opening the top on a hinge, as opposed to Pleiadian, Vegan, and Lyrians ships that can teleport you inside or raise you up on a beam of light. When a civilization first explores space or develops technology in general, they tend to fully embrace it, but later after they evolve even more, they become more grounded and "return to their roots", especially when they're getting ready to transition away from the physical plane altogether. This process is similar to human life. At first we can't wait to live away from our parents, but later we form a more mature relationship with them.

Zeta Reticulans and Hybrids

The Zeta Reticulans are an extraterrestrial civilization interesting enough that they deserve their own section. They come from the star system Zeta Reticuli, and for that reason are often called just Reticulans (sometimes spelled Reticulians) or Zetas. However, the most common name for this civilization is the "Greys" because of how they look. Reticulans are humanoid but appear very different from Earth humans. A typical Reticulan is three to four feet tall, has whitish-gray skin and no hair, a large head with small facial features, and large black lidless eyes. Their eyes are very light sensitive, so they tend to only visit Earth at night. They are small and frail; however, they can move swiftly in motions that would appear jerky to us.

Just as there are different ethnicities of humans on Earth, so are there a few different types of Reticulans. Some have more brownish skin or other varying features, and not all reside in the Zeta Reticuli solar system. They are part of a Confederation of Planets known as the "Network." The Network relates to the larger Intergalactic Confederation in a manner similar to the way the European Union relates to the United Nations.

The Reticulans are a few hundred years ahead of Earth in technology and a bit behind the Pleiadians. Unlike many races that are so far ahead of us it's mind boggling, the Reticulans are close enough to Earth that it's not hard to visualize ourselves at their level in a few centuries. They're focused on technology to what most of us would consider an unhealthy extreme. They no longer have any obvious sexual organs and only reproduce themselves in the lab or through cloning. Reticulan beamships are rather Spartan and are usually triangular or cylinder shaped.

Reticulans are called Greys not only because of their appearance, but also due to their disposition. The Reticulans have a "hive" mentality and are completely devoted to the needs of their collective race. They work together extremely well and have little sense of ego or personal individuality. They are basically all the same and to us would seem boring or even dreary. There are virtually no disagreements among them of any kind since they all serve the collective needs. The Reticulans are very unemotional with concepts like smiling or laughing completely alien to them. Although the Reticulans are humanoid, they also have characteristics of a highly evolved insect race. This would account not only for their jerky movements but also their unemotional and hard working collective mentality.

The collective consciousness and Oneness of the Reticulans has many good assets, such as high productivity, psychic connection, and clarity of direction. There is always concern for the future and the environment, and there are rarely any conflicts because they all work for the group. Negatively, they can be seen as detached "sheep" that allow themselves to be dominated by their society. On Earth, our individuality also has many good assets, such as accelerated soul growth, here and now aliveness, and a uniqueness that makes each person special. Negatively, we are seen as overemotional people who are dominated by passions, care only for today, and only do what enhances our separate egos.

It is interesting to compare ourselves to the Reticulans since we are very different from each other. Humans represent the individual, while Reticulans represent society. We are emotional, while they are detached. Our emphasis has been on personal growth, while theirs has been on unified growth. In other words, Reticulans and humans are exact opposites of each other; together we form a duality. This duality is the ultimate reason we and the Reticulans are interacting with each other. Like attracts like, but opposites attract, too, because they're different sides of the same coin.

Unfortunately, the Reticulans are a dying race because their collectiveness is to such a degree that they have stifled individual life; hence, the *cells* that make up their race are becoming ill. We of Earth, at least in our recent past, were also an unhealthy race due to selfishness and greed of all kinds combined with more and deadlier weapons without respect for others or our environment. We were both headed toward extinction (or at least a massive planetary cataclysm along the lines of Atlantis in our case) where the only thing that could save us was each other!

The Reticulans have been visiting Earth for one primary purpose: To create a new race of beings. Entities of this new race are called Hybrids because they are a cross between Reticulans and humans in both looks and in behavior. The Hybrid race is populating a planet called Essassani, which means "place of living light." Essassani is an etheric planet, meaning it can't be seen from Earth. Hybrids are being created to provide a future for the Reticulans and to also help our planet move into Oneness. The Hybrid civilization represents the best of both worlds: individual freedom and uniqueness combined with a strong inclination to work together harmoniously. As the "children" of humans and Reticulans, they have discipline and technology combined with love and enthusiasm. In a Hybrid body, spiritual growth is easier due to the increased emphasis on the One, more natural psychic faculties, and a more loving etheric environment. Perhaps some human and Reticulan souls will actually be in Hybrid bodies in future incarnations. Perhaps Hybrid bodies or bodies like them will be used in future Root-Races on Earth, or on future Globes in our current Chain.

Along with the Pleiadians, the Reticulans are the civilization that has the most involvement with Earth, and visits our planet most often. Most extraterrestrial races merely observe Earth and follow a non-interference policy, or at least limit their activities to spiritual planes. The Reticulans, however, are basically the only race that is actively involved in physical projects on our planet, meaning they're allowed to interfere and affect the lives of people on Earth to a greater extent than other races.

The Reticulans are behind most of the extraterrestrial "abductions" taking place, during which people are seemingly detained against their will, and subjected to various examinations and procedures. Afterward they sometimes end up having marks on or implants in their bodies. One thing that goes into the creation of Hybrid bodies is the merging of human and Reticulan DNA. A common task done by the Reticulans during detainments is sampling of a human male's sperm which then gets united with a Reticulan egg, or else the sampling of a human female's egg which is united with Reticulan sperm. This combining is usually done in a laboratory; however, technology can only do so much. Sometimes a more spiritual or natural approach is needed. In other words, sometimes a human female actually gets impregnated with alien sperm. The fetus is then "stolen" from the uterus in a later detainment. This is why extraterrestrial examinations often seem to be of a sexual nature. Of course, the process has lots of complexity where the Reticulans need to be attuned to the growth of the human detainees over time since they can't just fly in and randomly beam up someone off the street. This can explain the purpose of implants as well as contacts throughout life all the way back to childhood.

People detained are usually made to remember nothing of the experience, except for perhaps noticing missing time, strange scars, or other symptoms. Most detainees never know what they're involved in, but some are able to eventually recall their experience through hypnosis or other methods. Much of what is experienced is understandably difficult to process and has lasting effects. Love and patience is essential in helping to recover and integrate. Why are people seemingly abducted without consent, and why are they not consciously asked for permission beforehand? It is important to remember that all "abductions" are based on agreement. In other words, anyone detained by extraterrestrials has agreed on a soul level, probably before their present incarnation, to make it their mission to help Earth in its work with the extraterrestrials. Most of the people being detained are advanced souls, even if they aren't consciously aware of it, and are close to overcoming the last of their fears. Detainees deserve deep thanks for the sacrifices they're making in service to both races.

The Reticulans are ahead of us in technology due to their ability to work together and because they never repress technology or have wars with each other that would require them to redevelop it. However, their society is in more of a crisis than ours on Earth, which means they need the Hybrids more than we do. Due to these reasons, the Reticulans are detaining us and are primarily responsible for creating the Hybrid race, and not the other way around.

The Reticulans are also believed to be behind many of the so-called "cattle mutilations." This is where a cow or related farm animal is found killed in a precise manner with various organs removed or blood drained and with evidence of surgical cuts not unlike those seen in some detainments. Human and Reticulan DNA aren't the only things going into the Hybrids. A few other creatures, such as Earth cattle have also been used or researched. Why are the cattle killed and just left lying there? Reticulans are so detached and down to business that they're probably wholly devoted to their task at hand, meaning cleaning up is irrelevant to their mission. Precise cuts and hard to duplicate biological modifications can also be done to help promote speculation among us about the presence of extraterrestrials, as a way of gradual introduction. Before judging the Reticulans as negative, it should be noted that they are far more humane and serve a higher purpose than the ways people butcher cattle for meat.

Based on things the Reticulans are doing, some fear them to be an evil race with malicious schemes and intentions. Fortunately, that's not true. The Reticulans are not here to harm us in any way whatsoever, and are rather here to help us as friends (at least as much as an unemotional race can express friendship) in our growth taking place during these important times in Earth's evolution.

Many of the suspected conspiracies concerning the Reticulans focus on their involvement with Earth governments. Starting in the 1940's, the United States and other governments have received definite evidence of extraterrestrials, either through direct meetings with the Reticulans and other races, or occasionally when one of their beamships crashes on Earth and dead or still living extraterrestrials are recovered at the site. The Reticulans have secretly met with various Earth governments. Again the rationale is for a higher purpose, and most of the stories one hears about such meetings are distorted or highly exaggerated. The crashes were truly accidents, although again on a high level they served a purpose. Those Reticulans did agree in some form (even if they were consciously unaware of what was going to happen, like how human detainees usually are) to give their lives to show our governments the first evidence that we aren't alone.

Although the Reticulans formally showed themselves to governments, they along with the Pleiadians and other extraterrestrial races are waiting for our governments on their own to admit to the extraterrestrial presence. Like it or not, our governments (elected or not) are representative of the collective consciousness of the people. When enough of the population believes extraterrestrials exist, that will cause the governments to release the information, since it will cause no social problems with most knowing the facts already. Even though our governments can certainly use improvement in many areas, we have to remember that we are a part of them. Through our actions and inactions, we allowed what we currently have to be manifested. The extraterrestrials know and respect that.

Hence, it's desired to have a gradual introduction of extraterrestrials into our society, or ultimately have Earth's integration with the galactic community come about through our own deduction and acceptance, rather than having it forced upon us by some public landing. This is part of the purpose behind many of the sightings, visitations, and detainments, as well as most of the crop circles: to get us thinking and questioning.

Any maliciousness on the part of the Reticulans is illogical. If they wanted to conquer or establish control, they could have done so much more easily a few centuries ago when they first started observing our planet. (Actually that isn't true either, since the Intergalactic Confederation prohibits and prevents any such imperialism that isn't part of the karmic evolution of the civilizations in question.) What the Reticulans are doing is too precise and calculated to simply be harassment. If they wanted to cause fear or take over, there are much more effective methods then doing detainments in the present manner or taking an occasional sample from cattle.

It is important to realize that the Reticulans are as afraid of us as we are of them! On an inner level, some of our fear in connection with the Reticulans is the fact that they are here to help bring unity and Oneness to us, and we are concerned that we might lose our individuality and personal power. The Reticulans represent the collective mind, and that frightens many of us. We, however, represent the individual mind, and that greatly scares them (at least to the extent that an unemotional race can be afraid). The Reticulans having to meet with individual humans and with relatively self-centered governments is a good way for the Reticulans to be put in touch with and overcome their own denial of individuality. Remember the Reticulans are not any better than we are, and we should not give up our individual freedom nor do anything other than what we choose or agree to do. After all, that very quality is the asset we are contributing in our interaction. Nobody is coming to enslave us, and nobody is coming to save us either. Rather we are co-creating with various civilizations to the benefit of all parties.

Examples from science fiction can help us understand the Reticulans better. The Reticulans behave a lot like the emotionless characters Spock or Data from Star Trek. The Star Trek race that comes closest to the Reticulans is probably the Borg, which is short for cyborg. The Borg were a leaderless group with control being spread throughout the collective consciousness of their ship. Thus, it's almost impossible to seriously harm them since they have no critical sections. The many half-organic and half-robot beings aboard the drab, gray, geometric Borg ships fit the Reticulans very well, too. About the only difference is that the Borg were a hostile race that absorbed or assimilated races it conquered, which is probably similar to what some fear the Reticulans are like in real life.

Comparing the Pleiadians and the Reticulans, one can see why the Pleiadians are seen as friendly while the Reticulans seem untrustworthy. The attractive Pleiadians look like us, and are more like cousins than aliens since we come from a similar source. The headstrong, enthusiastic nature of the Pleiadians isn't threatening to our individualism. However, the Reticulans, like the Reptilians, behave and look different and are often treated the way one would treat a foreigner or someone of a different ethnicity. Earth's interactions with the various extraterrestrial races can be seen as a macroscopic version of the interaction between different ethnic or national groups on our own planet. In both cases, acceptance and mutual cooperation helps each side. We can't have effective relationships with extraterrestrials until we have healthy relationships between groups on our own planet. Although we shouldn't condemn the Reticulans, such reactions are understandable and even natural during our growth process.

It is important to remember the big picture. Just as our planet Earth is alive, so is the entire galaxy one giant living creature, with different parts serving different functions. Just as a growing being learns different things in different times and places, so do different planetary civilizations develop and represent different characteristics. Earth and Zeta Reticuli have developed two polarized concepts of how an individual relates to society. Having completed our evolutionary tasks, now we are unifying and passing on our fruits to future and higher civilizations.

11: Metaphysical Phenomena

"Those who dance are considered insane by those who can't hear the music."
- George Carlin

Of all the different areas of spirituality, one of the most interesting is metaphysics. Metaphysics or the paranormal refers to manifestations or abilities beyond that which is understood by mainstream science. The word occult (Latin for "concealed") is frequently used to refer to metaphysics because it describes that which is hidden from normal understanding and also frequently studied in secret. Metaphysics is often practiced privately to avoid persecution and unwanted attention from those who might fear or misuse it.

There are two types of metaphysics. Internal metaphysics means personal abilities that aren't visible outside of oneself, such as psychic perception. External metaphysics means phenomena that are visible to anyone, such as telekinesis or techniques of divination. Some instances of metaphysics are both internal and external. For example, a ghost is an external phenomenon; however, most ghosts are only perceivable by one who is psychically sensitive.

Metaphysics may seem special; however, ultimately metaphysics is just a form of physics. All psychic and spiritual phenomena have a rational explanation although they involve things common science hasn't proven yet. At our present time in history, metaphysical manifestations are still relatively rare although that will change in the future. Everybody has psychic potential, and psychic abilities in general will increase as humanity continues to evolve. The human species gradually evolved the sense of sight, and now we're gradually evolving foresight.

Presently psychics are to ordinary people as a person with sight is to a society of people blind from birth. Such a blind person has difficulty learning about an object a hundred yards away because he/she can't easily hear it, touch it, or use other senses he/she considers normal. People used to laugh at those who thought heavier than air flying machines were possible or who believed in plate tectonics where continents could actually drift across the Earth's surface. The same analogy applies to psychic abilities and other forms of metaphysics that people often don't believe in.

Psychic senses have limitations just as standard vision isn't effective all the time. For example, a sighted person can't tell what someone's doing at night or behind a wall. If one sees a meteor in the sky, he/she can predict that a rock will hit the ground in a few seconds. Someone who can't see or doesn't bother to look up has no way of knowing about the incoming meteor. Also, like every prediction, it needs to be properly interpreted and it isn't guaranteed to happen. The meteor may burn up in the atmosphere before it hits the ground.

Although truly metaphysical phenomena do exist, very often what one thinks is metaphysics has a mundane explanation. People may attribute things to metaphysics out of wishful thinking or arrogance, because they think it would be desirable to have such experiences or abilities. Unfortunately, many demonstrations of metaphysics are intentionally faked. Therefore, a certain degree of skepticism is healthy. Unfortunately, there are people who want to make you think they're powerful, control your life, or at least part you from your money.

However, just because most apparent instances of metaphysics have a mundane explanation or are outright fraudulent doesn't mean that's true in all cases. It's important to believe in metaphysics or at least not outright deny the possibility. Metaphysics allows us to appreciate the mystery of life and be inspired to investigate more, and it keeps us questioning boundaries of our knowledge. Metaphysics is the true final frontier because it's always a step beyond our current level of understanding. No matter how advanced technology becomes or how much of the Universe we explore and understand, there's always the potential for magic. Ultimately, Spirit is metaphysical because spiritual concepts are by definition beyond the mental levels of intellect. Hence, to deny metaphysics is to deny spirituality.

In spite of the above, there's an important distinction between metaphysics and spirituality. A psychic person isn't necessarily spiritual. Psychic abilities have the potential to actually distract one from true growth because the increased personal power can cause arrogance and pride. That doesn't mean such abilities should be avoided either. There's significant good that can be done with psychic abilities if used properly. For a simple example, such abilities can expose people to spiritual realities. Metaphysical exploration is an interesting area. Some pursue it as a hobby like any other simply because it's interesting. However, metaphysics shouldn't be considered a spiritual Path even though it often leads one to the Path. A number of seekers started out with a desire for metaphysical experiences, which later evolved into a desire for wisdom and other spiritual virtues.

Similarly, being spiritual doesn't necessarily mean one is psychic. Some of the most evolved people on this planet are very humble and have no abilities beyond the miracle of their love. However, after a certain point along the Path one unavoidably has what would be considered metaphysical experiences because they consciously connect with their soul or higher energies. Hence, they develop what can only be considered psychic powers, even if such powers are subtle like being sensitive and wise.

Divination

"A wise man rules by the stars. A fool is ruled by them."
- Anonymous

Divination is using spiritual techniques to learn about one's environment or oneself. The word "divination" has the same Latin root as "divine," which emphasizes its spiritual origins. Divination is calm observation and interpretation, as opposed to more active or interactive means of acquiring information such as channeling. People often use divination to help find answers to specific questions, such as whether they should do something. They may also attempt to use divination to foretell the future and determine what will happen in it.

A potential downside with divination is that it can be disempowering. Trying to determine the future assumes that it's fixed, fated, and can't be avoided. Energy spent toward trying to read the future is often better directed toward actually living life and working toward making a desirable future happen. Similarly, trying to answer personal questions through divination has the potential to remove one from a proper decision making process. Divination is best used as a way to learn more about one's inner characteristics and motivations. Such a usage is more subtle, but ultimately more effective and more conducive to personal growth.

There are numerous forms of divination. The following are a few of the most common techniques:

Astrology: Astrology is divination based on the positioning of planets and other celestial bodies. The primary elements in astrology are the background signs of the zodiac, the locations of planets in the zodiac, and the angles or aspects planets make with each other. Planets are much more than just chunks of rock and gas, but are living entities expressing on all planes up through the Logos. The positions of planets and the angles they make with each other give off powerful spiritual influences, and in effect indicate part of the Divine Will. Similarly, the zodiac is more than just space and random stars, but is an expression of the Galactic Logos whose physical body consists of the various stars. Dividing the celestial sphere into the twelve signs of the zodiac is a way to help classify what would otherwise be the overwhelming infinity of the Universe.

Astrology and other forms of divination don't describe a fixed fate. Astrology is more like a weather report; it indicates the energies one is likely to encounter in their life and receive from their environment. Astrology can help one understand life goals and karmic influences, although again each person has a choice of how to respond to given situations. To use an analogy from playing cards, astrology is the hand of cards you're dealt; however, it's up to you how to play that hand you're given. For example, an astrological weather report can state that rain is likely. An astrologer can conclude that energies are not conducive to having an outdoor picnic or even predict with reasonable certainty that one is not likely to have a picnic. However, there's nothing preventing one from doing it anyway if they're willing to put up with the rain. One's personal astrology chart is more a reflection of their existing personality as opposed to something that determines it. In other words, being born under the sign of Aries doesn't make one actively assertive, as much as many actively assertive souls choose to be born as Aries.

Numerology: Numerology is divination based on numbers. Numbers aren't just inert quantities. Like the planets and Rays, each number has its own unique energy and influence. Common numerology techniques involve considering the numbers in one's birthday and getting a result not unlike astrology or converting the letters in one's name to numbers and interpreting those energies.

Just as there are higher chakras and Rays beyond the standard seven that have more spiritual qualities, so are their higher numbers beyond the standard digits normally used in numerology. A Master Number is a double digit number using the same digit, such as 11 or 22. One may notice Master Numbers or encounter them in their life, especially in pairs such as 11:11. Instead of just accidental coincidences, such synchronistic events can be useful divinatory messages.

The prime number 109 has special qualities and can represent spirit and evolution in several ways:

- 109 starts with the digit "1." Being a straight line, "1" represents the ordinary physical or intellectual state of being. The seeker then discovers intuition or spirituality, represented by the circle or digit "0." Finally one blends the two aspects of life together with spirit on top, represented by the "0" over the "1" to form the digit "9."
- 109 starts with first digit "1," ends with the last digit "9," and has the empty digit "0" in the middle. This sequence represents the spiritual Path from beginning to end that each soul fills in with his/her own unique journey.
- 109 can also be considered the number of love because it's similar in shape to a heart. The digit "9" looks like the right half of a heart while the digits "1" and "0" if pushed together can make a backwards "9" or the other half of a heart.
- A mala (Sanskrit for "garland") is a beaded string commonly used by Buddhists and Hindus when repeating mantras. It has 109 beads total when including the head bead.

Tarot: Tarot cards are a form of divination based on shuffling cards, laying them out, and interpreting the meaning of each card in its given position. The different cards in a tarot deck represent the various archetypes of life, forming a rich psychological language not unlike the zodiac in astrology or the digits in numerology. There are a number of divination systems that use cards, but tarot is probably the oldest and most popular.

Tarot readings can be accurate for several reasons. Metaphysically, the symbolism of a tarot card is powerful enough to have spiritual energy attached to it. This is especially true if one works with their deck, consciously helping to charge their cards and get familiar with the energies. That allows the right cards to be selected due to energy affinity when meditating on a question. Tarot can also work simply due to synchronicity. Everything happens for a reason; ultimately some cards have to appear, so they're likely to have important messages or at least present an interesting option to consider.

Even from a skeptical point of view, tarot can be valuable due to the reader simply interpreting the cards appropriately in the context of their question. For example, in a reading about romance, both positive and negative cards can be interpreted similarly and have a similar psychological benefit. A positive reading about a new or improved partnership presents a possibility, and can make one work to make it happen. A negative reading about a breakup or being alone is a warning and can make one work to avoid that unwanted outcome.

Sacred Space

"Someone's sitting in the shade today because someone planted a tree a long time ago."
- Warren Buffet

Sacred space is any area that has positive spiritual qualities. Sacred space can be created through actions, such as by a one time or repeated event. A religious house of worship is sacred space, due to both the reverent thoughts and actions that have taken place there over time, as well as the respect that most have when interacting with it. Sacred space can be personal or only significant to certain people. For example, the site of a marriage proposal is sometimes very meaningful to the couple involved. At high levels of consciousness, everywhere and everything can be sacred.

Sacred space can be found in the natural world. For example, large trees, gardens, waterfalls, mountain summits, and natural arches have obvious physical majesty along with inner qualities that one can benefit from, such as the oxygen generated by plants and ions generated by moving water. Natural sacred space also tends to attract fairies or other nature spirits of a positive quality. Sedona, Arizona is an example of an entire district of sacred space, due to the red rock formations and the spiritual “energy vortexes” for which the area is famous.

Some areas are sacred even if they seem ordinary on a physical level. Ley lines are channels of energy that crisscross the planet, similar to nerves in the physical body. Ley line endpoints and intersections have especially strong energy; where often things such as stone circles or houses of worship are built at such sites by those who are consciously or subconsciously aware of their qualities. Note that most ley lines go through the middle of the earth; the ones people interact with are on or near the surface. Ley lines may also slowly drift over time; sometimes the most energetic location is now actually nearby as opposed to in the middle of an ancient site.

Sacred geometry refers to symbols, mandalas, or other designs that have special properties or can generate sacred space. Sacred symbols can be found in almost every religion or spiritual society, and sometimes in everyday culture. Some symbols have actual metaphysical qualities due to their designs representing Universal concepts or having numerological ratios. Other symbols have significance due to the many people that are aware of it. There are large emotional and thought forms connected with the design on the astral and mental planes with which one can connect. Sacred geometry can also be found in many constructions, from modern buildings to ancient sites such as Stonehenge in England.

A talisman is an object that generates sacred space around it by attracting wanted influences, such as healing or repelling unwanted influences, such as negativity. There are numerous examples of talismans. Many are specific to particular cultures or belief systems. For example, in Western culture, horseshoes and rabbits’ feet are supposed to increase luck. Some talismans are merely superstition while others have actual metaphysical effects. Even for inert talismans, they often have a positive psychological effect like a placebo. A talisman to ward off evil can make one feel more confident and less likely to fear, which prevents them from being controlled by negative influences.

Crystals: A crystal is one of the most universal talismans. Crystals are tools that can radiate, direct, and store energy. They can be worn, used as focus points in meditation, and even used for healing. Many crystals are connected with the Rays, as described in the chapter "Rays of Divinity." Clear crystals and those connected with the 1st Ray of will tend to act as amplifiers and magnify whatever energy is present. Hence, like any tool, a crystal can potentially be used negatively as well as positively.

"Crystal power" becomes apparent when one considers a crystal's properties. Crystals are one of the few objects in nature which are produced along perfectly straight lines, as opposed to curved or irregular like plants. Even in mainstream physical science the organized nature of crystals has interesting effects. Crystals can create electricity at very precise frequencies, and hence are used in watches, lasers, and other equipment. Crystals can even output electricity through the piezoelectric effect where pressure on the crystal generates an electric charge.

Pyramids: A pyramid is an object with a flat base and triangular faces that gradually rise to a point. The base is usually square, but may also be triangular or even any polygon. Pyramids are a good balance between the physical and spiritual. They are grounded, with a flat face touching the earth, and they point up toward the sky, representing growth and reaching toward Spirit. Pyramids also symbolize the mystery of life, especially with ancient life sized versions around the world having special or secret chambers. Among the best examples of pyramid sacred space are the Great Pyramids of Giza, Egypt. A pyramid can be a talisman if carried around or used like a crystal, especially when already made out of crystal. A pyramid is also an instance of sacred geometry when considering the properties of the pyramid shape itself.

Labyrinths: A labyrinth is a meandering path without any junctions. The word "labyrinth" is based on the Greek word "labrys" meaning a double headed axe. The labrys was a common symbol in the ancient Minoan civilization which originated the Greek myth of the Labyrinth, in which King Minos kept the Minotaur.

Labyrinths are a perfect example of sacred space. They are a near universal symbol. Classical labyrinth patterns have been found around the world in many separate cultures dating back hundreds of years. Labyrinths symbolize the twists and turns of life's journey. Navigating a labyrinth can be done with sacred intent like a meditation. Walking a life-sized labyrinth is a unique experience because it amounts to a walking meditation, involving the body in addition to the soul. The following is a famous labyrinth pattern with the earliest example seen in Chartres Cathedral, France.

Mazes: A maze is a puzzle with choices and false paths. The word "maze" is based on the old English word for confuse or confound. Although mazes and labyrinths are synonymous in the dictionary, modern spiritual writers usually use the term labyrinth to mean a single unicursal path without junctions, and maze to mean a puzzle with choices.

Like labyrinths, mazes are an excellent metaphor for life. There is a goal to be reached, but the real experience is the journey. Mazes are a balance between fate and free will where the walls force us down certain paths, but we still have choices to make among the options available. Just as we often don't know where we are in a maze, so do we often get lost in life. Every person must walk the path themselves, but one can travel with others and there can be multiple valid ways to reach the goal. Occasionally, one runs into a dead end and has to backtrack; however, that's part of the learning process so shouldn't be considered negative.

A standard maze with a single solution has passages and walls that resemble a branching tree. A number of things in life have a tree structure. In the body, one's bloodstream and the respiratory passages within the lungs form a mazelike tree structure. A maze on paper is frequently formed of black walls on a white background, with the entrance and exit at the top and bottom. Such a maze resembles our spiritual nervous system. The white colored solution path through the maze is like the spinal column, or the spiritual sushumna, descending from the head with all the other passages leading off the route through forming the rest of the cerebral nervous system. The black colored walls form a tree structure too, in two halves divided by the maze's solution. This is like our sympathetic nervous system or the spiritual ida and pingala on either side of the spine.

Extrasensory Perception

"I am become a transparent eyeball; I am nothing; I see all..."
- Ralph Waldo Emerson

Extrasensory perception (ESP) is a category of metaphysics dealing with the ability to perceive things beyond that which can ordinarily be picked up by the five physical senses. A person with any form of extrasensory perception is called a psychic.

Auras around the body are one of the most common things a psychic can perceive. Auras are often perceived as colors which indicate different emotions or states of being. Metaphysically, seeing auras happens when one can sense the emanations of a body's etheric double. Ordinary objects can also emanate psychic energy, and people can leave behind energy on objects they touch.

Psychometry is a form of psychic reading where one perceives things about someone from objects that person owns.

Foretelling or precognition is using psychic senses to predict the future. Foretelling is a type of divination that takes place internally, which doesn't rely on any external tool such as astrology to provide data to interpret. Events that happen on the physical plane are effects whose causes were originated on higher planes. Psychic foretelling is merely perceiving and hopefully accurately interpreting such energies. For example, before two people or nations fight, their dislike and hatred for each other exists and can be seen on the astral plane. This foretelling is similar to radar on a ship detecting an oncoming ship through fog. The radar acts like a psychic sense allowing one to predict that another ship will physically appear soon. A psychic can sense upcoming events like a lover or other significant person coming into one's life, by perceiving incoming energies.

Psychically seeing into the past is similar, and involves perceiving what amounts to higher plane footprints or echoes. Just as future events manifest on higher planes before the physical, so do past events have effects on higher planes long after there's nothing apparent anymore on the physical. For example, a broken heart can easily be seen on the astral plane in one's aura, even through on the physical plane the person looks normal. The most accurate way to see into the past is by reading the Akashic Records, which contain a perfect record of everything that's ever happened. The Akashic Records are on the Buddhic plane, which is hard for all but the most spiritual to perceive; however, they have semi-accurate reflections on the mental and astral planes.

Some dreams foretell the future, although most dreams are just mental processing. Unfortunately dreams tend to be so vague and symbolic that they're difficult to interpret correctly. Most everyone dreams, and billions of dreams happen every night, so many dreams that come true are just coincidences. Even when dreams are truly prophetic, they're often allegorical and use real world things to represent abstract concepts. This is similar to how in the Bible, Jesus used parables and allegories of things in physical life to describe spiritual truths. For example, one may dream about a physical tsunami flooding an area. In reality, what happens is people in that area experience strong emotions, which are represented by water.

Clairvoyance is seeing something which isn't normally perceivable by the physical eyes. Clairvoyance is popularly known as "having a vision." Some things attributed to clairvoyance are actually just physical hallucinations that result from mental illness or drug abuse. On the other hand, some people get diagnosed as having a mental illness when in fact they're actually psychic.

Clairaudience is hearing something which isn't normally perceivable by the physical ears. If one hears other people talking through their inner ear, then their clairaudience is a form of channeling. As with clairvoyance, clairaudience may be valid psychic input, or it may just be "hearing voices." A true clairaudient experience is unmistakable. It's like someone's talking when there's obviously nobody there.

Clairsentience is simply knowing something which isn't normally deducible by logic or perceivable by other senses. Clairsentience is using one's intuition, as opposed to receiving input from outer or even inner vision. Clairsentience can be considered the highest form of extrasensory perception. It ultimately emanates from the Buddhic plane of intuition; however, it also requires the most discernment. It's challenging for even an experienced clairsentient to separate true knowing from their own biases about what they want to be true.

A clairvoyant or clairaudient experience is interesting because the psychic impression goes directly to the consciousness and doesn't activate the parts of the physical brain that normally process vision or hearing. For this reason, such experiences are frequently forgotten quickly since there's no context that one can use to remember. In other words, the brain wasn't already working along those lines. A clairvoyant experience may feel like one's consciousness was interrupted. One was thinking and seeing in a normal fashion when suddenly something inserted itself right before one's consciousness. When the impression passes, normal thinking continues where it left off. Hopefully, one will be aware that an impression came in.

Psychic senses tend to be developed gradually. For example, clairsentience often goes unnoticed. One just considers himself/herself sensitive or intuitive until the coincidences become too strong to be ignored. Clairaudience tends to develop gradually as well. For example, initially while in a relaxed state, one may hear what sounds like quiet static. Later, one may pick up individual words, and eventually short phrases will be heard that have little relation to anything going on at the time. Finally, words can be perceived while doing other things, and one can hear answers to questions they mentally ask.

Channeling

"We don't do good works, God does good works through us."
- Robert Firth

Channeling is a type of psychic perception where one communicates with a spiritual entity. Channeling is an active way to gain wisdom, as opposed to divination which is a more passive observation and interpretation. Those who are able to channel are called mediums because they act as the middle point between the spiritual source and the physical plane. One can channel an external being, or channel within and communicate with aspects of themselves.

In order to channel, the medium relaxes and may even enter a trance, blanking his or her mind so other input can come in. The best way to channel is to get one's personality out of the way, so the message can come through undistorted. The image of a glass tube may be helpful. The tube is unobstructed so communication passes through, and uncolored so the message isn't biased. Channeled information can be perceived strongly and accurately, or it can manifest in a subtle fashion. Even when one actually connects with an external entity, sometimes the communication comes through as impressions, which the medium must verbalize on his or her own.

Like all expressions of metaphysics, channeling is sometimes fake. The medium may be connecting with their own soul or intuition, which they incorrectly believe is coming from a source outside themselves. The channeler may also intentionally make the whole thing up with the intent to deceive others. A fake channel may not be openly malicious but may wrap up his/her own genuinely positive ideas in the guise of an entity in order to attract more attention or make his/her message seem more exciting. Other people are more likely to want to listen or pay money to hear an extraterrestrial from Venus or a million year old warrior from Atlantis than John Doe's common sense.

One way to express channeling is with automatic writing where one sits in a trance with a pen or pencil and writes down the messages that come from his/her inner voice or from another entity. Automatic writing is useful because the act of writing gives a physical record of such psychic impressions which might otherwise be quickly forgotten.

A Ouija board is a device with letters, numbers, and simple words such as "yes" and "no." A person or small group sits before the board with a planchette or pointer, which seems to move around the board on its own volition as it spells messages. The word Ouija (pronounced "wee-gee") most likely comes from the words "oui" and "ja", the French and German words for "yes," which indicates the Ouija board's ability to answer questions. The Ouija board is one way to channel other entities. That entity may guide your subconscious or even be able to manipulate the planchette itself. Note that the Ouija board often works with your own subconscious moving the planchette. The lack of conscious awareness makes it seem like some disembodied entity is guiding it.

The downside to an Ouija board is that there's no guarantee about the quality of the entity attracted. It's like getting advice in a chat room on the internet; you have no idea whether the person on the other end is who they say they are. There have been attempts to create more spiritually oriented boards to attract entities of a higher vibration. For example, several companies have produced "Angel Boards" designed to connect with Angels or other guides, similar to how there are different divination card decks other than traditional tarot. Note that with more spiritually oriented boards, the improved results are due to the user as much as the board itself. The user is likely to want to connect with higher entities for a higher purpose. He/she asks for guidance and suitably protects himself/herself, as opposed to seeking cheap excitement from dabbling in the occult.

A pendulum is a crystal or stone suspended from a string or chain. The pendulum can be used for divination by holding it steady and letting it swing. Different directions indicate yes, no, and other answers. Like the Ouija board, a pendulum can be a form of channeling, using one's subconscious muscles or an external entity to make the pendulum swing.

A séance is a gathering of people that channel a disembodied entity. It consists of a primary medium and other people called sitters. Usually a small number of individuals gather in a circle or around a table. A real séance is an intimate and private affair and often results in visible metaphysical phenomena. Note the contrast to a standard public channeling where the medium has someone appear to speak through them. In a public channeling there's nothing physically visible and nothing other than the medium's word and the integrity of the message to prove that it's real.

Possession is a form of involuntary channeling where the channeler seems to be controlled by an outside source. Fortunately, it's virtually impossible for an entity to possess someone without permission having been given on some level. The person's guardian Angel or other spiritual guides tend to put a stop to such things quickly. Possession usually happens when people open themselves up to outside energies, such as they weaken themselves through drug abuse, or they just want to channel and don't care with whom they connect. Possession is more likely to affect teenagers or young adults because youth tend to have more turbulent emotions and hence rapport with the lower astral plane where negative entities often dwell. There's nothing special about possession; people often allow themselves to be controlled in negative relationships or by other people on the physical plane. The best way for people to avoid possession is to vibrate on higher levels to begin with, so they'll only attract and be responsive to entities of a higher nature.

Metaphysical Entities

"There are more things in heaven and earth, Horatio, than are dreamt of in your philosophy."
- Hamlet

A metaphysical entity is any being not yet proven by mainstream science. This term usually refers to spiritual beings that exist on the etheric or higher planes, such as fairies and Angels. Metaphysical entities also cover physical creatures from other realms, such as extraterrestrials. Fairies and Angels are described in the chapter "Kingdoms of Nature" and extraterrestrials in the chapter "Our Extraterrestrial Cousins."

A ghost is any being without a physical body, who normally inhabits one. Most ghosts are people who have physically died but haven't yet made their full transition to the astral plane. They're sometimes referred to as earthbound souls since they're still connected to the physical plane. Often they remain because they're afraid of the afterlife or have attachments to physical life. For example, a ghost may have unfinished business on earth. They'll stay stuck between worlds until they decide to let go, or some other spirit convinces them to do so. A ghost may also be a positive spirit who has properly made its transition but has temporarily returned to the surface of Earth in order to visit or provide guidance to loved ones. It may also be a soul about to be reincarnated into a new physical body.

Ghosts or other spiritual entities with metaphysical talents are sometimes able to affect physical objects, for example, by drawing denser matter around their spiritual body. This can be done to a lesser or greater degree, ranging from vague lights to a full materialization that can manipulate and pick up objects. The matter in a metaphysical materialization is called ectoplasm.

Often what appears to be a ghost is just an apparition or psychic echo from the past. For example, an old house may seem haunted because one psychically or even physically hears footsteps or gets a glimpse of a human figure. However, instead of an actual entity, it's just an extended echo from someone in the past that regularly walked there.

A vampire is a negative entity that steals vitality from others. An energy vampire or psychic vampire takes prana or other life force from another person. The energy drawn may be physical, emotional, mental, or a combination. Energy vampires may be physically alive, or they may be disembodied ghosts who try and attach themselves to people. Some energy vampires are conscious of what they do, and enjoy the feeling of power they get from psychologically manipulating others or stealing from them. Other energy vampires are completely unaware of what they do, either because they don't know the effect they have on others, or because they have a physical or psychic disease that causes them to have low vitality, and hence to subconsciously compensate by grabbing energy from any nearby source.

How does one deal with energy vampires? The simplest method is to just avoid them or not have negatively-oriented people in your life. When you vibrate at a high level, you only attract and are responsive to entities of a high nature. Another method is to form a psychic shield around yourself to protect your energy from negative sources. However, that may indirectly give them influence since you're considering energy to be a scarce resource. The best way is to connect with the Universal source and let power come from the infinite instead of your limited self. An energy vampire can't drain you or anybody else if they're drinking from the ocean.

A more extreme type of vampire is a ghost. In this situation an evil person, especially one who has some occult knowledge, wants to avoid judgment in the afterlife. Upon physical death, they resist the call of the afterlife, and cling to their dead physical body. The way to force beings to move on is to destroy their dead body. Cremation, as opposed to burying a body and allowing it to slowly rot over time, has the advantage of not leaving behind a corpse to which a newly transitioned soul might form an unnatural attachment. The above may be the cause of certain myths about vampires or other undead creatures, such as a vampire can be killed by a stake through the heart, by burning, or by exposure to sunlight. The ghost wants to preserve their dead body as long as possible, which can explain why vampires traditionally seek blood, and why zombies seek brain matter. Corpse vampires were common during periods of Atlantis, but today are almost nonexistent, due to the increased evolution of even the most negative people, combined with occult development being less common compared to that era.

Metaphysical Feats

"If you want to do a certain thing, you first have to be a certain person. Once you become that certain person, you will not care anymore about doing that certain thing."
- Dōgen Zenji

The deepest category of metaphysics is personal achievements that are seemingly superhuman or miraculous. Such feats are certainly possible on the physical plane, but most are very hard to accomplish successfully. They require extreme amounts of knowledge and discipline, so few ever successfully do them. Some also require near Master levels of spiritual evolution, and most Masters have more important things to do with their time on Earth than play with occult powers.

Firewalking: Firewalking is being able to walk on burning coals with one's bare feet without getting burned. Firewalking classes are sometimes used as a personal growth technique to convince people to overcome fear and realize they can do things they didn't consider possible.

Firewalking usually doesn't involve the occult, and can be explained with normal physics. Both human skin and charcoal are poor conductors of heat, meaning touching coals won't burn one immediately, especially if they're walking through the coals and hence not touching them for long. This resistance is heightened if one's feet are wet in any way, such as if firewalking is taking place in a wet grassy field. There are, however, metaphysical ways that one can enhance their firewalking, such as working with certain metaphysical entities. Fairies that work with fire could decrease or deflect heat, fairies that work with water could create a liquid barrier between oneself and the fire, and so on.

Telekinesis: Telekinesis is being able to move objects with the mind without actually manipulating them through obvious physical means. The classic example of telekinesis is bending a spoon, which is sometimes seen in demonstrations (frequently faked, unfortunately). Real telekinesis usually involves using the body's subtle energy fields to create electricity, air currents, or other physical effects. It can also be accomplished by enlisting the aid of metaphysical entities who can affect physical matter.

Pyrokinesis: Pyrokinesis is being able to start fires through metaphysical means. This often manifests in subtle ways, such as being able to generate heat. Few people have ever been able to create massive fires or throw fireballs with their minds. Spontaneous human combustion (abbreviated SHC) is where a human body catches fire and burns without any obvious external source of ignition. Presumably, these cases are caused by people manifesting pyrokinesis within themselves. This doesn't mean that all or even most cases of SHC have a paranormal explanation. It can be caused by various physical reasons. For example, extreme static electricity can start fires. Since much of the human body is fat, the human body can actually act like a candle in special circumstances.

Invisibility: Invisibility, as the name implies, is not being detectable by normal vision. One way to accomplish invisibility is by bending light rays around one's position. This feat is challenging to do accurately to avoid any distortion of the image on the other side. It's also challenging to do in all directions at the same time and more or less impossible to do completely if one is standing on the ground since there's no light coming up from the ground directly under one's feet to bend. Hence, this form of invisibility works better when one is flying. A more complete form of invisibility is to partially etherealize oneself, so light rays simply pass through one's location normally. Invisibility is more often accomplished through advanced technology then by a person. Extraterrestrial beamships frequently employ invisibility to avoid being seen by humanity.

Levitation: Levitation is hovering in the air without being supported by the ground and without obviously propelling oneself upward against the force of gravity. The metaphysics behind levitation are very similar to the technology of anti-gravity. Extraterrestrial beamships use anti-gravity to silently hover in the air, while anti-gravity was also used in Atlantis for the airships they had at that time.

Some anecdotes of levitation may not be physical levitation, but rather a description of one's spiritual evolution. A seeker may be so lighthearted and full of love he/she is practically floating. Levitation can be an analogy showing no attachments to the physical world; it no longer holds them down or attracts them.

Walking on water: Water walking is being able to physically move across the surface of a body of water without sinking into it. The classic example is from the Bible where Jesus and His disciple Peter walked on water (Matthew 14:25-31). The simplest way to walk on water is to use the same technique as in levitation, except that one changes their weight so that they're lighter than water, but not light enough to be floating in the air.

Some anecdotes of water walking may not be the physical act but rather an allegory to indicate that one has mastered his/her emotions. Walking on top of water represents being above the watery astral plane of emotion. For example, Jesus and His disciple may have actually walked on water; people at their level of evolution certainly have the ability of doing so should they choose. However, the story may just demonstrate Jesus' complete mastery of emotion, and the struggles of Peter who was able to walk on water briefly until he started sinking and needed his Master's help.

Phasing: Phasing is being able to move solid objects, such as your own body, through other objects. Phasing is readily accomplished on the astral and all higher planes; however, it's extremely hard to do on the physical plane with physical objects. In fact, the concept of "walking through walls" is almost synonymous with doing the seemingly impossible. One who's extremely talented may be considered to be able to walk through walls, whether or not their available talents actually include phasing. For example, the 1972 television series Kung Fu had the classic quotation, "A Shaolin priest can walk through walls."

How is phasing accomplished? Physical matter can be considered mostly empty space. The nucleus of a hydrogen atom is 100,000 times smaller than the width of the atom itself, meaning only one quadrillionth of an atom can be considered solid. Because moving through objects is readily accomplished on the less dense astral and higher planes, if one can somehow temporarily etherealize physical matter, then one could move through another physical object, and then snap back into the physical plane afterward. For example, if one could apply psychic pressure to separate each physical plane particle into the seven astral plane particles that compose it, then one could phase as easily as is done on the astral plane. Phasing in this manner needs to be done very carefully and accurately. Prematurely returning to physical solidity would be deadly if an individual is inside a wall. Allowing the temporary astral matter to drift so the physical body becomes scrambled would also be deadly. The classic government conspiracy theory of the Philadelphia Experiment concerns paranormal research aboard a United States Navy ship that ended badly with the bodies of several crewmembers fusing with the ship's hull.

Teleportation: Teleportation is the act of moving objects from one location to another, without traveling through the intervening distance. Teleportation is one of the hardest metaphysical feats to accomplish because there are many challenges with it. When teleporting your own body, it's possible to leave your clothes behind, or even worse, parts of your body. Arriving at the destination is just as risky, and may involve getting your body subtly or very obviously scrambled along the way, or accidentally appearing in a deadly location such as half way inside a wall or at the center of the Earth. It's easier to teleport yourself than other objects or other people because you can work with your own body's energy field and don't have to interact with anybody else's will. This is similar to why it's easier to move your own physical body than it is to use your body to pick up objects or move other people.

Astral projection isn't the same as physical teleportation; however, it's important to realize that it's much easier to teleport on the astral plane. On the astral plane one can travel at near instantaneous speeds, such as reach the other side of the world in about the time it takes one to think of the idea. Being out of body at all is close to an act of teleportation because the astral and all higher bodies along with consciousness are at some alternate location; it's only the physical body that hasn't moved from its original position. With the proper technique, it's possible to "pull" the physical body to where the astral body currently is, instead of the usual conclusion to an out-of-body experience which is flying in the astral body back to the physical.

Another form of teleportation is accomplished by manipulating time. Time is relative and can seemingly or literally pass faster or slower depending on one's consciousness. Einstein's relativity gives insight into teleportation with time passing faster or slower in different reference frames as one approaches relativistic velocities near the speed of light. This is apparently how extraterrestrials are able to visit Earth and other planets in a way that would seem to imply they're moving faster than the speed of light. They more or less just normally fly their beamships from their world to ours, but with appropriate technology it seems to happen instantaneously from both their time frame and our own, which is in effect teleporting. They cease to be at one location and become at the next. Unlike other forms of teleportation, this method would still be obstructed by walls.

Understanding the fourth dimension (a fourth dimension of space as opposed to time) gives additional insight into teleportation. Consider the relation of the 3rd dimension to the 2nd, to understand how the 4th dimension relates to the 3rd. You can take a two dimensional "universe" on a piece of paper, and by folding it cause two distant points to come together, teleporting from a 2nd dimensional perspective by jumping through the 3rd. The astral plane has four dimensions. The mechanics of this allow astral entities in spiritualistic séances to apport objects from a distance and accomplish other metaphysical feats. Philosophically, to teleport you need to detach from your limited self that sees itself as a separate entity at a single point in space, and embrace the Oneness of the Universe, so you're equally at all positions in it. This idea demonstrates how many metaphysical feats require a high level of spirituality, which in turn means the best way to evolve into being able to accomplish such feats is to work on spiritual growth.

12:
Astral Projection

"The best way to make your dreams come true is to wake up."
- Paul Valery

Astral projection is a metaphysical phenomenon interesting enough to deserve its own chapter. Astral projection is where consciousness temporarily leaves the physical body and enters the astral body. The astral body, which normally occupies the same location as the physical body, detaches from it. One is then able to perceive the astral plane and move around using his or her astral body.

Astral projection is sometimes called an out-of-body experience. An out-of-body experience is any event where consciousness leaves the physical body. Astral projection is the most common form of an out-of-body experience, but not all out-of-body experiences are astral projection. An out-of-body experience can also be projection to a plane higher than the astral, a near-death experience, or actual death.

Remote viewing is a psychic ability similar to astral projection. In remote viewing, one is able to psychically perceive current events happening at a distance. Usually remote viewing is a vivid clairvoyant image like watching an inner television screen, as opposed to just intuitive impressions. In remote viewing, one remains in the physical body and sees a distant location while in astral projection, one's consciousness actually travels to another location.

Dreams

During astral projection the physical body is still as if one is in a deep trance or asleep. To understand astral projection, the seeker should begin by understanding standard sleep. People on average sleep eight hours a night. In other words, people spend about one third of their entire lives asleep. Hence, there's great potential benefit if one can effectively use this time.

Sleep is only needed by the physical body. The physical brain is made of matter dense enough that it periodically needs time to rest and organize. In contrast, the astral and higher bodies don't ever become tired and can work ceaselessly for days or years without problem. After an out-of-body experience where one is completely free of the dense and confining physical form, one often feels very refreshed as if a full night has been slept.

During sleep, the astral and higher bodies are released from being bound to the physical body. In other words, technically, everybody astral projects, but only a few remember it. Some people perform valuable service on higher planes every night but aren't yet aware of it. A major part of spiritual evolution is becoming consciously aware of one's higher aspects that are already present.

Sleep can help one solve problems or make decisions. Sleep allows one to reorganize internal thoughts, which can often provide fresh insights upon awakening. Because the higher bodies are still active during sleep, they may actually be working on finding answers. In other words, sleep on a problem and let your astral self work on it for you.

Dreams are caused by one's relaxed consciousness being aware of the reorganization process. Subjects of dreams are frequently related to random things one saw or thought about during the day. That is why dreams so often appear random—they rapidly morph from one thing to another. Being asleep is like standing on the edge of a mental warehouse as forklifts and other vehicles move boxes of memories around within it. A dream image is just a particular box that happened to get moved in front of a person in their warehouse.

Dreams allow one to explore and learn from things that aren't possible or would have serious ramifications if done in real life. For example, one can dream of being the opposite gender, and benefit some from that experience without having to wait until a future incarnation. One can dream about getting in a fight or even killing someone and experience the ramifications without the significant karma that would manifest if that were done in real life. Dreams are often about past experiences or potential futures. Dreams about the past can allow one to learn wisdom from them while dreams about the future can be inspirational or serve as a warning. Dreams also let one explore inner motivations or desires. For example, it's possible to manifest superpowers, such as flying.

Dream symbology is personal because dreaming about certain subjects means different things to different people. Dream dictionaries that claim dreaming about a particular topic always means something in particular should be treated skeptically. For example, dreaming about being naked traditionally means one is feeling exposed or defenseless. However, to one who appreciates nudity, being naked likely means freedom and openness.

The seeker should pay attention to their dreams. The best introductory exercise for one who wants to astral project or become more aware of alternate levels of consciousness in general is to work with their dreams. For example, keep a dream journal, and write down your dreams immediately upon awakening. Dreams are frequently forgotten as one moves into the day's activities, so dreams should be recorded as soon as possible. Everybody dreams; however, not everybody has developed the ability to remember their dreams.

Lucid Dreaming

A lucid dream is one in which people are consciously aware that they're dreaming. In most dreams, people are trapped in the illusion of their dream world and believe that what they're experiencing is real. That's what makes nightmares so frightening. For example, in a dream you actually think a two-headed monster is chasing you and will eat you if it catches you.

In a lucid dream, people know that they're in a dream environment and are no longer afraid when in scary situations. For example, they know the monster can't actually hurt them. More importantly, a lucid dream allows one to control his or her dream environment. One can do almost anything in a lucid dream, such as make a monster disappear or change into a kitten. In lucid dreams one is only limited by his/her imagination and beliefs. Like meditation, lucid dreaming is an excellent method to train the will and concentration and to get familiar with more spiritual energies.

Once people achieve lucidity in dreams, they tend to act out their desires. For example, they may choose to manifest superpowers, or find a sexual partner. Perhaps the most common activity for a lucid dreamer is to start flying through the air because it's so free and fun. Physical life is very limited compared to life on the higher planes where flying is very similar to how one moves on the astral plane.

A lucid dream can start out as a normal dream then one suddenly realizes that they're dreaming in the middle of it. One may also go directly into a lucid dream upon falling asleep if one maintains focus, avoiding the usual period of unconsciousness or unawareness. Lucid dreams can happen spontaneously; however, with practice they can also be generated.

There are several tricks people can use to become aware that they're dreaming. Dreams often feature illogical or unexpectedly changing environments. If people get in the habit of checking whether their reality is consistent, they can start doing it in their dreams and quickly realize they're in a dream world. For example, they know that two-headed monsters don't exist on this planet; therefore, the presence of one means they must be dreaming. Also, physical stimuli, such as sound or light, is frequently sensed while asleep and interpreted in context of the current dream. For example, the rumble of a passing train in the real world may manifest as an avalanche in a dream. People can set up equipment in the real world to emit special sounds or lights while they are asleep with the intent to influence their dreams in a particular way. This allows them to realize they're dreaming.

Lucid dreaming is halfway between normal dreaming and astral projection. Both lucid dreams and astral projection involve one being fully conscious and perceiving things while the physical body is at rest. The only difference is that while lucid dreaming, consciousness is still within the physical body and experiencing the personal dream world.

Leaving the Body

Everybody can astral project although like other metaphysical talents such as extrasensory perception, some people find it easier than others. An emotionally oriented person tends to more easily enter and maintain astral consciousness than a mentally oriented person because the emotional person is already so active on the emotional plane. On the other hand, a mentally oriented person tends to have an advantage when overcoming fear and facing illusions since they're already calm and detached. Young adults are more likely to astral project because older people tend to be more centered in their heads and focused on physical plane issues, such as career. Spiritually oriented people are much more likely to astral project since they're naturally drawn to and already have sensitivity to things beyond the physical.

Sleep paralysis is where the body becomes rigid to minimize physical movement and potential injury during dreams. Before people lose consciousness or fully enter a dream world, they may consciously experience sleep paralysis where they seem unable to move. This situation can be frightening. If sleep paralysis is combined with dream images that can be partially active at the time, it can feel like one is being attacked by demons, abducted by aliens, or similar situations. Sleep paralysis is, however, a significant state because it means one is still alert while leaving ordinary physical consciousness. If one can maintain this alertness, he/she can move straight into a lucid dream or astral projection.

Sometimes while falling asleep, one may hear an inner hum or feel the "current" of an invisible river. In some cases this is sensing actual astral phenomena while in others it's just a psychological effect. Just as the physical plane has rivers of physical matter, the astral plane hosts currents of various types which flow and change over time. Occasionally, it may feel like an astral current is flowing through one's room. During such times astral projection is much easier.

If people maintain their conscious awareness during meditation or while falling asleep, they can astral project from full consciousness. One can also astral project from a dream or lucid dream where one transitions from the sleep state to astral consciousness. If one astral projects from the middle of a dream, the dream may seem to freeze and dissolve or *crack* like a seed ready to sprout. As one leaves the body, one will often feel the inner hum or roaring of the inner river become much more intense. When consciousness leaves the physical plane, it can feel like you have gotten the wind knocked out of yourself because you're disconnecting from the physical body which is maintained by breath. One may also feel a slipping or tug within the solar plexus chakra, and that chakra will seem full of electric energy or on fire.

Astral consciousness is normally prevented due to a psychic barrier in the etheric double of the physical body. This barrier may seem annoying to one who wants to experience higher realms, but it serves an important purpose in allowing us to live our physical lives and learn our lessons here, without being disturbed by ghosts or other phenomena. This is why one often needs to fall asleep in order to astral project, because one needs to get themselves past the barrier. One of the characteristics of Masters is they no longer experience this barrier. They're always fully conscious and are able to move awareness effortlessly from one plane to another or even experience both at the same time. In this sense, a true Master never sleeps.

Astral projection helps prepare one for physical death because one already familiar with the astral world tends to be unafraid of the death process. Astral projection is often frightening at first because the experience is similar to actually dying. In both cases you leave your physical body and enter the astral plane; however, with astral projection, you have a path back to your body via the *silver cord* that connects the physical and astral bodies. In spite of this, nothing can fully prepare one for the actual experience of death. Most astral projection is only a partial experience of astral consciousness because of the silver cord's attachment to the physical body and because one hasn't yet gone through the death bardo. Astral projection is like visiting a university while death is like actually enrolling in classes.

The Astral Body

The astral plane is the plane of emotion. While in the physical body, emotions are watered down by the time consciousness experiences them because they need to be filtered through the dense physical brain. When a beginning astral projectors first leave their bodies, they will likely experience extreme emotion, perhaps more intense than anything they've felt before because there's no longer any filter. Emotions on the physical plane are like sipping from a drinking fountain while emotions on the astral plane are like drinking from a fire hose. Initial astral projections are often filled with strong fear because the experience is so new and very similar to dying. After one becomes used to astral projection and no longer experiences as much fear, the next most common emotion is strong sexual desire or arousal. The seeker will want to have sex with somebody, perhaps anybody they can find.

Beginning astral projectors will likely find themselves on one of the lower subplanes of the astral plane although usually not in the "hell"-like lowest realms. That is because they're often just beginning their spiritual Path. After people work on themselves spiritually, a process which discards many of the lower vibration particles in their emotional body, they'll be able to experience the higher realms of the astral plane.

When a baby is born into the physical plane, it needs to learn how to walk and coordinate itself. Beginning astral projectors face similar issues when they first become aware on the astral plane. For example, people may be conscious on the astral plane but not able to see anything. They have to open their astral eyes and do so without returning to physical consciousness and opening their physical eyes. Similarly, the process of moving one's astral limbs to separate them from their physical counterparts can also be a challenge.

On the astral plane one can fly; however, flying rarely comes automatically. Astral projectors may find it difficult to move where they desire and may seem to get caught in invisible astral currents (which may be real or imagined) like a balloon in the wind. After physical death, using the astral body will be easier; however, while still physically alive, it tends to take some adjustment. Experienced astral fliers can move at speeds nearly indistinguishable from teleporting.

While astral projecting, one can visit almost any location. Although it takes practice, it's simpler to focus on the vibration of where you want to go as opposed to trying to fly the whole way while navigating like you would in a private plane. This technique is also the fastest way to return to one's body. An astral projector can even visit other planets although that's more difficult since one needs to leave the astral atmosphere of our own planet, and the vibration of another planet is very different and harder to focus on. It's much easier to find an appropriate guide than try to do things like this on your own. Visiting the Moon is a bit easier, since it's related to the Earth, and the Moon is obvious in the sky. Because objects on higher planes have wider auras, the astral atmospheres of Earth and the Moon actually touch sometimes.

Astral objects can interpenetrate one another. An interesting thing one can do while outside the physical body is move body parts through each other, such as move one forearm through the other or insert a finger through the palm. This activity understandably feels very weird, as if one's astral body were made out of liquid. One can also move the astral body through other objects, such as go right through a closed window without breaking it and feel the glass moving through the interior of one's body. That also feels unusual and may make beginning astral projectors concerned the glass will break inside their body and injure them. One can feel pressure from touched objects, which is what allows things on the astral plane to still be picked up and manipulated; however, if proper pressure is applied then interpenetration happens.

The astral body is connected to the physical body by means of the silver cord. The silver cord connects the physical head to the back of the astral heart and feels like a wet umbilical cord. The silver cord is almost invisible and easy to miss since it can stretch indefinitely and isn't obstructed by astral objects. The silver cord can be followed back to one's body if a person wishes to stop astral projecting although an easier way to return is to simply focus on the vibration of the physical body. Upon physical death, the silver cord breaks. The silver cord, however, can't be severed as a way to cause death.

The astral plane has four dimensions of space. A beginning astral projector usually won't sense the fourth dimension right away. When one is aware of all four dimensions, it's a wonderfully indescribable state which makes one acutely aware of how limiting the physical plane is in comparison. One can only describe things as appearing *roomy* but still fundamentally the same. For example, feeling the fourth dimensional astral equivalent of your bedroom compared to the physical third dimensional version of it is analogous to being in your physical third dimensional room versus just looking at a picture of it. One of the more uncomfortable things one can experience related to astral projection is leaving the exquisite freedom of the fourth dimension and being forced back into three dimensions and a physical body.

While astral projecting you can visit other people. If a visited person is asleep at the time, his or her own astral body often appears to be hovering unconsciously, as if in a trance. While out of body you're very similar to a ghost, with the only difference being you still have a physical body to return to. If the other person is also astral projecting, you can interact with him or her in a way you both should remember upon returning to your bodies.

Deeply heightened opportunities for intimacy are available out of body. Hugging someone astrally compared to hugging physically is like hugging someone when you're both naked compared to hugging with clothes on. Astral sex is indescribably intense. A downside of astral sex is that an astral climax will often reflect in the physical body, awakening one from the astral state.

The physical world contains physical matter, such as rocks, which belong to the mineral kingdom of nature. Similarly, the astral world contains astral elemental essence, which belongs to the less evolved elemental kingdom. Astral elemental essence is very fluid and responsive to external stimuli, such as the emotions of people. There are great reservoirs of positive and negative feelings on the astral plane where emotions people give off tend to collect. These collections can appear like beautiful artifacts or disgusting smog, depending on their nature. A number of Masters and other servants of our world dedicate themselves to helping cleanse and improve the vibration of the dirty parts of Earth's astral plane.

Although much more spiritual than the physical plane, the astral world is still one of the lower planes of the Universe, hence it's like the physical world where not everybody you meet is good. On the lower subplanes of the astral, one may encounter malicious entities who want to frighten you, steal vitality, or control you in other ways. Negative astral entities may be disembodied ghosts who are trying to stay in touch with the physical world, mischievous fairies, or even other astral projectors. Like all negatively behaving entities, such astral spirits shouldn't be hated or feared but rather recognized as fellow beings working through their current level of evolution.

The astral world is often called the plane of illusion because your feelings and desires strongly affect your experience. One can manifest scenery or even entities from their own feelings, hopes, or fears, which need to be discerned from the true astral environment. For example, an attacking monster may be a creation of one's fear, which disappears like a popped bubble once one realizes it's just an illusion or otherwise adjusts their inner state.

Because the astral plane is the world of illusion, a negative astral entity may make itself appear like something fearsome in an attempt to scare you or may try to appear like a loved one or other respected person in order to gain your trust. Fortunately, such ruses are easy to see through, especially with a little experience. The astral plane is the world of emotion. Everything on that plane, including illusions, technically must be composed of emotion which understandably won't feel right. Negative entities may also attempt to flatter you to engage your ego. In this respect, astral entities are no different from negative entities on the physical plane.

Astral projection can be frightening to the beginner because the experience itself is so intense. In addition, one might encounter negative entities or be worried they might encounter them. The best way to handle potential fear is to know that you're never alone in life's journey, whether in or out of body. If you're intentionally astral projecting, it's recommended that you ask for guidance from your Guardian Angel or other positive beings, just as you would before any other meditation. If you spontaneously have an out-of-body experience, mentally ask for protection, and trust that you've been heard even if it doesn't seem like it.

Guidance isn't just something to invoke when one is worried but can be used to learn on the astral plane in general. For example, astral projectors might be able to encounter or communicate with their Guardian Angel or other teachers. One can even find dead relatives that have passed on earlier although there are limitations with this. Those who have died within the past few days can be difficult to contact because they're still in the middle of their bardo transition to the astral plane. Similarly, those who have been dead for years can also be hard to contact because they've risen to a higher astral subplane that's harder to connect. They might even be above the astral plane altogether.

Visiting the astral plane can be beneficial to one's spiritual growth and offer special opportunities for service; however, one shouldn't focus on it to the detriment of physical life. Each of us incarnated in order to learn lessons only available on the physical plane, and to serve in ways best done on Earth. To use an analogy, if the higher planes and bodies are like mission control, then the physical plane and body is like the spaceship projected from it. Mission control is more comfortable; however, the spaceship is what actually accomplishes the mission.

13:
Spiritual Practices

"The more I learn about myself, the more I become a different person."
- Ashliegh Brillent

Once one becomes aware that spiritual realms and levels of consciousness exist, what follows is the long process of attaining them. A spiritual practice is any exercise or discipline one undertakes in order to evolve. There are many examples of spiritual practices, such as meditation, diet, faith, and various philosophies. Even concepts, such as studying, expressing love, and sexuality can be spiritual practices. The specific practices of learning, Oneness, and intimacy are covered in later chapters.

Spiritual practices frequently involve working in one area to cause change in another. For example, physical behavior like yoga can result in emotional peace. Similarly spiritual behavior like prayer can result in the physical benefit of lower blood pressure or improved health in general. One can also grow by directly focusing upon the area in question. For example, the best way to become a good painter is to spend time painting. Related activities, like reading about painting are certainly useful, but they can only assist to a certain extent. If one engages in a behavior enough, it becomes a habit and eventually an innate part of one's being.

Spiritual teachers frequently recommend establishing a daily practice. This habit ensures the activity is actually done. Being practiced at the same time every day in a regular schedule makes one get used to it faster. A daily practice also demonstrates one's commitment to spirituality as a way of life, as opposed to one doing spiritual things as an occasional hobby when convenient. However, as with everything else in life, there's the need to seek balance. One can go too far, even with a spiritual practice. Doing the same thing for too long results in one no longer growing and indicates lack of newness and change. The most successful people focus on their ultimate goal. Although they may engage in practices, they don't let themselves be defined or get distracted by them. For example, if they seek money, their main focus will be on actually getting out and earning it as opposed to just doing meditations to attract it. In other words, faithfully do a practice for as long as you're benefiting from it but also know when one has served its purpose and it's time to move on to other things.

Are spiritual practices necessary in order to evolve? Ultimately, the answer is no, where evolution can still happen without them. Spiritual practices are only useful if one wants to grow faster. We can allow the Divine River of which we are all a part to eventually carry us to the ocean, or we can row forward with the current or Divine Will in order to reach the ocean faster. Spirituality is the journey, and the process should be enjoyed. There's no need to rush to the top of the mountain, which ultimately will never happen because there are always additional levels of growth. The human experience, and even Mastery and Enlightenment, is just one state of consciousness among many that we go through.

Any spiritual practice should be done for the right reasons. Practices are frequently challenging and require discipline. However, they are best done out of appreciation instead of forced and are best done out of love for the new result instead of dislike of one's current state. Technically, a practice means one is working toward something they don't have. That can imply one doesn't like the way they are now, which is a subtle form of hate. Zen author Alan Watts summarized this warning with the quotation, "Self improvement is a dangerous form of vanity."

Not all spiritual practices people engage in are beneficial. There are certainly a number of unusual or even harmful activities people get involved with that have little benefit to their growth beyond them eventually learning that such a path isn't the best way to grow. Ultimately, validity or success of a practice can be measured in how well it is applied in your day to day life. Does it make you better in any way, such as nicer, calmer, or stronger? The same concept applies to any spiritual insight or revelation one may receive. Deep secrets about the Universe are interesting, but unless they can benefit yourself or others, they're basically just trivia.

Meditation

"First you are in the light, then the light is in you, then you and the light become one!"
- Shirley MacLaine

Meditation is probably the most common spiritual practice. Human lives are too often filled with physical activity, emotional turmoil, and mental chatter, leaving little or no room for spiritual considerations. Meditation allows one to stop continually running around and to become quiet, which allows one's inner voice to be heard. In typical meditation, one focuses upon a particular object, like a candle flame or crystal ball, or a particular concept, like peace or God. This exercises one's ability to stay focused and avoid external distractions. One gently refocuses attention on the subject at hand should his/her attention wander. Hence, proper meditation is about actively tuning in and focusing, not passively tuning out and disconnecting from the world. One might think those who meditate aren't accomplishing anything useful; however, nothing could be further from the truth. Inactivity on the physical plane can mean one is more active on higher spiritual planes, which have greater opportunities for service.

Meditation can lead to higher states of consciousness. Samadhi (Sanskrit for "integrated wholeness" and sometimes called Cosmic Consciousness) is one of the highest states one can experience in the physical body. Samadhi can be described as there no longer being a dualistic separation between the individual and the object of their meditation. They're truly one with it or even one with the Universe as a whole. Samadhi is an utterly still state of one-pointed consciousness and pure awareness. It transcends the consciousness of the physical, emotional, and mental planes of personality and touches the higher spiritual planes.

Centering is a meditation exercise that clears the consciousness and brings awareness back into oneself, which creates a space for deeper meditations or other spiritual disciplines. For example, it's hard to receive intuitive or psychic impressions when one's consciousness is wrapped up in thoughts and emotions about external issues. Centering exercises usually involve one focusing upon the heart area and breath while breathing in peacefulness and breathing out restless energy.

Grounding is a meditation exercise that connects individuals with the earth and their physical body. This practice keeps them physically alert but doesn't disconnect them from the potential of receiving higher influences. Grounding can be considered similar to an electrical ground, allowing energy to flow, making both receiving and sending easier. Grounding exercises usually involve sending energy down from the root chakra or soles of the feet into the earth. They can also involve connecting with the heavens in addition to connecting with the earth, creating a balance.

Yoga is meditation that is combined with physical postures and movements. The term yoga is Sanskrit for "yoking" or "joining." In other words, yoga means union with Spirit. Properly done yoga fully engages one on all levels, physical as well as mental and spiritual. Although some yoga is little more than exercise, even standard exercise can put one in a meditative state and result in inner benefits due to increased health. Physical practices also are effective because we're currently incarnated in physical bodies and should take advantage of the opportunities they offer while we have them. Advanced forms of yoga can cause psychic awakening or other very real effects. These are considered secret knowledge and not shared publicly to ensure the ignorant don't hurt themselves or otherwise misuse the results.

Martial arts can be considered similar to yoga since it's also a discipline involving the body. When it is practiced properly, it involves other levels as well. Martial arts have a practical benefit in self-defense and increased confidence, which can be useful in today's world. Another benefit of martial arts is it takes the aggressive or competitive instinct that many of us have and channels it productively, transmuting it instead of just trying to starve it out.

Philosophy

"If you wish to reach the stage of enjoying everything, then seek enjoyment in nothing."
- Saint John

The various attitudes one can hold form a major category of spiritual practices. The philosophy of spirituality can be interesting in its own right and yields excellent subjects for meditation. However, ultimately the effectiveness of having any philosophy is determined by whether one is able to actually follow and live it. Below are a few major spiritual concepts.

Here and now: The philosophy of being here and now is simple to describe but challenging to practice. It means staying real and focused on what is actually before one in the present moment. Many continually regret the past or worry about the future, forgetting that consciousness exists in an eternal moment of now. Being here now doesn't mean avoiding consideration of the past or future. Rather, it means being able to do so in a healthy fashion from a centered consciousness.

Non-attachment: Attachment is when individuals try to focus on or maintain a particular concept of themselves; often, this is motivated by fear or ego. All earthly states are temporary; ultimately, nothing is permanent beyond the essence of Spirit. Hence, attachments are inherently false or illusions, and trying to maintain them eventually results in stress or suffering. This causes one to react negatively in certain circumstances, primarily when one's desires aren't being met. For example, an attachment to always being right makes individuals upset when they're wrong, so they attempt to cover it up, explain it away, or find some other place they can reinforce their ego and make themselves feel better. Non-attachment is a state where one accepts whatever comes in life, is content with being nothing beyond their spiritual essence, and isn't wrapped up in the eternal striving that so many do. Non-attachment doesn't mean laziness but rather being able to work without attachment to the results. Complete non-attachment includes not even being attached to whether one is embodying non-attachment.

Surrender: Surrender or letting go is a process leading to non-attachment. It means releasing all the desires, fears, and attachments one might have. Letting go doesn't mean pushing away things that you love or prefer, but it does mean not being addicted to whether or not you have them. Letting go may be difficult, but it results in true freedom and liberation. Complete surrender includes letting go of even the desire to let go. Surrender can be summarized with the classic quotation, "If you love something, set it free. If it comes back to you, it's yours. If not, it never was."

Virtue: Even a simple virtue can be a philosophy if one values it. Developing a virtue can be a spiritual practice where the virtue can be meditated upon or simply applied in everyday life. There are many virtues that the most evolved are able to embody. However, just like standard talents, people tend to focus on or specialize in certain areas.

Most virtues are related to discipline, love, clarity, or appreciation and can be divided into four main categories. These four categories are aligned with the four classical elements: 1) discipline is Earth or physical; 2) love is Water or emotional; 3) clarity is Air or mental; and 4) appreciation is Fire or spiritual. Each category can be applied to oneself or practiced in relation to others. Some virtues have a balance and need to not be overdone. For example, assertiveness is a virtue as long as one doesn't become aggressive or dismissive toward others. Both assertiveness and humility can be forms of self-love. A lack of assertiveness implies low self-esteem; however, a lack of humility also implies low self-esteem since one is trying to compensate by inflating his/her ego. The following table summarizes the categories of virtues and gives examples of each type.

Virtues		
	Within Self	**Toward Others**
Discipline (Earth)	patience, diligence, perseverance, focus, purity, serenity	reliability, responsibility, loyalty, service
Love (Water)	confidence, assertiveness, contentment, humility	tolerance, gentleness, consideration, kindness, compassion, charity
Clarity (Air)	alertness, awareness, intelligence, wisdom, detachment	integrity, discernment, honesty, openness, acceptance
Appreciation (Fire)	enthusiasm, optimism, curiosity, hope, courage	thankfulness, gratitude, respectfulness, faith, reverence, devotion

Purity

*"A monk asked Zen Master Joshu, 'To be holy - what is it like?' Joshu replied, 'To dump a mountain of sh*t on a clean plain.' In Zen language that means if we do not divide the world into 'holy' and 'unholy,' there is nothing to stain it."*
- Dick Sutphen

Purity is the state of being free of both internal and external negative influences and results from the practice of refining oneself. Even physical purity or cleanliness is beneficial because a clean body or environment results in being surrounded by clean energy, which helps facilitate spiritual awakening.

Physical purity includes avoiding addicting substances, such as alcohol, tobacco, and drugs, or even caffeine and sugar if seriously abused. Such substances can deaden higher influences or even make people do things they regret later. Drugs can also unnaturally open psychic senses and keep them forced open and tuned into lower energies whether one likes it or not. A strong addiction to a physical substance can also result in a negative withdrawal experience after death. One can no longer fulfill a physical craving since one no longer has a body, but the desire is still present and much stronger since one has transitioned to the astral world of emotion.

Purity should be balanced and not taken to extreme levels. Appreciation of purity should not degenerate into dislike of impurity. There is always imperfection in the physical world. Excessive dislike of impurity may fill one with negativity, which is impure. A mistake some seekers make is to focus on an outer discipline, ignoring the spiritual qualities the discipline is supposed to bring forth. For example, they may be strictly celibate or militantly vegetarian with their desire to avoid things being as strong as any hedonist's desire to indulge. Ultimately, purity is more of an inner attitude than anything one does or doesn't do externally. Purity should be a tool used to lead one to spirituality, as opposed to an end in itself.

Innocence is a type of purity, and is often an underestimated virtue. Innocence means being gentle, optimistic, and open minded to new ideas and concepts. This is opposed to letting life experiences make one act skeptical, cynical, or overly cautious. Innocence in this context doesn't mean living a sheltered life and missing out on opportunities to learn and grow or having a lack of experience which may cause one to blindly make a big mistake. Proper innocence is being able to combine wisdom and street smarts with a sweet and childlike attitude. Innocence is also inherently humble, which is the origin of the verse in the Christian Bible: "Unless you change and become like little children, you will never enter the kingdom of heaven" (Matthew 18:3).

Vegetarianism

"You are what you eat."
- Victor Lindlahr

Vegetarianism is the practice of not eating animal flesh. There are many different degrees of vegetarianism, ranging from just cutting red meat out of one's diet to excluding all animal products and only eating raw plant-based foods. There are also different levels of commitment. One may strictly avoid eating meat at all costs or only do so occasionally.

Vegetarianism is an extension of the practice of having a good diet in general. Nutrition has a major effect on health. Taking the right vitamins and minerals through food or supplements can greatly benefit how one feels. Similarly, many diseases or other maladies are caused by a simple lack of something in the body where the body isn't receiving it in the first place or is unable to properly digest or absorb it.

There are a number of good reasons to be vegetarian. Vegetarianism has less impact on the environment because it takes less land, water, and energy to produce an equivalent amount of food through growing crops than raising animals. The unpleasant condition in which many animals are kept, and the suffering they endure while being raised and slaughtered has a negative effect upon those subsequently eating their flesh. Fear and pain can be stored in an animal's body, acting as astral attachments that enter our bodies when we consume the meat. There can even be a small amount of negative karma for being part of the demand for flesh products, which results in the mistreatment of animals.

Although vegetarianism is recommended, it is important not to enter it haphazardly or force it before one is ready. Vegetarianism needs to be practiced properly to ensure the individual is getting enough protein, iron, and other minerals. Although many people could benefit from the lighter energy of vegetarian food, some spiritual seekers are so disconnected from the world that they can actually benefit from the grounding effect of meat. In addition, although vegetarianism avoids killing animals, people shouldn't think they're morally superior just because they are vegetarian. The vegetarian still kills plants, which have life force, too. Plants at least are from an earlier kingdom of nature that lacks a nervous system; hence, they don't have the same capacity for suffering. One is always killing something when eating. In fact, just walking around can result in one inadvertently stepping on insects. We can, however, minimize the degree of our impact or the amount of suffering we cause and avoid killing intentionally.

Even spiritual Masters occasionally eat meat. Tenzin Gyatso the 14th Dalai Lama is vegetarian at his home in Dharamsala but not always while traveling abroad. Once during a lecture he was asked about the virtues of the vegetarian lifestyle. Rather than take a strict stance, the Dalai Lama mentioned that he decided to be vegetarian every other day. As with all things, balance is good.

Hunting animals may seem morally negative; however, it isn't as bad as one might think, especially if one hunts for food as opposed to only cutting off the head for a trophy. Seeking out an animal in the wild has the benefit of putting one in touch with nature, which today many are too disconnected from. Hunting is no worse than picking up meat at the market or ordering it in a restaurant. In fact, it could be considered better because one knows where the meat is coming from, as opposed to letting someone else do the killing for them.

Faith

"Pray to God but keep rowing to shore."
- Russian proverb

Faith is directing trust, belief, or devotion toward something, usually a higher power. Faith is frequently underestimated since it may not seem logical and isn't directly related to personal growth. That, however, is what makes faith one of the strongest and most powerful practices. Faith is beyond intellect. The focus outside self helps one transcend pride and egotism, which are some of the biggest challenges to overcome on the spiritual Path. There is genuine wisdom behind and benefit in concepts, such as "putting faith in Christ," to use an example from religion. Of course, it's best to put one's faith in a higher concept, as opposed to Earthly organizations or individuals, some of which are less virtuous and likely to take advantage of blind devotion.

Prayer is an expression of faith where one makes a request of a higher power. Prayer can be on a personal level as when one merely asks for something for himself/herself or on a selfless level where one seeks something to benefit others or the world. Similarly, one can pray individually or in combination with others. Group prayer has the potential to be much more powerful. One benefit in prayer is that it's a clear statement of desire and intent, which is an important step toward building a fulfilling life.

Prayer is like planting a seed where its effect rarely happens immediately. The Universe, along with the Angels, Masters, and other Spirits that help administrate the Universe, don't necessarily give you exactly what you ask. They're more likely to give you what you need as opposed to what you want. However, when you connect with higher powers, they can ensure things turn out all right in the end—at least when you look back on the situation later (even if it may not have seemed like you were being helped at the time).

Faith can be summarized by the classic poem "Footprints in the Sand" by Mary Stevenson, which depicts a seeker walking with God where two sets of footprints could be seen. However, during challenging life periods, he felt separate from God because during those times, he only noticed one set of footprints. Of course, that was when God was carrying him. He was never alone even if it seemed like it.

14:
Learning and Teaching

"A poor disciple utilizes a teacher's influence. A fair disciple admires a teacher's kindness. A good disciple grows strong under a teacher's discipline."
- Gasan

No treatise on evolution would be complete without covering the methods by which we evolve. One of the primary ways to evolve is via learning. We can learn through experience or even just grow over time as we age, but one of the most effective ways to learn is by intentionally becoming a student and studying the subject of interest. The other side of the coin of being a student is having something else play the role of a teacher. One of the most significant relationships is that between student and teacher or between disciple and master. Both roles are interrelated. Often you can learn about being a student by considering what it's like to be a teacher, and vice versa.

Being a Student

One of the most effective ways to evolve is through an eager willingness to learn. Not everyone has a desire to learn. This aspiration is a quality that one may develop over time. In other words, one learns how to learn! Just as not all children in school want to study, so is it the case that not all adults want to continue their education. It doesn't matter if you're currently ignorant or even if your current understanding of things is wrong because continuing to learn will eventually overcome or correct both.

There is benefit to casually or informally learning; however, to seriously evolve requires a more focused and disciplined approach.

If you want to reach the top of a mountain, it's necessary to choose a particular path and actually follow it up. In spirituality this concept is represented by one finding his/her spiritual path by following a philosophy or religion, getting involved with a small or large spiritual group or otherwise establishing a plan of action. A religion is basically just a spiritual philosophy combined with a particular set of practices or a cultural framework. Some people appreciate the ritual and benefits of fellowship that comes from an established religion or path while others are more independent. It's simplest to follow an existing path, but occasionally one creates a completely new path, either just for himself/herself or as a benefit to others. Even when following an existing path, no two people follow it the same way. Every person must walk his/her own path, so ultimately every person's path is unique.

Most people follow established religions, and most follow the religion of the area they grow up in. Many don't bother to question whether the religion of their parents is the right one for them. In other words, they take what they're given and don't bother to consider whether other religions or philosophies might be better. That isn't necessarily unevolved or limited thinking on their part. Again, a religion is spiritual philosophy with a particular cultural framework wrapped around it. Most religions cover the same truths in different ways and aren't fundamentally better or worse than one another. Hence, it makes sense for people to be drawn to the religion that represents the environment in which they've grown up if for no other reason than it's what they're most familiar and comfortable with.

Although there are no bad spiritual paths, it is important to realize that different paths can take one up different mountains, can be faster or slower than others, and can result in different experiences along the way. Hence it's important to know exactly what your objective in spirituality is and to keep aware of what you're doing along the way (even if as you become wiser, you update your objective or methods).

Following a path takes discipline and it's important for a student to have a commitment to it and appreciation of it. At the same time, one doesn't want to become too fanatical about or otherwise attached to his/her path. Spiritual growth is like taking a path to a friend's house. The goal is to get to your friend; it doesn't matter which way you take to get there. You certainly won't be worrying about which way is *right* once you're there. In other words, let your path help you but don't become too defined by it. John F. Kennedy said, "Ask not what your country can do for you - ask what you can do for your country." That wisdom, of course, applies to service in general, not just patriotism to one's country. However, on a spiritual path the reverse can also be true. Start by asking how a particular path can help you. Sometimes you've learned all you can from a path, meaning it's time to leave it for your next step. Beyond that, ultimately everything is within you. Remember that a spiritual path is just a way to awaken the potentials that are already present.

One of the deepest ways of being a student is to become a disciple of a master or guru. Just as one of the safest ways to climb a mountain is to get a guide who has already climbed that mountain to accompany you, one of the most effective ways to learn is by facilitating a relationship with someone who already knows. The master and disciple relationship is a time-honored tradition going back thousands of years. The concept isn't just limited to spiritual learning but applies in many other areas, such as being an apprentice on a job or even a child in a family. You can learn on your own, but there's no replacement for the continuous feedback you can get from a relationship with a teacher. If your teacher has other students, being in an environment with fellow seekers also has benefits.

Learning from a master isn't easy and requires a lot of discipline. Being a disciple is not for everyone; it's only one form of being a student. It's natural for a student to disagree with or sometimes even dislike his/her teacher. Like a rebellious teenager, it's part of their growth process whether they're learning to be more independent or learning to overcome their combative separateness. Some teachers even encourage this to ensure the student doesn't become unhealthily attached to them. If one does challenge the teacher, it should of course be done respectfully. It may feel unpleasant to have a teacher criticize you, but it's even harder to be a teacher yourself with the continuous integrity and receiving input from all directions. Usually the teacher does know best even if at the time it doesn't seem like it to the student.

How do you know when you've found the right teacher or path? Finding your path or your teacher is like choosing a romantic partner. In other words, the path should just feel right and have an excitement or good chemistry to it. Like romantic partners, a path that's wonderful to you may seem repulsive to others, and vice versa.

Similarly, the wrong path for you should intuitively feel wrong even if it seems attractive on the outside. Ultimately there are no bad paths or teachers; however, some, like potential partners, are less evolved or have coarser energy.

Cults

"In the entire history of man, no one has ever been brainwashed and realized, or believed, that he had been brainwashed. Those who have been brainwashed will usually passionately defend their manipulators, claiming they have simply been 'shown the light,' or have been transformed in miraculous ways."
- Dick Sutphen

In seeking their path, students should be wary of teachers or groups that don't have their best interests in mind. Some groups are cults. The word cult (Latin for "worship") simply refers to a religious group and its belief systems. Modern interpretation of the term *cult* tends to be negative. To many a cult is a group with obsessive devotion to a person or thing that doesn't deserve such veneration and conducts weird practices. A cult isn't a yes or no distinction where some groups have some but not all characteristics of one. Founders and members of cults, whether intentionally malicious or unaware of what they're doing, seldom think they're a cult or a part of one. The ways of a cult aren't limited to spiritual groups but can also be found in certain clubs, communes, and even some business or government organizations. A cult can be identified by five primary characteristics: uniqueness, isolation, hierarchy, tension, and negativity.

1) Uniqueness: Cults think they're special and believe that only they have the highest truth, and all other groups are wrong or otherwise less evolved. For example, only they have a true Master guiding them, only they can prevent the world from being blown up through their prayers, and so on. Some good groups really do accomplish significant things, but they recognize other groups serve in similar ways, or at least they're humble about what they do.

2) Isolation: Cults disconnect themselves from other groups or society. For example, there's a focus on special retreats or even people living in an isolated environment where having friends or contact outside the group is discouraged or forbidden. This allows them to ingrain their message without exposure to other points of view. They tend to have a specific set of beliefs they expect everyone to follow with little room for diversity of opinion. In addition, cults often make heavy use of special jargon, unique practices, and secret information, which are also ways of making a distinction between themselves and others. Good groups may be unique, but they maintain a connection with and acceptance of the world they want to benefit.

3) Hierarchy: Cults have a definite hierarchy and are usually centered on a charismatic figure or original founder. There's a distinct boundary between being a member of the group and not being a member of it. There's also a focus on recruiting new people to be a part of their group and getting members to preach or convert other people to it. Cults also want to hold onto their members. They try to keep people from leaving or else dislike former members when they do leave. Cults ask for more than they return, and they have an unhealthy focus on money and trying to acquire it. They also make decisions for their members or maintain control in other ways. Good groups have humble leaders who encourage you to do what's best for yourself, even if that means taking a different path. Although all groups have financial needs, a good group's focus is more on how they can use money for positive causes.

4) Tension: Cults maintain an element of emotional tension within them. Cults often use techniques to cause stress in their members or recruits, such as making people do rigorous exercises, have restricted diets, have little time of their own, or have a general sense of uncertainty about their own or the group's future. Cults, like an abusive romantic partner, may alternate between very positive and very negative feedback, keeping members confused about where they stand. Good groups are a peaceful influence and are more laid back with respect to their specific practices.

5) Negativity: Cults focus more on the negative or on things not to do. For example, don't miss prayer, don't get angry, don't listen to rock music, don't feel guilty, and many other rules. Cults often focus their attention on a visible or invisible enemy that threatens their existence or goals. Examples of enemies include the *devil* himself, prophesized negative events like *Earth Changes* or alien invasions, the government, other people or groups with different views, or even anybody who's not yet a member of their group. Good groups may face challenges, but they're more positive and open-minded in their approach to them.

Cults sometimes have access to the most accurate information or the highest wisdom, but they interpret it badly or wrap it in a negative framework. Other cults start out well, but later their leaders or members fall into common traps, such as a certain amount of success causing them to think they're the best group in the world or the only ones with access to the truth. Although there certainly have been and will be great spiritual leaders in the world, spiritual wisdom usually manifests through multiple equivalent channels, like trees in a forest as opposed to relying on one single tree.

The most successful world religions (where *successful* means those with the most members) are not necessarily ones that have the best practices or the truest philosophy but rather tend to be those that are able to attract and retain the most people. For example, many religions (even those that are full of love in other areas) disagree with the practice of homosexuality. A likely reason (even if they say something else) is that homosexual relationships don't result in pregnancy and birth and therefore more children likely to get indoctrinated into that religion. In other words, powerful religions tend to be ones that encourage their members to have large families or to otherwise direct their sexual energies to the group instead of themselves. Paradoxically, in today's more open-minded world, a philosophy that said they weren't the only or even the best path and recommended people shop around would likely become very popular.

Another characteristic that defines long lasting religions or philosophies is adaptability or a willingness to change. Charles Darwin said, "It is not the strongest of the species that survive, nor the most intelligent, but the one most responsive to change." However, organizations often resist change. That which is unwilling to change becomes rigid and inflexible and eventually dies and gets replaced by something more effective in meeting modern needs. This leads to the concept of a lifecycle for a religion or group, which tends to happen in five stages: inspiration, expansion, maintenance, rigidity, and dissolution.

1) Inspiration: A prophet or other truly inspired person or small group comes up with something new. Their ideas begin to be shared. Any organization surrounding them is non-existent or small. Their message is likely to be resisted by older and more rigid organizations.

2) Expansion: The new philosophy fulfills a need for many people and starts expanding and becoming popular. There is a well-defined group of people that follow the philosophy and an increasingly large organization with layers of administration surrounding it.

3) Maintenance: The original founders of the philosophy die or are otherwise no longer involved. They attempt to pass on ownership of the organization to trusted successors. Dogmas and rituals get established as a way of maintaining and preserving the message. The concepts originally introduced are no longer new, and other organizations appear that present a similar message or incorporate it into their own teachings.

4) Rigidity: Eventually, people forget the original message of the founders and focus more on the dogma or established practices, or they get bogged down in trying to correctly interpret the original philosophy. They attempt to hold onto the successes they had in the past or even disagree with other organizations that have alternative approaches to that area.

5) Dissolution: Finally, the philosophy starts dying out as most people give their attention to newer philosophies that better reflect the current reality or take into account the current culture.

A similar lifecycle concept applies to other areas. For example, consider businesses (especially in high technology areas, such as computers) that start out being innovative, become successful, expand into large corporations, get bogged down in their own bureaucracy, and finally get replaced by new innovative small companies that better reflect the changed times. The concept can even be seen in nature. A tree sprouts, grows, becomes big, eventually rots from within, falls down, and then becomes life for new seedlings.

The organization lifecycle may seem negative, but it's really quite natural, and should be embraced more than resisted. Philosophies and organizations shouldn't attempt to exist forever (they can try, but they'll eventually fail) but rather fulfill their original purpose and then move on, allowing their "children" (or new philosophies based on them) to grow in turn. The same applies to our own lives; we shouldn't be afraid of death and try to live forever but rather focus on having a fulfilling life in the time we're here.

The most inclusive philosophies are those which can be deduced independently. For example, extraterrestrials on another planet that have never had contact with Earth could come up with something very similar. Any system that requires faith in or blessings from a particular individual (as opposed to embracing their teachings, which could be learned from anybody else at that level of wisdom) excludes the vast majority of the Universe.

The most inclusive philosophies also tend to observe, appreciate nature, or develop science which is ultimately a description of nature. In the past, there has been a gap between science and spirituality. As science continually expands, more and more things that at one time seemed mystical, are being explained. In actuality, everything is science for science and spirit are one.

Being a Teacher

"The mediocre teacher tells. The good teacher explains. The superior teacher demonstrates. The great teacher inspires."
- William Arthur Ward

Eventually students learn enough to be able to assist others with one or more subjects. The students then have the opportunity to pass on knowledge or wisdom and become teachers themselves. Being a teacher, whether of spiritual wisdom in a temple or worldly knowledge in a school, is one of the most positive ways to serve and one of the most honorable things one can do (even if modern society frequently doesn't seem to respect the role of the teacher).

Teachers can take many forms. Some are teachers and don't know it as they teach through example. Sometimes the most irritating or even unevolved people make the best teachers because they let us know what we need to work on in our lives, or they at least act as bad examples not to follow. Individuals are the most common type of teachers; however, groups can also be teachers. For example, powerful countries should take care in how they act and present themselves to the world because developing countries look to them as examples.

If you choose to become a teacher, it's important to do so for the right reasons. Some teach just to enhance their ego and make themselves feel important while other teachers frankly don't know what they're talking about. At the same time, some people are very wise and would make great teachers but don't think they are worthy enough. If you are concerned about whether you'd be a good teacher or if your pride would get in the way as one, that humility and self-reflection is probably enough to ensure you will be a good teacher.

As a teacher, it's also very important to continue learning on your own. Never think you know it all because then you stop growing yourself and become stagnant. Spirituality is like an endless ladder. No matter how high you climb, there's always another rung, and beings on that rung who can teach you how to climb up to that level. Eventually, we become the Masters who have taught us in the past. The ladder analogy not only shows that everyone is a student but also shows that everyone has the potential to be a teacher. There are always people on rungs below us that can be helped up to our rung.

Teachers are sometimes inspired by higher sources where they consciously or subconsciously channel higher wisdom. In this sense the teacher is acting as a student as well as a teacher by passing on what they receive to others. Thus a teacher's success is sometimes not entirely due to his/her own talent but rather partly due to the source working through them. Similarly, the most successful teachers and other leaders are supported and assisted in many ways by their families or staffs. Sometimes we wonder how famous people accomplish what they do when in fact what we're seeing is the result of a group effort.

Good teachers don't want students to follow them but rather want students to find their own paths. The primary goal in teaching is not to make your students be copies of yourself. Instead you want to inspire students to awaken their own true selves, which may or may not be like you. Don't tell students what to think or spoon feed them facts and philosophies. Instead, teach them to think for themselves. Like good parents with their children, good teachers want their students to eventually equal them in knowledge and ability or, better yet, to surpass them. A teacher can be the "giant upon whose shoulders their students stand," allowing the students, if not socicty as a whole, to see farther than they ever could before.

Teachers specialize in certain areas. For example, if you're a teacher of a certain type of yoga, you may be excellent at sharing that particular path. You should, however, recognize that the path you teach isn't necessarily the only path and isn't the best path for every person. Sometimes teachers hope the entire world will listen to them and visualize the utopia that would come about if only that would happen; however, their message or at least the way it's presented is only beneficial for certain types of students. For example, intellectually-oriented people and emotionally-oriented people respond better to different styles of teaching. Hence, it's preferable for teachers to have their students come to them when they are ready, as opposed to a teacher trying to acquire students.

Teaching often seems like a thankless job. If you want glory or acclaim or even credit or appreciation, don't expect teaching to bring it to you. Don't expect everyone to immediately accept your message. Some may not understand it for many lifetimes. Students may seem slow or forgetful, but that's understandable since it takes a long time to learn something new. Just keep trying and trust that the right people will listen, and the people who are listening are benefiting even if it doesn't seem like it. Teaching is less about immediate results and more like planting seeds in a garden.

Teachers sometimes get rejected or receive negative reactions from either their direct students or from others who hear about their teachings. Often the greater the teacher, the more radical the message and, therefore, the more hostile the reaction. The most recent lifetime of Jesus was a perfect example of this. Initial non-receptivity is also expected since the teacher is of course teaching those who don't understand yet.

On the other hand, teachers are often highly revered or even considered gurus whether or not they want to be seen that way. Like it or not, being a teacher also means being a leader. Hence, it's even more important for a teacher to demonstrate spiritual virtues than the average person because so many are looking to them as an example of how to live their lives. For example, as a popular teacher it's good to be unattached to physical things since people are likely to want to give you gifts. If you're greedy or materialistic, your students are being taught to be the same, regardless of what you're trying to teach them. Good spiritual teachers don't order other people around unless they want their students to behave the same way when they become teachers. Of course, sometimes the best virtue for a teacher to demonstrate is humility and self-awareness of personal faults and foibles. If a teacher wants his/her students to equal him/her, that teacher must emphasize their similarities as opposed to differences.

Even when one is an excellent teacher, things don't necessarily stay that way. A teacher should constantly stay vigilant to ego or attachment, which can result in a moral downfall. For example, a teacher may produce an inspired book, which makes him/her famous. If the teacher grows attached to that fame, once the book is no longer new, he/she may produce other works that aren't inspired but are merely attempts to remain in the spotlight. Sometimes teachers are revered for their wisdom; however, their information eventually becomes outdated, and other people or even their own students equal or surpass them. The teacher needs to have enough humility to accept that and adjust to the new reality and not become jealous or try to discredit the newcomers.

Secret Knowledge

"Never teach a pig to fly. It wastes your time, and it annoys the pig."
- David Hatcher

Secret knowledge refers to information that individuals or groups refuse to share with others, at least until those others prove themselves worthy to receive it. In popular culture, secret spiritual knowledge implies cults or secret societies knowing metaphysical truths that they keep hidden from those who aren't a member of their group. One might think all knowledge should be public; indeed, in most cases that's true. However, secrecy is preferred or even necessary in certain situations. Secret knowledge consists of five types: protection of others, protection of understanding, protection from misuse, protection of self, and protection of community.

1) Protection of others: Some practices are potentially dangerous and can cause harm if done incorrectly or when one isn't properly prepared for them. For example, certain methods of yoga (especially techniques related to kundalini) have a very real effect on one's physical and spiritual bodies. Therefore, they should not be practiced or even learned about until one is ready. Other techniques for growth, such as practicing celibacy, need to be done in the proper environment in order to do more good than harm. These practices are like putting a knife or instructions for building a bomb into a child's hands. Such things should be prevented or kept private until one is mature enough to use them wisely.

2) Protection of understanding: Spirituality often presents deep philosophical truths which can be misunderstood by the masses. For example, the concept that we are all one can be corrupted into trying to force everyone to be the same way or be like a particular individual. The concept that everything is ultimately good can be corrupted into thinking it allows you to do whatever evil things you want. This is part of the reason behind the Biblical verse, "Do not give what is holy to dogs, and do not throw your pearls before swine, or they will trample them under their feet, and turn and tear you to pieces." (Matthew 7:6). In this context "dogs and swine" isn't meant to be an insult but merely refers to people with less understanding. Students shouldn't be exposed to quantum mechanics until they've learned basic science.

3) Protection from misuse: Some information needs to be understood in context and can easily be distorted by the unintentionally ignorant or those intentionally seeking to further their own agendas. For example, metaphysics can present histories of the planet, which includes those of races, religions, or other groups, and the positive or negative things they've done or what has happened to them, along with how such events fit into the larger picture of our collective evolution. Unfortunately, people can take such information and try to prove certain ethnicities or philosophies are better or worse than others. Merely having spiritual information doesn't make one a good or wise person. In fact, it can lead one astray if one is exposed to it at the wrong time. For example, Nazi leaders during the Third Reich had access to lots of occult information, but it was filtered through their own biases and did more harm than good.

4) Protection of self: Some practices or beliefs aren't harmful in and of themselves but need to be kept secret because they're unpopular with the majority, the government, or the dominant religion of the area. Especially in past centuries, metaphysical groups needed to remain secret to avoid being branded as heretics and persecuted or even killed. Fortunately, such biases, although still present in many people and locations, are becoming less common and less severe. Pagans and other groups that have suffered in the past are increasingly accepted and are able to openly practice in many parts of the world.

5) Protection of community: Finally, groups can keep information or practices secret as a way to differentiate their members from others, which can be used to create or emphasize a particular community. This can be done for good or bad reasons. Positively, a well defined community is one way to learn about unity, similar to the way nice uniforms help a team's morale. Having oneness within a branch allows people to better understand the rest of the tree. Families certainly have no reason to share private family secrets or history with strangers. On the other hand, some groups do exist entirely or partly as a way to make their leaders and members feel better about themselves with all the maturity of a boys' secret club that says "no girls allowed" on the door. Even when a group has integrity, some people seek to join it for the wrong reasons because they want to know things others don't as a way of enhancing their ego or because they lack their own direction and seek it outside themselves.

15:
Mastering the Personality

"Irrespective of different philosophies, the most important thing is to have a tamed and disciplined mind and a warm heart."
- Tenzin Gyatso, the 14th Dalai Lama

Physical existence is only a small part of the vastness covered by our souls, Spirits, and Divinity itself. However, that doesn't change the fact that incarnated life is what we're experiencing at this time. In life we express through our personalities, which are the combination of our bodies, emotions, and minds. Hence, a major part of growth for us at this time is refining and evolving our bodies, emotions, and minds. This work may seem less glamorous than deep philosophy or metaphysical phenomena. Nevertheless, mastering the personality is the foundation upon which all higher experiences are based.

The personality should be a reflection of the soul because ultimately, it's a projection of the soul into the lower planes in order to grow. The lower planes are a pale imitation of the higher. By definition, higher planes have additional dimensions and forms of expression not possible at lower levels. Although the personality can never fully express the soul, in the ideal case nothing exists in the personality that doesn't also exist in the soul. The personality can reflect the soul just as a two dimensional photograph can accurately portray a three dimensional realm. All souls and Spirits are inherently good. Personalities who express evil are merely inaccurate representations of their pure souls where their lower bodies contain distortions and haven't been brought under control yet.

Body, emotions, mind, and even soul and Spirit are ultimately just different vibrations of the whole; ideally our different aspects all work together. That means we shouldn't focus too much on dividing ourselves into boxes or disregarding the interrelatedness of all things. Nevertheless, the aspects that compose our personality are still useful to consider individually and are more readily understandable that way.

On the most common path of evolution, a being or species first evolves the physical body, then the emotions, the mind, and finally the spirit. People do, however, sometimes grow in a different order or specialize in different areas. They also tend to go through phases as to which aspect of their personality they focus on. Children and teenagers tend to express more through their emotions. In contrast, as one gets older, the mental bodies become more used. On a wider scale a particular incarnation may focus on one aspect or another. There's nothing wrong with the different approaches, as long as one maintains at least some balance.

For example, some dislike the coldness of intellect and prefer to live in their feelings. Artistic or sensitive people tend to evolve their emotions and intuitions before their minds, resulting in a kind and spiritual person who's not necessarily intelligent. They may make what seems like bad choices or dumb mistakes until their intelligence catches up with the rest of their otherwise evolved state. Other people dislike the lack of control in emotion and prefer the clarity of intellect, such as scientists who focus on developing their minds. Some intellectual people have completely neglected anything spiritual and have repressed anything emotional. This state is potentially dangerous since it results in the growth of technology and power without the balance of emotional maturity or wisdom to use them properly.

Mastering Emotion

"Anybody can become angry - that is easy, but to be angry with the right person, and to the right degree, and at the right time, and for the right purpose, and in the right way - that is not within everybody's power and is not easy."
- Aristotle

An emotion is a reaction to external stimulus. Emotion is similar to the physical sense of touch; however, emotion also interprets the stimulus, such as judging it to be positive or negative. There are a wide variety of emotions or ways things can be interpreted, some more healthy than others. A master of emotion has awakened and cultivated four qualities, which are described below. These qualities tend to be developed in sequence during one's evolutionary journey.

Emotional Qualities		
#	**Quality**	**Explanation**
1	Variety	Capable of expressing different emotions
2	Appropriateness	Emotions are appropriate for the situation
3	Control	Emotions are calm and controlled
4	Refinement	Emotions are more positive than negative

Individuals begin their emotional evolution by being able to express emotions in the first place, and then they move on to being able to express a wide variety of emotions. Unevolved souls aren't yet capable of expressing certain emotions. For example, they may see someone in pain and not feel compassion, or not be capable of feeling love beyond a muddy sense of desire.

Most people on Earth at this time are able to feel all emotions, but many don't express them appropriately. They may be capable of expressing anger, but it erupts uncontrolled and for unnecessary reasons. For example, one gets mad at a car that cuts them off on the road, even though such an action only delays them a few seconds. Their anger is misplaced. The other driver may have any number of good reasons to cut them off, such as they honestly didn't see them, or they're speeding to the airport so they don't miss their plane. Even if other people are openly rude, it may be something that shouldn't be taken personally, such as they had a very bad day or just got fired from their job. Emotions can also linger longer than needed, which can cause individuals to take out their frustrations on other people who had nothing to do with the original source.

Emotions are a sensory tool that lets people know how they feel about something. Although very useful, individuals shouldn't let emotions run wild or control them, any more than a horse should be out of control of its rider. Emotions are also an individual experience; hence, emotion has a measure of self-absorption to it. Too much emotional expression is a form of narcissism, like overindulgence of any other type.

Although emotional control is a very good thing, often when people attempt to control or calm their emotions, they're actually just repressing them. The emotion is still there, just not being expressed outwardly. Repression isn't necessarily bad, as long as it's done consciously and in moderation. Certainly, it's useful to keep anger in check so people doesn't do something they regret later. However, repression is very different from having a better emotion to begin with.

Because emotions are reactions, they are inherently uncontrolled. Once present, they shouldn't be judged but rather observed and noted because they often have valuable messages to teach us about ourselves. Because emotions come from within, the best way to control emotion is to work to change one's inner nature so one reacts differently initially. Calm and controlled emotions are the outer effect seen when one is already evolved. Emotions are not something one should try to manipulate in order to become evolved in the first place.

Proper control of emotion doesn't mean a lack of emotions. We still want to be able to express them when appropriate. Emotions, such as anger, aren't negative in and of themselves and only become harmful when expressed improperly or when one loses control. Even spiritual Masters get angry; however, they do so for meaningful and unselfish reasons. For example, Jesus expressed anger or at least took assertive action when He overturned the tables of the moneychangers in the temple. (Matthew 21:12)

Developing emotional qualities like compassion takes hundreds of lifetimes. We should be patient with ourselves during our own growth process and patient with young souls still expressing negatively. If we show them kindness, our example helps them grow slightly, like sun or rain on a seedling. To use an cxample from Jesus again, there is wisdom in His philosophy of "turning the other cheek" (Matthew 5:39), assuming it's done not out of meekness, fear of standing up for oneself, or out of pride because one thinks such an action implies they're spiritually superior.

Negative emotions are associated with superficial things on the lower planes; thus, such emotions are like fireworks: they erupt quickly in response to external events and go out just as quickly when those events change. A negative emotion rarely lasts long. If it does, it's only because the fire is continuously given new fuel, which generates a different series of emotions in response to the same stimulus. Higher emotions are associated with more permanent or spiritual qualities in something, making them much more powerful and longer lasting. Deep feelings from the heart or Spirit are like stars in the night sky. They slowly rise and shift slowly, only seeming to fade if something else rises to block them.

The changeable nature of emotion means that a good way to make a difficult decision, such as whether to buy something expensive, is to wait overnight. If the inclination to buy it was an impulsive emotion, it should dissipate over time. If, however, the inclination to buy the item is based on a more meaningful feeling, it should remain just as strong if not grow stronger.

Once emotions are expressed appropriately and in a calm and controlled manner, the emotions one generates naturally become more positive. This results in an inner happiness which is almost always present because it isn't dependent upon external things that may or may not conform to one's demands. This optimistic viewpoint isn't wishful thinking or a denial of negative situations but a reality once one sees the spiritual purpose and perfection in everything.

Most people are happy when something good happens to them and are sad or angry when something bad happens. In other words, we tend to let things outside of ourselves control our attitudes. In the ideal situation, emotions come from within and are more a conscious choice as opposed to something dictated by external circumstances. The individual experience of emotion transmutes into the altruistic feeling of love, which is ultimately a level beyond emotion altogether.

Classifying Emotion

"Praise and blame, gain and loss, pleasure and sorrow come and go like the wind. To be happy, rest like a giant tree in the midst of them all."
- Buddha.

There are many types of emotions; however, most fall into several categories. Knowing the general categories is useful for individuals to better understand their own emotions and those of others. All emotions include either liking or disliking something. In addition, emotions either exist within oneself or are directed toward others. Emotions within oneself are concerned with something that's happening now, something that happened in the past, or something that one expects might happen in the future.

Emotions within self			
	Past	**Present**	**Future**
Like	Appreciation, Nostalgia, Pride, Gladness	Happiness, Contentment, Joy, Euphoria, Ecstasy	Excitement, Enthusiasm, Confidence, Hope
Mixed	Sadness, Grief	Ambivalence, Surprise, Loneliness	Anticipation, Suspense, Desire
Dislike	Disgust, Horror, Embarrassment, Guilt, Regret, Remorse, Resentment	Hate, Anger, Annoyance, Depression, Boredom, Apathy	Fear, Dread, Anxiety, Worry, Nervousness, Paranoia

Although most emotions are either positive or negative, some are mixed and have both positive and negative aspects to them. For example, sadness of a pet dying is dislike of their death combined with loving the pet. General desire is liking something combined with dislike for not having it already. Other emotions, such as surprise, may be positive, negative, or both depending on what caused the surprise.

Embarrassment is disliking something you've done in the past combined with wanting to forget about it or cover it up. Guilt is disliking something you've done in the past combined with wanting to punish yourself for it. Guilt isn't as negative an emotion as it's frequently portrayed since at least one is feeling remorse for something negative he/she has done and wants to put things back in balance. The negativity comes when one allows others to make him/her feel guilty or responds to the guilt by punishing himself/herself as opposed to actually making amends for whatever he/she did wrong.

Emotions that cover dislike of the present are primarily distinguished by how one reacts to that which is disliked. Hate is dislike of something combined with wanting that which is disliked to go away. Anger is dislike combined with wanting to force change in the situation, such as by violently fighting it. Disgust is dislike combined with wanting to get away from that which is disliked but not out of fear. Apathy is dislike combined with not caring about changing anything. Depression or boredom is dislike of one's condition combined with not knowing how to change it. Loneliness is a type of depression; however, it's really a mixed emotion since the depression is combined with like of others and wanting to connect with them.

Fear is dislike of the future and not wanting something to happen. One is never afraid about something unpleasant actually happening now or about something that happened in the past but only about something that might happen in the future. A typical example is a horror movie where characters (or viewers) are afraid that a monster will jump out at them. Then a monster jumps out at them, and then one is afraid that the monster will catch them. If the monster catches them, then they are afraid that the monster will eat them. If the monster does eat them, then they go to the afterlife and are no longer afraid.

Most "like" emotions are positive; however, this isn't always the case. For example, the emotion of pride means liking yourself or appreciating things that you've done, such as looking back with pride upon a job well done. If individuals feel pride when they don't deserve it or take their feelings of pride to an extreme, then it becomes unhealthy.

The other main category of emotions is emotions directed toward others. One way of subdividing such emotions is based on whether the like or dislike is directed toward someone perceived to be in a superior, equal, or inferior position to himself/herself. This classification was originally described in "The Science of the Emotions," by Bhagavan Das, which was later summarized by Katherine Browning in "An epitome of the Science of the Emotions."

Emotions directed toward others			
	Inferior	**Equal**	**Superior**
Like	Compassion, Sympathy, Tenderness, Pity	Love, Affection, Empathy	Respect, Reverence, Adoration, Devotion, Worship, Lust
Dislike	Arrogance, Contempt, Scorn, Condescension, Schadenfreude	Hostility, Enmity	Fear, Envy, Jealousy

Note "superior" and "inferior" as used here only refer to the context that generated the emotion and not one's general level of evolution. For example, if you dislike the power your boss has over you at work, your fearful feelings are based on his/her superior position to you on the job, even if your boss is mean and an unevolved young soul. However, if you dislike your boss because you believe him/her to be stupid, then your contemptuous feelings are based on what you perceive as their inferior position to you intellectually.

Again, most "like" emotions directed toward others are positive although this isn't always the case. For example, lust is liking or desiring someone or something; however, the emotion is less controlled, and the reasons behind it are selfish and motivated by self-gratification.

The "Dislike of Superior" category can be extended to include all the emotions in the "Dislike of Future" category in the previous table. One may have any of the fear-based emotions about a superior, out of concern that they may do something in the future you dislike. Jealousy is a type of fear that's a combination of desire for what you don't have, hate that someone else has it, and fear that they're better than you.

Schadenfreude (German for "harm" and "joy") is getting satisfaction from someone else's misfortune. This emotion involves a slight amount of positive *like;* however, what's being appreciated is very negative. Schadenfreude is rooted in sadistic egotism, a situation in which one lazily improves his/her position because others fail. Because we know it's negative, schadenfreude is often kept within and not openly expressed. However, many of us experience it in certain circumstances, especially if we think the other person deserves his/her misfortune. For example, movies frequently climax with a villain experiencing misfortune or getting killed by the heroes after committing evil acts, which is designed for the audience to appreciate.

The movie "Monsters, Inc." (2001) is a cute yet insightful example of the power of positive emotions when compared to negative emotions. The film featured various monsters intentionally scaring children. The children's screams would generate power for the monsters' city. Eventually, the monsters realized that if a child laughs, it would generate much more power than a scream.

Mastering the Mind

"You may control a mad elephant;
You may shut the mouth of the bear and the tiger;
Ride the lion and play with the cobra;
By alchemy you may earn your livelihood;
You may wander through the universe incognito;
Make vassals of the gods; be ever youthful;
You may walk on water and live in fire:
But control of the mind is better and more difficult."
- Thayumanavar

All thought is analysis and comparison. That ability allows us to learn and make decisions. Unlike emotion, thoughts aren't easily divided into categories. Certainly, there are many types of positive or negative things that can be thought about, but thought itself is inherently neutral. The mind is a tool, which should be used by the Spirit and consciousness when appropriate. Like a tool, the mind may be rusty, overused, or used for the wrong purpose. A mentally-evolved person has awakened and developed four qualities, which are described below: intelligence, creativity, flexibility, and control. As with emotional qualities, these mental qualities tend to be developed in sequence during one's evolutionary journey.

Mental Qualities		
#	**Quality**	**Explanation**
1	Intelligence	Express raw smarts, and apply such talents in life
2	Creativity	Imagine new concepts, and contemplate abstractly
3	Flexibility	Think for oneself, and consider many points of view
4	Control	Calm the mind, keeping attention focused on a subject

Standard intelligence is one aspect of mental development and probably the most readily understood. Intelligence is raw intellectual ability, such as memory, reason, calculation, and the ability to think concretely in general. Intelligence here also means having applied such abilities in life. Having a good memory is a talent but so is using whatever capacity one has to memorize something. When used properly, intelligence can assist one with their spiritual Path as much as emotional virtues. However, intelligence on its own is neither good nor bad. Evil people may be highly intelligent intellectually even though they're severely lacking in other areas.

Intelligence can be grown even though we're often taught to think otherwise. Frequently, early in school students get divided into *smart kids* and *dumb kids*. Unfortunately, the *dumb kids* may forever think they have to stay that way, so they stop trying to grow. Like physical muscles, the mind can be strengthened and should be regularly exercised in order to stay healthy and effective. Learning and acquiring new skills is a lifelong process and shouldn't be something that ends once one no longer has to go to school.

The next level beyond static intelligence is being able to think abstractly instead of just concretely. Abstract thought includes philosophy, as well as creativity and being able to invent new ideas on your own. Metaphysically, concrete thought or raw intelligence is expressed on the lower subplanes of the mental plane while abstract or truly creative thought is expressed on the higher Causal subplanes of the mental plane. Abstract thinking not only develops the mind, but it's also inherently non-material, which helps lead one to spiritual thoughts and experiences.

A mentally-evolved person is able to conceive of a wide variety of thoughts. Although the mind is a very useful tool, its conclusions can be wrong. One should remain flexible and not put too much emphasis on intellect. One should also be able to think dynamically in a conscious fashion in the present moment as opposed to just automatically regurgitating facts or preformed opinions. Finally, one should think independently instead of just responding to external stimulus. For example, passively watching television, which merely presents things to the senses, doesn't exercise the mind nearly as much as reading a book does because you visualize things yourself. Reading, in turn, doesn't exercise the mind as much as writing and thinking up new content yourself.

One manifestation of a lack of mental evolution is being stuck on a particular line of thought. For example, those who are prejudiced and refuse to or are unable to consider things outside their worldview have what appear like warts on their mental bodies, which is a manifestation of their rigid thought forms. Having an unwanted song stuck in one's head is a lack of mental control similar to how staying angry is a lack of emotional control. In both cases one has something appear in their consciousness that they didn't choose, and that stays in spite of their wants.

A mentally-evolved person is able to stay focused on a particular line of thought; however, in this case the focus is disciplined and a conscious decision. Proper mental focus is very different from obsessing or worrying about a particular subject, which is an uncontrollable urge usually rooted in emotion.

Often people "live in their heads" where their minds are continually babbling about something, flitting from one thing to another like a butterfly in a windstorm. At home, they may think about what they have to do at work, or at work, they think about what they'd rather be doing at home. They find activities like meditation very challenging. To them, meditation feels like trying to tell a hyper puppy to sit still. Attempts to quiet the mind immediately result in the mind babbling about how uncomfortable it is trying to be quiet or trying to decide whether or not it's quiet yet!

Calming the mind can be very challenging. Most find it takes much more effort than calming emotions, and many never attempt trying to calm the mind to begin with. It takes years if not lifetimes for the mind to become peaceful like calm reflecting water. Once the mind does evolve into Spirit's efficient servant instead of being the master of one's consciousness, one can more easily experience intuition and other spiritual energies beyond the personality.

The best way to control the mind is to keep it focused on something. Trying to blank the mind and keep it empty is nearly impossible, at least in the earlier stages of development. Besides, people shouldn't turn off their minds any more than they should turn off their emotions. Inner idleness is one of the main causes of the mind finding something random to think about, such as internal tapes from the past to replay. By keeping the mind focused, it stays out of trouble and develops discipline. The mind can't wander when it's actively involved with something constructive. Similarly, on the emotional front, one can't act in anger when their heart is already expressing love.

Some think being completely intellectual is a good thing and consider a lack of emotion to be like a badge of honor. That, however, is the wrong approach to growth. Too much focus on the mind or rather too little focus on feelings can result in coldness and detachment, which is just as bad, if not worse, than turbulent emotions. It's important to be able to be sensitive to different vibrations and to be able to respond appropriately to them, instead of numbly cutting oneself off from everything. For extreme examples, a calculating person completely lacking in compassion has arguably strayed from the path more than a hotheaded person full of rage. Lack of emotion can also make people so detached and apathetic that they no longer have any desire to grow, resulting in eons of stagnation.

One can never be fully mental or completely non-emotional, like a member of the Vulcan race from the Star Trek science fiction television series, because one still chooses to do things in life. Any physical action taken is because one wanted it to happen. Wanting something is a subtle emotion even if one chose it due to logical reasons. A desire for a lack of desire is still a desire. Metaphysically, the astral plane of emotion lies between the physical plane of action and the mental plane of thought. As a result, any physical action taken due to thought had that impulse transmitted through the astral plane; hence, it has an emotional component to it.

Spiritual Struggle

"If I were offered a perfect life, I would be tempted, but I would decline, for a perfect life would teach me nothing."
- R. Milner

Evolution and growth means changing from one state of being to another. For this change to happen effort must be expended; otherwise, one would already be in the other state to begin with. Change is a process and struggle, which frequently involves growing pains or making mistakes along the way.

Spiritual growth (and life in general, for that matter) is frequently very difficult. It's challenging to determine which practices are effective, which groups are beneficial, and what to believe in general. It's also challenging to find enough time to devote to a spiritual Path or to actually have the discipline to follow one even when a clear Path is available. None of this should be considered a bad thing because the journey is what causes evolution in the first place. If growth were easy, there'd be little reason to do it.

We often learn more from our mistakes than our successes, for a hard lesson is better remembered than an easy one. Sometimes we learn just as much from bad paths or even lifetimes as we do from good ones. One may look upon the negative things people are involved with or on all the other inefficiencies in the world and wonder why things are like that or whether they can be changed. What they fail to realize is that on a deep level the world is already perfect and is proceeding exactly as it should. For example, dead end jobs or annoying aspects of work help us learn discipline and strength, death makes us appreciate life and not take our loved ones for granted, and so on.

If you solve a maze too quickly, you should be doing harder mazes. Similarly, if life is too easy, we're not learning anything from it. This doesn't mean one has to experience negativity or should seek it out in order to grow, of course. One can acquire wisdom first hand, or one can learn it from reading about someone else's experience. However, even the latter case has some amount of struggle because one is spending energy to read and contemplate their experience.

To solve a maze, one takes their best guess and tries out passages. Frequently, he/she takes wrong passages that lead to dead ends, which then force him/her to backtrack. The dead end paths may seem negative since taking them moves one farther away from the goal. However, ultimately dead ends move one toward the goal because one is learning which paths not to take. Life is the same. The seemingly bad choices individuals, groups, or nations take are all part of the natural growth process.

In fact, evolution requires dead ends. Physical evolution is full of species that have become extinct for one reason or another. Corporate evolution is full of failed companies that didn't have viable business plans or didn't adapt to changing markets. Evolution in life is full of all the crazy choices we made in our youth or in past lives in order to arrive at the wisdom we have today.

Evolution of a group occasionally requires sacrifice from members of the group. For example, it sometimes takes a deadly accident for a dangerous crosswalk to get a traffic light or for a new safety regulation to get made into law. The development of new technologies, such as air and space travel, results in accidents as we learn what works and what doesn't. A person's body is a group of many cells. Sometimes evolution requires the death of certain cells while a person is growing up, such as when a child loses baby teeth to make way for permanent teeth or even when a child skins a knee while playing.

People are frequently critical of themselves or others for the mistakes they make because they consider mistakes to be a bad thing as opposed to part of the Divine like everything else. Individuals may feel guilty, thinking they could be or should be Ascended Masters already instead of trapped on Earth. We're not *fallen Angels,* and we're not disconnected from our true selves, other than being projections of our souls which always happens during physical incarnation. We certainly didn't do anything wrong to get to where we are now. What we are doing is continually awakening into being stronger and truer expressions of ourselves.

Spiritual growth, whether individual or planetary, is a gradual process. Although many writings refer to discrete stages of evolution, much of that is just a way to try to classify our long journey in order to more readily understand it. Enlightenment is more something that one emerges into or that sprouts and grows like a tree, as opposed to a yes or no condition where one suddenly transitions from one state to the other. Becoming spiritual is like becoming an adult; it partly happens naturally, and there's no need to rush.

Spiritual Mistakes

"The only man who makes no mistakes is the man who never does anything."
- Theodore Roosevelt

In general, when working on yourself or working toward a goal, it's best to focus on what to do, as opposed to what not to do. It's better to give attention to role models than villains, and focus on the positive instead of the negative. Nevertheless, there is some value in considering mistakes one can make on the spiritual Path. A mistake in this context means something that results in direct or indirect harm to oneself or another, something which makes the growth process take longer than it would otherwise, or something that in general is deluded or inefficient. Although mistakes, like other challenges, can help one grow, that doesn't mean one should seek to make mistakes or intentionally commit them, of course.

Most of the ways people *stray from the Path* are related to one of six different areas: pride, individuality, attachment, indulgence, structure, and assessment. Each area can either be focused upon too much or too little, resulting in twelve possible spiritual mistakes. Most problems are caused by being too extreme in one direction or another. As in many other areas of life, balance is good to avoid such problems.

Spiritual Mistakes		
	Too much	**Too little**
Pride	"Obviously, my path is the way to change the world."	"What are you asking me for? I can't change anything."
Individuality	"My growth, my feelings, my life—get get out of my way."	"Shut up! You're wrong and you're rocking the boat."
Attachment	"Aaah, if we don't stop global warming now, we're all going to die!"	"Who cares about the world? It's all an illusion anyway."
Indulgence	"What's on TV?"	"Sex is for inferior people who can't control their desires."
Structure	"This is the way things have always been done properly."	"What should I do today? I haven't done this before."
Assessment	"I am two incarnations away from becoming a Master."	"One can't ever understand the Universe, so why try?"

Pride (too much): Seekers may focus too much on their own importance, whether or not they actually have significance. Pride can also be directed to one's spiritual Path, making one a proselytizer who thinks his/her way is the best way or the only way. Both cult leaders and their followers consider their path to be the best, not just for themselves personally, but for everyone else as well. Even good groups and genuinely evolved people can fall into the trap of pride because they actually are on a quality Path. Because of this, they want others to benefit as well, and get annoyed when other people don't change or don't want to change.

Pride (too little): Seekers may deemphasize themselves and their abilities too much, often out of a misguided attempt to avoid seeming arrogant. Many people suffer from low self esteem and don't realize how much they can benefit or even change the world if they'd only bother to try. There are many people who are wise, but they keep their wisdom to themselves because they mistakenly think stepping forward is a manifestation of egotism.

Individuality (too much): Seekers may become self-absorbed and make everything about themselves. Growth is all about how they themselves are becoming better. True spiritual evolution is more about the world than the individual and more about serving others and the One Being of which we're all a part than enhancing self. This mistake also covers general selfishness, such as being mean or seeking personal power.

Individuality (too little): A seeker may become too conformant or too involved with whatever groups to which they subscribe. This mistake also covers unhealthy selflessness where one serves to such a degree he/she ignores his/her own needs or allows himself/herself to be taken advantage of. Such behavior is a corruption of Oneness where the individual either tries to deny his/her own needs or gets his/her needs denied by the group's hierarchy. Cults fall into this category, as does general crowd consciousness where people follow whatever the group says or does and adopt the group's positions without thinking for themselves. Examples of crowds that people often blindly follow are local sports teams, their ethnicity or culture, the nation they live within, and the dominant religion of their region.

Attachment (too much): A seeker may become too attached to the world. For example, they obsessively worry about "Earth Changes," contemplate whether Earth will ascend to spiritual levels or destroy itself, watch the news continually, or get too involved in various good vs. evil dualities. Even if their worries are accurate or their causes are valid, they let themselves become defined by and unhealthily driven by their concerns. They forget that our planet is a classroom and has been in many positive and negative situations over its lifetime. We shouldn't let the fact we're currently expressing through human bodies control us or make us forget that ultimately everything is an illusory drama designed to help us grow.

Attachment (too little): A seeker sometimes withdraws from the world, often out of dislike of how challenging it is to change or deal with. We're in physical human bodies in order to be human or at least to help evolve what it means to be human. It's up to us whether we take advantage of the unique growth opportunities being here offers. Some people are so detached they do nothing but continually meditate. Although there are exceptions that do useful work on higher planes, some such people are about as useful as bags of rice, or even worse because at least a bag of rice can be eaten! If people withdraw too much, the world may change for the worse around them and eventually catch up to where they're hiding. In extreme cases, it's possible for seekers to detach from the world to such a degree that they stop incarnating since they no longer have any desire for rebirth. That, however, isn't Enlightenment but rather a stall in one's evolution that may last for eons before they finally crawl out of their hole and decide to start growing again.

Indulgence (too much): This mistake is obvious and covers people not trying to grow in the first place or being lazy about their growth. They may be too indulgent with pleasures or distractions or continually focusing on entertaining themselves. Taken to an extreme, this can harm others because expending too many resources damages the environment. These are significant times in Earth's history, and everyone should take advantage of the unique opportunity offered by being alive at this time. One positive side to indulgence is that a person sometimes learns faster because of it, even if it's only due to hitting "rock bottom" sooner.

Indulgence (too little): Seekers may become too ascetic and be too hard on themselves or others. Although asceticism can be useful behavior from which one learns discipline and non-attachment, it shouldn't be considered a spiritual Path in and of itself. The way to overcome material attachment isn't necessarily by getting rid of material things because that just creates a new attachment to being non-material. Instead of renouncing material things as evil, we should learn to do positive things with what we have or make the most efficient use of what's available. Examples of over-asceticism are those who never have any fun, parents who are overly critical of their children, or those who refuse to allow medical science or anybody else to help them because they don't want to appear weak. This mistake also covers trying to grow too fast. Working too hard results in burnout, like a butterfly prematurely forced out of its cocoon which could result in its being crippled or killed. Slow and steady is more effective, especially since spiritual growth shouldn't be considered a race. We are all One. Often over years or lifetimes individuals or groups of people leapfrog each other with first one seeming more evolved and then the other.

Structure (too much): Like dried branches, seekers may allow themselves to become static and rigid. They may embrace tradition to such a degree they get stuck in a rut, stop growing, fail to understand changing conditions, or take advantage of new opportunities. This state can be motivated by too much pride about one's Path; however, more often seekers gets stuck because they honestly think their Path is the best way or because they're afraid to let go of the old and familiar.

Structure (too little): Novelty is good; however, it can be taken too far if people reject the old for the new to such an extreme that they "throw the baby out with the bathwater" or aren't careful about the new beliefs they embrace. Some seekers are like butterflies, constantly flitting from one thing to another, never having the attention span to follow one Path for too long. Spiritual evolution is like a growing tree since we build on ourselves and our past successes. Spiritual growth is 10% inspiration of new ideas and 90% perspiration as seekers work to implement existing ideas. Some novelty seekers look forward to a revolution where the existing social order gets overthrown. This is often motivated by not wanting to have to deal with their existing problems or address their inner weaknesses. This state can be motivated by too much pride or individuality when individuals seek to make themselves look good by doing something that nobody has done before. This mistake also covers having too much personal freedom with no goals and nothing providing discipline.

Assessment (too much): Seekers may think they know it all. That is impossible because no one can fully understand the mystery of the eternal. Seekers may also focus too much on classifying themselves or others into levels or castes. Attempting to classify spirituality can be beneficial; for example, much of this book does that. However, one should always remember that the infinite depth, changeableness, and diversity of people can never be totally described. This mistake sometimes affects seekers who are highly developed in general and have mastered the techniques of their chosen Path. Because they understand their particular Path, they think it's the right way or the only way. That behavior isn't pride as much as individuals honestly thinking that they have a complete view of the Universe.

Assessment (too little): Seekers may believe that it's impossible to know the mysteries of the Universe and feel they shouldn't try. However, a seeker who appreciates mystery should realize that things only get more mysterious the more you learn and discover. Seekers may also think everyone's equal and any attempt to classify levels of growth in people is discriminatory. Such a philosophy can be problematic because it can make one less tolerant of those who aren't spiritual yet. Like different grades in school, there are many different ages of souls and types of souls inhabiting human bodies. That, however, doesn't mean it's easily determined who's more advanced since true evolution isn't connected to outer characteristics or even things like accomplishments. Even on the same evolutionary level, people specialize in different areas, like being a math professor or an English professor. A seeker who appreciates equality should realize that the best path to true equality is to understand the Divine essence we all share and then allow everyone to work on filling in the outer areas where they still need to grow.

16: Love and Oneness

"Love is the answer..."
- Karen Millar

We are all One and the meaning of life is to express and experience love. The preceding sentence is the primary message in this chapter and, for that matter, the main message of the entire book. All the technical information about spirituality and metaphysics is ultimately a way of leading the seeker to that conclusion. If you remember that core message, the rest of the book could be considered unnecessary. If you're still reading, that means you're interested in details, examples, or supporting data about love.

What is love? Simply stated, love is consciously liking something. Love means one has concern for something or wants to be more connected with it, which results in their consciousness expanding around it. The opposite of love is hate where one dislikes something and emotionally withdraws from it. Love is inherently an expansive vibration while hate is a contractive vibration. Hence, love means expanding consciousness. Since evolution is about expanding consciousness, it follows that love is the primary key to evolution.

Love is very different from simple desire. Love is conscious, comes from within, and often involves self-sacrifice where one is willing to put effort into helping or caring for that which is loved. Desire is more subconscious, is aroused by external stimuli, and tends to be motivated by selfish pleasure. Love is usually directed toward other living beings or focuses on the non-physical qualities of something. Desire is usually about something physical, and if desire concerns other people it tends to objectify them. You love a cherished pet but you desire chocolate. Love and desire are frequently present at the same time; for example, love for a romantic partner is mixed with lustful desire.

True love is unconditional. It's easy to express love for things we already like or love those people who agree with us; however, that's no more than external input conforming to desires. Good parents love their children just as much even when they're naughty. This concept can be found in many sources. For example, the Bible has the verses: "In that way, you will be acting as true children of your Father in heaven. For he gives his sunlight to both the evil and the good, and he sends rain on the just and on the unjust, too. If you love only those who love you, what good is that? Even corrupt tax collectors do that much." (Matthew 5:45-46)

Unconditional love can be applied to oneself. When people value love, they often judge themselves too harshly when they don't love. In other words, they love themselves when they express love, and they dislike themselves when they find themselves expressing hate. However, one can unconditionally love even their hatred and appreciate the vibration of hate and the unpleasant experiences that result from it because of the unique learning process it provides us. If you find yourself in an unloving state, the first thing to do is love yourself for it. To be filled with love, you don't cast hatred out of your being as much as you love yourself the way you are, warts and all.

Loving hatred does not mean individuals don't work to improve themselves or the world. Parents who unconditionally love their children will still provide them with discipline when necessary. You can love hatred even while you work to overcome it or even fight it when there's no peaceful alternative.

Oneness

"We really are all one being. We are the universe manifesting as individuals."
- Deepak Chopra

Love goes hand in hand with the concept of Oneness. Oneness means seemingly separate things being connected into a larger whole. It's a macrocosmic view that sees us as forming a much larger being together instead of being separate from one other. Like love, Oneness is an expansion of consciousness; therefore, understanding, valuing, and experiencing Oneness is another primary key to spiritual growth. Oneness exists whether or not we're aware of it. We are all One, always have been and always will be. Evolution just means becoming more consciously aware of our inherent Oneness and acting to benefit the One instead of just our separate selves.

Practical examples of Oneness are trees forming a forest, stars forming a galaxy, cells forming a physical body, and people forming the human race. Common analogies used to depict Oneness are rays of the Sun, petals of a flower, and branches of a tree. For example, a ray is a distinct object; however, it was sent forth from the Sun and can't exist without it. Follow any two rays backwards, and they will eventually meet and merge together in the center of the Sun. Similarly a branch is a separate object, which was created by its tree; any two branches of that tree will eventually meet at the trunk.

Oneness and the connection of an individual being to the One are more readily apparent when considering plants. A plant has its roots embedded in the earth. The boundary between where the plant ends and the earth begins is indistinct and occurs gradually as the roots spread outward. The interconnectedness is even stronger with plants that have runner roots; a root from one plant can be followed some distance after which it sprouts up as another plant. For animals and humans, Oneness is a bit harder to grasp since we seem to have distinctly separate bodies which move around. Oneness is still present because on a spiritual level each creature can be considered a cell in the body of its species. The species as a whole has consciousness and is evolving, similar to how the individual beings within it are evolving.

There are many levels of Oneness. A person can experience Oneness within himself/herself, with a lover, within a family, with a spiritual soul group, with the world, or with the entire Universe. Many virtues start at home, and the same is true with Oneness. A person starts by making their body, emotions, thoughts, and Spirit consciously work together instead of being disconnected or behaving erratically. Oneness can be experienced with a close friend or a lover. Sexual union is one way of expressing Oneness on the physical plane. Oneness can also be cultivated within groups, such as families, spiritual organizations, or nations. Eventually one can experience oneness with the consciousness of the world and the Universe.

The different levels of Oneness are like branches on a tree. Consciousness starts in an individual leaf. Soon the leaf becomes aware of and connects with other leaves attached to the same twig. That cluster of leaves then becomes aware of other leaf clusters attached to the same branch. The branch becomes aware of nearby branches, and eventually a large branch becomes aware of the trunk. Finally, consciousness expands to encompass the entire tree and knows that everything is part of a greater organism. The concept of beings forming a larger being together is similar to fractals where a graphic image is composed of smaller copies of itself.

If an incarnated human is like an underwater plant, the human Spirit is like the water surrounding the plant with the human race being the entire lake. When a person becomes conscious of his/her own Spirit, they unavoidably feel connected with other Spirits. In other words, we are all cells in the body of a *Heavenly Man* or leaves on the tree of the human lifewave. On a higher level, all the different species are parts of the body of the planet on which they live. To use examples from the physical body, your unique function in the *Heavenly Man* may be as an ear or an elbow; you're much more effective when you can serve and be a part of the whole body instead of just doing things on your own.

The Universe, which by definition includes everything, is the ultimate concept of Oneness. Similarly God, by definition the ultimate Being, is the ultimate in conscious Oneness. One way of looking at God is as the consciousness of the entire Universe. Just as individual drops are part of the ocean so is everything in the Universe ultimately a part of God. This concept is sometimes expressed as "The One and the Many."

Communication is an important part of conscious Oneness. Communication allows the different parts of the One to be aware of and coordinate with each other. Conversely, non-communication is a form of separation. Individuals or groups frequently cut off communication with those with whom they disagree; however, all that does is allow false ideas about other people to fester and grow. Consider politics where those of a particular viewpoint usually consider those of other viewpoints to be wrong, so they rarely communicate with them except when trying to change them. For an extreme example, the beginning of war is often marked by the end of negotiation and a tendency to dehumanize those on the opposing side.

Oneness does not mean lack of disagreement or a seeming utopia where everyone believes the same thing, and there's never any debate. In fact just the opposite can be true. Increased interaction and communication often raises issues that wouldn't come up if people were unaware of each other. Marriage is an excellent example that shows both the importance of mature communication and how Oneness doesn't necessarily mean there's no conflict. Oneness means knowing how to handle conflict effectively and dealing with issues in an open manner that takes all sides into account.

The concept of Oneness sometimes causes apprehension because it can it seem like a person is giving up his/her power. Proper Oneness does not mean central control or blindly following the orders or some guru or government. Cults and tyrannies often preach that they're about Oneness because they want everyone to be the same. Such organizations are actually a form of separation because they push away those with alternate viewpoints or persecute those who don't obey their own rules.

Similarly, proper Oneness doesn't make you feel guilty about your individuality. (Many belief systems seem to involve restrictive *shoulds*—one should do this or should not do that.) Oneness doesn't deny your individuality but rather means recognizing the larger picture of which your individuality is a part. True Oneness feels very freeing because one is no longer trying to reinforce the ego or holding onto the illusion of the separate self. Oneness doesn't mean a person stops doing things to benefit himself/herself. Egocentric individuals ignore others and only focus on themselves; however, a soul who ignores his/her own needs is also misguided because in both cases part of the whole (whether others or the individual) is being disregarded.

Oneness means diversity. People not only can support different causes, but should. In a healthy tree, the branches point in different directions; in a healthy body, different organs serve different functions. Another good analogy for Oneness is pieces in a puzzle. Each piece is unique and plays a role that only it can fulfill in making the completed picture. The pieces separate aren't worth much, but as they align with each other, they produce something beautiful. A big part of evolution is not just focusing on our one little piece of the puzzle but being conscious of and able to consider the puzzle as a whole. Oneness isn't a lack of difference. Instead, Oneness is coming together in spite of our differences.

Since we grow into Oneness, that implies we're separate in earlier parts of our evolutionary journey. Hence, separateness is natural and shouldn't be disliked in ourselves or others. Disliking people who express separateness is like being angry with a child because he/she hasn't learned how to drive a car yet. We all grow up in the proper timing and at the proper rate. The separateness that we experience now isn't due to us falling from grace or forgetting our Oneness. That would imply guilt because we did something wrong in the past or that there's something wrong with us now. On a Universal level, the Divine intentionally projected itself, which resulted in the creation of young souls. However, that's as natural as parents having children or a gardener planting seeds and letting them grow.

Duality

"As long as one is in the position of 'choosing' to view life from either a dualistic or non-dualistic perspective, then the decision has already been made in favor of the dualistic perspective."
- Gerald Bryan

Duality is a form of separation. Duality means focusing on opposites in life. There are many types of dualities, such as good and evil, light and dark, right and wrong, love and hate, male and female, yin and yang, spiritual and physical, new and old, and birth and death. Duality frequently manifests as personally identifying with one of the polarities and disliking or otherwise excluding the other. In other words, duality means focusing on a part of the whole without remembering that everything is part of the whole. Duality is, of course, more common and apparent on lower planes; however, it rapidly becomes less significant and eventually ceases to exist on higher planes.

Non-duality is a unified view of opposites. However, it's much more than just a balance between them. For example, a non-dualistic view of good and evil isn't a simple blending of the two into a morally muddy position with both good and evil qualities. Rather non-duality sees the big picture behind good and evil and sees them both as expressions of the Divine, and as tools that allow us to grow or test our growth.

Since non-duality is all-inclusive, aspects of its wisdom can be expressed by certain self-referential statements. For example, hating hatred is still hate. Intolerance for those who are intolerant is still intolerance. Judging that judgment is bad is still a judgment. Complaining about people who complain is still complaining.

To be truly loving, one shouldn't dislike hate and try to avoid expressing it at all costs because it's "bad" but rather allow himself/herself to feel dislike of things. To be truly tolerant, one should be tolerant of people and philosophies they disagree with, which includes people who are intolerant. Intolerant people are merely younger souls in an earlier stage of evolution or may even be on a different branch that's equal but has a different focus than ours. To truly transcend judgment, people should not only avoid judging others or themselves too harshly when they make mistakes but also not judge people who make judgments in the first place.

Even dividing the world into duality and Oneness is a duality. Hence, if one *tries to be non-dualistic*, that effort is doomed from the beginning because it's already dividing the possible states of being into *dualistic* and *non-dualistic* and is judging *dualistic* as bad and *non-dualistic* as good. Achieving non-duality does not leave duality behind, but rather non-duality includes duality and all other potentials within it. Becoming non-dualistic isn't like becoming rich, which means one isn't poor anymore. Rather, becoming non-dualistic is like a crawling baby learning to walk; they still have the potential to crawl if they want.

Non-duality is challenging to truly understand and extremely difficult to actually apply in one's life. Advice on non-duality is like saying one can climb Mount Everest by putting one foot in front of the other. That's technically true; however, it takes a lot more training, planning, and effort to actually accomplish.

Perhaps the biggest duality and the one hardest to overcome is that between self and other. Normal consciousness has individuals experience themselves in a particular location in the Universe where they consider everything else in the Universe as outside of and not part of themselves. Ultimately, individual consciousness is an illusion, only a piece of the Universal consciousness. The Universal consciousness is always present; one just needs to awaken to it. Individual consciousness shouldn't be considered as something distinct from it; instead, it's a part of the Universal consciousness that's not fully conscious of itself yet.

Similarly, when individuals truly become non-dualistic and One with everything, they question the concept of free will. Free will implies that people make choices to determine their actions and can do so independently in a way that can't be predicted. This concept is opposed to predestination which states that things are guaranteed to happen in a particular way. If this is true, then on some level it's possible to predict exactly what will happen for the rest of time and/or some higher power predetermined exactly what will happen.

Free will means that when making choices, individuals choose based on their individual bit of consciousness. However, consider that any act of choosing is based on one or more reasons. If that's all that's involved in the decision, then it's really the reason making the choice, not the individual. When a being becomes truly One with all, there's no longer an individual consciousness or free will as we think of it. In other words, individual will has been replaced with Divine will.

Truly transcending free will only happens at very late stages of evolution after one is a Master. People shouldn't fall into the trap of thinking at some point that their will has turned into Divine will so they can tell others what to do. Similarly, as with Oneness itself, individuals shouldn't let others tell them to give up their power. Seekers may think their free will is bad and try to repress it, which can be taken advantage of by unevolved gurus who want control. Moving beyond individual consciousness and free will is best thought of as something that happens naturally after one is already a Master, as opposed to something that the seeker tries to do in order to become one.

Duality is natural and plays a necessary part in our evolution. Although duality eventually gets transcended, it shouldn't be treated as an evil influence. Duality is like living with parents – a very positive thing in a child's development even though we outgrow it. We can appreciate the old roles played in our past even as we grow up and embrace new levels of being.

The movie "The Dark Crystal" (1982) does a wonderful job depicting a journey into non-duality. In its story, excessive pride caused a race of beings to split into two new races, the evil Skeksis and the gentle Mystics. Each Skeksis had a corresponding Mystic with whom they were connected on all levels. In fact, they were so connected that if one were injured or killed, the other would be as well. At a special time of conjunction between the realm's three Suns, the Mystics and Skeksis met and aligned with each other and merged back into their original states. Good didn't defeat evil; instead, they combined together into a greater good.

Fellowship

"My religion is very simple. My religion is kindness."
- Tenzin Gyatso, the 14th Dalai Lama

Fellowship means connecting with others in a positive manner; hence, fellowship is a form of expressing love and Oneness. Interacting with others allows one to receive ideas and inspiration and to share insights. Common forms of fellowship include holding family or community gatherings and joining clubs or organizations with those of similar disposition. Spiritual seekers may join a traditional ashram, which allows them to grow in a special environment. More importantly, joining groups puts them in contact with others of like mind. Societies, such as the Freemasons and the Rosicrucian Order, act as spiritual schools; however, ultimately they're places of fellowship.

Service is doing something to benefit other people or groups or at least doing something beyond merely trying to advance one's individual interests. There are many forms of service and many areas where one can choose to assist. Ultimately, service is doing what needs to be done and not just those things you want to do. Frequently service is tinged with personal interests, for example, by serving in an area that you enjoy. There's nothing wrong with that because we each have our areas of talent where we can best help out.

Valuing and doing service is one of the best indicators of evolution. First, service means one is actually accomplishing something, as opposed to just thinking about things they'd like to do or wasting time in frivolous pursuits. Second, service implies one is no longer focused entirely on ego and instead is able to see the larger picture. Service may seem boring or even threatening to the lower self since one seems to be working for others instead of themselves. However, since we are all One, helping "others" is actually helping ourselves.

Of all the virtues one can have, perhaps the simplest and yet most significant is kindness. There are many possible talents one may cultivate but being nice to others is frequently underrated. Many can make themselves powerful or even wise, but one of the best signs of true Mastery is simply being kind to others. In relationships, the most important aspect of compatibility is whether the two people get along, which mainly means whether they're nice to each other. In this sense, kindness can be considered more important than talent or even spiritual attainment (although kindness is a spiritual quality in its own right).

When a group works together it can do much greater things than individuals can do. For example, to land a person on the Moon required thousands of people working together to finance the operation, build the spacecraft, and run Mission Control. Although most focus on the people who actually stepped on the Moon, they were the tip of a very big iceberg where everyone involved deserves credit. Even people not directly aware of the Moon mission helped make it happen by developing technology and being willing to share it with others.

Considering Oneness or the greater good helps prevent what's called The Tragedy of the Commons. The Tragedy of the Commons, as popularized by authors such as Garrett Hardin, means each person trying to get the most for themselves even at the expense of others. Eventually, this creates a worse situation for the individual than if he/she agreed to cooperate initially. For example, consider a common resource, such as a lake with fish. If no individual catches too many fish, there will be enough for everyone. However, if everyone tries to grab as many fish as they can, there will be few left to spawn for next year. Each person greedily thinks he/she can take one more fish and not affect the whole much. However, if everyone does that, then a problem arises. The only way to avoid degenerating situations like this is for everyone to understand and value the One Being they all form to begin with.

Environmentalism is an expression of Oneness since it's considering the health of the planet that contains us all. Individual people, corporations, or nations sometimes exploit resources for short-term profit at the expense of long-term health or sustainability. Fortunately, increasing numbers of people are becoming aware of and caring about our environment. If you want to save the world, work with others who also want to do so. The planet is alive just like we are. Another good example of Oneness is the planet itself because our physical bodies are formed from the matter of the Earth's body, and our Monads are spiritual projections sent forth by our Planetary Logos.

17: Understanding Evil

"When you learn to love hell, you will be in heaven."
- Thaddeus Golas

This book is about evolution, spiritual growth, and love. These are all things that are usually classified as positive or *good.* We can also increase our understanding by considering that which is not good; in other words, let's examine things that are negative or *evil.*

In the English language, the word "good" is "God" with an extra letter "o," and the word "evil" is "live" spelled backwards. Another way of looking at it is that the word "evil" rearranged spells "vile." Although those are coincidences as opposed to actual etymologies of the words, they're still insightful. What we consider good is that which leads to God or spirituality. What we consider evil is backwards living or those things which are harmful to life or move oneself or the world backwards. Hence, good is to be embraced and expressed, and evil is to be resisted and overcome.

Love and goodness are inherently linked with Oneness; increasing love makes one expand and feel connected with more around themselves. God is the ultimate expression of love where God's consciousness encompasses the Universe. Similarly, evil is linked with separation. For example, hate makes one disconnect and withdraw from things around them. Note: this doesn't mean a hermit or introvert is bad, only that they just choose to connect with different things. Similarly, a socialite or extrovert isn't necessarily better. Some merely desire to appear better than others which reinforces separation.

Just as Cosmic Consciousness makes one blissfully feel connected with everything, an opposite experience called Avichi is the ultimate separation. Avichi (Sanskrit for "waveless" or "without happiness") is a state where one's consciousness is in a void, disconnected from everything. This state is much more extreme than being in a sensory deprivation chamber or isolation tank, which some actually enjoy because it allows them to get in touch with inner energies. In Avichi one is separate even from their soul, making it one of the worst "hell" experiences possible, similar to a more extreme version of the lower astral plane. It can happen to a practitioner of black magick who follows the path of evil and separation to the most extreme state possible. This experience will often be a "rock bottom" situation and cause him/her to journey back to the light. Avichi can also be temporarily experienced by a spiritual person during their Fourth Great Initiation.

Everything is a part of the Divine, even those people or situations we perceive as evil. Every spirit's destiny is to be unified with the Divine at the end of its evolution. The only difference between positive souls on a spiritual Path and negative souls doing bad deeds is that the former will finish their evolutionary journey faster than the latter. In other words, the concept of evil only exists in the framework of linear time. On higher planes that are beyond time there's no worrying about faster or slower evolution. Similarly, the concept of evil only exists in the framework of duality. On higher planes that are beyond duality, there's no distinction between "evil" and "good;" rather, everything is One and part of the Divine. In other words, evil only exists on lower planes, such as the physical and astral because those are the areas where beings are able to commit evil acts and where beings are able to be perceived as evil by others.

Evil serves several useful purposes in our evolution. The presence of evil makes us appreciate the good and not take the positive things in life for granted. Evil also acts as a force to push against or an influence to be tested with in order to grow. Physical exercise requires effort or something to resist over time in order to grow strong. Without exercise our bodies would be weak and have little energy. Similarly spiritual growth happens much faster when we struggle against what not to do. Without the presence of evil, we wouldn't be nearly as conscious of the good within ourselves.

Although the presence of evil isn't strictly necessary in order to grow, it does make evolution through certain levels of awareness happen faster than it would otherwise. Painful lessons are remembered the best by those souls taking roundabout paths to Enlightenment. In other words, when souls do evil acts and pay the karma for them, they learn their lessons better than those who just read wisdom in books and choose to follow it. We often learn more from our failures than our successes. In the grand scheme of things, evolution doesn't come from success as much as from what we learn in the process. For example, you can be generous in life and appreciate what you did when looking back on it in the afterlife, or you can be selfish and regret in the afterlife the positive opportunities you didn't take advantage of. The negative outcome isn't as bad as one might think because they both result in one becoming aware that generosity is a good thing and intending to be more generous in the future. If you don't make a mistake or experience a negative emotion at least once a day, your life isn't challenging enough.

All things in the Universe have value in our evolution. If something that we consider unpleasant happens, we're just being given a positive opportunity to grow more. For example, falling off a bicycle a few times is necessary when learning to ride it, which means a seemingly negative event like falling has value. Traffic jams help us learn patience, periodic forest fires help giant sequoia trees grow better, losing loved ones makes us appreciate each other more, and criminal acts make us see the difference between right and wrong. It all comes down to how one chooses to view things. Every event can be considered enjoyable, educational, or both. And if it's not, then it still helps us get in touch with our emotions or at least shows us what things are more effective than others. From a high level, no matter what happens, something good is happening. From a high level, everything is a perfect expression of the Divine and a part of the unified being that everything forms.

The above philosophy can be easily misunderstood. With everything being good, one might think that means bad actions are condoned, or people can do whatever evil deeds they want. Technically, you can do whatever you want, and it will be "good" in the grand scheme of things. However, your own negative karma that happens as a result of those actions and the resulting learning experiences will also be "good."

Similarly, everything being positive may make one think they don't need to take action to improve the world or grow themselves or that one shouldn't be compassionate to those who have bad things happen to them. Again, one has the freedom to do nothing if they choose; however, seeing the beauty in everything can actually make people much more effective at actually implementing change because they're doing it out of love for the way things can be instead of dislike for the way things are now. If we don't like what we see in the world or in ourselves, then we should work to change it. That, of course, is best done from a standpoint of love and understanding lest one become just as negative as that which they desire to change. We can work to change the world or even fight for what's right, but we should do so with love in our hearts.

Everything being positive doesn't mean one should only express happy emotions. Individuals shouldn't put themselves down or think they're doing something wrong if they're not able to see the good in something. We tend to be happy when things that we want happen in our lives and are sad or angry when they don't or when unwanted things happen. Negative reactions have their place and shouldn't be considered "bad" any more than anything else. In other words, if we learn to see happiness in sadness, we'll remain happy no matter what. How do Masters stay calm and serene? They don't prevent bad things from intruding into their lives as much as they don't let bad things bother them or judge them as bad in the first place.

The Devil and Fallen Angels

"The seduction of evil is precisely in that it involves us in trying to get rid of it."
- Thaddeus Golas

Any consideration of evil should include the traditional being of ultimate evil: the devil itself. The word devil is Old English for "evil spirit." In the English language, the word "devil" contains the word "evil" within it. The devil is frequently named Satan, which is based on the Hebrew word for "adversary."

Different religions have different views concerning the devil, but in general the devil is described as an irredeemably evil being who opposes God, rules over "hell," and tries to tempt and gain control of human souls. Traditional Christianity says the devil along with one third of the Angels in heaven rebelled against God. As punishment for their pride, they were cast out of heaven. Some go so far as to consider the devil equal to God in power and claim that they're both locked in an eternal struggle.

Fortunately, the devil as described doesn't exist. What do exist are our own internal negative tendencies, which can be personified as an inner devil. Our individual and collective potentials for evil are the most important thing to overcome as opposed to fighting some external force of darkness. Some actually like the concept of an external devil (even if they won't admit it) because it's nice to have a scapegoat to blame for external problems or internal shortcomings. Some even use the threat of a powerful soul-stealing devil to scare and manipulate people. Good and evil form the ultimate duality with the concept of the devil as the ultimate manifestation of evil. Being able to transcend limited views of a polarized "devil" goes a long way toward transcending other forms of duality as well.

Not all belief systems even have the concept of a devil. It's mainly seen in monotheistic religions with both God and the opposite concept being seen as individual entities. Although a personified devil doesn't exist, what does exist is the "trickster." Many Native American and other faiths feature the concept of a trickster, who is basically a teacher that uses methods we might consider negative, such as playing tricks, causing trouble, or in general being chaotic as a way to get people out of their ruts and old ways of thinking. A trickster may be conscious of their role and intentionally playing it or be a seemingly unevolved fool.

In traditional Christianity, Satan offered an "apple" to Eve. Her taking it caused humanity to be kicked out of the spiritual and dreamlike Garden of Eden and develop free will where we have knowledge of good and evil and freedom of choice to express both qualities. This story appears in other faiths, such as the Greek god Prometheus who stole fire from Mount Olympus and gave it to humanity, allowing us to develop civilization. Both Satan and Prometheus were punished for their actions. Like many such stories, these are based on true concepts, namely the growth process of individuals or the human race as a whole. We leave a relatively immature or carefree state of being, like childhood where we are being taken care of by parents and emerge into young adulthood where we have increased responsibility and become more accountable for our actions.

People being tempted by the devil, especially while they're on a spiritual Path, is an archetype appearing in many religions. For example, in Christianity the devil tempted Christ in the desert with suggestions He should use His powers selfishly, put God to the test, and receive the world's riches. In Buddhism, when Gautama Buddha was approaching Enlightenment under the Bodhi tree, the devil figure Mara attempted to seduce Him with beautiful women. In Zoroastrianism, the devil figure Angra Mainyu or Ahriman tried to tempt Zoroaster with rulership over the world.

Interestingly, the devil is sometimes called Lucifer, a name which means "lightbringer." When the Earth was first created, the Divine wanted someone to serve the role of tempter and tester. Lucifer, the brightest of God's Angels, volunteered along with other beings. This willingness shows the devil and his associates weren't cast out of heaven but intentionally left the beauty of the higher planes in order to serve on Earth. Even this depiction of the devil is a story although it's probably the most accurate. It is true that some spiritual beings coordinate challenges for individuals or groups of humanity. Some spiritual beings work in the high heavens while others help with issues lower down on Earth.

The above means one can actually appreciate these "devils" and the serious sacrifices they've made in order to help us evolve. Few like playing the villain and being hated for the necessary position they're filling. It's like being an army drill sergeant, who serves an important role in helping soldiers grow, but is often disliked for their hard methods. This appreciation can even be taken as far as the radical concept of "worshipping the devil;" however, this love is of a very different sort than what's usually meant by "devil worshipping." Most who consider themselves Satanists want to embrace hedonism or other animalistic qualities or are that way just out of youthful rebellion because they want to shock their peers or make themselves seem intimidating. Of course, one shouldn't actually worship the devil, even with a more positive understanding of its role, just as they shouldn't worship any other spiritual teacher. The best way to honor the work and sacrifice of these beings is to overcome their temptations, just as the best way to please a school teacher is to do well on the tests they give you.

What things might tricksters do to help us evolve? One of our biggest tasks in Earth school is to learn discernment or wisdom about what is true and how best to approach things. It follows that tricksters can present us with false paths and distractions, such as cults, conspiracy theories, or negative events designed to draw us into their drama. It's especially challenging when the truth is mixed with falsehood or presented in a negative manner, although learning to extract one from the other is an effective way to grow. Wisdom isn't supposed to be easy to acquire. One of the most insidious goals of tricksters is to make you hate them in order to demonstrate that you're not fully expressing love yet. In other words, the whole concept of an evil devil could be considered a conspiracy perpetrated by the devil itself! Of course, we cause enough of our own problems and distortions so we don't need external teachers to provide them for us. False paths like the above don't need to be intentionally created although higher beings are very aware of them and their effect on us and how we ultimately grow from them. Instead, tricksters are just an aspect of our One Being and the world getting involved with such problems is like the One Being itself making a mistake and learning from it.

Tricksters may seem to try to tempt us or lead us astray, but they want us to resist them. We can "fight the devil," not out of hatred or fear, but from a sense of mutual understanding and appreciation of our respective roles. Once all of humanity is Enlightened, we can have what amounts to a big party with all the various Angels and teachers and look back with fondness upon all the fun roles we played back in the day.

The Dweller on the Threshold

"Tough assignments are only given to the best students."
- The Transformation Game

When spiritual seekers are about to resolve the last of their karma or fully embrace a deep level of love, they are on the threshold of one of the biggest boundary points on their evolutionary journey. Before stepping through the doorway into a new state of being, they must demonstrate that they're able to exist in the new room, and that there's nothing in the old room still holding them back. Before crossing the boundary point, one has intense experiences that can be referred to as facing the "Dweller on the Threshold."

The Dweller (or Dwellers) on the Threshold is a guardian standing in a doorway who ensures that only the worthy can pass through. The dweller usually isn't an actual external being but is rather just a personified name for the internal things that must be addressed. These experiences can be dramatized as "resisting the devil," "slaying the dragon," and so on. They are like a final examination that you take when you want to graduate from a class. All the intensity of the school year comes to a focused point, and it's time for you to demonstrate your mastery of the subject matter. If you want to fully release something, you need to embrace it one more time in order to carry it to the trash.

If individuals want to balance their karma, they must face any remaining karma. If they want to move beyond karma altogether, then they must release all their accumulated bad deeds over all their lifetimes, which means seeing them one more time. If they want to live in love, they must prove they can be unconditionally loving even in midst of extreme negativity. For this reason, spiritual individuals often have challenging lives or difficulties that people might think they don't deserve. These challenges are because they're actively working on their issues and pushing themselves.

The Dweller on the Threshold can refer to any other challenging spiritual test that seekers face on their evolutional journey. For example, when they first astral project, they're likely to encounter a number of repressed emotions, passions, and fears, which need to be faced, accepted, and released in order to have quality experiences out of body. Similarly, the bardo experience after physical death where individuals review their life experiences is like a dweller that must be faced before moving on to a new life on the astral plane.

Some spiritual Mystery Schools intentionally facilitate initiations that involve challenging tests. The book "Initiation in the Great Pyramid" by Earlyne Chaney, co-founder of the Mystery School Astara, contains an excellent depiction of (among many other things) one facing the Dweller on the Threshold during a spiritual initiation in the subterranean chamber of the Great Pyramid.

Black Magick

"Do not be a magician, be magic."
- Leonard Cohen

An important aspect of evil to consider is metaphysical force used negatively. Black magick refers to occult powers or abilities directed to selfish purposes or motivated by lower desires, such as hate or greed. Black magick is sometimes called dark magick or evil magick to avoid using the word “black”. Black shouldn’t be considered a bad color, and, of course, black magick has nothing to do with skin color. The word “magick” is spelled with a “k” to distinguish actual occult phenomena from the tricks of stage magic.

Black magick usually takes the form of psychic attack where one directs negative energies at someone they dislike in an attempt to harm them. The user of black magick may be what we’d consider an “evil” person, but usually they’re just someone who finds a reason to rationalize his/her actions. For example, that person insulted me, so I’m justified in attacking him/her. It’s important to remember that in conflict, people often think they're good and the other side is evil, but from the other’s point of view, the opposite is true. Sometimes it’s necessary to stand up for oneself, but it’s better to know how to deescalate or resolve conflicts in a healthy manner. If one is forced to fight, it’s important to keep love in one’s heart.

The fact that black magick is never a good idea hardly needs mentioning. It creates negative karma for reasons beyond just causing harm to someone who may not even deserve it. You’re creating a reality where people can be adversely affected by magick, which is likely to manifest in your own future. Black magick corrupts the real spiritual path by reinforcing the selfishness which one should be trying to overcome. Most methods of trying to metaphysically affect someone you dislike are based on ego where you want to make yourself feel better by having power over someone or powers in general.

How do you protect yourself from psychic attack or other unwanted vibrations, such as unpleasant entities on the astral plane that may be encountered while out of body? Once individuals learn that the spiritual side of life actually exists, they may become concerned about potential dangers they never considered before. Since metaphysics concerns the laws of the Universe that science doesn’t fully comprehend, ultimately there’s no difference between using magick to affect someone and simply attacking him/her physically or verbally. We often make more fuss over metaphysics than we need to.

Psychic attack is primarily based on fear. Most black magicians have no actual ability to manifest anything, but they want you to think they have powers. They may dramatically cast a spell or do something flashy to make you think they’ve actually accomplished something serious. They're no different from a schoolyard bully who wants you to think he can beat you up, so you'll be afraid and he can have control over you. As with the bully, if you refuse to be intimidated or stand up to him/her, you'll find he/she is not so scary after all. For individuals to be attacked psychically is extremely rare, especially in modern times; however, if people think they're being attacked, their own paranoia can make them manifest health problems or see any undesired event as the effect of a curse.

One way to defend against psychic attack is to form a psychic shield around yourself to block undesired vibrations from reaching you. The shield can also act as a psychic mirror to reflect such vibrations back where they came from, or, better yet, direct them down into the earth to be transmuted. This is analogous to using a physical shield to protect from physical influences. A shield can also be used to help against other disruptive energies, such as those felt in a busy city. Note: a psychic shield often functions like a placebo due to one's confidence that the shield will help, as opposed to having an actual metaphysical effect.

A different approach for dealing with those who have wronged you is to "invoke their karma." That means directing your will or energy or casting a spell that the karma between you two will be resolved (or in other words accelerating its schedule). That can sometimes be very effective, and might seem to quickly cause something bad to happen to them. Like any other form of magick used in conflict, this method has potential drawbacks. First, by creating a reality where people can have their karma invoked, you can expect the same to happen to you with your own karma that may come up faster than you might be ready for. Also, that person who slighted you may be someone you've terribly wronged in the past and thus the event you dislikc was part of you paying back your own negative karma. However, by invoking karma, the quick resolution of the remaining issues between you means everything blows up in your face where suddenly a bunch more unpleasant things happen to you! In other words, it's best to trust higher sources and not play with the workings of karma.

The best method to defend against psychic attack or help yourself in any other challenging situation is to connect with something greater than yourself. Connect with your soul, your Guardian Angel, with a positive group of people, or with God, and realize that they care about you, are there to help you and won't ever let anything happen to you that's not part of your karma. Trying to hurt someone who's on a high vibrational level is like trying to hurt a person in a television broadcast by flailing your fists at the radio waves flying through the room. Don't try to hold onto personal energy, which is finite and limited, but rather connect with the spiritual ocean. Nobody will be able to "steal your energy" or "drink all your power" if you're a channel for the Divine.

Black magick, like other forms of negativity, serves a purpose when considered from a higher level. In learning the wisdom of cause and effect, sometimes a soul will consider black magick or other disharmonious actions as the way to get what it wants and will experiment for a few days, years, or lifetimes. However, involvement with such things is always temporary; eventually we all develop love and healthy practiccs. Disharmony around us helps us grow stronger, appreciative, and more harmonious after we face it in others or ourselves.

Cosmic Evil

"When it is dark enough, you can see the stars."
- Ralph Waldo Emerson

Growing into goodness and spirituality and the corresponding concept of overcoming evil are natural parts of human evolution. Just as it's expected for growing children to play in the mud and get some answers wrong on school tests, it's expected and natural for all to express and work through negativity and selfishness or what we'd call "evil energies." This can be called Planetary Evil because overcoming it is part of the evolution taking place upon this planet.

There is, however, a deeper kind of evil that is not inherently part of our planet. Cosmic Evil refers to certain negative energies outside of our planet altogether which are not intended for the human kingdom to experience. Cosmic Evil happens when a large group chooses negativity together with full awareness and intelligence. Oneness is the strongest force in the Universe, so only when a group goes down the wrong path is there enough power to connect with similar energies off the planet. Individuals and small groups can't invoke Cosmic Evil, no matter how bad they are on their own.

Earth is like an elementary school with humans as students in it and the Masters as teachers and other faculty. In school we're supposed to work on our lessons. Related challenges might involve fighting on the playground or dealing with bullies. Fighting on the playground, although negative, is natural and even expected, and most schools are equipped to deal with it. Opening the door to Cosmic Evil is like children digging under the fence and leaving school property altogether. They're no longer under the protection of school employees. Outside the school, a wayward child may get hit by a car or encounter a child molester. It's not intended for children to ever encounter these things because such events don't effectively serve their evolution.

Children shouldn't leave school or play in the street, but eventually they grow up and have to graduate and learn to drive. Only Masters and other Enlightened Spirits are advanced enough to directly deal with Cosmic Evil. Masters help us as much as they can, but ultimately we have free will and have to deal with our own karma. The Masters are like courts ruling it's against the law to drink alcohol and drive or like parents warning teenagers to not drink and drive when they go out. That guidance helps but doesn't totally prevent people from driving drunk.

The Great Invocation contains the dramatic line "and may it seal the door where evil dwells." Behind "the door where evil dwells" is Cosmic Evil. The door itself refers to the barrier between our planet and those negative influences; "opening the door" to Cosmic Evil means groups choosing to express and connect with those energies to a greater or lesser degree.

The Roman Empire was the first semi-modern society to connect with Cosmic Evil. The Axis powers during World War II connected with it to a significant degree. Even a few modern countries who should know better are at risk of opening the door. However, nothing going on today comes close to the wild things that took place during Atlantis. At times during that civilization, the door to Cosmic Evil was not only fully open, but the surrounding walls were knocked down as well! Tyrannical dictatorships that suppress the majority of their population aren't really connected with Cosmic Evil, not even when the population is drafted into the army and forced to invade others. The danger comes when the society freely buys into the message of imperialism as opposed to being forced into it, meaning the leaders and a significant percentage of the population are working together toward negative ends.

Cosmic Evil and the spiritual beings connected with it aren't openly malicious. It's more like water behind a dam; if one stupidly pokes a hole in the dam, raw destructive energy pours forth. Cosmic Evil can be considered an energy the planet pushes against in order to grow. When building a tower, you work against gravity. Gravity isn't evil but is rather an impersonal force. If Earth is an anthill, and people are ants, Cosmic Evil is like the freeway next to the anthill and the cars on it. If an ant leaves its safe home and wanders on the freeway, it's likely to get squished, not due to intentional maliciousness of the cars, but simply due to cause and effect because it got in the way. Note the risk of "wandering off" here means the moral sense of leaving the will of the Planetary Logos, as opposed to a physical risk to space travelers.

Spiritual beings that can be considered "Lords of Cosmic Evil" exist but shouldn't be thought of as traditional devils that want to conquer Earth. One might think these ancient entities are like dramatic fictional monsters or gods, such as Cthulhu from H. P. Lovecraft's mythos where if we're not careful, they might awaken and crush us. Instead, these beings are like construction workers or car drivers on the freeway next to our anthill who are just doing their jobs and are ultimately a part of the Divine like everything else in the Universe.

Even Cosmic Evil plays a role in our evolution just as children get taught not to accept rides from strangers and to look both ways before crossing the street. In that sense, there's no difference between Planetary and Cosmic Evil—both are energies we overcome in order to grow. The energies of Cosmic Evil aren't obscure; instances of it mostly consist of separation, materialism, and a desire to control others, only on a larger scale. That's little difference from the individual issues with which we each struggle and overcome during our own evolution.

Just as we expand our awareness through the planes of the Universe and evolve through and beyond the dense energies of the lower astral plane, so do aspects of the Universe itself evolve on a higher level. Cosmic Evil can be considered the energies of the lower Cosmic Astral plane, something a Planetary Logos and the lifewaves in it evolve through. An individual learns through making a mistake like touching a hot stove and getting their finger burned.

Similarly, the One Being sometimes learns through an aspect of it (such as a nation or other group of people) making a mistake and having that "body part" get hurt in some way.

Like evil itself, Cosmic Evil has the potential to be misunderstood and misused. For example, people may accuse groups they dislike of not only being evil but of being agents of Cosmic Evil. Cosmic Evil is not something to be feared and one shouldn't be concerned that the planet is being attacked or will be attacked by outside forces. It exists only in an energetic sense and is more a negative potential. However, it's still useful to know about the concept and what's meant if one hears the term.

18:
Spiritual Intimacy

"Across the years I will walk with you - in deep green forests; on shores of sand; And when our time on earth is through, in heaven, too, you will have my hand."
- Robert Sexton

Until beings reach levels of consciousness where they're one with everything, there will be an apparent distinction between themselves and others. A significant part of spirituality is how we relate to other beings, and an important part of evolution is how we grow those relationships. Just as spirituality can help us with our relationships, so can our relationships help us along our spiritual Path. A soul's connection with and love of someone can be a reflection of its oneness with the Divine.

Relationships can be classified as vertical or horizontal. A vertical relationship is with a being on a higher or lower level of evolution or influence. Vertical relationships include those with parents, teachers, and even God, as well as with children, students, and pets. A horizontal relationship is with an equal, such as a friend or spouse.

Vertical relationships with beings or concepts more evolved than us, such as God, are somewhat abstract due to the different levels of existence. Horizontal relationships with peers are the most concrete and readily apparent; in these relationships, love directed toward and received from peers is the most capable of being understood. Love with family and teachers can be just as strong, but the potential for romance and intimacy with peers adds an extra dimension to such relationships that's worthy of consideration.

Romance

Everybody wants to love and be loved although some certainly do a good job of hiding it or expressing their desires in unusual ways. A relationship is one of the best ways to fulfill this inner need where a partner can both appreciate you and be appreciated. Even those who are happy being single are expressing love, too. Their love is directed toward non-romantic relationships, such as with friends, family, or themselves.

Attraction on higher levels is deeper and longer lasting than attraction on lower levels. For example, a simple physical attraction is literally only skin deep and will change or end once a person gets older and their body changes. However, an attraction to someone's spiritual principles continues after the death of the physical body and is likely to continue across multiple lifetimes, regardless of what bodies the souls in question inhabit.

Many romances start with lust on the physical level, graduate to the emotional level once they realize they're infatuated with each other, change to the mental level when they develop shared interests together, and only in later life develop real love and a deep spiritual connection. However, the best way to form a partnership is to blend aspects from higher planes to lower as opposed to from the bottom up. For example, find your soulmate or someone with whom you connect on a spiritual level and then mentally see how your lives connect and how you can work together in life. Next, emotionally realize how much you enjoy being with the person and finally develop a physical attraction to each other.

The best relationships connect on all levels and have both physical and spiritual qualities where the spiritual shouldn't be considered strictly better than the physical. Many just care about attractiveness or other physical qualities. On the other hand, some deny the physical, which can be just as bad if not worse because we are now in physical bodies. All relationships require change; however, it's easier to change physical aspects than spiritual aspects to form and maintain a relationship. A physically dirty person can just bathe and change into new clothes to be more attractive; however, a negative or spiritually dirty person can't easily change themselves into a sweetheart.

Simplistic relationships usually end early after the lustful *in love* state ends. More evolved relationships aren't necessarily long lasting; they end at the appropriate time, often after the parties learn what they need to from the relationship. The deepest type of relationship is based on love. It's not about what you're getting or even learning from it, but rather it's about sharing the journey with your partner without judgment or condition through good or bad times, as well as educational or boring times.

More spiritually-evolved people may tend to find it harder to find romantic partners since they usually want fellow spiritually-evolved people to relate with on that level, which can be hard to come by. The average person can just go to a neighborhood bar and quickly find someone on a similar level that they have a lot in common with. In the distant future when a larger percentage of humanity is Enlightened, the situation will be reversed. Most will want deep spiritual relationships, and it will be more difficult to establish a more superficial connection. In addition, a spiritual person is usually pickier about finding someone they're compatible with since they're active on many levels, meaning there are more aspects being affected by and linked up with the other. An unevolved person only sees and looks for physical compatibility; the average person wants emotional and mental compatibility as well while only an evolved person seeks all of the above plus spiritual compatibility.

If you're a unique person, it's better to intentionally seek out a partner as opposed to hoping to meet one randomly. Personal ads and related services are an effective way of seeing or being seen by numerous people, and working with such services indicates to both yourself and others that you're ready for a relationship. That increases your chances of finding the right person, as opposed to hoping one of the relatively few people you come across during the day is not only compatible but also looking. The internet has made personals very effective, so individuals can connect with thousands of people around the world. On the astral plane this has been taken to a whole new level where one can be introduced to people based on soul vibration. If you don't ever find a good partner in physical life, trust that it's much easier to hook up in the afterlife!

Finding and maintaining a relationship requires taking action on both physical and spiritual levels because we're both physical and spiritual beings. Finding true love requires first loving yourself and working through most of your issues, so they won't interfere with a relationship. Ultimately, love is an attitude held inside more than something found or expressed outside. Relationships also require physical seeking, which means placing yourself in environments where you can actually meet someone of similar vibration. Praying or visualizing drawing romance to you can certainly help, but eventually one needs to take physical action in order to have physical results. Don't just settle for anyone out of a need to not be alone because that will make you unavailable when an appropriate person does come along. Instead, insist on finding the right person for you. We're eternal souls, which means even searching for multiple lifetimes is only a drop in the bucket of our infinitude!

Soulmates

A soulmate is one's ultimate partner on a soul level. Soulmates will have a stronger connection and be happier with each other than with anybody else in the cosmos. This link spans multiple incarnations and is on a deep level beyond simple desire although there's definitely attraction on all levels.

Not everybody has a soulmate. Some souls are relatively independent and don't want such a relationship while others are equally connected with multiple souls. Like standard relationships on earth, soulmate relationships can be sought; it depends on what one wants to have in his/her existence. If you want a soulmate, trust that you already have one out there somewhere or can find someone who wants to become yours.

Soulmate relationships can be born or created. Some soulmates were literally born together with their Monads as two halves of the whole. Other soulmates came about through a conscious decision of the souls in question. In other words, an existing relationship can be turned into a soulmate relationship if both parties are willing. Also, a soulmate relationship isn't a yes or no distinction. Not only can existing relationships become soulmate relationships, but existing soulmates can explore ever deeper levels of love together.

Soulmates are almost always on the same evolutionary level even if it may not seem like it at first. Your partner may be almost exactly like you, be your complement in certain ways, or more likely be a mixture of both. In a particular incarnation, one may be emotional while the other mental, one may act as the teacher while the other the student, or one may be alien and the other earthy. However, these are usually just temporary roles. Soulmates (and larger soul groups for that matter) are often like children playing leapfrog; first one will be in front, and then the other. We shouldn't focus too much on who happens to be in front now, as much as we should contemplate the larger game being played.

A soulmate relationship is a blessing and a gift, not only to you and your beloved but also to the world. If you have a soulmate, you should expand your love for your partner into love for everyone and seek to use your relationship to benefit the world. Even if nobody else knows about your relationship, it can still act as a channel for love to enter the physical plane. Your love will radiate out from your sacred union and warm the world like sunlight.

A soulmate relationship usually has instant attraction; the thought of separating or ending the relationship is as inconceivable as splitting yourself in two. However, even if you're with your soulmate, that doesn't mean the relationship won't lack challenge or require effort. It's very hard to hide things from someone or maintain any illusions when your partner is such a close reflection of yourself. It's like he/she can read your mind and won't hesitate to call you on your issues. A relationship is a beginning, not an end, and soulmate relationships especially necessitate sharing, honesty, modesty, kindness, and balance.

Sex

Sex scenes in a book or movie are often considered the "good parts." Although one reader might believe this to be true, another may not; however the fact remains that this book has sections about sexuality. Few things in life attract people's attention, create as strong desires, or cause as much diversity of opinion as sex.

Where does sexual desire come from? What actually causes one to be attracted to other people and not attracted to things such as rocks or driftwood? Part of attraction is simple bodily instinct that is based on the hormonal or emotional desire to procreate and/or knowing that physical pleasure comes from sex. On a metaphysical level, part of sexual desire is due to an ancient and powerful thought-form produced by the great spiritual beings that created the human race and other species to ensure we'd reproduce. In other words, some aspects of sexuality aren't necessarily one's own desire but are merely an environmental broadcast being tuned in to. Many just blindly seek to fulfill their desires, but it can be useful to meditate on where such desires originate and how and whether one should continue to follow them. Ultimately, sexual attraction is a desire for love and oneness on a physical level. Sex is a physical plane manifestation of love and a physical reflection of the beautiful lovemaking that happens on higher planes.

One of the biggest issues surrounding sex and sexual desire is whether it's a positive or negative influence on people. There's a wide diversity of beliefs concerning whether people should "do it" or "not do it." There's no single correct answer, regardless of how one chooses to answer it for himself/herself. It all depends upon how sex is approached. Like a relationship itself, sex can either be a harmful distraction or a powerful tool for evolution.

Although sex isn't a bad thing in and of itself, practice of it is best done consciously with focus and attention, as opposed to just getting carried away by passion. In other words, sex best comes from the soul instead of the body. Letting soul love awaken bodily pleasures is far more satisfying than focusing on bodily pleasures which may or may not bubble up to higher levels.

The best way to approach sexual desires is to use them as a tool to express love. Don't try to destroy or repress desires, which are a valuable tool in the manifest world but rather transmute them into love. Let sexual energies flow through you, not emanate from you personally. The point of transforming our sex lives is to avoid selfish lust and to increase creative loving compassion. In that sense, there's nothing special about sex because spiritual Paths have us refine our actions and feelings in many areas.

Sex has a number of beneficial effects. Just as crying is healthy since tears release toxins and going to the bathroom is healthy since it releases toxins in a more direct manner, sex helps one relax and release physical and emotional tension. Done right, sex can actually be "making love" or adding loving energies to the world. Even lustful sex can be beneficial since it at least exercises the emotional body.

Tantra is an esoteric tradition that uses sex as a tool for spiritual growth. The word Tantra is Sanskrit for "weave" or "loom," which implies the interconnectedness and continuity of all things. Tantra is much more than just a sexual practice and is actually a much wider philosophy that sees the Universe as Divine energy and seeks to creatively and sacredly express that energy.

One should have discernment when getting involved with any spiritual group, and especially exercise caution if that group works with sex. The leaders of such groups need to have high integrity and maintain strict boundaries in order to avoid abusing their position and taking advantage of their students. There's already such devotion from disciple to master that if a teacher is having sex with his/her students, there's risk of the student forming an unhealthy level of dependence. The teacher could also develop an unhealthy level of pride due to having what amounts to his/her own harem.

Celibacy or chastity is the practice of not engaging in any sexual activity or doing so minimally. Celibacy can be a beneficial spiritual practice if approached correctly. Simply trying to deny sexual desire is about as effective as trying to deny eating or going to the bathroom. It's possible for advanced yogis to sustain themselves through water and their breath alone and avoid eating and defecating. Being able to do that generally implies one is a Master although not all Masters choose to undertake this discipline or express themselves on the physical plane in this manner. People don't learn to transcend food by starving themselves; similarly, one shouldn't learn celibacy by repressing themselves. If one chooses to become celibate, the best way is to become so full of love and discipline that all desires are met, leaving no need to satisfy desires sexually.

Sexuality is centered in the root chakra. This chakra is also the seat of kundalini, the Divine force of evolution, which moves up from the root through the other chakras and out of the crown. There's great power within the root chakra; in most individuals that energy just goes into sexual desire, but in a few it also awakens kundalini. Certain forms of kundalini yoga are based on celibacy where one doesn't expend the root chakra's energy in sexual activity but rather directs it upward. Kundalini eventually awakens on its own. One certainly shouldn't try to force it, but one can certainly do things to prepare for or smooth the process. For example, certain Tantric practices involve sexual intimacy that is combined with sexual continence (where one controls their fluids and avoids ejaculating). This technique allows sexual expression where one is still able to attain orgasm but without the physical draining that happens afterward. It can even cause sexual energy to rise from the genital area up through the body. Such a practice can help lead one to Enlightenment, but, as with all spiritual Paths, shouldn't be considered the only way.

Many have much guilt surrounding sex. Some traditional religions consider sex or sexual desires to be sinful. Since most individuals have sex or want to at some point in their lives, that would make everyone sinful. Negative religious philosophies don't want their followers to have sex for any reason other than reproduction in order to prevent people from having sex for pleasure. Some religious organizations are even against birth control because they hope to cause pregnancies and create additional followers of that religion. If people feel guilty and sinful, they'll seek redemption and hand over their power to that religious system.

Guilt surrounding sex isn't limited to traditional religions. People on spiritual Paths can have just as much if not more guilt around it. Spirituality often suggests you control your desires or conserve the sexual energies and redirect them to spiritual purposes. Unfortunately, this concept frequently manifests itself as repressing desires and sexual energy, and, hence, potential for love, which does more harm than good.

After physical death, one enters his/her astral or emotional body where feelings are far more intense. During the death bardo experience, the various chakras get stimulated, which may arouse sexual feelings. Some sources talk of the dangers of letting those sexual feelings distract you because they have the potential to cause one to skip the heaven worlds and have a premature rebirth. The time of death is indeed very significant so it's important to remain focused on what really matters. Fortunately, such feelings won't affect anything other than the smoothness of the bardo experience itself. Such an admonishment is just another form of guilt, making one ashamed or worried about conquering their sexual feelings so they won't be "damned" when they die.

Alternative Sex

The concept of alternative sex refers to any sexual preference or practice that's outside what the majority of people do. Note: the label *alternative* is based on the majority view. To those who actually engage in alternative sex, they're the *normal* ones, and everybody else is unusual. Assuming the practices don't harm any of the people involved, they should generally be welcomed as an expression of diversity.

Homosexuality, where individuals are attracted to members of their own gender, is one of the most common alternative practices. As with most preferences, homosexuality shouldn't be considered a black and white distinction but rather a gradual continuum between heterosexual and homosexual attraction. Bisexuality is a preference roughly half way between pure heterosexuality and pure homosexuality.

Some religions and spiritual philosophies (including some otherwise enlightened ones who should know better) are against homosexuality for the same reasons that some are against birth control: it can't increase population and, hence, result in more people who are likely to subscribe to their belief system. They may also be against it simply because they're disturbed by those who are different. The only potentially negative aspect of homosexuality is something that can happen with any other practice. If individuals consider themselves special or better than others, they tend to proudly separate themselves from others. Note: as people focus less on the physical flesh before them and more on the immortal characteristics of their beloved, gender and sexual orientation becomes less and less of an issue.

People often debate the reasons behind homosexuality. The reasons given are frequently designed to reinforce whether they think homosexuality is a positive or negative practice or whether they want it to be a behavior that can be changed. In actuality, homosexuality can be due to any number of different reasons, and there are many different forms of it. The answer varies for different people since no one size fits all. For example, a person's sexual orientation may be caused by genetics, learned behavior, a simple choice, an expression of the soul, or connecting with one of the spiritual thought-forms that helps drive sexual desire. If a person switches physical body genders between lifetimes, he/she may have an attachment to the former gender. Sometimes that results in transsexuality, a person having the desire to be the opposite gender and/or get a sex change operation.

One interesting potential cause is that homosexuality is a short term survival mechanism in response to the overpopulation of our planet. Our planet could effectively support many more people with the right technology and arrangements; however, in our current society and with our current consumption, the problem is too many people. Species adapt to their environment, and a homosexual relationship doesn't result in new babies to feed. Although homosexual couples may choose artificial insemination, they may also choose to adopt or not raise children at all.

This idea can explain why homosexuality seems more prevalent in dense population centers because the throngs of people are more apparent there than in rural areas. Another reason is that rural areas tend to be more conservative, and people may be less tolerant toward those who are different. In a rural area you're more isolated and dependent upon your neighbors while in a city it's easier to express your beliefs and explore alternative beliefs. Since it’s harder to distinguish yourself in a city, living in one actually encourages going against the norm.

In the long term (as in tens of thousands of years from now) homosexuality, and more significantly bisexuality, is a first step on humanity's evolution to hermaphroditism. In the distant future, we won't have dualistic genders anymore. Everybody will have both male and female integrated within both their physical and spiritual bodies. In the distant past before the Lemurian civilization, humanity didn't have genders because the sexes hadn't separated from each other yet. Similarly, in the future the sexes will merge and unify into one; we will reproduce by the power of the mind and spirit instead of bodily. Having separate genders is an important (and fun) step during our evolution, but it's ultimately just one phase of many. Homosexuals deserve credit for being on the challenging cutting edge of evolution and for getting the rest of us to meditate upon these issues.

Polyamory is where three or more people are all intimate with each other. Polyamory is a voluntary practice and should be distinguished from a situation where one person in a power position acquires multiple dependent spouses. Polyamory should also be distinguished from the practice of “swinging” where a person has casual encounters with potentially many people with or without knowledge or approval of a primary partner. Just as homosexuality challenges us to be more tolerant of other people’s beliefs, polyamory challenges us on a deeper level. Polyamory may just be an experimental phase one goes through, or it may be representative of a deeper aspect of their soul and more complex soul relationships. Polyamory may be suitable for those who don’t have a single soulmate, which can’t be expressed as a simple dyad relationship between two beings.

The most extreme forms of alternative sex are the various practices that are often considered kinky. Such practices include bondage, sadomasochism, or various forms of domination and submission, regardless of whether one is the giver, receiver, or both. Kinky sex may seem negative, especially to a spiritually-oriented person who tends to focus on behaving well. However, as with every other practice, the important thing is whether it's being done for healthy reasons. If it's consensual between both parties and not harming anybody else, they have the right to do as they please. It's just another art form among the many diverse forms of expression in our world.

The biggest danger in kinky sex also applies to standard sex. If individuals merely focus on their personal sensations as opposed to love, then the passions can be inflamed to an unhealthy degree and cause objectification of other people or at least a distraction from evolution. Those seeking the most extreme sensations possible may gradually develop a need to continually seek kinkier or harder core stimulation to arrive at the next high, a situation similar to drug use.

Kinky sex, like sex in general, can be used for positive spiritual growth even if it may not seem like it. Role-playing can put people in touch with different aspects of themselves, such as inner motivations or even past lives, which may be useful to get to know themselves or their partner better. Sex is already a very vulnerable act and requires opening up to one's partner, which means deeper activities can increase trust and intimacy even further. Finally, individuals might ask why people would want to place seeming limitations or hardships on themselves. Physical incarnation is already a painful limitation and form of bondage; however, it is one of the best ways to grow. Hence, if one seeks out more extreme forms of limitation, it can potentially be a useful discipline for growth like any other practice.

Autoeroticism or masturbation is where individuals sexually stimulate themselves without involving a partner. Some consider autoeroticism to be kinky or deviant; however, it's hardly an alternative practice since almost everyone does it. Autoeroticism is frequently considered bad; few things seem to cause as much guilt as it. Some think it implies a person is worth less since he/she doesn't have anybody who's willing to have sex with him/her. Autoeroticism may also seem like the ultimate in succumbing to lust. Also, since the practitioner is alone, it may seem devoid of love.

In actuality autoeroticism can be as valuable as any other form of sexuality. Everyone has the occasional long periods between partners, especially those who want to find the right partner as opposed to just grabbing the first person that comes along because they don't want to be alone. One can visualize and make love with one's soulmate if they're not physically with you at this time or even make love with aspects of yourself and bring spiritual love into the world just as you can with another person. The Universe is composed of many interconnected forms of life. When considering relationships, we shouldn't only consider the level of personalities. Not only do groups of people form one larger being together, but the reverse is true where individual beings are also formed of many other life forms.

19:
Spiritual Politics

"The penalty good men pay for not being interested in politics is to be governed by worse men than themselves."
- Plato

Politics means relationships; however, these relationships are between groups of people instead of individuals. On higher planes, spirits more often consider macrocosmic interactions between lifewaves of souls, as opposed to focusing on personal issues. Hence, understanding politics can actually help an individual grow spiritually by making him/her more aware of group service. If world leaders had and applied spiritual values, then the planet would benefit greatly, especially if those values were not forced upon the populace like some fundamentalist religion.

The concept of *spiritual politics* may seem like an oxymoron. Many spiritually-oriented people (and non-spiritual people, for that matter) avoid politics because it so often seems negative. The endless debates or even hateful "mudslinging" between the various philosophies can drive away the more sensitively oriented. Nevertheless, such interactions have a purpose and can be seen in a positive light. Political activists try to change the world in the way they see best, which is a form of service. Of course, an important part of changing things for the better is being able to interact with others positively, a policy which would certainly be nice if more people followed. However, it's also important to realize that growth takes time.

In our long term evolutionary journey through the human kingdom, there are various stages. First, one develops his/her physical body and the ability to do things with it. After many incarnations one can start developing emotions, then intellect, and finally spirituality. When one develops intellect, it's first used as a tool to compare things against each other and make judgments based on those comparisons. In other words, there's a natural period where one tends to be overly intellectual and argumentative for a number of incarnations. That plays an important part in the large picture of one's overall growth just as second grade and playing in the mud during childhood does to one's education. There are much higher grades, of course, but one can't get to the higher until one works through the lower. Negative intellectual warriors shouldn't be considered a problem; those who are calmer or more positive are probably just farther along the Path and acted the same way in past lives.

Although many dislike politics, it's important to talk about and be involved with the political process and always exercise rights, such as voting. Ignoring politics is done at one's own peril because it allows the situation to deteriorate and get further out of control. If a leaky roof is ignored for too long, it will collapse in a soggy mess that could have been avoided with a little maintenance. Similarly, if the world is ignored too long, it will eventually result in a tyrannical dictatorship or needless war. At Earth's current stage of evolution, there are still negatively-oriented people in positions of power. Only in the distant future when the majority of society is well on its way to Enlightenment can we ignore the workings of government and trust that it will take care of itself. James Madison said, "If men were angels, no government would be necessary."

A job in politics is a great way to serve although it's very challenging and usually unappreciated, like being a school teacher. Politics can also be difficult, at least in our developing world where many are still learning virtue because it requires incremental improvements. (The alternative is to try to force change through some sort of revolution, but that almost never happens without violence and mass devastation.) The fact that we don't evolve all at once but do so gradually, applies to society as well as individuals. Politicians often must make deals, temporarily sacrificing one issue, so they can get enough support to implement another. Politicians must also sometimes compromise on positions so they can get elected in the first place. Spiritual people are often outspoken about the way the world should be and have a utopian vision that they want to have implemented right now, which makes politics difficult for them. The best politicians are able to do what's necessary without compromising their core values. They realize they can't create their utopia, but they can at least make improvements or push things in the right direction.

Another interesting aspect of politics is the concept of being a representative of the people. Many enter politics because they want the opportunity to implement the views they personally think are right. However, some politicians act as pure spokespersons for the people they represent; they work for those things their people want without letting their own opinions intrude. Good politicians are able to act as representatives and do what the people want, but they also know when to do things that may go against the majority. Sometimes a politician needs to do what's best for the people although few are able to separate that from their own biases.

Government

"Charity enslaves people. To share your wisdom with others, so they are enabled to help themselves, is greater than any material gift."
- Paramahansa Yogananda

All well-defined groups have some form of central administration. This is similar to how all trees have trunks, which provide support for trees as centralized ways of distributing nutrients to the branches. For groups of people this role is filled by government.

The main function of government is collecting resources from people and spending or otherwise redistributing them. For example, collecting taxes and using them to build roads. Of course, there are numerous arguments about how much should be collected from which people and especially how those funds should be used. In other words, government is inherently a means of deciding which people give up assets and which people receive benefits. Political arguments (whether simple disagreements within a group or wars between groups) are inherently struggles over limited resources. This is one reason there's very little politics on the astral plane. The after death world is so vast that there's plenty of room for everyone; it's also so abundant that there are none of the struggles for survival currently felt on the physical plane, which means nobody interacts unless they want to. It follows that improving the standard of living on Earth will go a long way toward resolving many political problems.

Most people in politics have agendas, ideas they wish to push upon others. Of course, most people think their own views are enlightened. They believe they're not trying to force anything but are rather "sharing the love" or some other positive effect. A common way to implement political views is by having policy taught in schools. For example, wanting to have prayer in public schools or wanting to keep religion out of schools are both cases of people trying to force their opinions. The politician wants everyone's kids to be indoctrinated with his/her beliefs, so the children will hopefully grow up supporting the politician's interests. The best way to handle education is to teach children how to think for themselves and how to think in general. That way the next generation doesn't grow up blindly towing a party line but is able to evolve and make changes based on things their parents weren't aware of. The author recognizes his own views in this chapter are just as biased.

Although there are many ways to define governments and political philosophies, perhaps the most fundamental consideration is the effect they have on their citizens. Governments can exercise control or allow freedom in economic and personal matters. These two axes can be combined in a graph, resulting .in four quadrants or basic effects of government. The following graph shows the types of government, and is most similar to the Nolan Chart popularized by American libertarian David Nolan.

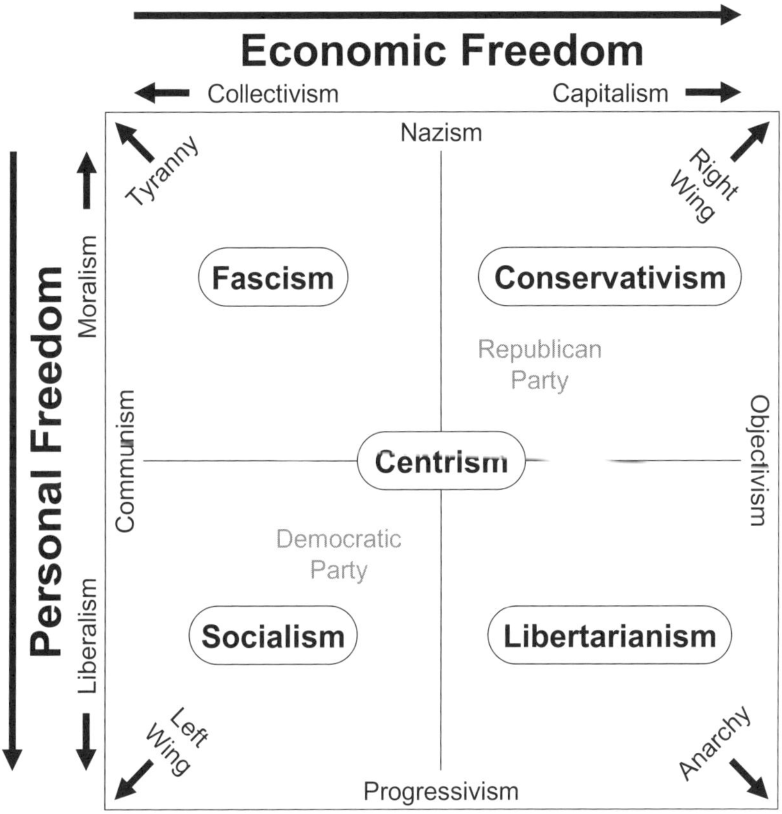

The four halves of the chart (left and right, and top and bottom) can be enumerated as collectivism, capitalism, moralism, and liberalism.

Collectivism involves a government having high control over economic matters. The government takes most of a person's resources and redistributes it, hopefully in an equal manner. This philosophy implies high taxes but also a large number of government services. For example, jobs and health care are generally provided to everyone; however, there's less choice in the matter. People are rarely rich or poor because wealth is redistributed from the rich to the poor. A collectivist society works well if the centralized government isn't corrupt and doesn't abuse its increased power and if people don't take advantage of government handouts or use it as an excuse to stop working hard. Metaphysically, group souls tend to follow a collectivist concept. After death the experiences of the animal go into the group soul to benefit equally all the entities evolving in it.

Capitalism is the opposite of collectivism; a capitalistic government has little control over economic matters. It takes little of an individual's resources, which implies low taxes, but also few government services. Capitalism allows people to gain (and lose) wealth in a free market environment and profit from the fruits of their labors and innovations. This philosophy results in rich and poor classes, meaning the poor receive assistance from voluntary charity more than public programs. Government is small, but companies are unchecked, so they can potentially become powerful controlling influences on their own. Capitalism usually has high efficiency; however, sometimes it can become inefficient if a monopoly tries to starve out competition or prevent new innovation. Capitalism is a Darwinist or natural selection "dog eat dog" philosophy; this can result in problems if all individuals or corporations are only looking out for themselves instead of society. A capitalist society works if the companies and people have compassion for those less fortunate and for the world in general. Metaphysically, individualized souls tend to follow a capitalist concept where each human soul must evolve on its own.

Moralism or authoritarianism is seen in a government that has high control over personal or social matters as it promotes a set of conduct or values for the people to follow. For example, it features state-sponsored religions or other ways of promoting behavior, which hopefully are non-discriminatory. This is government *guiding the people*. A moralist society works if it promotes general virtue and doesn't degenerate into discriminating against people of certain religions or other minorities. Metaphysically, any religion or organized spiritual Path is a form of moralism where the group is seeking to establish and expand values.

Liberalism is the opposite of moralism. A liberal government has little control over personal matters, which means it lets people believe and behave as they wish, provided they aren't harming others. Liberalism implies philosophies, such as *separation of church and state* and *keeping the government out of people's bedrooms*. People usually appreciate the freedom liberalism offers although it also challenges people to accept things with which they may personally disagree. For example, liberalism tends to legalize things, such as drug use, gay marriage, gun ownership, and prostitution. Liberalism works well if the people don't take their freedoms so far that they collapse in reckless hedonism and stop evolving.

The four different quadrants of the chart can be enumerated as fascism, conservatism, socialism, and libertarianism.

Fascism is a government that has great control over both economic and social matters. It is as large as possible; individual interests are considered secondary to those of the state. This philosophy is the ultimate in statism or *state worship*. Taken to the extreme, fascism becomes tyranny. This quadrant may seem like the worst because the individual has minimum freedom; however, it can receive popular support if the government's biases align with those of the individual. For example, a fascist government may promote a particular religion or race, which will likely be supported by members of that group assuming they only care about their own interests. Most religious cults with strong leadership combined with strong standards of conduct belong in this quadrant. Fascism can be efficient because the government has no impediments or opposition and can even work well if the government is unbiased and beneficent to all. That rarely, if ever, happens in the physical world; however, on higher planes where souls work together in unity, there are wonderful spiritual hierarchies that technically belong in this quadrant.

Conservativism is where government has little control over the economy but firm control over social matters. In other words, conservatism is capitalism combined with a moral majority, or what's commonly called the *right wing*. It can be considered a traditional *fatherly* philosophy that combines survival of the fittest in the market with standards of behavior. Conservatism tends to be more popular in rural areas because government is distant, and people rely on each other to have the same values. The Republican Party in the United States mostly falls in the conservative quadrant since it combines a capitalist philosophy with Christian or family values.

Socialism is the opposite of conservativism. A socialist government has firm control over the economy but little control over social matters. This philosophy is often expressed as "from each according to his ability, and to each according to his needs." It is commonly called the *left wing*. It can be considered a traditional *motherly* philosophy that combines the government unconditionally caring for everyone with permissive behaviors. Socialist viewpoints tend to be more popular in urban areas because many people are present; thus, there's a more obvious need to address the poor and deal with a wide diversity of personal habits. The Democratic Party in the United States mostly falls in the socialist quadrant since it combines many government services with liberal ideals. Many spiritual leaders, such as Gandhi and the Dalai Lama, have political views similar to socialism since they focus on the ideal of people helping each other.

Libertarianism is the opposite of fascism. A libertarian government has little control over both the economy and social matters, beyond providing basic services is as small as possible. This is a laissez-faire philosophy of everyone having the right to do whatever he/she chooses as long as he/she doesn't harm another human being. It is a "live and let live" form of government. Libertarianism may seem ideal since it allows maximum freedom in both areas; however, it can result in isolationism or people being disconnected from each other. Taken to the extreme, libertarianism becomes anarchy, which paradoxically eventually results in little freedom because the lack of government and structure allows other groups to establish themselves and take over.

The four different edges of the chart can be enumerated as Communism, Nazism, Objectivism, and Progressivism.

Communism: In its ideal sense, communism is just a more extreme form of socialism. In actual implementation, it tends to be tyrannical, such as seen in former East Bloc countries. Although collectivism had been taken to the extreme in such countries, they were authoritarian and didn't provide any extra personal freedom.

Nazism: National Socialism is more commonly called Nazism. Although it has "socialism" in its title, it has little to do with true socialism. Nazism is an example of a philosophy that takes moral authoritarianism to the extreme (persecuting and even killing those who don't meet their standards). Nazism is actually near the middle with respect to economic freedom; an example is the corporations during the Third Reich which were largely left alone as opposed to being absorbed and run by the government.

Objectivism: Author Ayn Rand developed the term objectivism as an example of a philosophy that takes capitalism to the extreme;

however, it's balanced on the moral scale since it dislikes both religion and anarchy.

Progressivism: An example of a philosophy that takes liberalism to the extreme is progressivism or more specifically social progressivism. It is continually focused on social change and working to allow more civil liberties; however, progressivism is more balanced or at least variable in its approach to economics.

Note: the effects of government described above are different from the actual form a government takes or the procedures they follow. For example, democracy doesn't appear in the chart because it isn't an effect but rather a method of implementing effects. Democracy is a quality form of government because its elections give power to the people and tend to keep the government from becoming too authoritarian. However, even a democracy is limited by the virtues of those within it. It can suffer from a *tyranny of the majority* where the majority vote themselves privileges at the expense of minorities or take advantage of other countries or the environment. Sir Winston Churchill summarized the issues well with the quip, "Democracy is the worst form of government except all the others that have been tried."

Centrism

"Moderation in all things, including moderation."
- Mark Twain

Is there a correct political philosophy? The simple answer is no. There's no perfect system that if everyone supported would magically solve all the world's problems and create a utopia on Earth. The most one can say is that each philosophy has its own benefits and only starts becoming a problem when taken to extremes. Centrism is the philosophy of balance between the various systems and belongs in the center of the chart. The concept of a compromise between the various systems may seem simplistic, but there's a lot of wisdom in it.

Note: trying to define where the center is can be a challenge. Most people or political groups think their own ideas are centrist, and anybody who disagrees with them is on the fringe in one direction or another. For example, the centrist position in the United

States is half way between the Democrat and Republican parties; however, both parties are considered in the right wing conservative quadrant when compared to most European governments. To those in the United States, European governments, in turn, seem closer to socialism.

A healthy society has a balance of individuality and economic freedom, as well as regulation and group goals. Too much government control, too much corporate power, or too much anarchy are all equally bad. However, we need at least some form of government, a decent market economy, and freedom to do what we want as long as it doesn't harm others if we are to prosper and evolve. Of course, actually implementing this philosophy and determining where to draw the lines between the polarities is a challenge and subject to debate. However, that's not a bad thing; healthy competition between political parties or points of view is good to ensure society doesn't become too stagnant.

Centrism is more than just a balanced position between the various political extremes. Centrism also recognizes the value of some people having extreme positions. It's good to have different people or groups focusing on different areas, suggesting ideas from them and ensuring they don't get overlooked. It's important to remember that all do what they think is right. It's comforting to know that all are ultimately good, even if their methods are different. All believe their own positions are correct, which should be respected because inconsideration for others is one of the main causes of problems in the world.

In addition to general acceptance, centrism also means being aware of and exposed to the various positions. A situation frequently found in politics and life in general is the concept of *cocooning*, originally popularized by marketing consultant Faith Popcorn. Political cocooning involves people only associating with like-minded people and avoiding other points of view. That results in people reinforcing their own viewpoint and marginalizing and disliking any alternative viewpoints. Hence, if one is actually wrong or needs to make adjustments, he/she continues to try to hold onto his/her incorrect position, often well after the bad effects of it have manifested.

The philosophy of balance can be extended to other areas in life beyond politics. For example, consider the personal immune system. If individuals expose themselves to toxins or have dirty habits, their immune system will be overworked, and they'll become ill. On the other hand, if individuals are obsessive about washing, and they clean too excessively, their immune system can also become weak due to its being out of practice. Then the first germs that do come along will wreak havoc and cause illness.

A tree is healthiest when its roots go deep down into the ground, and its branches reach high up into the sky. If a tree doesn't have the diversity of extremes and has shallow roots or a short trunk, it will more easily fall over or be eaten by animals. Considering a tree's branches, it's best if they're all reaching in different directions to provide balance for the trunk, allowing some leaves to face light wherever the sun is positioned. For another analogy, tightrope walkers have the best balance with their arms extended far out to the left and right, as opposed to trying to walk with everything together in the middle. A rainbow is beautiful because all the colors are separate and pretty in their own ways. If all the colors were blended together into gray, the result would be boring. Of course, the best balance of colors includes a bit of gray, black, and white in addition to the hues of the rainbow.

World peace isn't achieved by everyone unifying and being the same standard way. Peace comes about from accepting others for their differences and not judging them. A big step on the way to achieving Oneness in our world is to realize there will never be one way of doing things and to stop trying to force other people to change. There will always be different cultures, philosophies, and as many opinions as there are people. Accepting that and coming together in spite of our differences is the true way to have Oneness.

More evolved societies, such as advanced extraterrestrial civilizations and our own planet in the future, are or will be very different; however, don't expect them to be completely unrelated to what we have on Earth today. Such societies still have challenges and differences of opinion; the significant change is they are able to resolve these differences in a healthy and efficient manner.

Many activists want to change the world for the better. Activists are generally positive because they want to serve; however, they should ensure they're doing it for the right reasons. It's better to work motivated by love toward a desired ideal than work motivated by hate against what one might perceive to be a dysfunctional society. Technically, the concept of *saving the world* means manipulating and changing other people while not saving the world means accepting and loving it as it is.

It's good to want to serve and to aim high, but it's also important to be grounded. For example, there were still wars and differences after great Masters like Buddha and Christ came to Earth. Not everyone accepted their teachings during or after their lives. In other words, we shouldn't expect everyone to follow our views either or for our activities in isolation to change the world. Of course we can, especially when unified with others, benefit significant parts of the world.

Political issues

"It is the mark of an educated mind to be able to entertain a thought without accepting it."
- Aristotle

Perhaps the most fundamental part of politics is the issues or specific rules a society enacts and makes people follow. People often try to use laws to manipulate others into behaving certain ways. However, they don't understand that people will still act according to their beliefs which may reduce or even reverse the effect of a law. In other words, political policy often results in unintended consequences or backfiring karma. For example, laws for mandatory safety equipment in cars and boats may actually result in more accidents if people then think they can go faster or otherwise take more risks. Building more roads to address traffic problems may actually increase traffic because then people find it more convenient to drive. Charity programs to help homeless people get back on their feet may actually increase the number of homeless because people migrate to the community from surrounding areas in order to take advantage of the benefits. That doesn't mean such policies should be avoided, of course, but rather that one should consider their true consequences.

What follows is how various political issues can be seen from a centrist or metaphysical perspective. There are, of course, many other issues than the short list here. In addition, there is much more depth to each issue and arguments for both sides than the quick summaries presented. Ultimately, each issue comes down to a matter of balance, which may include individuals accepting their own views and realizing that they help represent a particular side in the debate.

Gun control: The moralist view is that one shouldn't use violent means to solve problems. There's opportunity and potential to cause harm when keeping guns for self-defense or sport, so they should be banned. At the very least there should be limits on what can be owned—of course, people shouldn't be able to own missiles or nuclear weapons. One needs to take a drivers license test before they can operate a car, so it makes sense to have similar tests in order to operate other powerful equipment like a gun.

The liberalist view is that owning a gun and using it safely doesn't hurt anyone, so owning guns shouldn't be restricted by others. Fighting, whether on an individual or group level, should, of course, always be a last resort; however, it shouldn't be ruled out altogether lest unevolved people or groups notice and take advantage of the easy prey. One of the oldest quotations in support of gun rights says, "When guns are outlawed, only outlaws will have guns." For the balanced viewpoint, people should be able to have a certain amount of self protection. One can't rely solely on external sources, such as the police, or internal concepts like loving thoughts to protect one from harm.

Drugs: Morally, drugs are just a form of escapist pleasure that distracts people from useful work and evolution. They can be very addictive if not deadly, so they should be banned. The liberalist view is that drugs are a personal decision, so individuals should be able to make their own choices. Spiritually, Rastafarianism and certain Native American belief systems have a long tradition of *sacred medicine* where certain substances can be smoked as a spiritual act or method to raise consciousness.

From a balanced perspective, it doesn't have to be all or nothing; drugs can be regulated and licensed like any other potentially dangerous activity. Outlawing drugs just creates an underground economy for them, which gets fought over by criminal elements. The United States tried to ban alcoholic beverages during Prohibition; this resulted in the rise of mobsters and other organized crime. It's best to hold people liable for causing accidents or otherwise harming others while their judgment is dulled, regardless of the source of their distraction.

Prostitution: The moralist view is that prostitution indulges desire which isn't virtuous and doesn't result in love which is what most people really want inside. That combined with the fact that the majority of people involved in this field are exploited by pimps or are victims of human trafficking means it's degrading for all involved and should be banned.

The liberalist view is that *the world's oldest profession* is a voluntary act between two people, and *victimless crimes* shouldn't be illegal. As can be seen in society, sex is one of the strongest drives people have; they'll seek it out one way or another. Even something as simple as buying someone a drink in a bar in the hope they'll go home with you can be seen as paying for sex. Prostitution can be legal and, hence, properly regulated or driven underground where there's a lot less oversight. Acts that actually cause harm are what should be prosecuted, such as people exploiting each other or knowingly passing on diseases. This policy should be combined with economic programs to ensure that sex workers are only those who actually want to express themselves and earn a living that way, as opposed to people being forced into it because they have no other choice.

Abortion: This issue is notable because the rights of the mother to choose her own life and the rights of the fetus to have a life seem in conflict. Both sides have a slippery slope. Few are extreme enough to support late term abortions in the third trimester; similarly, few are extreme enough to consider abortion to be murder if it's performed in the case of rape or incest right after pregnancy is detected. It's best to find a balance and draw the line at the half way point. For example, abortion is allowed for any reason in the first half of pregnancy and restricted in the second half, except for special cases like saving the life of the mother.

Metaphysics allows the abortion issue to be looked at from additional perspectives. A soul reserves an embryo at conception and gradually occupies it more and more until birth when it permanently moves in. If a pregnancy ends through abortion or miscarriage, the soul will find another pregnancy to reserve and isn't really inconvenienced other than losing a little time. It's possible to channel the soul of a fetus and discuss the matter with it and basically get its approval to have an abortion. One can even ask the soul to leave on its own if it can, resulting in a miscarriage. This communication, of course, requires one to have reliable intuition or work with an impartial external channel that doesn't let his/her personal biases influence the message.

Feminism: In views concerning this issue, one extreme has *traditionalists* who believe in a cultural system where women should be inferior to men and can only be mothers and housewives. The other extreme says women must be warriors and fight their oppressors; those on this side sometimes look down on women who do choose to stay at home or raise a family. Note: in both cases women are having people (whether men or fellow women) trying to tell them what to do. The ideal situation is for women (along with men and every other cultural group, for that matter) to have the freedom to think for themselves and live their own lives. Some people honestly want to follow a *traditional* role or even be what some might consider being submissive, and we should respect that even if we disagree. This philosophy of acceptance can be summarized with the humorous yet profound saying by Thaddeus Golas which goes, "Giving others the freedom to be stupid is one of the most important and hardest steps to take in spiritual progress. Conveniently the opportunity to take that step is all around us every day."

Affirmative action: This issue refers to programs that help disadvantaged minorities who sometimes have been discriminated against in the past. Affirmative action ensures enough minorities get college positions, jobs, and so on. One view is that affirmative action is bad because quotas are basically another form of discrimination, often "reverse" discrimination against certain individuals who happen to be in the majority. Also, giving a minority extra help can be seen as condescending, which in a sense reinforces the discrimination by implying they're inferior or less capable of succeeding on their own. In other words, assistance should be based on economics, independent of whether one is or is not a member of a particular group.

Although nice in theory, the above colorblind view ignores certain realities and the fact that groups and by extension individuals in them often became disadvantaged in the first place due to past injustice. Things shouldn't only be looked at from an individual standpoint where groups are entities on a different level. When a species is endangered, members of it get special protection compared to common species. In summary, both affirmative action supporters and detractors serve a role in preserving the balance and ensuring the pendulum doesn't swing too far in either direction.

Capital punishment: From a metaphysical standpoint, capital punishment or the death penalty should be avoided, making this issue different from others that benefit from a more balanced viewpoint. All life is precious, and less evolved people can benefit more from physical life than spiritual people who are focused more on higher plane energies. If a criminal is executed in the prime of their life, their consciousness will go to the lower astral. On that plane, their violent emotions will be more intense and pollute the astral plane with emotion forms which may adversely affect or even influence impressionable people on Earth. It's best to let the most hardened criminals live out their lives in jail, which allows their passions to cool down before they die. They still won't escape their karma, but the time passed will result in smoother transition for them and everybody else still on Earth.

Even from a practical standpoint, the death penalty is challenging to implement. It costs a government more money to do all the appeals and go through the process, than it does to simply support a criminal in prison for life. Also there are a number of cases where innocent people have been convicted, especially those from disadvantaged groups; execution, of course, prevents the chance of overturning a wrongful conviction. From a standpoint of Oneness, we want to rehabilitate criminals, since they're just as much a part of our One Being, even if they are younger souls on the "tail" end of it. As part of our extended families, they will be connected with us in one form or another until they evolve.

Overpopulation: This issue is perhaps the single biggest challenge facing us on a global level. Most other issues can be reduced to the concept of there being too many people fighting over too few resources. For example, the environment is at risk because the throngs of people are consuming too much, which isn't sustainable. Issues like immigration cause disagreements because immigrants don't have enough at home, and current residents fear the newcomers will take their jobs or otherwise use limited resources, so there's less to go around.

Although overpopulation seems bad, it does serve a positive purpose or at least can be understood. When a world has lower population, everybody forms separate communities, which don't have much in common and hence are likely to fight when they do eventually meet. This situation describes much of the history of our planet up through the 20th century. Once the world becomes populated enough, and technologies such as the internet cause information to be exchanged worldwide, the concept of one world becomes more apparent. Once resources are no longer plentiful, there may be a certain amount of competition over what's left. However, the situation also causes the rise of environmentalism where people become aware of and start caring about the world and learn to behave more efficiently. In other words, overpopulation can be seen as a natural part of a planet's evolution, or at least a cause of it. From a metaphysical standpoint, Earth is in a period of significant change and close to what amounts to a spiritual graduation day. Numerous souls want to incarnate now during this important time, either to help out during the transition or to try to quickly learn enough so they can graduate or not "get held back a grade."

Poverty: This issue is perhaps the most fundamental to address on an individual level because if people are dying of hunger, they're unable to benefit from any other rights. Spiritual fulfillment in life comes after physical needs like food are met, meaning if we want to feed the spirits of people, we first need to feed their bodies. Although it is true that spirituality tends to make one less materialistic where some seekers live a very ascetic life, that's due to their personal choice. Disciples in ashrams and such are in a positive environment, compared to a family in the poorhouse.

It is worth noting that spiritual guidance often acts as if one has lots of money, free time, or living space. For example, teachers suggest things, such as buy organic, meditate every day, or create a sacred space. That's certainly good advice; however, in reality most people struggle to make ends meet, are short on time, and come home from work exhausted. That doesn't mean one can't grow in spite of adverse situations. Challenge is often the cause of evolution; however, prosperity does make growth easier. It's easy for me to sit here and write books like this; however, I recognize it would be much harder to walk a spiritual Path if my economic situation were different and that many others currently not on a Path could do so if given the means.

20:
A Vision of our Future

"The best way to predict the future is to invent it."
- Alan Kay

Few topics capture people's attention as much as the future. The past is dead and can't be changed. The future, however, is yet to be determined, and making the right choices can bring happiness or at least help avoid problems. The past is interesting and important to study but mostly in relation to what we can learn from it and how we can do better in the future. Spiritual evolution is the process of growing over time. One works on himself/herself in the present in order to be better in the future. In other words, it's better to look forward than look back.

Because the future by definition is yet to be determined, nobody can definitively say what will happen in it. Many try to prophesize the future, but few are correct to any significant level of detail. Spiritual growth is a personal journey; individuals ultimately have to decide for themselves what their Path will be in spite of what others may say or want them to do. Therefore, one should maintain a healthy skepticism of any claims about the future. That includes everything in this chapter! All writings are opinion, but this chapter is more opinion than any of the others. As the title indicates, this chapter presents a particular vision of the future, as opposed to the one true fated explanation of the future. In spite of the vague nature of any prediction, the future is still important to consider, and there are a number of things that can be said about it.

End of the World?

"The children now love luxury. They have bad manners, contempt for authority, they show disrespect to their elders.... They no longer rise when elders enter the room. They contradict their parents, chatter before company, gobble up dainties at the table, cross their legs, and are tyrants over their teachers."
- Socrates

"What is happening to our young people? They disrespect their elders, they disobey their parents. They ignore the law. They riot in the streets inflamed with wild notions. Their morals are decaying. What is to become of them?"
- Plato

"The world is passing through troublous times. The young people of today think of nothing but themselves. They have no reverence for parents or old age. They are impatient of all restraint. They talk as if they knew everything, and what passes for wisdom with us is foolishness with them. As for the girls, they are forward, immodest and unladylike in speech, behavior and dress."
- Peter the Hermit, A.D. 1274

The quotations above demonstrate that many of the issues we deal with and the things we complain about now aren't unique to our time period but are truly universal and existed as far back as Ancient Greece and the Middle Ages.

Many see our world in or approaching a crisis. They look at war, disease, morality, and the environment and see the world falling apart or even headed toward destruction. Different people have different issues they're concerned about. For example, political liberals frequently see the world approaching an environmental crisis caused by greed, or a crisis of war caused by religious fanaticism and other forms of bigotry. Political conservatives frequently see the world approaching a moral crisis, with youth being increasingly corrupted by all manner of influences, such as those seen in the quotations at the start of this section.

Fortunately, the world situation isn't as bad as we might think. The world is not going to end, in spite of what some say or even hope for. Yes, on a subconscious or even conscious level, some actually want the world to end or at least have some major crisis. If the world ended, that would mean an end to one's problems and the challenges of life in general because one would no longer have to endure humanity's seemingly slow or non-existent progress. People would no longer have to work to raise themselves up or be envious of other people's successes because everyone would be starting over at the same level. An apocalypse provides a convenient and obvious distraction from working on personal issues, which some would rather avoid facing.

Today we're concerned about the spread of new viruses, such as HIV. However, previous generations struggled with polio, smallpox, and typhus, which are no longer problems today. In the 1300's roughly half of Europe's population was killed by the Black Plague. An equivalent epidemic today would kill over three billion people around the world. Disease, although still a concern, doesn't affect nearly as many people as it used to.

Today we're concerned about developing nations acquiring nuclear weapons. However, previous generations faced the Cold War where the entire world was at risk of nuclear annihilation. The worst that can happen now is terrorism or a localized war may destroy a city or two, which is certainly a concern, but no longer something that threatens all of civilization.

Today we're concerned about intolerance, such as religious fanaticism, racism, and sexism. Religious bigotry is a problem today; however, during the Crusades of previous centuries, conflict between religions was much worse. Racism is a problem today; however, things have improved in many areas, such as the end of slavery in the United States and the end of apartheid in South Africa. Sexism is a problem today, especially in certain parts of the world; however, today's imbalances are much less than in previous centuries when women couldn't even vote.

Today we're concerned about natural disasters, such as earthquakes and hurricanes. However, today we have much better building codes, early warning systems, and nations around the world willing to quickly help with relief efforts. Since 1960 the world population has risen by over 200,000 people per day or a billion people every 13 to 14 years. The worst disasters in recent history (the 2004 Indian Ocean earthquake and tsunami and the 2010 Haiti earthquake) each killed about 230,000 people; however, in spite of their horror they only caused blips in our rising population curve for one day.

Today we're concerned about various wars around the world; indeed, our planet may seem full of conflict. However, the number of wars is decreasing. The world has gone from two World Wars in the first half of the 20th century to only local conflicts for the last seventy years. In addition, the wars that do happen are becoming less deadly and have less of an impact on society.

For example, consider major wars experienced by the United States. Over 4000 Americans were killed in the Iraq War and subsequent occupation. However, that's far below the 58,000 Americans that died in the Vietnam War. The Vietnam generation also faced a forced draft, which modern youths in the United States have never experienced. The deaths in Vietnam were far below the 400,000 Americans killed in World War II. That, in turn, was fewer than the 600,000 people that died in the American Civil War. The differences between old and new wars are even greater when considering how much larger the population is today than in previous centuries.

Future wars will cause fewer and fewer deaths until finally our planet will achieve the long awaited era of no more war. Some visualize war suddenly stopping, and everyone just as suddenly evolving after some miraculous Earth changing event. However, war is not going to stop immediately but will rather have continually less impact over time. War will also move from physical conflict to mental conflict, such as propaganda, before it disappears altogether. For example, election battles between political candidates are a war like any other, just conducted with words and emotions instead of swords or bombs.

None of the above is meant to disregard the suffering that's still going on in many parts of our world. Certainly if we or a loved one experiences one of the misfortunes above, it's a tragedy regardless of how many other people are experiencing it. Similarly, none of the above is meant to deemphasize the importance and significance of the challenges we face today. We can, however, put our problems in perspective and remember to acknowledge the hardships of previous generations and the sacrifices they've made to give us the civilization we have today. Today's challenges aren't insurmountable and can be improved and even resolved. Many dedicated souls have been and are working on the issues, and they can use our help. Certainly we don't want to stop and forget about the people still suffering just because things have mostly gotten better.

Some believe the world is approaching a major test in the near future to decide its ultimate fate and survival. Based on the above, the biggest tests have already been overcome. If people want to worry about the future, they can be concerned about all the work still ahead of us. When an apocalypse happens, we get to start fresh after it's over. Our current situation is perhaps more frightening because it means we're stuck here until we fix the rest of our problems.

Today's society has become soft in certain respects. Previous generations had to work much harder for everything—for physical needs, such as food, and emotional needs, such as freedom. This isn't bad but is rather a measure of our success, which shows how much society has improved in recent decades. Today's pessimism may seem like whining and complaining; however, that's also a demonstration of success since more voices are being heard. The media may seem bad with all its negative and sensational reporting; however, that's better than silence where people of previous generations never knew about many of the tragedies going on around them. The increased reporting is another reason why things may seem hectic today.

Apparent softness or lack of appreciation for what we have may seem negative where one might think society should grow stronger or return to core values. However, trying to force virtues like that is dangerous, as is trying to control people in many other areas or getting them to change before they're ready. People will make their own lives challenging when they want to. Many seek thrills, such as bungee jumping, roller coaster riding, or other activities to bring uncertainly and danger into their lives. Others join ashrams to live a more ascetic life in order to grow stronger.

Are you still depressed over the state of world? That's not a bad thing, as it shows that you care. Many souls are incarnating now in order to provide assistance during these significant times. Of course, it's better to help out in whatever way we can instead of just complaining about the world situation or wondering what will happen in the future.

For an extreme example, who cares even if the world gets destroyed? That's not going to happen; however, if it did, our eternal spirits would just move on to a new form of existence. Ernest

Hemmingway said, "One thing about life, it goes on." Regardless of whether the situation in the world or in our own lives seems to be heading toward paradise or heading toward destruction, we should still do whatever we can. At the same time, we should understand that success doesn't necessarily mean lack of strife or even survival. What happens on an outer level isn't as important as what we learn from it.

Beginning of the World!

"Be the change you wish to see in the world."
- Mahatma Gandhi

This chapter is more about how to live life and how to approach the future, as opposed to trying to explain the mundane details of what will happen in it. Nevertheless, it's useful to understand some of the directions toward which our world is headed. If we're not going to destroy ourselves, then what are we going to do?

The most significant change happening in our world today is an increased sense of Oneness. This feeling is primarily caused by greater global awareness. Earth's increased population is creating many challenges; however, it's also bringing us together whether we like it or not. For example, many don't care about the environment or find it necessary to work with others until resources start becoming scarce. Increased Oneness is also caused by the rise of technologies, such as the internet, which allow the free exchange of ideas and a rising standard of living around the world which gives people time to devote to personal growth. Because Oneness is an integral part of spirituality, our planet is also becoming more spiritual.

The European Union consists of countries that used to almost constantly be at war with each other. Now they're inseparably connected although each country still has its own unique culture. As time progresses, our planet will establish or improve other alliances, such as the African Union, which will bring a stop to all the local conflicts going on there. Eventually our world will be fully connected as exemplified by the current United Nations, a foreshadowing of the future.

Increased connection between cultures makes people more tolerant of various lifestyles in everything from religion to sexual preference. However, when cultures initially contact each other, there's sometimes conflict where each side tries to spread or reinforce their own beliefs. In other words, there's sometimes a bit of a backlash before acceptance sets in. To use Europe as an example again, thousands of years ago it was a bunch of disconnected tribes. Later it expanded into a set of distinct cultures, which eventually ran into each other and conflicted for several centuries, all the way up until the end of World War II. Only then did the European Union form. The same thing is happening today with the world as a whole.

One example of social tolerance is that people will become more comfortable with their bodies. The ever more revealing clothing available today will go to its logical conclusion where eventually public nudity becomes acceptable. The popularity of naturism and nude beaches in many parts of the world is already a demonstration of this; such acceptance will continue to spread. Less clothing implies fewer emotional barriers between people. For example, it's easy to get angry at other drivers on the road because there's no intimacy; people in other cars are like impersonal objects. Similarly, if world leaders conducted negotiations naked, they would see each other more as people instead of adversaries.

In coming decades, the world will finally address global warming and by extension, non-sustainable energy resources, such as oil. There won't be a sudden switch away from such sources. Rather as oil gradually becomes rarer and hence more expensive to acquire, it will become more economical to acquire energy from a variety of other methods. The planet goes through many natural cycles, such as Ice Ages; in the distant past and future, Earth's climate has been and will be very different from the way it is today. Global warming has a number of different causes; however, we'll accept responsibility for our own role in seriously contributing to it.

Vegetarianism will become much more common. This will be more due to economic necessity than a moral desire to prevent animal suffering or to have a "spiritual diet." It takes much more land, water, and energy to raise animals than crops; increased population will make vegetarianism more efficient to provide food for everyone. Also, the spread of infections, such as e. coli, salmonella, mad-cow disease, hoof-and-mouth disease, avian bird flu, and others yet to appear will make meat eating more hazardous.

Vegetables aren't free of pollutants, but they are at least much easier to clean. Meat substitutes such as tofu, seitan, tempeh, and other soy products will be available in forms almost indistinguishable in taste from the meat they simulate and will be much cheaper to produce and environmentally sustainable.

Space exploration will continue. It may seem to be happening at a slow pace today, but it's really only just started. We took centuries to learn how to cross the oceans in ships, and the same is true for space travel. The International Space Station is an excellent example of our interconnected society. Nations that used to be rivals in space exploration are now cooperating to build something better than any one nation could do on its own. Eventually we'll have massive space stations in orbit and throughout the solar system and beyond, whose quality of life will be just as good if not better than life on the surface of Earth. The only reason we're on Earth is because we need its resources to survive, just as a baby needs its mother's milk to survive. In thousands of years we'll know how to get most of our energy and resources in ways that don't impact Earth's environment, such as from asteroids, nebulas, and interstellar dust.

Extraterrestrials will land and formally introduce themselves. Contact will be slow at first, but gradually we'll exchange goods and culture. Earth will receive ambassadors from other solar systems, and we'll send our own ambassadors. Eventually Earth will integrate with the galactic society, just as we are now blending different local cultures into a world society. Extraterrestrials won't publicly land until our planet has evolved enough that we won't panic, attack them, or worship them. In other words, we shouldn't wait for them to appear because they're already waiting for us.

The human body will continue to evolve. Over millennia the physical forms we currently inhabit evolved from the Neanderthal and Cro-Magnon species, and they are continuing to change. One readily apparent outer difference in the future is that our bodies will have no hair. That state will be a logical extension of how we've lost body hair while evolving from earlier primates. In the future, we'll first lose the light hair we have on our bodies, and eventually even the hair on top of our heads. Many extraterrestrial races are hairless, which is a likely outcome for the human race as it continues to evolve. Today many men shave their beards, and many women shave their legs. This may be due to a desire to appear less like earlier primates and to look more civilized and evolved. The next major change in the human form will be when the sixth Root-Race begins several hundred years from now. (See the chapter "Cycles of Evolution" for more about the Root-Races.)

Genetic science will be much more developed, and we'll learn the true potential and limitations of what it can do. Some people are concerned about genetically modified food and other uses of genetics, and for good reason; it is a powerful tool that needs to be used properly and which we're only just beginning to understand. However, genetics isn't going away. It will still be researched even if parts of the world attempt to ban it. We'll be able to do wondrous things with genetics, such as regrow amputated or damaged body parts. We'll also be able to grow entirely new biological forms that can perform various functions like a machine. For a simple example, we'll be able to grow meat cells instead of having to raise animals for meat, to simulate it even more accurately than vegetarian meat substitutes. Genetic programming will become a career similar to how computer programming is today. This programming, however, will only be taken so far because highly advanced body forms will attract incarnating souls and we don't want to create a slave race. We'll also learn the limitations of genetic alteration; moral development is more important here. Trying to create a "superior race" with genetics is as effective as trying to make a person better by giving them money and power.

Space and genetic exploration will be fully embraced by our current fifth Root-Race; however, not everyone will be interested in such intellectual pursuits. Those incarnating in the upcoming sixth Root-Race will live a more grounded life on Earth focused on spiritual evolution. They're likely to be seen as ascetics by everybody else, similar to how a person today might consider one who chooses not to partake of modern society and instead lives in an ashram or on a mountaintop. Members of this new Root-Race won't dislike technology; however, they won't let technology control them or interfere with their spiritual growth.

Distractions will become ever more prevalent. These distractions are one challenge with the convenience of modern society. Television brought the benefit of increased and faster communication; however, it also caused some to spend most of their time in passive entertainment and to become disconnected from their families, neighborhoods, and the benefits of physical activity. Computers and the internet are like television on steroids. They've provided even more benefit, but like all technology, they sometimes get misused. Computer games and other online activities will become ever more impressive and addictive. Computers can be very educational, but they can also just waste time. People of the future (as well as the present to an increasing extent) will need to consider carefully how they want to spend their lives.

A classic adage says, "The only thing that never changes is change itself." The most important thing to remember about change is that it's happened before and will happen again. Empires will rise and fall, and humanity will both make mistakes and do wonderful things. As time passes and cycles turn, there are eras of young souls and eras of old souls on our planet. Everything that happens or doesn't happen has a purpose. It's all part of our grand evolutionary journey.

Evolving Spirituality

"You may give them your love but not your thoughts.
For they have their own thoughts.
You may house their bodies but not their souls,
For their souls dwell in the house of tomorrow, which you cannot visit, not even in your dreams."
- Kahlil Gibran in "On Children"

This book is about spiritual evolution, not just spirituality. In spiritual evolution not only do we grow as individuals, but our environment itself changes. In other words the very concept of spiritual growth evolves over time. The ways we evolved in the past aren't necessarily valid now; similarly, the ways we evolve today won't necessarily be what we'll do in the future.

As spiritual growth is a journey, wisdom or writings that help one grow are very much like a road map. Some spiritual practices that we make use of today are similar to a 200 or 2000 year old map. The map was accurate at one time and is still useful for certain unchanging natural features; however, one should realize that quite a few things have changed since the map was made.

The changing face of spirituality is one of the most important and exciting trends of the current era. Perhaps the single most significant thing to happen in the future will be a revolution of spirituality. Today's seekers are spiritual frontiersmen and will likely be seen as such by those in future generations. This is similar to how we today view physical frontiersmen and settlers from previous centuries.

Although we can and should embrace the coming changes, we don't need to force them. In our eagerness for change, we shouldn't throw out what we have just because it is old because much of the old contains a lot of wisdom. Doing so haphazardly is what's called "throwing out the baby with the bathwater." People often appreciate tradition and seek out their cultural roots; thus, many aspects of today's practices can and should be honored and retained. The improvement is that the old will no longer be a restrictive influence that perpetuates inaccuracy or prejudice.

One spiritual change in our world is the arrival of "Indigo Children." Indigo Children are highly intuitive and compassionate; concepts like spirituality come naturally to them. The extremely sensitive nature of Indigo Children can make them more affected by negative energies or negative physical effects, such as pollution. Indigo Children can be seen today and are increasingly incarnating because only now is the world evolved enough to be ready for them. This is changing the dynamic of parenting because sometimes our children are older souls than we are. Children still need our loving guidance and constructive discipline; however, we can often learn just as much from them as they can from us.

The name indigo for such children is due to their often having indigo in their auras—indigo is the color of the third eye chakra of intuition. Indigo is also appropriate because it's the sixth color of the rainbow. Presently the sixth subrace of the fifth Root-Race is making an appearance on the planet, and soon after the new sixth Root-Race will follow. Indigo Children are sometimes called Starchildren, especially if the child seems to have a connection with celestial energies, such as extraterrestrials or Angels.

Note: the concept of Indigo Children has the risk of creating separation because it implies there are children who aren't Indigo Children and, hence, aren't "special." All children are special; the only difference is the age of the soul expressing through them. Those who are parents of Indigo Children or even are Indigo Children themselves should not arrogantly consider themselves better than others. Of course, a defining characteristic of Indigo Children is they don't have large egos to begin with. Because other children are younger souls than Indigo Children, they need just as much if not more love and attention to navigate these intense times.

Traditionally, a spiritual seeker moves to an ashram and studies under a guru. Now students are often not physically in the presence of their teachers. Modern technology allows seekers to study through correspondence. Even the most committed Disciples aren't necessarily with a living Master; instead, their Master works with them on the higher planes. Related to this situation, instead of detaching from the world, most seekers are staying involved with the world. Indeed, everyday life is one of the best teachers.

Traditionally, spiritual initiation happens to individuals. For example, a Disciple is initiated separately or even achieves Enlightenment individually. Now initiation frequently happens in a group context where multiple people join together and move as a whole to their next level. This phenomenon is happening due to increased awareness and expression of Oneness and because there are many more seekers advancing today. Initiation used to be rare but is now much more common. Initiates are batched together similar to how a bus takes a group of people at the same time to a new location.

A visualization that may be useful to show how spirituality is becoming more common is that of a sheet of paper held up to the Sun. The Sun represents Enlightenment while the paper is the barrier of ignorance between it and society. The earliest seekers were able to reach up and poke holes in the paper and achieve illumination on their own. This then effectively allowed a narrow beam of sunlight to shine down to others. Now groups of people are coming together, and their collective effect acts like scissors and cuts lines across the paper. Eventually, once enough lines are cut, large sections of the paper can be removed altogether, and Enlightenment will happen on a mass level. The paper will effectively no longer be present. The human race will have achieved its goal of collective Enlightenment and bringing that light to Earth.

Traditionally, once individuals become Masters, they Ascend and no longer return to Earth after the death of their physical body. Now increasing numbers of Masters aren't "Ascending" in the classic manner but rather are staying with the world. As our world evolves and becomes more spiritual, it becomes a more suitable place for the Master. Also, as the number of Masters increases, many of the spiritual jobs on higher planes are filled so there's no longer an urgent need for the Master to go elsewhere. A high school graduate has no reason to stay in a first grade classroom; however, if that classroom holds more evolved 12th graders about to graduate on their own, then there's reason to remain in contact.

Related to the above, traditionally a single Master holds a spiritual position, such as World Teacher. Now more Masters are serving in areas that individual Masters used to cover on their own. When Masters finally do move on, they're increasingly passing on their work to groups instead of individuals, which is necessary because the positions themselves are increasing in responsibility. This situation is similar to how it takes more people to administrate a large group than a small one where Earth is now a much larger group than before with respect to the number of people spiritually aware.

The changes in spiritual growth described in this section are summarized in the following table:

Changes in Spirituality	
Old concept	**New concept**
Parents teach ignorant children	Parents and children learn from each other
Seekers study under guru	Seekers study on their own or with peers
Seekers detach from the world	Seekers live in and are involved with world
Initiation happens to individuals	Initiation happens to groups
Masters ascend from the world	Masters stay with the world
Individuals hold positions	Groups serve positions

The Age of Aquarius

"When the moon is in the Seventh House, and Jupiter aligns with Mars.
Then peace will guide the planets, and love will steer the stars.
This is the dawning of the Age of Aquarius."
- Hair

As Earth spins on its axis, the north and south poles point at the same fixed spots in space. The North Star is the star located directly above the North Pole. As a result, the North Star stays in the same spot in the sky while the other stars appear to revolve around it. However, our planet's axis wobbles over time, meaning the points above the poles aren't permanently fixed, but rather they slowly mark out circles on the celestial sphere. This movement is very gradual and takes approximately 25,765 years to make a complete cycle.

Earth's axis defines the seasons. In Western astrology, the spring equinox in the northern hemisphere defines when the Sun enters the zodiac sign of Aries. Traditionally, at the beginning of spring the stars next to the Sun form the constellation Aries. However, as the planet's axis moves, the stars behind the Sun at certain points of the year also move. Presently the spring equinox no longer happens in the star constellation Aries but rather in previous constellations along the zodiac.

This movement is called the precession of the equinoxes. While the spring equinox happens in a particular constellation, our planet is considered to be in an Age named after the corresponding zodiac sign. With twelve signs in the zodiac, that makes each Age approximately 2,147 years long. Changing from one Age to another marks a new era in Earth's history.

For the past two millennia, Earth has been in the Age of Pisces. Pisces (the fishes) describes much of our history in the past Age, such as the rise of shipbuilding, exploring the oceans, and military might determined by control of the seas. Pisces is a sign in the element of water and is associated with emotional qualities, such as devotion and compassion. This era has also seen the arrival of faith based religions; for example, the fish is a common symbol of Christianity. The birth of Jesus is sometimes considered to mark the beginning of the Piscean Age.

Earth is in the process of entering the Age of Aquarius. Aquarius is an intellectual, inventive, independent, and humanitarian sign in the element of air. The Age of Aquarius is covering the rise of air and space travel, mental phenomena like the internet, along with increased freedom around the world. More significantly, the Age of Aquarius is bringing increased compassion for other people, fellowship, and working together in groups, and Oneness in general.

The term "New Age" as a spiritual movement refers to this change in era.

Before the Age of Pisces was the Age of Aries, which roughly spanned the first and second millennia B.C. Aries (the ram), an active and aggressive sign in the element of fire, saw the rise of desert civilizations such as Egypt, other military empires such as Rome, and a de-emphasis of feminine values. Before the Age of Aries was the Age of Taurus, which roughly spanned the third and fourth millennia B.C. Taurus (the bull), a serene and practical sign in the element of earth, saw improvements in agriculture and more peaceful civilizations with traditionally feminine values like the Minoans, who considered bulls to be sacred.

The Age of Aquarius as a whole will be a positive era of peace and spirituality. However, it won't be without its challenges, and the peace won't manifest until we work to make it happen. Two thousand years ago, many believed the upcoming the Age of Pisces would be an era of spirituality and compassion. Indeed it saw the rise of major religions; however, it also featured blind fanaticism and illusion. Similarly the Age of Aquarius is certain to bring in new challenges related to the negative aspects of that zodiac sign. For example, those influenced by Aquarius can isolate themselves from others or only interact in an impersonal manner. We should ensure we know our neighbors and meaningfully interact with each other instead of letting ourselves be absorbed by our televisions and computers.

The date when the Age of Aquarius begins is unknown, but we do know that we're near the beginning of it. The exact moment isn't that important because the changing of an Age is more a process than a sudden jump from one state to another. The year 2012 is one good candidate for the start of the Age of Aquarius. (The significance of this year is described in the next section.)

The solar eclipse on February 5, 1962, is another good candidate for the start of the Aquarian Age. That day featured all seven classical planets (Sun, Moon, and Mercury through Saturn) in the zodiac sign Aquarius, and all within a narrow 16 degree span.

The North Star alignment on March 24, 2100, may also be the start of the Age of Aquarius. On that date, Polaris the North Star reaches its closest distance from the north celestial pole. As the poles move due to the precession of the equinoxes, various stars become pole stars. Currently Polaris is very close to being the North Star, and over the next century it will gradually become closer. The year 2100 is also significant because it's close to 2,147 years after the birth of Christ and other Biblical events. Because such events are likely starting points of the Age of Pisces, the start of the Age of Aquarius should be close to the proper interval after it.

The song lyrics from the 1960's at the beginning of this section don't indicate the start of the Age of Aquarius on their own because they're too general. Jupiter and Mars conjunct each other every two years. The "seventh house" merely refers to a section of the local sky near the western horizon, meaning the Moon is always in the seventh house in some part of the world.

2012 A.D.

"Destiny is no matter of chance. It is a matter of choice: It is not a thing to be waited for, it is a thing to be achieved."
- William Jennings Bryan

Any future prediction involves specifying an event, a date, or both at the same time. It's easy to predict an event without saying exactly when it will happen. It's much harder to predict an event and an exact time for it because one has a chance of being wrong. Recent history is filled with predictions of earthquakes, extraterrestrial landings, and other flashy events; however, the suggested day came and went like any other. When a prediction (whether valid or not) involves a specific date, it causes anticipation as that date approaches. Unscrupulous individuals may attempt to take advantage of people's emotional excitement to gain attention or money. A common tactic of cults is to make up events in the first place and claim that Earth changing disasters only get averted at the last minute through the cult's "positive energies."

Although all predictions of upcoming events should be taken with a grain of salt, one year is too significant to ignore: 2012 A.D. This year is described as important by a variety of historical, spiritual, and scientific sources.

Perhaps the best known event happening in 2012 is the end of the Mayan calendar. Specifically, the Mesoamerican Long Count calendar ends on December 21, 2012, completing a 5,125 year cycle.

The Mayan Calendar was popularized in the New Age community by José Argüelles, who organized the Harmonic Convergence event on August 16-17, 1987. The Harmonic Convergence signified the beginning of a more spiritual era; indeed, 1987 saw the New Age movement really become popular. The twenty-five year period between the Harmonic Convergence and the end of the Mayan Calendar is said to mark the collapse of old structures until a "new world" begins in 2012. December 21, 2012 is also the day of that year's winter solstice, which happens at exactly 11:11A.M. GMT.

Another significance of 2012 is its proximity to the closing of the Doorway of the 11:11 at the end of 2011. "11:11" is a double instance of a Master Number in numerology. In recent decades many people report seeing 11:11 and related numbers unexpectedly on digital clocks and in other situations. 11:11 is like a sign or trigger that encourages us to wake up spiritually and be more real on all levels. The 11:11 Doorway was organized by the visionary author Solara and is a series of eleven events called Gate Activations, ranging between January 11, 1992, and November 11, 2011, (11/11/11). The 11:11 Doorway facilitates our collective journey of leaving behind duality and moving into greater love, Oneness, and previously unknown levels of being. Instead of people doing things separately during each Gate Activation, the 11:11 Doorway focuses on unified movements and coordination where the One Being we all form gets awakened and activated.

A related event happening near 2012 is the Galactic Alignment. The Galactic Alignment is when the Sun's position at the winter solstice is aligned with the center of the galaxy. During the 25,765 year cycle of the precession of the equinoxes, the Sun's position at the solstice gradually moves around the Celestial Sphere. The Galactic Alignment actually took place in 1998; however, due to the width of the Sun, the Sun actually overlaps the center of the Milky Way for nearly 36 years. The total time period covered is between 1980 and 2016. This is another period similar to those described above.

Another notable event in 2012 will be a transit of Venus over the disk of the Sun. Venus transits happen in pairs, with the pairs happening 105 to 122 years apart. There was a transit on June 8, 2004, and there will be another one on June 5, 2012. After 2012 there won't be another Venus transit until the year 2117. Happening every century or so, Venus transits are common enough not to indicate fundamental planetary changes on their own; however, combined with other events the Venus transit lends additional significance to the period around 2012.

There are additional things happening in 2012. For example the 11 year sunspot and solar activity cycle will next reach its peak that year.

All these events are summarized in the following table. Interestingly, they are all periods of approximately a decade or two leading up to a point near 2012. This shows how different sources and cultures can tap into similar energies even if they focus on different aspects of what's going on. Note that many sources have attempted to describe 2012. Some sources are pure and clean expressions while others allow fear or ego to distort their communications. This variety is no different from standard religions or spiritual teachings in any other context.

Timeframes of Spiritual Transition			
Event	**Start**	**End**	**Years**
Harmonic Convergence & end of Mayan Calendar	1987	2012	25
11:11 Doorway	1992	2011	20
Galactic Alignment	1980	2016	36
Venus transits	2004	2012	8
Sunspot cycle	2001	2012	11

With all the significance of 2012, the big question is what exactly will happen in or near that year? Some suggest positive or negative external events such as the coming of the next World Teacher, extraterrestrials revealing themselves to the public, or any number of Earth Changes. However, the most likely thing that will happen is: Nothing! 2012 signifies an unprecedented spiritual change; however, being spiritual, it may or may not have any reflection on the physical plane. 2012 will come and go. Some will be disappointed that, after all the hype, nothing more exciting than usual seemed to happen. However, none of this diminishes the significance of 2012. In fact, it means just the opposite, for a true spiritual change is more meaningful than mere external phenomena.

Special events aren't something to passively watch or wait for but are opportunities to take advantage of. Ultimately what happens during 2012 and related events are up to each of us. If we want something momentous to happen in 2012, then we should work to make it manifest.

The impact of 2012 and how it affects our evolution is depicted in the following graph. The horizontal axis is time, and the vertical axis is level of consciousness. Consider 0 to be the old level of consciousness, and 1 to be the new level of consciousness toward which our planet is transitioning. The formula chosen for the graph is based on doubling or powers of two where every 100 years the level of consciousness doubles. This graph describes the accelerated growth Earth has been going through for the past few centuries. 2012 is the half way point between the levels of consciousness after which we're closer to the new level than the old. 2012 is the point of the steepest slope of the curve, which indicates the highest rate of change and features the most intense time of transition. After that time, the graph levels off as it approaches the new level.

This representation is a gross simplification of the complexities of collective spiritual growth. Something as deep as level of evolution can never be reduced to a simple number or formula, but it does give a general idea. The graph should also be considered an average because different individuals and areas may be ahead or behind the curve.

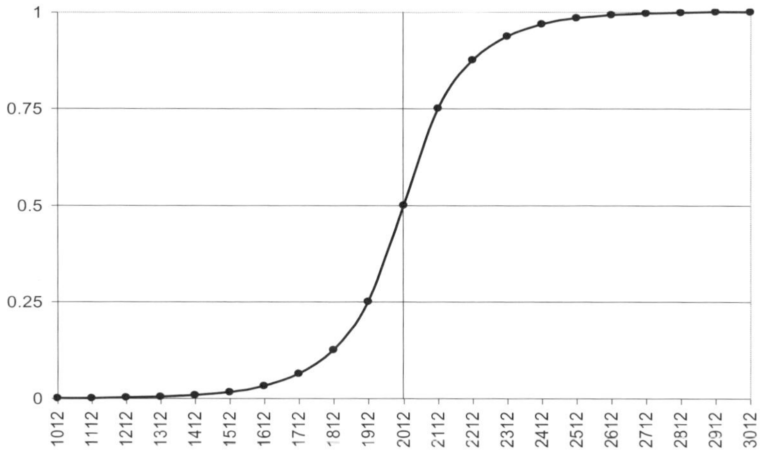

This graph spans two thousand years. If it were expanded to ten thousand or ten million years, the graph would seem to be entirely flat at level 0 for a long time. Afterward it would make a sudden vertical jump to level 1. To any scholar looking ahead from the distant past or looking back from the distant future, the period around the year 2000 would seem to be a momentous change, which it most definitely is. However, near the point of change where we are now, one can see that the transition isn't instantaneous but has been going on for a few centuries. It will continue to progress for a few more centuries before stabilizing.

The following is the same as before, except it only spans 200 years, and zooms in on the two centuries in the middle of the first graph. In this narrower timeframe, one can see that 2012, although slightly steeper than surrounding decades, isn't that different. Each decade features its own unique challenges and growth.

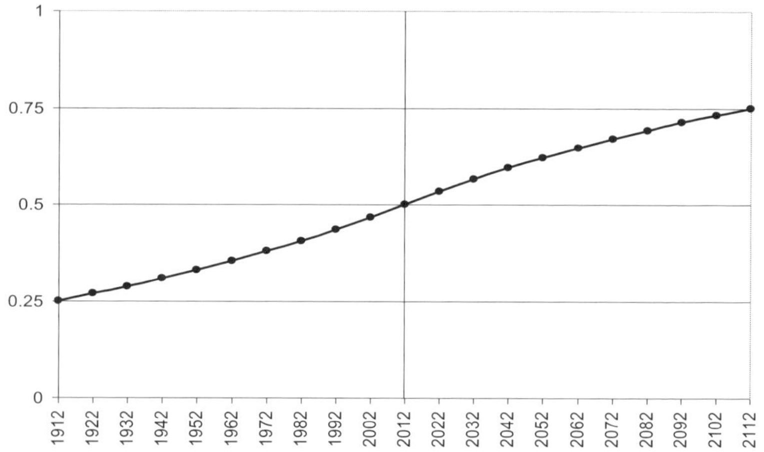

21:
God and Consciousness

"Why believe in God when you can experience God? Belief is a poor substitute for experience. If you want to know, don't simply believe. You can only believe things you don't actually know."
- Dick Sutphen

Of all the questions contemplated by philosophers, perhaps the greatest concerns God. Does God exist, and if so what form does it take? Many traditional religions say there's a single Deity, a form of belief called monotheism. Other polytheist religions believe in multiple gods. Atheism is the belief that God doesn't exist at all, which is often combined with a scientific mindset that rejects most other aspects of spirituality. Agnosticism is where one keeps an open mind about God's existence. Agnosticism has certain amount of wisdom in it because one isn't steadfastly defending an opinion which may be wrong; however, some use agnosticism as a means to avoid considering the matter and related spiritual topics.

The most important thing to remember concerning God is that it's so much beyond our understanding that we can't hope to conclude much by contemplating it. Humanity trying to understand God is like a bacterium trying to understand quantum mechanics. God is the ultimate mystery and the ultimate unknown because no matter how evolved one becomes, the level of God is still higher. People sometimes try to personify God by treating it like a merely powerful person, calling it by a gendered pronoun such as "He." If one doesn't like the word "God" due to the personal implications of it, he/she may prefer to use Divine, Great Spirit, the Universe, or other terms.

God is often called the Creator because it created the Universe. On a deeper level, God didn't just Create the Universe but rather

God is the Universe. God, being the Supreme Being, encompasses absolutely everything. God must be everything because, if it weren't, then one could visualize a new being greater than God that includes more which, of course, contradicts the concept of the ultimate Being. Because God is all, all individuals in the Universe are a part of God and contain a spark of Divinity within them. This connection shows the power of Oneness since a group of people coming together is a microcosm of the unified consciousness represented by God.

Most arguments concerning God are merely a matter of semantics or how one chooses to define things. If people see God as the Universe, then they can say definitively that God exists because the Universe obviously exists around us. Similarly, if God is indeed the Universe, one knows that God isn't a simple personified being and can, therefore, say definitively that form of God doesn't exist. Monotheism and polytheism don't have to be mutually exclusive either. Many polytheistic arrangements have an original God that created the others or a supreme Deity that rules the others. If one chooses not to define lesser or later beings as gods, then polytheism becomes monotheism. If one chooses to define a single Deity's assistants or aspects as also gods, then monotheism becomes polytheism.

God is traditionally considered omnipotent, omniscient, and omnipresent. This is true; however, God, being everything, is also not these things and covers more limiting concepts. The Divine is all things, meaning the Divine is both lacking in certain ways yet at the same time is never lacking. A classic philosophical puzzle asks, "Can God create a stone so heavy that even He can't lift it?" The answer is yes since God can do everything and covers all potentials. God is traditionally the ultimate force of good. However, because God is everything, in an abstract sense one can also say God is "evil" as well as good. What we consider evil certainly exists in the Universe; however, even evil can play a part in the Divine Plan since it challenges us to grow.

Metaphysics allows the concept of God to be looked at from a somewhat practical level. Any being that touches the Divine Logos plane can be considered a "god." A Planetary Logos or the spirit of a planet is the first being on this level or the first level at which a being is able to act as a Creator in its own right and breathe forth new Monads to create new spirits. A Solar Logos or the spirit of a star and solar system is also on this level and contains several Planetary

Logoi within it like organs in its body. Similarly, a Galactic Logos or spirit of a galaxy has many Solar Logoi acting as cells in its body. Eventually we have a being spanning the entire Universe, and that ultimate being of Oneness that encompasses the Universe can be considered God.

The Universe

"Who am I, What am I? As I am, I am not. But as we are, I AM. And to you my creation, My Perfect Love is your Perfect Freedom. And I will be with you forever and ever, until the End, and then forever more."
- God as quoted in "Pyramid Energy: The Philosophy of God, The Science of Man"

Any consideration of God should include the Universe. What purpose does the Universe serve, and why was it Created in the first place, or why does God express itself as the Universe? If you were omnipotent, omnipresent, and omniscient, perhaps one thing you would want is to temporarily give up a bit of power or knowledge. Would it be any fun playing a game if your infinite ability to see into the future allows you to know what's around the next corner or how the game is going to end?

Because God is everything, God can't readily experience anything that isn't a part of itself. In order to experience any sort of mystery, there must be a fragmentation; the One separates into individual components, such that different parts can experience each other. The manifest Universe was created in a spewing forth of independence and separation and is a projection of the Divine. From the physical standpoint, this initial creation appeared as an explosion which we call the Big Bang.

In other words, God wants to experience itself. God experiences the Universe, and, just as important, the separate parts of the Universe experience God. The path of evolution is a spark of God being projected and then returning to the whole, which allows the part to experience the whole. God as the ultimate in Oneness and yet also composed of the individual pieces can be summarized with the phrase "The One and the Many."

The purpose of the Universe shows the importance of freedom. Freedom is that which allows an individual and by extension God to have experiences in the first place. In this sense freedom is just as important as spiritual growth. Unity or a return to Divine levels is everyone's eventual and ultimate destiny. Freedom can be considered a separation or lack of Oneness; however, that isn't a bad thing because lack of Oneness is merely a delay in time of evolution.

Another way of looking at God and the Universe is that God is the parent, and the Universe is God's child. Everything in the Universe is alive, from atoms to Archangels. Everything contains the Divine life principle that swims through all parts of the Universe. In Creating the Universe, the Divine intentionally projected itself, which resulted in the creation of young Monads and souls.

God is like a Divine Gardener, and each of us is a plant growing in the garden of the Universe. The number of Monads and souls increases over time just as the number of plants in a garden increases over time. Older earlier plants can eventually grow enough to help out in the garden by going to seed and causing additional plants to sprout themselves. God is also like a Divine Painter with our Universe as the next painting God is Creating. Or rather, God is the Painting Instructor, and we are the next class destined to become painters or painting instructors ourselves.

Evolution is both a journey of awakening as well as a journey of remembering. In one sense, we're all Divine projections; our Monads are all equal and perfect, and evolution is simply the journey back home. In another sense, we're awakening principles that have never been awakened before. Because the lowest planes are part of the Divine plan, they shouldn't be disliked or avoided. The spiritual journey isn't leaving the realms of matter for the realms of the Divine, as much as it's bringing the Divine into matter.

What happens after one completes their evolutionary journey and returns to the Divine? Does one stay in Divine realms forever, or start over again from the beginning? If the Universe is an ocean, an individual entity is a drop of water sprayed forth. When the drop returns to the ocean, the drop and the ocean become One. Future activity is perceived from the vantage point of the ocean itself. Even when the ocean sends forth more drops, such activity is still perceived from the ocean's point of view; the drops are just aspects of the ocean projected forth which will soon return.

What happens after the end of the Universe? Do we create another Universe and go through the whole journey again? These questions have no real answers because they involve time where time is an aspect of and was created along with the rest of the Universe. In other words, on high levels, time as we know it no longer exists; it's really only an effect of our human level of consciousness. There are countless Divine manifestations; however, the Infinite is much more than a simple process of creating and evolving Universes over and over again. The Divine is more an eternal dynamic spiral or helix, spiraling up and out and within, than a simple static circle chasing its tail forever.

Consciousness

"Seems it strange that thou should live forever? Is it less strange that thou shouldst live at all? This is a miracle, and that no more."
- Edward Young

One of the biggest mysteries of the Universe is consciousness. What exactly causes a being to be aware? What makes you who you are, as opposed to somebody else? Why is your piece of consciousness within your specific body, and not in some other location in the Universe? These are significant questions, and true meditation upon them can be very illuminating.

Consciousness is perhaps the most fundamental reason the soul exists, and why there's more in the Universe than just physical plane phenomena. Consciousness is much more than just a side effect of chemical reactions occurring in the brain. If chemistry were the only thing happening in the world, then although there could be physical bodies running around like machines doing things in response to stimuli, there would be no real awareness or consciousness inside those machines.

Thoughts and feelings are merely stimuli that can impact consciousness where consciousness exists behind them on a more fundamental level. Consciousness is an aspect of the creation of the Universe, when the One separated into the many. Consciousness is identification with or focusing on something in particular, and by extension, disregarding everything else. Consciousness consists of a continuous vibration of assertion and negation where one is continually declaring "I am this" or "I am not this."

A major part of spiritual growth is expanding consciousness. As consciousness expands, it encompasses more aspects of the Universe. In other words, higher consciousness is inherently linked with love and Unity. It follows that loving more and identifying with more of the Universe is a way to expand consciousness. The highest levels of consciousness are achieved on the Buddhic plane of Oneness, when individuals are able to identify themselves with everything.

When one first learns a skill, such as driving a car, it's new, unfamiliar, and exciting, and one has to consciously work at it. Later, when one is more experienced, the activity becomes automatic. At extremely high levels of evolution, expressing love and Oneness becomes inherent, like breathing or the beating of one's heart; where it's done without having to consciously expend effort at it. Once a being has mastered love and consciousness, its next era of growth is learning how to use it in the Universe. In other words, beings start learning how to embody higher or Divine will, as expressed by the Atmic plane of will and Spirit.

On the highest planes, consciousness as we know it is transcended altogether. High consciousness means individuals identify themselves with the rest of the Universe; however, there's still a separate self feeling that identification. On the highest planes, consciousness is replaced with what can only be described as a unified feeling or essence shared by all. Similarly, free will as we know it disappears at the highest levels because eventually one's individual will becomes replaced by Divine will, or more accurately unified with Divine will.

The Spiritual Hierarchy

The Spiritual Hierarchy or Occult Hierarchy is a group of Enlightened spirits who coordinate spiritual evolution on Earth. After a Master graduates from the human kingdom, they can join the Hierarchy. More technically, the Hierarchy consists of beings at the level of the Sixth and Seventh Initiations, who have started their true Path of service.

The word hierarchy is based on the Greek words for "sacred" and "to lead." The Hierarchy plans and directs spiritual activities; however, the Hierarchy isn't about ruling or control, which one might associate with that word. A seeker isn't supposed to submit to the Hierarchy, but rather awaken their inherent connection with it. The Hierarchy is like humanity's parents, who guide us until we grow up enough to be a part of the Hierarchy ourselves.

Just as humanity is centered on the physical, astral, and lower mental planes of the personality, the Hierarchy is centered on the Causal, Buddhic, and Atmic planes of the Spirit. In other words, members of the Hierarchy are based on levels far above the physical plane, and presently they only incarnate when there's a special need. Note that as humanity evolves, higher energies and souls are able to express on the physical plane. An important aspect of the spiritual changes taking place in our world at this time is that humanity and the Hierarchy are becoming more aware of each other and forging stronger connections. This activity or change is sometimes called "The Externalization of the Hierarchy."

The primary service the Hierarchy performs is implementing the Plan. Evolution is an expression of Divine will. The specific processes spirits implement to bring forth evolution are collectively called "The Plan." The ultimate energy or essence of the Hierarchy is love and consciousness. On levels as exalted as the Hierarchy, we are all One. The Hierarchy not only works with humanity, but also with Angels and a variety of other spiritual beings, including non-physical entities from other planets.

The Hierarchy is sometimes called the "Great White Brotherhood." Note that this name has nothing to do with specific ethnicities or genders. The color white represents the Brotherhood's inherent goodness, while also representing unity, just as white light contains all colors. Brotherhood indicates beings working together as One Being. The Hierarchy is the ultimate spiritual Ashram of which all Earthly ashrams are ultimately a part. If the various spiritual Paths are branches of a tree, the Hierarchy is the trunk.

The Spiritual Hierarchy contains a number of roles and positions. These exalted offices are hard for us to understand, but we can still attempt to say a few things about them. Most world religions have been founded by these beings on the occasions that they physically incarnate. The primary offices in the Hierarchy are as follows:

- The Manu (Sanskrit for "man") is a Master who among other important purposes incarnates to help set the physical form of a new Root-Race. Manus express on the 1st Ray energy of will and power.
- The Bodhisattva (Sanskrit for "essence of perfect knowledge") or World-Teacher is a Master who incarnates in order to teach humanity. Bodhisattvas express on the 2nd Ray energy of wisdom and love. The Bodhisattva referred to here is a specific title; however, the term "bodhisattva" is sometimes used in a general sense to refer to any Master who postpones the Nirvana they've earned in order to help other beings attain Enlightenment.
- The Mahachohan (Sanskrit for "great Chohan") is the leader of the various Chohans or higher Masters. The Mahachohan works with the seven Rays, especially the 3rd through 7th Rays. Each Ray has an individual Chohan administering it. These seven Ray Chohans are overseen by the supreme lords of the Hierarchy: The Manu, Bodhisattva, and Mahachohan.

Shamballa

Shamballa (sometimes spelled Shambhala or Shambala) is the highest realm and level of consciousness related to our planet. The word Shamballa is Sanskrit for "place of peace." Like the Hierarchy, Shamballa can be considered a spiritual Council; however, at such a high vibration that it's staffed with beings just shy of Divinity. More technically these are beings who have taken the Eighth or Ninth Initiations, and are close to the Planetary Logos level.

While the Hierarchy implements the Plan of evolution, Shamballa radiates the Purpose behind the Plan. Many effects that manifest on Earth are reflections of causes that originate from Shamballa. For example, Shamballa may focus on the essence of it being time for Earth to move to its next level in evolution. The Hierarchy will take that directive and formulate plans to make it happen, such as bringing in new energies and discarding old elements. Finally, humanity will take specific actions on the physical plane in alignment with these plans.

Humanity's alignment with the Hierarchy and Shamballa happens to different degrees. Souls on a spiritual Path will often incarnate with a mission to move things in a desired direction. Most of humanity isn't yet aware of the higher influence behind many changes taking place within ourselves and happening externally on Earth; however, they're still subconsciously affected by these directives, like a boat in an ocean current. Because change implies effort, the physical plane reflection of the spiritual causes may temporarily manifest as struggle or even suffering as old elements get transformed.

Shamballa is more evolved than the Spiritual Hierarchy to the same degree that the Hierarchy is beyond humanity. Shamballa also guides the Spiritual Hierarchy in a manner similar to how the Hierarchy guides humanity. Each group assists the next group lower; even humanity stewards the animal kingdom and the earlier kingdoms of nature. Properly caring for the natural world is a potential humanity is increasingly embracing.

The energy of Shamballa usually reaches humanity through the Hierarchy; however, there's also potential for direct contact between Shamballa and humanity. The connection between Shamballa, the Hierarchy, and humanity isn't merely linear, but properly evolved, the three groups form a triangle. One of the inner causes behind the extreme changes and growth happening within humanity in recent centuries is an infusion of energy from Shamballa. Ultimately the three groups, along with the earlier kingdoms of nature, are all One and are all an expression of the Planetary Logos.

Since the beings of Shamballa directly assist the Planetary Logos of our world, the things they do are beyond comprehension or at least on an incredibly vast level. For example, they maintain an open channel between our Planetary Logos and the Solar Logos, similar to how a child maintains a relationship with their parents. They also maintain a channel with Venus, the one planet or Scheme of evolution in our solar system more evolved than Earth, in a manner similar to how a child maintains a relationship with and receives assistance from an older sibling. Some of the more readily definable roles in Shamballa are as follows:

- The Lord of the World is the Manu of our World-Period or the entire era spanning our journey on this planet through seven Root-Races. The Lord of the World administrates the seven lesser Manus in the Hierarchy that look after the seven Root-Races. In a higher sense, the Lord of the World is an avatar or expression of the Planetary Logos. The relationship between the Lord of the World and the Planetary Logos is similar to the relationship between each person's projected personality and their unified soul. Earth's Lord of the World is named Sanat Kumara, whose name is Sanskrit for "eternal youth" or "eternal virgin." Like all Manus or spiritual leaders, the Lord of the World expresses on the 1st Ray.

- The Buddha (Sanskrit for one who is enlightened or awake) is a higher form of the Bodhisattva from the Hierarchy. The Buddha is the supreme teacher for our planet, which includes the beings of the Hierarchy as well as non-human kingdoms such as the Angels. When a Buddha graduates from their role to still higher positions, the Bodhisattva becomes the next Buddha. An analogy is the Buddha is the president, and the Bodhisattva is the vice-president. When the president's term ends, the current vice-president becomes the next president. The Buddha referred to here is a specific title; however, the term "buddha" is sometimes used in a general sense to refer to one who has achieved an enlightened level of awareness. Like the Bodhisattva, the Buddha expresses on the 2nd Ray.
- Round Manus and Chain Manus are semi-Divine beings even more evolved than the Lord of the World. A Round Manu coordinates a lifewave's journey across the seven Globes of a planetary Chain, and hence administrates seven different Lords of the World. A Chain Manu coordinates a lifewave's seven journeys around the seven Globes and hence administrates seven different Round Manus and the globes themselves. A Chain Manu is one step shy of being a Planetary Logos itself. For more about Root-Races, Globes, Rounds, and Chains, see the chapter "Cycles of Evolution."

Humanity, the Hierarchy, and Shamballa form a trinity. If humanity is the body of our stream of evolution, then the Hierarchy is the soul, and Shamballa is the Spirit. If the human race is the root chakra in the collective life of our planet, then the Hierarchy is the heart chakra, and Shamballa is the crown chakra. Humanity is centered in the physical, astral, and mental planes (the bottom three), the Hierarchy is centered in the mental, Buddhic, and Atmic planes (the middle three), and Shamballa is centered in the Atmic, Monadic, and Logos planes (the top three). Humanity uses bodily forms, the

Hierarchy expresses as spiritual consciousness, and Shamballa is identification with the Divine. The essence of humanity is the individuality of personality, the Hierarchy's essence is love and Oneness, and Shamballa is Divine will. These relationships are summarized in the following table:

Centers of Evolution on Earth			
Group	**Humanity**	**Hierarchy**	**Shamballa**
Analogy	Body	Soul	Spirit
Expression	Form	Consciousness	Identification
Essence	Individuality	Love	Will
Service	Action	Plan	Purpose
Planes	Physical-Mental	Mental-Atmic	Atmic-Logos
Initiations	Up through 5th	6th-7th	8th-9th
Guides	Animal Kingdom	Humanity	Hierarchy
Guided By	Hierarchy	Shamballa	Divine

In popular culture, Shamballa has been rumored to be a physical city or kingdom hidden in the Himalayan Mountains. In the early twentieth century Europeans actually conducted several expeditions into Tibet in an attempt to find it. This, of course, is a misunderstanding. People sometimes try to find something externally through physical action which really exists internally and can only be known through spiritual growth.

Although Shamballa is the height of spirituality upon this planet, it actually does have what we would consider a focus point on the physical plane. This place is believed to be located in the Gobi Desert in China. Today this area is just desert, with nothing readily apparent physically. In the distant past however, such as during Atlantis, the location featured a great city. Like many aspects of spirituality, the physical reflection of Shamballa goes through cycles; sometimes it's very apparent and inhabited while in other periods, it's dormant and empty. In its most recent period of manifestation, the city existed on an island, with an enormous stone bridge connecting it to the mainland. Hence it was called the City of the Bridge, and the island was called the White Island. When the city is physically manifest, it usually corresponds to periods of history when the Manu and Bodhisattva are also choosing to express through physical bodies.

Planetary Chakras

The physical reflection of Shamballa can be considered the primary power point on Earth, or at least one of the planet's chakras. There are other very powerful points on the planet that also correspond to chakras. For example, the geographic poles are obviously significant. The magnetic poles are also significant, which shows that the location of power points can drift over time, just as the magnetic poles can move or even flip altogether via a pole shift. Egypt has a history much vaster than most modern archeologists are aware. The location of the Great Pyramids is also a primary power point and wasn't chosen by accident.

Outside of Shamballa, the most powerful point on Earth is probably the Big Island of Hawaii. Geometrically, if a tetrahedron were inscribed inside the sphere of our planet, and one vertex point was placed at the geographic South Pole, then the other three vertices would be at 19.47 degrees north latitude. Interestingly, that latitude intersects Hawaii, and more specifically goes through the middle of the Big Island. The volcano Mauna Kea on the Big Island is the tallest mountain on Earth when measured from base to top; it's even higher than Mt. Everest. Most of the Hawaiian mountains lie under the ocean, which is why their true height is often overlooked.

A planet is mostly liquid, and as it spins, it's affected by various laws of physics. A spinning liquid sphere manifests vortices of fluid; in computer simulations these vortices tend to flow into and combine with each other. (This is similar to how the initial matter and early planetoids combine together to make planets in the forming of a solar system.) The place with the best equilibrium for a final vortex in a spinning sphere to live is at the point as if a tetrahedron were inscribed in it, or 19.47 degrees latitude. On gaseous planets like Jupiter this vortex tends to manifest as a large stormy spot on the surface, while on planets with a hard crust like Earth there tends to be a large volcano over the more liquid mantle.

Bodies in the Solar System with prominent features at 19.47°		
Body	**Feature**	**Comments**
Sun	Sunspots	Most often appear 15-20 degrees away from equator
Earth	Mauna Kea	Tallest mountain on Earth when measured from sea bottom
Mars	Olympus Mons	Tallest mountain and volcano in solar system
Jupiter	Great Red Spot	Storm several times the size of Earth
Neptune	Great Dark Spot	Atmospheric depression the size of Earth

Hawaii consists of a row of islands. The largest and generally newest island is on the southeast end of the line, and the most active volcano is on the southeast coast of the Big Island. Over time the main volcanic pressure point has drifted, making the various islands. Similarly, the main volcano of Olympus Mons on Mars has also moved slightly over the eons; there's the main crater, and other much older craters nearby. Presumably as a planet's axis wobbles over time or its crust drifts via plate tectonics, the vortex moves to the new 19.47 degree spot.

Conclusion

"Reach high, for stars lie hidden in your soul. Dream deep, for every dream precedes the goal."
- Pamela Vaull Starr

The following chart summarizes the complete path of evolution, from an entity's initial beginning when its Monad was Created and breathed forth by a Logos, all the way to Divinity and the level of God itself.

The "Group" column shows the three main centers of evolution on our planet: Humanity, the Spiritual Hierarchy, and Shamballa, as described in this chapter. These centers are preceded by the earlier pre-human kingdoms of nature and are followed by Divinity itself.

The "Rank" column organizes the levels into seven categories in two different ways. The first ranking shows the seven kingdoms of evolution, starting with the mineral and ending with Divinity. This ranking skips the kingdoms of nature on the involutionary half of the journey that haven't reached the lowest physical plane yet. The second ranking shows the seven kingdoms of nature, which is balanced with three kingdoms on the involutionary half of the journey, the densest or mineral kingdom in the middle, and three kingdoms on the evolutionary half of the journey. This ranking ends with the human kingdom, not including the superhuman evolution that takes place after one becomes an Enlightened Spirit.

The "Era" column lists each specific level. It begins with the set of kingdoms of nature, and ends with the sequence of spiritual Initiations. The "Entity" column gives examples of beings that are on each level. These levels and entities are described in more detail in the chapters "Kingdoms of Nature" and "The Great Initiations." The average person in the human kingdom is working on developing their emotions and minds through the process of physical incarnation, but hasn't yet started on the spiritual Path as marked by the First Initiation, when one becomes interested in and starts developing higher qualities. The process of people developing emotional and intellectual virtues leading up to the First Initiation is described in the chapter "Mastering the Personality."

Finally, the "Plane" column lists the planes that entities on that level have reached on either their involutionary or evolutionary journeys or planes that they have fully mastered once they embark on the spiritual Path. These planes are described in more detail in the chapter "Planes of the Universe."

Levels of Evolution

Group	Rank		Era	Entity		Plane
GOD / UNIVERSE						
Divinity	7		4th – 7th Cosmic Initiations	Galactic supercluster & beyond		Mastered Cosmic Planes
Divinity	7		3rd Cosmic Initiation	Galactic Logos		Mastered Cosmic Planes
Divinity	7		2nd Cosmic Initiation	Solar Logos		Mastered Cosmic Planes
Divinity	7		1st Cosmic Initiation	Planetary Logos		Mastered Cosmic Planes
Shamballa	6		9th Initiation: Refusal	Round Manu, Chain Manu		Mastered Cosmic Planes
Shamballa	6		8th Initiation: Transition	Lord of the World, Buddha		Mastered Cosmic Planes
Hierarchy	5		7th Initiation: Resurrection	Manu, Bodhisattva, Mahachohan		Mastered Logoic
Hierarchy	5		6th Initiation: Decision	Chohan	*Higher Path Chosen*	Mastered Monadic
Humanity	4	7	5th Initiation: Revelation	Master	*Enlightened*	Mastered Atmic
Humanity	4	7	4th Initiation: Renunciation	Arhat	*Transcended Soul*	Mastered Buddhic
Humanity	4	7	3rd Initiation: Transfiguration	Initiate	*Perfected Soul*	Mastered Mental
Humanity	4	7	2nd Initiation: Baptism	Disciple	*Committed to Path*	Mastered Astral
Humanity	4	7	1st Initiation: Birth	Seeker	*Interested in Spirit*	Mastered Physical
Humanity	4	7	7th Kingdom: Human	People	*Individualized Soul*	Evolved to Mental
Early Kingdoms of Nature	3	6	6th Kingdom: Animal	Animal	*Group Souls*	Evolved to Astral
Early Kingdoms of Nature	2	5	5th Kingdom: Vegetable	Plant		Evolved to Etheric
Early Kingdoms of Nature	1	4	4th Kingdom: Mineral	Rock		Involved to Physical
Early Kingdoms of Nature		3	3rd Kingdom: Elemental	Astral elemental essence		Involved to Astral
Early Kingdoms of Nature		2	2nd Kingdom: Elemental	Mental elemental essence		Involved to Mental
Early Kingdoms of Nature		1	1st Kingdom: Elemental	Causal elemental essence		Involved to Causal
Monad Created by Logos						

Bibliography

Aligheri, Dante, Charles H. Sisson, and David H. Higgins. *The Divine Comedy.* New York: Oxford University Press, Inc., 1980.

Andersen, Hans Christian and Lisbeth Zwerger. *The Little Mermaid.* New York: Penguin Young Readers Group, 2004.

Anka, Darryl and Luana Ewing. *Bashar: Blueprint for Change.* Seattle: New Solutions Publishing, 1990.

Artress, Lauren. *Walking a Sacred Path.* New York: The Berkeley Publishing Group, 1995.

Bailey, Alice A. *The Externalisation of the Hierarchy.* New York: Lucis Publishing Company, 1957.

Bailey, Alice A. *The Rays and The Initiations.* New York: Lucis Publishing Company, 1988.

Browning, Katherine. *An epitome of the "Science of the Emotions", a summary of the work of Pandit Bhagavan Das.* London: The Theosophical Publishing House, 1925.

Chaney, Earlyne. *Initiation in the Great Pyramid.* Upland, CA: Astara, Inc., 1987.

Daniel, Alma, Timothy Wyllie, and Andrew Ramer. *Ask Your Angels.* New York: Ballantine Books, 1992.

Das, Bhagavan. *The Science of the Emotions.* Benares: The Theosophical Publishing House, 1908.

Fremantle, Francesca and Chögyam Trungpa. *The Tibetan Book of the Dead.* Boston & London: Shambhala Publications, Inc., 1975.

Giorgio, Gail. *Footprints in the Sand - The Life Story of Mary Stevenson, Author of the Immortal Poem.* Carson City, NV: Gold Leaf Press, 1995.

Golas, Thaddeus. *The Lazy Man's Guide to Enlightenment.* Layton, UT: Gibbs Smith, 1995.

Hardin, Garrett. "The Tragedy of the Commons." *Science*. Volume , December 1968: 1243-1248.

Hardy, Dean, Mary Hardy, Marjorie Killick, and Kenneth Killick. *Pyramid Energy: The Philosophy of God, The Science of Man.* Clayton, GA: Tri-State Press, 1987.

Keyes, Ken. *Handbook to Higher Consciousness.* Coos Bay, OR: Living Love Publications, 1975.

Leadbeater, C. W. *Man Visible and Invisible.* Wheaton: The Theosophical Publishing House, 1980.

Matteson, Barbara J. *Mystic Minerals.* Seattle: Cosmic Resources, 1985.

Powell, Arthur E. *The Astral Body.* Wheaton, IL: The Theosophical Publishing House, 1987.

Powell, Arthur E. *The Causal Body.* Manila: Philippine Theosophical Foundation, 1992.

Powell, Arthur E. *The Etheric Double.* Wheaton, IL: The Theosophical Publishing House, 1987.

Powell, Arthur E. *The Mental Body.* London: The Theosophical Publishing House, 1967.

Powell, Arthur E. *The Solar System.* London: The Theosophical Publishing House, 1930.

Rand, Ayn. *Introduction to Objectivist Epistemology.* New York: Meridian, 1990.

Silbey, Uma. *The Complete Crystal Guidebook.* San Francisco: U-Read Publications, 1986.

Solara. *11:11: Inside the Doorway.* Charlottesville, VA: Star-Borne Unlimited, 1992.

Solara. *Invoking Your Celestial Guardians.* Eureka, MT: Star-Borne Unlimited, 1987.

Stevens, Wendelle C. *UFO Contact from the Pleiades.* Tucson: U F O Photo Archives, 1978.

Sutphen, Dick. *Radical Spirituality.* Malibu: Valley of the Sun Publishing, 1995.

Van Gelder, Dora. *The Real World of Fairies.* Wheaton: The Theosophical Publishing House, 1977.

Video

2001: A Space Odyssey. Dir. Stanley Kubrick. Perf. Keir Dullea, Gary Lockwood, William Sylvester, Daniel Richter, and Leonard Rossiter. Metro-Goldwyn-Mayer, 1968.

2010: The Year we Make Contact. Dir. Peter Hyams. Perf. Roy Scheider, John Lithgow, Helen Mirren, Bob Balaban, and Keir Dullea. Metro-Goldwyn-Mayer, 1984.

Babylon 5: Into the Fire. Dir. Kevin Dobson. Perf. Bruce Boxleitner, Mira Furlan, Claudia Christian, Peter Jurasik, and Wayne Alexander. Warner Home Video, 2004.

Close Encounters of the Third Kind. Dir. Steven Spielberg. Perf. Richard Dreyfuss, François Truffaut, and Teri Garr. Columbia Pictures Corporation, 1977.

Communion. Dir. Philippe Mora. Perf. Christopher Walken, Lindsay Crouse, and Frances Sternhagen. Allied Vision Ltd., 1989.

Contact. Dir. Robert Zemeckis. Perf. Jodie Foster, Matthew McConaughey, and Tom Skerritt. Warner Bros. Pictures, 1997.

Defending Your Life. Dir. Albert Brooks. Perf. Albert Brooks, Michael Durrell, and Meryl Streep. Geffen Pictures, 1991.

Flatliners. Dir. Joel Schumacher. Perf. Kiefer Sutherland, Julia Roberts, Kevin Bacon, William Baldwin, and Oliver Platt. Columbia Pictures Corporation, 1990.

Monsters, Inc. Dir. Pete Docter. Perf. John Goodman, Billy Crystal, Mary Gibbs, Steve Buscemi, Randall Boggs, and James Coburn. Pixar Animation Studios, 2001.

Star Trek. The Next Generation. First Contact. Dir. Cliff Bole. Perf. Patrick Stewart, Jonathan Frakes, Marina Sirtis, George Coe, Carolyn Seymour. Paramount, 2002.

The Dark Crystal. Dir. Jim Henson. Perf. Jim Henson, Kathryn Mullen, Frank Oz, Dave Goelz, and Steve Whitmire. Universal Pictures, 1982.

The Five People You Meet in Heaven. Dir. Lloyd Kramer. Perf. Jon Voight, Ellen Burstyn, Jeff Daniels, Dagmara Dominczyk, and Steven Grayhm. Five People Productions Inc., 2004.

What Dreams May Come. Dir. Vincent Ward. Perf. Robin Williams, Cuba Gooding Jr., Annabella Sciorra, and Max von Sydow. Polygram Filmed Entertainment, 1998.

Index

About the Author

Walter D. Pullen is the latest incarnation of a soul on a long Path of evolution. An experienced astrologer, in 1991 he authored the freeware astrology software “Astrolog”. He also wrote the maze generation program “Daedalus” as a literal metaphor for the turns and choices of our spiritual “Path”. Walter combines writing, a degree in computer science, and love to serve our planet as part of an increasingly growing group of Lightworkers. He and his soulmate Jessica live in Seattle, Washington.

Other Books Published
by
Ozark Mountain Publishing, Inc.

Conversations with Nostradamus, Volume I, II, III................by Dolores Cannon
Jesus and the Essenes..by Dolores Cannon
They Walked with Jesus...by Dolores Cannon
Between Death and Life.. by Dolores Cannon
A Soul Remembers Hiroshima..by Dolores Cannon
Keepers of the Garden...by Dolores Cannon
The Legend of Starcrash...by Dolores Cannon
The Custodians..by Dolores Cannon
The Convoluted Universe - Book One, Two, Three..............by Dolores Cannon
Five Lives Remembered ....by Dolores Cannon
I Have Lived Before...by Sture Lönnerstrand
The Forgotten Woman..by Arun & Sunanda Gandhi
Luck Doesn't Happen by Chance...................................by Claire Doyle Beland
Mankind - Child of the Stars.............................by Max H. Flindt & Otto Binder
Past Life Memories As A Confederate Soldier.........................by James H. Kent
Holiday in Heaven..by Aron Abrahamsen
Is Jehovah An E.T.?...by Dorothy Leon
The Essenes - Children of the Light..............by Stuart Wilson & Joanna Prentis
Power of the Magdalene................................by Stuart Wilson & Joanna Prentis
Beyond Limitations ....by Stuart Wilson & Joanna Prentis
Rebirth of the Oracle..................................by Justine Alessi & M. E. McMillan
Reincarnation: The View from Eternity......by O.T. Bonnett, M.D. & Greg Satre
The Divinity Factor...by Donald L. Hicks
What I Learned After Medical School ....by O.T. Bonnett, M.D.
Why Healing Happens...by O.T. Bonnett, M.D.
A Journey Into Being...by Christine Ramos, RN
Discover The Universe Within You...by Mary Letorney
Worlds Beyond Death...by Rev. Grant H. Pealer
Let's Get Natural With Herbs..by Debra Rayburn
The Enchanted Garden...by Jodi Felice
My Teachers Wear Fur Coats.........................by Susan Mack & Natalia Krawetz
Seeing True...by Ronald Chapman
Elder Gods of Antiquity...by M. Don Schorn
Legacy of the Elder Gods..by M. Don Schorn
Reincarnation...Stepping Stones of Life ....by M. Don Schorn

Continue for more books by Ozark Mountain Publishing, Inc.

Children of the Stars .... by Nikki Pattillo
Angels - The Guardians of Your Destiny ....by Maiya & Geoff Gray-Cobb
Seeds of the Soul..by Maiya Gray-Cobb
The Despiritualized Church..by Rev. Keith Bender
The Science of Knowledge ....by Vara Humphreys
The Other Side of Suicide ....by Karen Peebles
Journey Through Fear ....by Antoinette Lee Howard
Awakening To Your Creation ....by Julia Hanson
Thirty Miracles in Thirty Days ....by Irene Lucas
Windows of Opportunity ....by Sherri Cortland
Why? ....by Mandeep Khera
The Healing Christ ....Robert Winterhalter
Morning Coffee with God ....Michael Dennis
Ask Your Inner Voice ....by James Wawro
Live From the Other Side ....Maureen mcGill & Nola Davis

For more information about any of the above titles, soon to be released titles, or other items in our catalog, write or visit our website:

OZARK MOUNTAIN PUBLISHING

PO Box 754
Huntsville, AR 72740
www.ozarkmt.com
1-800-935-0045/479-738-2348
Wholesale Inquiries Welcome